Lecture Notes in Computer Science 13592

More information about this series at https://link.springer.com/bookseries/558

Dalibor Klusáček · Corbalán Julita ·
Gonzalo P. Rodrigo (Eds.)

Job Scheduling Strategies for Parallel Processing

25th International Workshop, JSSPP 2022
Virtual Event, June 3, 2022
Revised Selected Papers

Springer

Editors
Dalibor Klusáček
CESNET
Prague, Czech Republic

Corbalán Julita
Polytechnic University of Catalonia
Barcelona, Spain

Gonzalo P. Rodrigo
Apple
Cupertino, CA, USA

ISSN 0302-9743 ISSN 1611-3349 (electronic)
Lecture Notes in Computer Science
ISBN 978-3-031-22697-7 ISBN 978-3-031-22698-4 (eBook)
https://doi.org/10.1007/978-3-031-22698-4

This Springer imprint is published by the registered company Springer Nature Switzerland AG
The registered company address is: Gewerbestrasse 11, 6330 Cham, Switzerland

Preface

This volume contains the papers presented at the 25th Workshop on Job Scheduling Strategies for Parallel Processing (JSSPP 2022) that was held on June 3, 2022, in conjunction with the 36th IEEE International Parallel and Distributed Processing Symposium (IPDPS 2022). The proceedings of previous workshops are also available from Springer as LNCS volumes 949, 1162, 1291, 1459, 1659, 1911, 2221, 2537, 2862, 3277, 3834, 4376, 4942, 5798, 6253, 7698, 8429, 8828, 10353, 10773, 11332, 12326, and 12985.

This year 19 papers were submitted to the workshop, of which we accepted 12. All submitted papers went through a complete review process, with the full version being read and evaluated by an average of 3.4 reviewers. Additionally, one invited keynote paper was included in the workshop. We would like to especially thank to our Program Committee members and additional reviewers for their willingness to participate in this effort and their excellent, detailed, and thoughtful reviews.

For the third time in a row the JSSPP workshop was held fully online due to the worldwide COVID-19 pandemic. Despite the obvious logistic problems, all talks were presented live, allowing for the participants to interact with the authors of the papers. We are very thankful to the presenters of accepted papers for their participation in the live workshop session. Recordings from all talks at the 2022 edition can be found at the JSSPP's YouTube channel: https://bit.ly/3mXyT8F.

This year, the workshop was organized into three sessions with 11 technical papers and one paper discussing open scheduling problem as well as one keynote talk.

The keynote was delivered by Lavanya Ramakrishnan who is a Senior Scientist and Division Deputy in the Scientific Data Division at Lawrence Berkeley National Laboratory. Her research interests are in building software tools for computational and data-intensive science with a focus on workflow, resource, and data management. In her keynote, Lavanya Ramakrishnan presented her take on the future of workflow scheduling. Workflows are important in scientific ecosystems that capture the relation between different steps of processing and data. Workflow tools have focused on providing automation and repeatability but mostly consider HPC resources as blackboxes. In her talk, Lavanya outlined the evolution of scientific workflow needs over the last 20 years and its impact on workflow scheduling on HPC systems. She outlined real science use cases with challenging scheduling problems and presented analyses of workloads on HPC systems over four different large-scale systems. She also discussed the implications of data, resources, networks, containers, and interactive notebooks on scheduling. The talk was concluded by discussing the future challenges of scientific workflow scheduling that supports autonomous experimentation and observation in concert with a self-driving infrastructure.

Papers accepted for this year's JSSPP covered several interesting problems within the resource management and scheduling domains and included one open scheduling problem (OSP). This year's OSP focused on the experience when using Kubernetes container orchestrator in an academic environment. Spišaková et al. demonstrated challenging problems when providing system resources "for free" to the scientific community, including poor resource reclaiming, overestimated resource requirements, and lack of fairsharing mechanism in current Kubernetes distributions.

The first full technical paper was presented by Tatsuyoshi Ohmura et al. and proposed to virtually reproduce job scheduling and power management choices of compute systems to determine optimal system parameters and policies. They applied this approach to the supercomputer AOBA, producing scheduling and power saving parameters that reduced job waiting time by 70% and energy consumption by 1.2%.

Kalogirou et al. proposed a VM allocation and node management system that increases utilization in active compute nodes through VM consolidation driven by load estimations based on runtime information and workload interaction models. Their simulations show that their policies closely match or overperform two state-of-art policies that combine VM consolidation with VFS.

The third paper by Klusáček et al. presented the real-life experience of deploying a walltime predictor using the soft walltime feature in PBS Professional. Their results show a significant increase in walltime accuracy over user-provided estimations and include a discussion on the effects on the system performance. This paper also included the publication of collected workload traces to allow other researchers to further study and extend this work.

Marta Jaros et al. described the use of a genetic algorithms and simulation to define execution schedules that reduce makespan and computation cost of complex ultrasound workflows based on moldable parallel tasks. The technique was validated by submitting the executing schedules to a real PBS job scheduler with a resulting maximum mean error of interpolation within 10%.

In the fifth paper, Nileshwar et al. proposed a set of deadline-based job-scheduling algorithms that consider power constraints. Their experiments show that their best approach combines greedy acceptance with a biased load allocation strategy, maximizing load and increasing energy efficiency.

Vanns et al. shared experiences of developing and running a resource manager that supports batch workloads for render farms to produce high-quality imagery for major motion pictures and television. They shared some recent changes to their production scheduler and discussed how their tooling for trace-based simulation allows them to gain confidence in production upgrades.

The last section of the workshop started with a paper about encoding schemes to represent the state of a cluster for reinforcement-learning driven scheduling. Li et al. argue that by using sparse representation, they can minimize the state vector size and accelerate training on the data.

In the eighth paper, Halder Lina et al. propose three scheduling algorithms for elastic message passing applications together with six methods to prioritize pending elastic jobs. The authors evaluated them through simulation and concluded that the suitability of the algorithms depends on the workload characteristics as well as the range of elasticity in the workload.

Venkataswamy et al. proposed RARE, a deep reinforcement learning job scheduler that maximizes the use of renewal energies whose power generation is intermittent. The experiment data indicate that RARE performs better than existing systems and it can learn from and improve upon existing heuristic policies using offline learning.

Mikhail Titov et al. presented a performance evaluation of the implementation of the Process Management Interface for Exascale integrated into a pilot-based runtime system called RADICAL-Pilot for the HPC platform Summit. Their experimental results show that it can run 65,500 tasks on 2,048 nodes while keeping resource utilization at 52%. At smaller concurrency, the system can achieve even higher utilization, reaching 85% at with 8,200 tasks over 256 nodes.

Last, but not least, Casanova et al. presented a study on the feasibility of simulation-driven portfolio scheduling for distributed cyberinfrastructure. They argue that online simulation can determine which scheduling algorithm will perform better for a given system state but inaccuracies in the simulations can greatly affect the results. Their main finding is that, even with large simulation inaccuracies, portfolio scheduling can outperform the best one-algorithm approach.

We hope you can join us at the next JSSPP workshop, this time in St. Petersburg, Florida, USA, on May 19, 2023. Enjoy your reading!

August 2022

Dalibor Klusáček
Corbalán Julita
Gonzalo P. Rodrigo

Organization

Program Chairs

Dalibor Klusáček	CESNET, Czech Republic
Julita Corbalán	Barcelona Supercomputing Center, Spain
Gonzalo P. Rodrigo	Apple, USA

Program Committee

Amaya Booker	Facebook, USA
Henri Casanova	University of Hawaii, USA
Stratos Dimopoulos	Apple, USA
Hyeonsang Eom	Seoul National University, South Korea
Dror Feitelson	Hebrew University, Israel
Jiří Filipovič	Masaryk University, Czech Republic
Liana Fong	IBM T. J. Watson Research Center, USA
Bogdan Ghit	Databricks, Netherlands
Eitan Frachtenberg	Facebook, USA
Alfredo Goldman	University of Sao Paulo, Brazil
Douglas Jacobsen	NERSC, USA
Cristian Klein	Umeå University/Elastisys, Sweden
Zhiling Lan	Illinois Institute of Technology, USA
Bill Nitzberg	Altair, USA
Christine Morin	Inria, France
P.-O. Östberg	Umeå University, Sweden
Larry Rudolph	Two Sigma, USA
Lavanya Ramakrishnan	Lawrence Berkeley National Laboratory, USA
Uwe Schwiegelshohn	TU Dortmund, Germany
Leonel Sousa	Universidade de Lisboa, Portugal
Ramin Yahyapour	University of Göttingen, Germany

Additional Reviewers

Matthew Dearing	Illinois Institute of Technology, USA
Devarshi Ghoshal	Lawrence Berkeley National Laboratory, USA
Boyang Li	Illinois Institute of Technology, USA
Diogo Marques	Tecnico Lisboa, Portugal
Ricardo Nobre	INESC-ID, Portugal

Abel Souza	Umeå University, Sweden
Xiongxiao Xu	Illinois Institute of Technology, USA

Insights and Requirements for Future Workflow Scheduling (Keynote)

Lavanya Ramakrisshnan

Lawrence Berkeley National Lab
LRamakrishnan@lbl.gov

Abstract. Workflows are an important construct in scientific ecosystems that capture the relation between different steps of processing and data. Workflow tools have focused on providing automation and repeatability but mostly consider HPC resources as black boxes. In the keynote talk, I outlined the evolution of scientific workflow needs over the last 20 years and its impact on workflow scheduling on HPC systems. My talk covered a) real science use cases with challenging scheduling problems, b) captured our analyses of workloads on HPC systems over four different large-scale systems, c) discussed the implications of data, resources, networks, containers, interactive notebooks on scheduling. I concluded the talk by discussing the future challenges of scientific workflow scheduling that supports autonomous experimentation and observation in concert with a self-driving infrastructure. This paper provides a few key details and pointers to supplement the keynote.

Keywords: Workflow scheduling · User research · Workfload analyses

Research Question and Background

Scientific advances increasingly depend on the ability of researchers to harness the power of high-performance and other computing infrastructure to operate on the large scientific data, produced by experiments, observations, and simulations. However, HPC systems have been designed for large scale tightly couple simulation jobs. The complexity of the data pipelines requires us to revisit the key research question of *How do we enable researchers to effectively and efficiently manage their computation and data on HPC and distributed resources?*.

Workflows are an important construct in scientific ecosystems that capture the relation between different steps of processing and data. Workflow scheduling has largely focused on distributed resource management (i.e., managing jobs across multiple sites) and job management (i.e., batch queue scheduling at a single site). Experimental data workflows require us to coordinate across organizations, support real-time data movement and computing, and manage moving data between storage systems. Additionally, the real-time and interactive nature of these workflows requires us to balance productivity and usability of scientific users with performance and utilization on the systems. Thus, human factors is a critical factor in addressing next-generation workflow challenges.

A Dual Approach

We need to take a dual approach to addressing the challenges of data in scientific workflows that considers both the quantitative and qualitative aspects of the problem. Our work has demonstrated that by using a mix of user research techniques [6, 7, 8] combined with workload analyses that informs the development of methods and tools results is effective to address the needs of scientific pipelines. Our work focuses on applying user experience research techniques to understand and enumerate user behavior, motivations, and their interactions with scientific data, workflows, and communities to inform the design of scientific software and infrastructure. Our work has helped us understand and address important user challenges - providing learnability as hardware and software changes, compatibility of new technologies with existing complex software stacks especially in large collaborations, and providing transparency on demand when building abstractions. We have combined these user insights with our quantitative workload analyses [2, 10] providing us a deep understanding of the needs of scientific workflows on HPC systems. Our analyses has informed our work in workflow scheduling [9], workflow management [3, 5], resource management [1], and data management [4].

Looking Forward

In the future, autonomous discovery and science will be commonplace in scientific work bringing together experiment/observation, theory, computation, and data together in ways that were not possible before. Our infrastructure and tools will need to support the different levels of automation and intelligence where systems can go from plain automation (where we have technology to assist the scientist), to self-driving, to autonomous as the system performs more tasks with lesser and lesser intervention from humans. These workflows need real-time access to resources at scale that need to be coordinated with the experiment/observation and the network. We have opportunities to look closely at workflow scheduling to address the challenges of these autonomous workflows. Coupled with the needs of the science, we have technology innovations with edge computing that will play a key role in the infrastructure fabric of the future. We will need to consider where data services (e.g., wrangling, search, storage and retrieval) tie in with the workflow and HPC systems. We will need to consider the synergy between data transfer and job scheduling on a programmable infrastructure. Autonomous science on a programmable distributed and high performance infrastructure provides a rich set of research challenges for the community.

Acknowledgements. This work has been supported by the U.S. Department of Energy, Office of Science and Office of Advanced Scientific Computing Research (ASCR) under Contract No. DE-AC02-05CH11231. This work would not be possible without the numerous collaborators, staff, postdocs, and students at Berkeley Lab and beyond.

References

1. Fox, W., Ghoshal, D., Souza, A., Rodrigo, G.P., Ramakrishnan, L.: E-HPC: a library for elastic resource management in HPC environments. In: Proceedings of the 12th Workshop on Workflows in Support of Large-Scale Science, WORKS 2017, pp. 1:1–1:11. ACM, New York (2017). https://doi.org/10.1145/3150994.3150996
2. Ghoshal, D., et al.: Characterizing scientific workflows on HPC systems using logs. In: 2020 IEEE/ACM Workflows in Support of Large-Scale Science (WORKS), pp. 57–64 (2020). https://doi.org/10.1109/WORKS51914.2020.00013
3. Ghoshal, D., et al.: Science capsule: towards sharing and reproducibility of scientific workflows. In: 2021 IEEE Workshop on Workflows in Support of Large-Scale Science (WORKS), pp. 66–73 (2021). https://doi.org/10.1109/WORKS54523.2021.00014
4. Ghoshal, D., Ramakrishnan, L.: MaDaTS: managing data on tiered storage for scientific workflows. In: ACM Symposium on High Performance Parallel and Distributed Computing (HPDC 2017). ACM Press (2017)
5. Hendrix, V., Fox, J., Ghoshal, D., Ramakrishnan, L.: Tigres workflow library: supporting scientific pipelines on HPC systems. In: 2016 16th IEEE/ACM International Symposium on Cluster, Cloud and Grid Computing (CCGrid), pp. 146–155, May 2016. https://doi.org/10.1109/CCGrid.2016.54
6. Paine, D., Ghoshal, D., Ramakrishnan, L.: Experiences with a flexible user research process to build data change tools. J. Open Res. Softw. **8** (2020). https://doi.org/10.5334/jors.284
7. Paine, D., Poon, S., Ramakrishnan, L.: Investigating user experiences with data abstractions on high performance computing systems. https://doi.org/10.2172/1805039, https://www.osti.gov/biblio/1805039
8. Ramakrishnan, L., Poon, S., Pastorello, G.Z., Gunter, D., Hendrix, V., Agarwal, D.: Experiences with user-centered design for the Tigres workflow API. In: IEEE eScience (2014)
9. Rodrigo, G.P., Elmroth, E., Östberg, P.O., Ramakrishnan, L.: Enabling workflow-aware scheduling on HPC systems. In: Proceedings of the 26th International Symposium on High-Performance Parallel and Distributed Computing, HPDC 2017, pp. 3–14. ACM, New York (2017). https://doi.org/10.1145/3078597.3078604
10. Rodrigo Álvarez, G.P., Östberg, P.O., Elmroth, E., Antypas, K., Gerber, R., Ramakrishnan, L.: HPC system lifetime story: workload characterization and evolutionary analyses on NERSC systems. In: Proceedings of the 24th International Symposium on High-Performance Parallel and Distributed Computing, pp. 57–60. ACM (2015)

Contents

Technical Papers

Technical Papers

On the Feasibility of Simulation-Driven Portfolio Scheduling for Cyberinfrastructure Runtime Systems

Henri Casanova[1](✉), Yick Ching Wong[1], Loïc Pottier[2], and Rafael Ferreira da Silva[3]

[1] Information and Computer Sciences Department, University of Hawaii, Honolulu, HI, USA
{henric,wongy}@hawaii.edu
[2] Information Sciences Institute, University of Southern California, Marina Del Rey, CA, USA
lpottier@isi.edu
[3] National Center for Computational Sciences, Oak Ridge National Laboratory, Oak Ridge, TN, USA
silvarf@ornl.gov

Abstract. Runtime systems that automate the execution of applications on distributed cyberinfrastructures need to make scheduling decisions. Researchers have proposed many scheduling algorithms, but most of them are designed based on analytical models and assumptions that may not hold in practice. The literature is thus rife with algorithms that have been evaluated only within the scope of their underlying assumptions but whose practical effectiveness is unclear. It is thus difficult for developers to decide which algorithm to implement in their runtime systems.

To obviate the above difficulty, we propose an approach by which the runtime system executes, throughout application execution, simulations of this very execution. Each simulation is for a different algorithm in a scheduling algorithm portfolio, and the best algorithm is selected based on simulation results. The main objective of this work is to evaluate the feasibility and potential merit of this portfolio scheduling approach, even in the presence of simulation inaccuracy, when compared to the traditional one-algorithm approach. We perform this evaluation via a case study in the context of scientific workflows. Our main finding is that portfolio scheduling can outperform the best one-algorithm approach even in the presence of relatively large simulation inaccuracies.

Keywords: Portfolio scheduling · On-line simulation · Workflows

---

This manuscript has been authored in part by UT-Battelle, LLC, under contract DE-AC05-00OR22725 with the US Department of Energy (DOE). The publisher acknowledges the US government license to provide public access under the DOE Public Access Plan (http://energy.gov/downloads/doe-public-access-plan).

D. Klusáček et al. (Eds.): JSSPP 2022, LNCS 13592, pp. 3–24, 2023.
https://doi.org/10.1007/978-3-031-22698-4_1

1 Introduction

Data processing and analysis applications that execute on parallel and distributed computing environments, or CyberInfrastructures (CI), arise in most fields of science and engineering. A key endeavor has been to develop CI runtime systems that make it straightforward for users to implement, deploy, and execute their applications. To this end, all these systems automate application execution, including the resource management and task scheduling decision making process. Specifically, decisions must be made along, at least, the following axes:

- Selecting hardware and/or virtualized resources;
- Picking application configuration options (e.g., pick numbers of cores that should be used by multi-threaded tasks);
- Scheduling application activities in time (when?) and space (which resource?).

Decisions along these axes must be made so as to meet user-level objectives and constraints, which can encompass notions of performance, monetary cost, energy consumption, reliability, etc. For simplicity, we call all above decisions *scheduling decisions*, which must be made using *scheduling algorithms*. Scheduling problems are generally NP-complete, and thus most proposed algorithms employ non-guaranteed heuristics.

The design of scheduling algorithms has received an enormous amount of effort. For instance, solely in the context of the popular "scientific workflow" application model [4], hundreds of research publications propose scheduling algorithms (see the many surveys on this topic [1,3,16,20,22,25,27]). Most of these proposed algorithms reuse ideas and principles from the age-old and extensive DAG (Directed Acyclic Graph) scheduling literature [28]. Yet, when examining existing workflow runtime systems, there is a clear disconnect between research and practice. Given the complexity of CI platforms and applications, research results are typically obtained based on simplifying analytical models and assumptions, so that scheduling problems are rendered more formalizable and tractable. For instance, ignoring network contention greatly simplifies application scheduling problems [13], but the computed schedules will perform poorly in practice when network contention does occur. Furthermore, published evaluation results for proposed algorithms cannot cover the whole range of situations a runtime system could encounter in practice. The literature is thus rife with scheduling algorithms that have been evaluated within the scope of their underlying assumptions, but whose potential effectiveness in practice is unquantified. There is thus little incentive for developers of CI runtime systems to pay close attention to scheduling research. Based on our own observation of production systems, it seems that developers often opt for simple scheduling strategies that are straightforward to implement but that may not lead to the most desirable application executions.

A way to resolve the above disconnect between scheduling research and practice is simply to obviate the challenge of picking one particular scheduling algorithm to implement as part of a CI runtime system. To this end, one can use *online simulations* for picking which algorithm to use at runtime. In other words, one executes fast simulations of the application execution throughout that very execution so as to "try out" many potential scheduling algorithms and automatically select the most desirable one. Based on simulation results, some of these algorithms may rarely (or even never) be used at runtime because simulations show them to be non-competitive. CI runtime system developers can incrementally add to their set of implemented algorithms, without ever having to decide at compile time which algorithm should be used. This approach has been referred to as "portfolio scheduling" [12] in the job scheduling literature, for the purpose of scheduling user jobs with known runtime estimates on a space-shared parallel computing platform. In this work, we instead consider a CI runtime system that automates the execution of an application workload that performs I/O, communication, and computation operations. In this context, many scheduling algorithms have been designed based on models and assumptions that are known to be not realistic, which are necessary for designing the algorithms, but which makes their effectiveness unclear in practice. The simulation can implement more realistic models and assumptions, and thus has the potential to give a more accurate measure of how these scheduling algorithms would actually perform in practice. But, conversely, no simulation can be perfectly accurate.

Our objective in this work is to assess the feasibility and potential merit of simulation-driven portfolio scheduling in CI runtime systems. Although the approach is general, we perform our experimental evaluations in the specific context of scientific workflows because they have become widespread as well as the CI runtime systems available to execute them. More specifically, this work makes the following contributions:

- We propose to use simulation-driven portfolio scheduling as part of CI runtime systems that automate the execution of application workloads;
- We evaluate the feasibility and potential merit of this approach via a case study to answer three main research questions: (i) What is the potential improvement over the traditional one-algorithm approach? (ii) How much of the upcoming application execution should be simulated? (iii) What level of simulation accuracy is needed?
- Our main finding is that, at least in the context of our case study, the portfolio scheduling approach outperforms the best one-algorithm approach even in the presence of relatively low simulation accuracy.

The rest of this paper is organized as follows. Section 2 discusses related work. Section 3 describes our approach, which we evaluate via the case study described in Sect. 4. Section 5 discusses experimental results. Finally, Sect. 6 summarizes our contributions and highlights directions for future work.

2 Related Work

The idea of adaptive scheduling at runtime has been explored in many previous works, typically to determine good values for parameters that define the behavior of the scheduling algorithm. While a number of techniques can be used to determine these values, some authors have used online simulation [7,14,15,29,30].

Some of these works target discrete parameters that drastically change the behavior of the scheduling algorithm (e.g., a parameter that defines the job ordering policy), and one could easy consider that these approaches select an algorithm from a set of possible algorithms. Doing so has generally been called "portfolio scheduling" and has been investigated in several works [12,31,32]. An important question is that of the method for selecting a particular algorithm within the portfolio. While many options are likely possible, such as machine learning [31], an attractive option used in previous works, and in this work, is on-line simulation [12,32].

The above works that use on-line simulation for scheduling algorithm adaptation and/or portfolio scheduling have shown that the approach can be effective. However, these works all target some version of the "job scheduling" problem. The goal is to allocate compute resources to jobs that request them for a predetermined time. As a result, the simulation boils down to merely computing the deterministic schedule (i.e., a Gantt chart) generated by each algorithm. The only source of inaccuracy in this computation is the job runtime estimates, which, notoriously, are overestimated. Some of these works examine the impact of inaccurate runtime estimates (e.g., [12,15]). Importantly, this inaccuracy does not correspond to the typical notion of simulation inaccuracy, i.e., that due to the simulation only approximating the real system. Instead, this is inaccuracy of the input to the simulation, which is no different than the inaccuracy of the input to the real-world system. In contexts more general than the job scheduling problem, sources of simulation inaccuracies arise because the simulation cannot perfectly capture the behavior of a complex system in which the simulated application workload uses and contends for network, I/O, and compute resources. Furthermore, information on the current state of the execution, on the platform configuration, and on the application's behavior, which are all needed to instantiate a simulation, is not perfect. In this work we investigate and quantify the effect of simulation inaccuracy by assuming that the performance metrics estimated via simulation are inherently noisy. This investigation is particularly relevant in this work as our case-study is in the context of workflow applications that perform communication, I/O, and computation activities in a distributed computing context. As a result, the sources of simulation inaccuracies are multiple and the magnitude of the error can be large. To the best of our knowledge, this is the first work that evaluates the potential merit of portfolio scheduling in this more general context, both in terms of the application workload and of the platform on which this workflow is executed.

A challenge for portfolio scheduling based on online simulation is that of the overhead of simulation. Several approaches to mitigate this overhead are possible, such as reducing the frequency at which online simulations are executed and pruning the algorithm portfolio [12]. In this work, we also experiment with reducing the simulation time horizon. As already mentioned, most of the aforementioned works target job scheduling, for which the simulation overhead is essentially that of executing the scheduling algorithm. This is because the simulation merely consists in computing job start and end times in a Gantt chart.

In our more general setting, the simulation must employ various models (e.g., to compute communication data transfer rates based on network topology, ongoing network flows, and network protocol effects), which increase simulation overhead. We discuss the simulation overhead challenge in more details in Sect. 5.5.

Many simulation frameworks have been developed that target the simulation of parallel and distributed applications and platforms [5,6,8–10,17,18,21,23,24, 33], and they each achieve different compromises between accuracy and speed. At one extreme are discrete-event models that capture "microscopic" behaviors of hardware/software systems (e.g., packet-level network simulation, block-level disk simulation, cycle-accurate CPU simulation), which favor accuracy over speed. At the other extreme are analytical models that capture "macroscopic" behaviors via mathematical models. While these models lead to fast simulation, they must be developed carefully if high levels of accuracy are to be achieved [34]. This work is agnostic to the simulation framework used to implement the simulation, but a more accurate and more scalable framework is obviously preferable. For the case study in Sect. 4, we implement a simulator using the SimGrid [9] and WRENCH [10] frameworks. SimGrid provides accurate and scalable simulation models and abstractions for simulating distributed applications, systems, and platforms. To date, it has been used to obtain simulation results for 570+ research publications. One drawback of SimGrid is that its simulation abstractions are low-level, meaning that implementing simulators of complex systems can be labor-intensive [19]. WRENCH builds on SimGrid to provide high-level simulation abstractions that make it possible to implement simulators of complex CI scenarios in only a few hundred lines of code [10].

3 Problem Statement, Approach, Research Questions

Consider a CI platform with hardware resources (compute, storage, network) accessible via various software services for starting computations, storing data, and moving data. Some application workload of interest is to be executed on this platform. A CI runtime system is used to automate this execution, and as part of this automation the system must make decisions regarding the allocation of application activities to the hardware resources in time and space. These scheduling decisions are made using some algorithm, with the goal of optimizing some metric such as overall execution time.

In the above context, we propose to use simulation-driven portfolio scheduling. The main caveat of scheduling algorithms in the literature is that they are developed with simplifying models and assumptions so as to make the scheduling problem algorithmically more tractable. By contrast, simulation does not need to make simplifying assumptions. For instance, it can easily capture stochastic platform and application behaviors, complex network sharing behaviors, or complex overlap behaviors between computation, I/O, and network communication activities. Although accounting for such behaviors makes the scheduling problem algorithmically more difficult, simulations merely output relevant application-level metrics (e.g., execution time, cost, energy consumption, reliability) for all candidate scheduling algorithms in a portfolio, and one can simply pick the most desirable one. All algorithms in the portfolio must be implemented in the runtime system. At the onset of application execution, a description of the application and the available hardware resources is constructed based on (likely imperfect) a-priori knowledge, so as to instantiate a simulator of the upcoming application execution. Throughout execution, scheduling decisions are made using one of the implemented algorithms, selected based on simulation results.

Realizing the above approach in practice entails addressing many research and engineering challenges that are outside the scope of this work. Our objective here is to determine whether this approach has potential merit in the first place. To this end, we focus on the following research questions:

How Much of an Improvement can the Online Simulation Approach Afford? We wish to compare our proposed approach to the traditional one-algorithm approach in which the runtime system uses a single scheduling algorithm throughout application execution. Assuming that a significant improvement is achieved, intriguing questions arise regarding the usefulness of individual algorithms (i.e., how many algorithms are never used? how many different algorithms are used throughout application execution?).

How Much of the Upcoming Application Execution Should be Simulated? In spite of advances in scalable simulation techniques for simulating distributed applications and platforms, online simulations do not take zero time. One easy way to reduce simulation overhead is to bound the simulated time horizon and not simulate the upcoming application execution until completion. We wish to quantify the impact of making simulations "short-sighted" on the effectiveness of our proposed approach.

What Level of Simulation Accuracy is needed? Simulations are never 100% accurate, because of inaccuracies inherent to the simulation models or because model parameters are not instantiated in a way that perfectly matches real-world settings. We wish to determine what level of simulation accuracy is needed for our proposed approach to outperform the traditional one-algorithm approach.

We answer these questions via the case study described in the next section.

4 Case Study

We consider the execution of scientific workflow applications on a multi-cluster CI deployment, where the goal is to minimize overall execution time, or *makespan*. Scientific workflows have been used by computational scientists to support some of the most significant discoveries of the past several decades [4], and are executed daily to serve a wealth of scientific domains. Many workflows have high computational demands and, as such, are executed in production on HPC clusters. Setting up, orchestrating, monitoring, and optimizing workflow executions on these platforms is challenging, and the way to address this challenge is to rely on runtime systems, or Workflow Management Systems (WMSs), that can automate workflow execution [26]. The past decade has witnessed a proliferation of WMSs [35], but there is no consensus on which scheduling algorithms should be implemented in these systems, which is why we picked this context for this case study.

4.1 Platform Configurations

We consider multi-cluster platforms. Each cluster hosts homogeneous 8-core compute nodes connected via a 100 GbE interconnect, as well as network-attached storage with I/O read/write bandwidths of 100 MBps. Core speed is measured in Gflop/sec, but our experiments are agnostic to the particular units since, as described in Sect. 4.2, workflow task compute times are given in seconds on a reference 100 Gflops/s core. That is, compute speeds are only used to scale task compute times based on the reference compute time. Each cluster is connected to the Internet on a network path with some bottleneck bandwidth. The network-attached storage is used to cache application data. That is, whenever a compute node in a cluster needs to write application data, it writes it to the cluster's network-attached storage. Whenever a compute node in a cluster needs to read application data, it does so from the network-attached storage if possible. Otherwise, the data is read from a remote location (the user's machine, where all input data is located initially, or another cluster's network-attached storage) and cached locally. We assume that storage capacity at each cluster is large enough to hold all application data.

We conduct experiments with the 9 synthetic 1-, 2-, and 3-cluster platform configurations listed in Table 1. These configurations do not correspond to particular real-world platforms and many other configurations could be considered. Our goal is to span a spectrum of diverse but reasonable platform configurations, over which different scheduling algorithms would likely make different decisions (e.g., due to the different ratios of compute speed to Internet bandwidth for the clusters in configurations P4 to P9).

4.2 Workflow Configurations

We consider 8 real-world scientific workflow instances, as listed in Table 2. These instances are provided by the WfCommons project[1] and were derived based on logs from actual executions [11]. Each instance defines a set of tasks, each with particular amounts of computation to perform, and input and output files of particular sizes. Some output files of a task are input files to other tasks, thus creating data dependencies between tasks. We selected instances whose work (i.e., execution time on a single 100Gflop/sec core) are in between 5 and 10 h. The metrics shown in the table show that the workflow instances correspond to a diverse set of configurations, with different structures and different computation-data ratios. As a result, we expect that different scheduling algorithms will fare differently across these workflow instances.

[1] https://wfcommons.org/instances.

Table 1. Multi-cluster platform configurations used for experiments. Each cluster is defined by a number of nodes ("nodes"), a core speed in Gflop/sec ("speed"), and an Internet bandwidth in MBps ("bdwidth").

Config	Cluster #1			Cluster #2			Cluster #3		
	Nodes	Speed	Bdwidth	Nodes	Speed	Bdwidth	Nodes	Speed	Bdwidth
P_1	96	100	100	n/a			n/a		
P_2	48	50	100	48	150	100	n/a		
P_3	48	50	100	48	400	10	n/a		
P_4	32	100	100	32	200	200	32	300	300
P_5	32	100	100	32	200	300	32	300	200
P_6	32	100	200	32	200	100	32	300	300
P_7	32	100	200	32	200	300	32	300	100
P_8	32	100	300	32	200	200	32	300	100
P_9	32	100	300	32	200	100	32	300	200

Table 2. Workflow configurations used in our experiments, indicating for each the application name ("name"), the application domain ("domain"), the number of tasks ("tasks"), the sequential compute time in hours on a single 100Gflop/sec core ("work"), the sum of all data file sizes ("footprint"), the number of levels ("depth"), and the size of the largest level ("max width").

Config	Name	Domain	Tasks	Work	Footprint	Depth	Max width
W_1	Montage	Astronomy	4,846	8.7	12.15 GB	8	3,411
W_2	Epigenomics	Bioinformatics	1,095	5.6	8.25 GB	9	271
W_3	Bwa	Bioinformatics	1004	3.7	56.89 MB	3	1,000
W_4	Cycles	Agroecosystem	874	5.2	6.17 GB	4	432
W_5	1000Genome	Bioinformatics	328	6.0	25.96 GB	3	208
W_6	Blast	Bioinformatics	303	8.7	0.47 MB	3	300
W_7	Soykb	Bioinformatics	156	6.7	2.82 GB	11	100
W_8	Srasearch	Bioinformatics	22	5.2	16.50 GB	3	11

The workflow instances available on the WfCommons collection do not include information about the execution of workflow tasks on multiple cores, but only give a single execution time t, which is a sequential execution time on a single core. Due to this lack of information, we assume an Amdahl's Law parallel speedup behavior [2]: a task that executes in time t on one core executes in time $\alpha t/n + (1-\alpha)t$ on n of these cores. For each task, we sample α uniformly between 0.8 and 1.0. This may not correspond to the actual speedup behaviors of workflow tasks in a real-world workflow, but in the scope of this case-study has no impact on simulation inaccuracy (since we use as ground truth the execution of the workflow assuming these very same task speedup behaviors).

4.3 Algorithms

We assume that the WMS used to execute workflows employs a typical list-scheduling approach for deciding, at runtime, which ready task should be executed on which compute resources, while enforcing that not two tasks run simultaneously on the same core. The scheduling algorithm proceeds in three steps as follows. While there is at least one ready task and one idle core on which no task has been scheduled:

1. pick a ready task using some criterion C_1;
2. pick a cluster with at least one idle core using some criterion C_2;
3. pick a number of cores for the task execution using some criterion C_3;
4. schedule the picked task on the picked cluster using the picked number of cores.

We consider the following options for each of the above criteria:

- Criterion C_1:
  - 0: Pick the task with the largest bottom-level (i.e., prioritize tasks on the critical path);
  - 1: Pick the task with the largest number of children tasks;
  - 2: Pick the task with the largest amount of input and output data;
  - 3: Pick the task with the largest amount of computation to perform.
- Criterion C_2:
  - 0: Pick the cluster that stores the largest amount of task input data in its network-attached storage;
  - 1: Pick the cluster with the most idle cores;
  - 2: Pick the cluster with the fastest cores.
- Criterion C_3:
  - 0: Pick as many cores as possible while ensuring that the task's parallel efficiency is above 90%;
  - 1: Pick as many cores as possible while ensuring that the task's parallel efficiency is above 50%;
  - 2: Pick as many cores as possible.

We denote each algorithm as A_x, where $x = 9 \times C_1 + 3 \times C_2 + C_3$, which gives us 36 different algorithms (A_0 to A_{35}). All above scheduling criteria have been proposed in the literature. Although many other options could be considered, these 36 algorithms provide us with a sufficiently large and diverse sample set to conduct our investigation.

4.4 Experimental Methodology

An implementation of our online simulation approach in this case study entails (i) an implementation of a WMS that executes workflows on multi-cluster platforms; and (ii) an implementation of a simulator of these executions that can be invoked at runtime by the WMS. We face two main technical difficulties. First, to answer the third research question in Sect. 3, we need to experiment with different levels of simulation accuracy to measure the resulting impact on the effectiveness of our proposed approach, including quantifying the best-case effectiveness when online simulations are 100% accurate. This is not possible with a real-world implementation since a given simulator is necessarily inaccurate. Second, we wish to evaluate our approach on a large range of workflows, platforms, and algorithms. For instance, in this particular case study, we evaluate a total of $9 \times 8 \times 36 = 2,592$ experimental scenarios (9 platform configurations, 8 workflows, 36 algorithms). Even if we had access to a large number of different platform configurations, it would be difficult to obtain all experimental results, not only in terms of time and energy consumption, but also in terms of ensuring that these results are repeatable. The need to obtain many diverse and repeatable experimental results is, incidentally, the main reason why researchers in the field resort to simulation.

Given the above, we perform our case study entirely in simulation. We implement a WMS simulator, with WRENCH[2] (v1.10) and SimGrid[3] (v3.29), that simulates a WMS that executes workflows on multi-cluster platforms using any one of our 36 algorithms. This simulator provides us with an analog of a production WMS implementation, which we enhance with our online simulation approach. That is, during its simulated execution, our simulator runs as many (online) simulations of its future execution as there are scheduling algorithms (36 in this case study). This is done simply by having the simulator call the `fork` system call to create a child process that is a clone of the simulator, for each algorithm. Each child then continues the simulated workflow execution and reports the simulated workflow completion date to its parent process. In this fashion, the simulator can explore all its possible futures for all algorithms. The WMS then picks the algorithm that achieved the fastest workflow execution in those simulations. The simulator outputs the workflow makespan, in seconds, based on the following input:

- **A workflow instance** – One of the 8 instances in Sect. 4.2, available as a JSON file using the WfFormat format[4]. We use w to denote the total amount of sequential work, i.e., the sum of the sequential task execution times on a reference 100 Gflops/sec core (the 4th column in Table 2).
- **A platform configuration** – One of the 9 configurations in Sect. 4.1.
- **A fraction of total work, α** – This parameter defines how often our online simulation approach is applied throughout workflow execution: it is applied at the onset of the workflow execution and subsequently each time an additional fraction α of the total work w has been completed. For instance, $w = 10,000$ Gflop and $\alpha = 0.2$, our approach will be invoked 5 times throughout workflow execution, once at the beginning of the execution, and once each time an additional 2,000 Gflop of sequential work has been performed. Note that the amount of work performed so far at any given time is known since the amount

[2] https://wrench-project.org.
[3] https://simgrid.org.
[4] https://wfcommons.org/format.

of work of each task in the workflow (i.e., its execution time in seconds on a single core) is also known.

- **A fraction of total work,** β – Each online simulation proceeds until execution of a fraction β of the total sequential work has been simulated and reports the current simulation date to the parent process. In other terms, β defines the time horizon of the simulations.

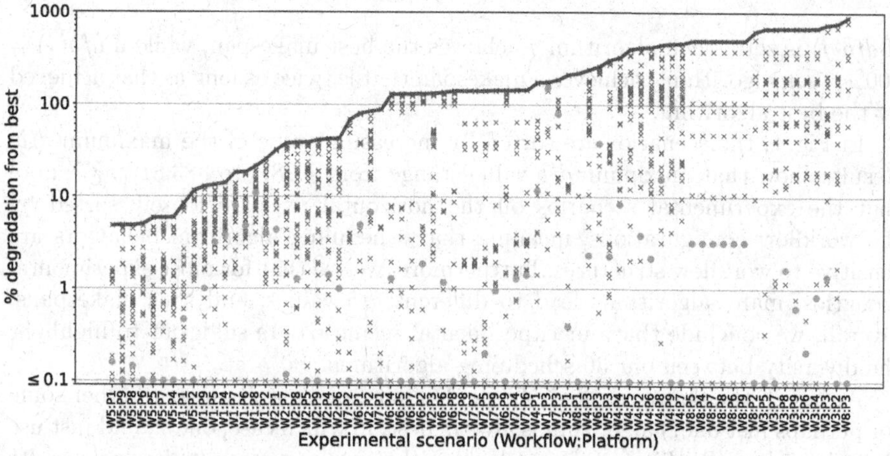

Fig. 1. Percent degradation from best for all algorithms over all experimental scenarios, sorted by increasing maximum values. Maximum values are shown as a blue solid lines. Data points for the A_8 algorithm are shown as red dots.

- **A relative simulation error,** e – This parameter denotes the relative range of an uniformly distributed simulation error. That is, when an online simulation determines that a fraction β of the sequential work was performed in time t, it reports, instead, a time $\max(0, t + \mathcal{U}(-t \times e, t \times e))$, where $\mathcal{U}(a, b)$ denotes the uniform random distribution on the (a, b) interval. For any experiment for which $e > 0$, we run 10 samples.

Simulator code and all simulation data are publicly available[5].

5 Results

5.1 Diversity of One-Algorithm Approaches

In Sect. 4, we claimed that our experimental scenarios (workflow and platform configurations) would lead our different algorithms to exhibit a range of behaviors. In this section, we verify this claim quantitatively. Figure 1 shows, for each experimental scenario (i.e., a workflow and platform combination) the relative

[5] https://github.com/wrench-project/jsspp2022_submission_data.

difference, in percentage, between the makespan achieved by each algorithm and that achieved by the best algorithm for this scenario, which is typically termed "degradation from best" or *dfb*. In other terms, assuming a set of n algorithms, if for a particular experimental scenario each algorithm i achieves a makespan m_i, then the dfb of algorithm j is defined as:

$$dfb(j) = 100 \times \frac{m_j - \min_i m_i}{\min_i m_i} .$$

If $dfb(j)$ is zero, then algorithm j achieves the best makespan, while if $dfb(j) = 100\%$, then algorithm j achieves a makespan that is twice as long as that achieved by the best algorithm.

In Fig. 1, the scenarios are sorted by increasing value of the maximum dfb. Results show that maximum dfb values range from 4.38% to 883.81%. We note that the experimental scenarios on the horizontal axis are loosely sorted by the workflow configurations, meaning that scheduling algorithm behaviors are sensitive to workflow structures. Furthermore, we see that for most experimental scenarios, many algorithms lead to different dfb values, and thus makespans. Overall, we conclude that our experimental scenarios are sufficient to highlight the diversity between our 36 scheduling algorithms.

Although the above results indicate diversity, one may wonder whether some (or perhaps just one?) algorithm is always best, in which case, one should just use that algorithm. To this end, for each algorithm, we can compute its average dfb over all experimental scenarios. We find that algorithm A_8 achieves the lowest average dfb at 6.47%. While this number is relatively low, it does not mean that algorithm A_8 is consistently a good choice. It happens to be the best (or within 1% of the best) choice for 37 of our 72 scenarios. However, it has a dfb higher than 10% for 7 of the remaining 35 scenarios, and as high as 159.60%. This is illustrated in Fig. 1 where the data points for algorithm A_8 are shown as red dots. We conclude that no single algorithm is best, and that although algorithm A_8 is the "best on average" choice, it can be vastly outperformed by other algorithms for some experimental scenarios.

5.2 Evaluation in the Ideal Case ($\beta = 1$, $e = 0$)

In this section, we compare our simulation-driven portfolio scheduling approach to the one-algorithm approach under ideal conditions, that is, with the two following assumptions: (i) each online simulation simulates the application execution until completion ($\beta = 1$); and (ii) simulations are 100% accurate ($e = 0$). In upcoming sections, we relax these assumptions. Unless specified otherwise, all results hereafter are obtained with $\alpha = 0.1$, i.e., online simulations are invoked 10 times throughout workflow execution.

Because of these two assumptions, given any experimental scenario, our approach is guaranteed to never be outperformed by any one algorithm: at the onset of the execution it simulates all possible algorithms and necessarily picks the best one. That is, if we were to plot the degradation from best of our approach

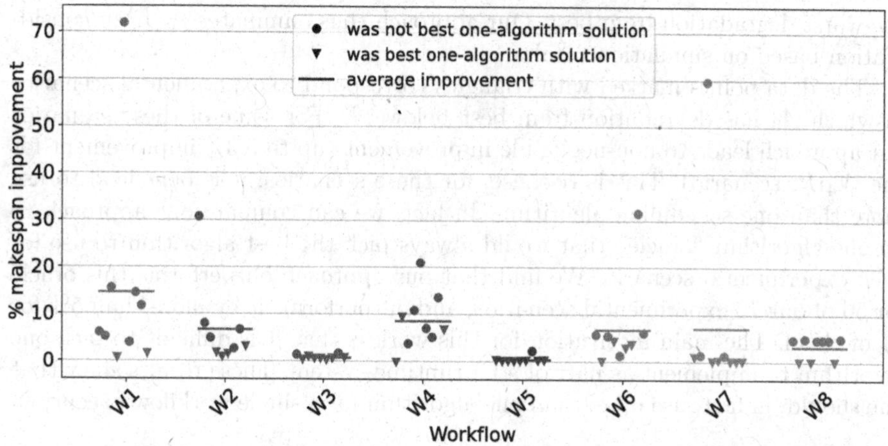

Fig. 2. Percentage improvement over the one-algorithm approach for each workflow (each data point is for a different platform configuration).

in Fig. 1, its data points would all be on the $y = 0$ line. In this and upcoming sections, we compare our approach to the one-algorithm approach that uses algorithm A_8, which, for simplicity, we term the *one-algorithm approach*. As seen in the previous section, A_8 is the algorithm with the lowest average degradation from best among all 36 algorithms. It thus corresponds to the best choice that a runtime system developer could make if asked to pick one algorithm to implement in their system, at least in the scope of this case study. Picking A_8 as our main competitor allows us to evaluate the effectiveness of our approach in the worst case. We note that, in practice, the runtime system developer may very well pick another algorithm, in which case all results hereafter would be more favorable (and often drastically more favorable) for our approach. Algorithm A_8 prioritizes tasks with the highest bottom-level ($C_1 = 0$), selects the cluster with the fastest cores ($C_2 = 2$), and uses as many cores are possible on a compute node ($C_3 = 2$).

Figure 2 shows relative makespan improvements over the one-algorithm approach. Results are grouped by workflow, showing 9 data points for each workflow (for the 9 platform configurations). Horizontal lines show average improvements. Relative improvement is always positive and can be large, and average improvement is above 5% for 5 of the 8 workflow configurations (Table 2).

Two kinds of data points are shown in Fig. 2. The data points marked with circles correspond to cases in which A_8 is not the best, or close to the best, of the 36 algorithms for that experimental scenario (i.e., its degradation from best is larger than 1%). For these data points, we expect our approach to provide improvement because it will simply use another algorithm. For instance, the data point above 70% for workflow W_1 corresponds to an execution on platform P_3. For this experimental scenario, Fig. 1 shows that algorithm A_8 has almost the worst degradation from best. Our approach thus eliminates A_8 from consideration based on simulation results.

The data points marked with triangles correspond to experimental scenarios in which A_8 has degradation from best below 1%. For some of these scenarios our approach leads to non-negligible improvement (up to 9.3% improvement for the W_4:P_5 scenario). This is because, for these scenarios, it is beneficial to use more than one scheduling algorithm. In fact, we can compare our approach to an one-algorithm "oracle" that would always pick the best algorithm to use for each experimental scenario. We find that our approach outperforms this oracle for 56 of our 72 experimental scenarios, and outperforms it by more than 5% for 11 of them. The main motivation for this work is that it is difficult to pick one algorithm to implement as part of a CI runtime system. These results show that one should, in fact, use more than one algorithm for a single workflow execution.

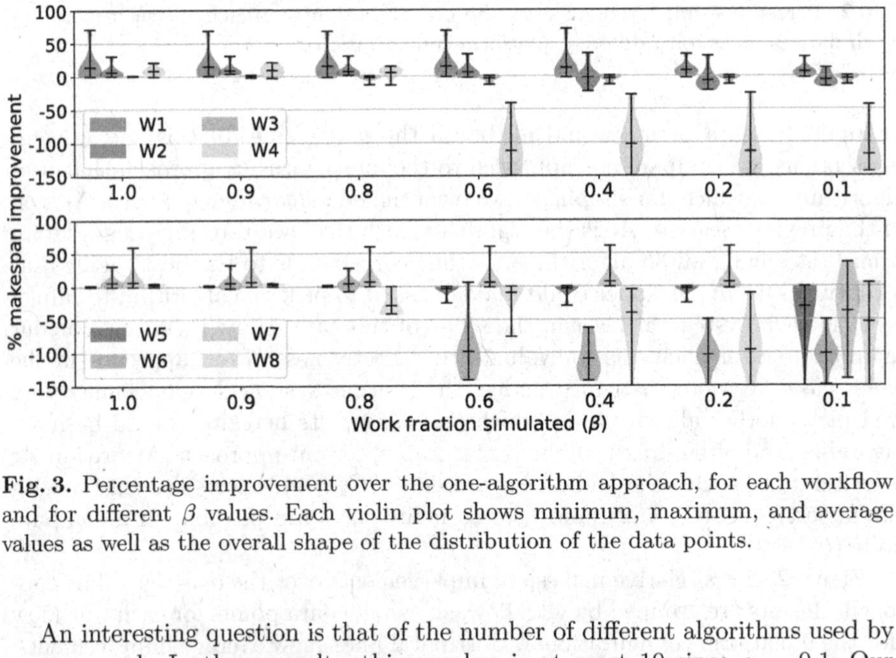

Fig. 3. Percentage improvement over the one-algorithm approach, for each workflow and for different β values. Each violin plot shows minimum, maximum, and average values as well as the overall shape of the distribution of the data points.

An interesting question is that of the number of different algorithms used by our approach. In these results, this number is at most 10 since $\alpha = 0.1$. Our approach uses a single algorithm for only 4 of our 72 experimental scenarios. Across all scenarios, our approach uses up to 6 different algorithms during a single workflow execution and 3.08 different algorithms on average. Overall, out of our 36 different algorithms 25 of them end up being used at least once by our approach. Algorithm A_8 is, unsurprisingly, the algorithm most used by our approach. But some algorithms that have poor average degradation from best are also used. For instance, algorithm A_0 is used for 12 of our 72 scenarios, but has the 4th largest average degradation from best at 176.26%.

5.3 Evaluation with Shorter Simulation Time Horizons ($\beta < 1$)

One may wonder whether it is necessary for online simulations to simulate the execution until completion. The results in the previous section are for $\beta = 1$, i.e., workflow execution is always simulated until completion. Given a value of β, a workflow, and a platform configuration, we measure the percentage improvement (or loss) that our approach achieves over the one-algorithm approach. Figure 3 shows results for several β value and workflow combinations. For each combination, there are 9 data points, one for each platform configuration. For better readability, these data points are shown as violin plots, which indicate the minimum, maximum, and average values as well as the shape of the distribution. Each data point below the $y = 0$ line corresponds to cases in which our approach loses to the one-algorithm approach.

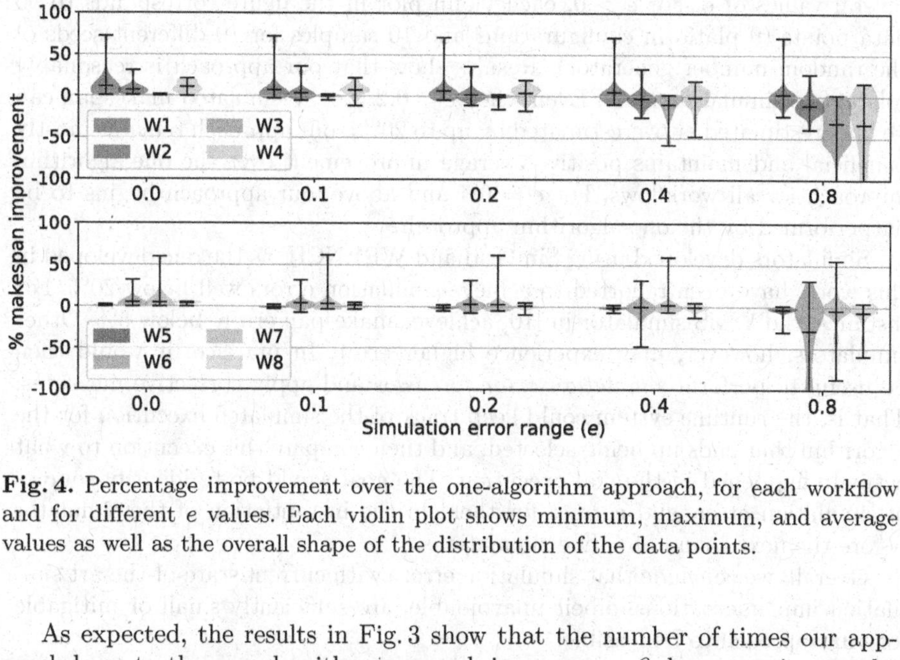

Fig. 4. Percentage improvement over the one-algorithm approach, for each workflow and for different e values. Each violin plot shows minimum, maximum, and average values as well as the overall shape of the distribution of the data points.

As expected, the results in Fig. 3 show that the number of times our approach loses to the one-algorithm approach increases as β decreases, i.e., as the simulation becomes more shortsighted. But the trends vary depending on the workflow. At one extreme, e.g. for workflow W_1, our approach remains beneficial for β as low as 0.1 (i.e., when only 10% of the total work is simulated). At the other extreme, for workflow W_8, as soon as β is 0.8 or below, our approach experiences losses. The fact that different workflows exhibit different behaviors is not surprising. Depending on workflow structures, scheduling decisions made at the onset of the execution may or may not have a large influence on the later phases of that execution. Given that, it is likely difficult to determine what level of shortsightedness is acceptable for a given workflow. We then conclude that simulating the entire execution of the application until completion ($\beta = 1$) is the safest option. All results presented hereafter, unless specified otherwise, are for $\beta = 1$. The downside of using $\beta = 1$ is that it maximizes simulation times, the implications of which are discussed in Sect. 5.5.

5.4 Evaluation with Simulation Inaccuracies ($e > 0$)

There are many sources of simulation inaccuracy, including: imperfect simulation models; imperfect instantiation of these models based on inaccurate information about the application, the platform, and the state of the ongoing execution of the application on that platform; and inherent platform/system noise. We need to ascertain whether our approach can tolerate a relatively high level of simulation inaccuracy. To answer this question, we apply uniformly distributed perturbations to simulated makespans in the interval $[-e, e]$, for various values of e (see details in Sect. 4.4). Figure 4 is similar to Fig. 3 but shows results for several values of e. For $e > 0$, each violin plot in the figure corresponds to 90 data points (9 platform configurations and 10 samples for 10 different seeds of the random number generator). Results show that our approach is reasonably tolerant to simulation error. Even when $e = 0.2$ (i.e., a simulated makespan can be underestimated or overestimated by up to 20%), our approach remains mostly beneficial and maintains positive average improvement over the one-algorithm approach for all workflows. For $e = 0.4$ and above, our approach begins to be outperformed by the one-algorithm approach.

Simulators developed using SimGrid and WRENCH, as the one developed in this work, have been reported to achieve simulation errors well below 20%. For instance, the WMS simulator in [10] achieves makespan errors below 5%. Other simulators, however, may experience higher error. In practice, it would then be useful to perform *simulation error forensics* and apply corrective measures. That is, the runtime system could keep track of the simulated execution for the algorithm that ends up being selected, and then compare this execution to what actually happened in the real execution. The goal would be to identify sources of simulation error, and correct for them in the instantiation of the simulator before the next round of online simulations.

Overall, we conclude that simulation errors with current state-of-the-art simulation implementations, albeit unavoidable, are sufficiently small or mitigable for our approach to be feasible.

5.5 Simulation Overhead

On-line simulations for driving portfolio scheduling do not have to hold up the application execution, but can be done concurrently with that execution, so that the simulation overhead can be fully hidden. One option, which we do not consider in this work, is to execute the simulations on the same resources as that on which the application executes. In this case, the simulation executions compete with and thus slows down the application execution, having a possibly large (and difficult to estimate) negative impact on application performance. Instead, we consider that the simulations execute on the host on which the CI runtime system itself executes (typically some multi-core hosts that orchestrates the application execution on other "remote" resources). Due to the overhead being hidden by application execution, its only impact is to delay algorithm selection. Since algorithm selection is performed at arbitrary times throughout execution, the only strong requirement is that the overhead be small (i.e., by at least one orders of magnitude) relative to the overall makespan. In what follows, we verify that this requirement can be achieved in practice.

Some parallel and distributed computing simulation frameworks, such as SimGrid, which we use in this work, have placed a large emphasis on scalability. To this end, analytical simulation models have been developed that have low computational complexity and that can be implemented efficiently. In Sect. 5.3, we saw that it is typically useful to simulate the upcoming application execution to completion. Furthermore, the number of algorithms to simulate could (and should) be large. Therefore, in spite of these simulations relying on scalable simulation models, simulation overhead could be large.

Table 3. Simulated makespan, simulation time, ratio thereof, and peak memory footprint of the simulation when simulating the execution of each workflow on platform configuration P_4 with algorithm A_8. Results obtained on a 2.3 GHz core.

Workflow	Simulated makespan (sec)	Simulation time (sec)	ratio	Peak memory footprint (MB)
W_1	338.77	29.35	11.5	149.95
W_2	221.67	2.86	77.5	36.19
W_3	170.63	5.58	30.6	65.98
W_4	57.62	4.48	12.9	65.58
W_5	5,618.07	3.20	1,755.6	16.96
W_6	57.21	0.77	74.3	19.32
W_7	4,887.52	6.97	701.2	28.96
W_8	416.16	0.11	3783.2	5.98

Most simulation frameworks implement discrete-event (as opposed to discrete-time) simulation. That is, computational complexity depends on the number of events to simulate and not on the length of time being simulated. Table 3 shows results obtained when simulating the full execution of each workflow on platform configuration P_4 using algorithm A_8. Simulations were executed on one core of a 2.3GHz Intel Core i9 and the results in the table are averaged over 10 trials. Since algorithm A_8 generally leads to shorter makespans than its competitors, the results in the table correspond to a worst case in terms of ratio of simulated makespan to simulation time. Also note that these results are for simulating the full workflow execution. As the execution progresses, online simulations only need to simulate the remaining application execution. That is, the simulation overhead decreases at each round of online simulation. Thus the results in the table correspond to the maximum (initial) simulation overhead.

We find that for most workflows the ratio of simulated makespan to simulation time is large. But for some workflows, such as W_1, the ratio is only 11.5x. This is because this workflow has a high number of tasks relative to its total computational work as well as a high data footprint (see Table 2), which increases the number of execution events to simulate. This is also the case for workflow W_4, and in this case is also due to the fact that the simulated makespan is low. As seen in Fig. 3, for these two workflows, it would be possible to reduce the fraction of work being simulated, so as to reduce the simulation time. In particular, our approach performs well for W_1 even when simulating the execution of only 10% of the total work.

The results in Table 3 are for the simulation of one algorithm. Our approach needs to run one simulation for each available algorithm (36, in this case study). These simulations are independent and can be executed in parallel on multiple cores, which is feasible due to the relatively low memory footprints reported in Table 3. For instance, running 36 concurrent simulations for workflow W_1, which causes the largest simulation memory footprint in our case study, only requires 5.2 GB of RAM. Running these 36 simulations concurrently on a 48-core Cascadelake 2.8 GHz machine takes only 23% longer than running only the slowest one of these simulations (simulations take different amounts of time depending on the scheduling algorithm in use).

Another option for mitigating simulation overhead is to reduce the frequency at which online simulations are executed [12]. All experiments presented so far have used $\alpha = 0.1$, that is, online simulations are invoked each time 10% of the total work has been completed. It turns out that, at least for the results in this case study, increasing α does not lead to significant performance degradation. We conducted experiments with $\alpha = 0.2$, so that online simulations are invoked only 5 times during the whole execution instead of 10 times with $\alpha = 0.1$. Comparing results between our approach and the one-algorithm approach, we find that there is at most a one-point decrease in effectiveness for 7 of the workflows and at most a two-point decrease for the remaining workflow. That is, if with $\alpha = 0.1$ our approach outperforms the one-algorithm approach by x%, then with $\alpha = 0.2$ it outperforms it by at least $x - 2$% and typically by at least $x - 1$%. In no instance does our approach lose to the one-algorithm approach with $\alpha = 0.2$. These results are obtained assuming that simulations are perfectly accurate. For a simulation error range at 20% ($e = 0.2$), then our approach experiences less than a one-point decrease in effectiveness for 5 workflows (instead of 7) and less than a two-point decrease for the remaining 3 workflows (instead of 1). Overall, at least within the scope of this case study, decreasing the frequency at which online simulations are executed, which reduces simulation overhead, does not have a large negative impact on the overall effectiveness of our approach.

We recognize that for a large number of candidate scheduling algorithms, i.e., well beyond the 36 used in our case study, it may also be necessary to investigate techniques for pruning the set of candidate algorithms (removing algorithms that tend to perform similarly, removing algorithms that tend to perform poorly) to avoid prohibitive simulation overhead. This could be done using, for instance, the technique proposed in [12] by which algorithms are placed in different categories depending on their past simulated performance, and a bounded amount of simulation time is allocated to each category.

6 Conclusion

In this work, we have assessed the potential merit of using simulation-driven portfolio scheduling in CI runtime systems that automates the execution of application workloads. The main goal is to obviate the well-known challenge of selecting a particular scheduling algorithm to implement in a runtime system. In a case study, we have shown that our portfolio scheduling approach outperforms the one-algorithm approach, even if this approach happens to use the algorithm that performs best, on average, across all experimental scenarios considered in the case study. Although in some cases our approach remain effective when simulating only a fraction of the upcoming execution, simulating the execution to completion is the safest option. Crucially, our approach retains its advantage over the one-algorithm approach even in the presence of relatively large simulation error, i.e., larger than what state-of-the-art simulators have been reported to achieve. Because simulation executions can be concurrent with the application execution, the simulation overhead only needs to be small relative to the overall application makespan. We have shown that achieving this requirement is feasible in practice by using simple techniques.

Recall that we have compared our proposed approach to the best possible rational choice a runtime system developer could make for implementing the one-algorithm approach in the context of our case study (i.e., pick algorithm A_8). It is not clear how this best choice could be made in practice (besides by conducting a full experimental case study as done in this work), hence the main motivation for this work. Were the system developer to pick a middle-of-the-pack algorithm, say algorithm A_{22}, which has an average degradation from best at 49.79% (the worst algorithm has average degradation from best at 179.23%), all results presented in Sect. 5 would be drastically improved. For instance, our approach would outperform the one-algorithm approach on average for all workflows for simulation error ranges up to 80% (instead of up to 20%).

The simulation-driven portfolio scheduling approach implemented for our case study, as described in Sect. 4.4, could likely be enhanced in several ways. For instance, instead of performing algorithm selection throughout execution based on amounts of work performed since the last algorithm selection, one could instead account for the structure of the workflow and perform it each time a workflow level has completed. This is because often different workflow levels have different data and computation demands, and thus can be better served by different scheduling algorithms. The main conclusion from the results presented in this work is that it is likely worth implementing simulation-driven portfolio scheduling in a real runtime system. We plan to do so as part of production Workflow Management Systems, so that we can reproduce in practice some of the results presented in our case study. A particularly interesting future work direction, to be pursued once a prototype implementation is available, is the investigation of simulation forensics techniques to detect and mitigate simulation error at runtime. Another interesting direction is the optimization of other metrics of application execution (e.g., energy consumption). Finally, although workflows are a general model of computation, it would be interesting to investigate whether the results in this work can generalize to other kinds of applications for which CI runtime systems must be developed that make scheduling decisions.

Acknowledgments. This work is funded by NSF contracts #2106059 and #2106147: "Collaborative Research: OAC Core: Simulation-driven runtime resource management for distributed workflow applications"; and partially funded by NSF contracts #2103489 and #2103508. This research used resources of the Oak Ridge Leadership Computing Facility at the Oak Ridge National Laboratory, which is supported by the Office of Science of the U.S. Department of Energy under Contract No. DE-AC05-00OR22725. Finally, we thank the NSF Chameleon Cloud for providing time grants to access their resources.

References

1. Adhikari, M., Amgoth, T., Srirama, S.N.: A survey on scheduling strategies for workflows in cloud environment and emerging trends. ACM Comput. Surv. (CSUR) **52**(4), 1–36 (2019)
2. Amdahl, G.M.: Validity of the single processor approach to achieving large scale computing capabilities. In: Proceedings of the Spring Joint Computer Conference, 18–20 April, pp. 483–485 (1967)
3. Arya, L.K., Verma, A.: Workflow scheduling algorithms in cloud environment - A survey. In: Proceedings of Conference on Recent Advances in Engineering and Computational Sciences (2014)
4. Badia Sala, R.M., Ayguadé Parra, E., Labarta Mancho, J.J.: Workflows for science: A challenge when facing the convergence of HPC and big data. Supercomput. Front. Innovat. **4**(1), 27–47 (2017)
5. Buyya, R., Murshed, M.: GridSim: A toolkit for the modeling and simulation of distributed resource management and scheduling for grid computing. Concurr. Comput. Practice Exp. **14**(13–15), 1175–1220 (2002)
6. Calheiros, R.N., Ranjan, R., Beloglazov, A., De Rose, C.A.F., Buyya, R.: CloudSim: A Toolkit for Modeling and Simulation of Cloud Computing Environments and Evaluation of Resource Provisioning Algorithms. Softw. Pract. Exp. **41**(1), 23–50 (2011)
7. Carastan-Santos, D., de Camargo, R.Y.: Obtaining dynamic scheduling policies with simulation and machine learning. In: Proceedings of the International Conference for High Performance Computing, Networking, Storage and Analysis, SC 2017. Association for Computing Machinery, New York (2017)
8. Carothers, C.D., Bauer, D., Pearce, S.: ROSS: a high-performance, low memory, modular time warp system. In: Proceedings of the 14th ACM/IEEE/SCS Workshop of Parallel on Distributed Simulation, pp. 53–60 (2000)
9. Casanova, H., Giersch, A., Legrand, A., Qinson, M., Suter, F.: Versatile, scalable, and accurate simulation of distributed applications and platforms. J. Paral. Distrib. Comput. **75**(10), 2899–2917 (2014)

10. Casanova, H., et al.: Developing accurate and scalable simulators of production workflow management systems with WRENCH. Future Generat. Comput. Syst. **112**, 162–175 (2020)
11. Coleman, T., Casanova, H., Pottier, L., Kaushik, M., Deelman, E., Ferreira da Silva, R.: Wfcommons: a framework for enabling scientific workflow research and development. Future Generat. Comput. Syst. **128**, 16–27 (2022)
12. Deng, K., Song, J., Ren, K., Iosup, A.: Exploring portfolio scheduling for long-term execution of scientific workloads in IaaS clouds. In: Proceedings of International Conference on High Performance Computing, Networking, Storage and Analysis, pp. 1–12 (2013)
13. Eyraud-Dubois, L., Legrand, A.: The Influence of Platform Models on Scheduling Techniques. In: Robert, Y., Vivien, F. (eds.) Introduction to Scheduling, chap. 11, pp. 281–309. CRC Press (2009)
14. Feitelson, D., Naaman, M.: Self-tuning systems. IEEE Softw. **16**(2), 52–60 (1999)
15. Gaussier, É., Lelong, J., Reis, V., Trystram, D.: Online tuning of EASY-backfilling using queue reordering policies. IEEE Trans. Paral. Distrib. Syst. **29**(10), 2304–2316 (2018). https://doi.org/10.1109/TPDS.2018.2820699, https://hal.archives-ouvertes.fr/hal-01963216
16. Gupta, A., Garg, R.: Workflow scheduling in heterogeneous computing systems: A survey. In: 2017 International Conference on Computing and Communication Technologies for Smart Nation (IC3TSN), pp. 319–326. IEEE (2017)
17. Hoefler, T., Schneider, T., Lumsdaine, A.: LogGOPSim - simulating large-scale applications in the LogGOPS model. In: Proceedings of the ACM Workshop on Large-Scale System and Application Performance, pp. 597–604, Jun 2010
18. Kecskemeti, G.: DISSECT-CF: A simulator to foster energy-aware scheduling in infrastructure clouds. Simul. Model. Pract. Theory **58**(2), 188–218 (2015)
19. Kecskemeti, G., Ostermann, S., Prodan, R.: Fostering energy-awareness in simulations behind scientific workflow management systems. In: Proc. of the 7th IEEE/ACM International Conference on Utility and Cloud Computing, pp. 29–38 (2014)
20. Liu, J., Pacitti, E., Valduriez, P., Mattoso, M.: A Survey of Data-Intensive Scientific Workflow Management. J. Grid Comput. **13**(4), 457–493 (2015). https://doi.org/10.1007/s10723-015-9329-8
21. Malik, A.W., et al.: Cloudnetsim++: A toolkit for data center simulations in omnet++. In: Proceedings of the 2014 11th Annual High Capacity Optical Networks and Emerging/Enabling Technologies (Photonics for Energy), pp. 104–108 (2014)
22. Nallakumar, R., Sruthi Priya, K.: A survey on deadline constrained workflow scheduling algorithms in cloud environment. Int. J. Comput. Sci. Trends Technol. **2**(5), 44–50 (2014)
23. Núñez, A., Vázquez-Poletti, J., Caminero, A., Carretero, J., Llorente, I.M.: Design of a new cloud computing simulation platform. In: Proceedings of the 11th International Conference on Computational Science and its Applications, pp. 582–593, Jun 2011
24. Qayyum, T., Malik, A.W., Khan Khattak, M.A., Khalid, O., Khan, S.U.: FogNetSim++: a toolkit for modeling and simulation of distributed fog environment. IEEE Access **6**, 63570–63583 (2018)
25. Rodriguez, M.A., Buyya, R.: A taxonomy and survey on scheduling algorithms for scientific workflows in Iaas cloud computing environments. Conc. Comput. Pract. Exp. **29**(8), e4041 (2017)

26. Ferreira da Silva, R., et al.: A community roadmap for scientific workflows research and development. In: 2021 IEEE Workshop on Workflows in Support of Large-Scale Science (WORKS), pp. 81–90 (2021)
27. Singh, L., Singh, S.: A survey of workflow scheduling algorithms and research issues. Int. J. Comput. Appli. **74**(15), 21–28 (2013)
28. Sinnen, O.: Task Scheduling for Parallel Systems (Wiley Series on Parallel and Distributed Computing). Wiley-Interscience, USA (2007)
29. Srinivasan, S., Kettimuthu, R., Subramani, V., Sadayappan, P.: selective reservation strategies for backfill job scheduling. In: Proceedings of Workshop on Job Scheduling Strategies for Parallel Processing, pp. 55–71 (2002)
30. Streit, A.: The self-tuning dynP job-scheduler. In: Proceedings of 16th International Parallel and Distributed Processing Symposium (2002)
31. Sukhija, N., Malone, B., Srivastava, S., Banicescu, I., Ciorba, F.M.: Portfolio-based selection of robust dynamic loop scheduling algorithms using machine learning. In: Proceedings of IEEE International Parallel Distributed Processing Symposium Workshops, pp. 1638–1647 (2014)
32. Talby, D., Feitelson, D.: Improving and stabilizing parallel computer performance using adaptive backfilling. In: Proceedings of 19th IEEE International Parallel and Distributed Processing Symposium (2005)
33. Tikir, M.M., Laurenzano, M.A., Carrington, L., Snavely, A.: PSINS: an open source event tracer and execution simulator for MPI applications. In: Sips, H., Epema, D., Lin, H.-X. (eds.) Euro-Par 2009. LNCS, vol. 5704, pp. 135–148. Springer, Heidelberg (2009). https://doi.org/10.1007/978-3-642-03869-3_16
34. Velho, P., Mello Schnorr, L., Casanova, H., Legrand, A.: On the validity of flow-level tcp network models for grid and cloud simulations. ACM Trans. Model. Comput. Simul. **23**(4) (2013)
35. Existing workflow systems (2022). https://s.apache.org/existing-workflow-systems

AI-Job Scheduling on Systems with Renewable Power Sources

Ganesh Kamath Nileshwar(✉) and Uwe Schwiegelshohn

TU Dortmund, Dortmund, Germany
{ganeshkamath.nileshwar,uwe.schwiegelshohn}@tu-dortmund.de

Abstract. The proliferation of edge data centers and the application of exhaustive tuning methods for machine learning with the use of large training data sets lead to increased power consumption of data centers. Even when considering improved operational efficiency, the conservative estimate of the power requirement for data centers in the year 2030 stands at 900 TWh. To comply with present political requirements, renewable energy sources must provide most of this power. The high volatility of these sources produces additional operational constraints for the data centers. In addition, the share of AI training applications is expected to increase in the years to come. On the one hand, those applications often require more data resources than typical interactive applications while on the other hand, they better tolerate execution delays. To exploit this tolerance, we represent it by introducing deadlines for the jobs and present simple scheduling algorithms that use this tolerance to better consider power constraints.

To examine those scheduling algorithms in a practical environment, we execute experiments with existing cloud traces. Since there are no traces available that include a significant portion of AI training jobs with explicitly specified timing flexibility, we use traces from Google clusters, extract the available information, and add any missing information subject to assumptions that are reasonable in practice. We specify in detail our motives for the extension of the trace data.

Our experimental results show that in practical cases, a greedy acceptance approach has a better performance than a threshold based job acceptance algorithm although the latter has a significantly better worst case performance. We obtain the best results when combining greedy acceptance with a biased load allocation strategy instead of using load balancing. Since some jobs may be highly parallel and rigid, we additionally consider an allocation algorithm that minimizes the intermediate idle times in order to achieve the best use of the available power. While the last algorithm achieves a small improvement over the other allocation schemes, it needs a significantly increased computational effort. The same is true when allocating jobs with the well known backfilling approach since deadlines require using the conservative variant of backfilling.

Keywords: Online scheduling · Jobs with deadlines · Power constraints · Evaluation with simulation

D. Klusáček et al. (Eds.): JSSPP 2022, LNCS 13592, pp. 25–46, 2023.
https://doi.org/10.1007/978-3-031-22698-4_2

1 Introduction

Advancements in the area of autonomous driving and smart cities demand an increase in availability of edge data centers, which is estimated to account for 30% of the total power consumption across data centers [15]. The total power requirement of data centers is estimated to be around 1% of the global power consumption: based on the reported data center power consumption of 200 TWh in 2018, a study by Andrae [1] in 2019 expects requirements up to 2000 TWh by 2030 whereas Masanet et al. [13] predict around 900 TWh. The latter more conservative estimate is based on observations from existing power utilization patterns at data centers and assumes further improvements of operational efficiency. The authors observed an increase in efficiency in the past 10 years due to better server virtualization, improvements in cooling and power provisioning infrastructure, more efficient processors, and reductions in idle power. They expect this trend to continue. The results of the SPEC power benchmark for many processors also emphasize the large contribution of idle power to the total power consumption. A further reduction of idle time in a data center requires a better scheduling of the computing jobs. Such better scheduling approaches are limited by the current computing on demand approach. Another restriction is the high volatility of the main renewable energy sources wind and solar that will be the dominating power producers in the future according to the plans of most governments.

As explained by Mastelic et al. [14], the inefficient consumption of energy in data centers can be mainly allocated to two components - energy loss and energy waste. Energy loss is the part of power lost during transport and conversion. It also includes the energy consumed by the cooling and lighting subsystems. Energy waste, on the other hand, is the energy spent for the main task in data centers without any useful output, such as the energy consumed during idle run times. We focus our study on second component, that is, the mentioned main task in a data center. For an efficient running of a data center, the critical IT load must be planned in advance. This is achieved by listing and aggregating the nameplate power rating and voltage rating of all hardware components such as computers, network devices, and storage devices and adjusting the information to match the anticipated load. Alternatively, we can define the total power requirement as the product of the power required for the normal functioning of a single core, multiplied by the total cores active in the data center.

Additionally, the increasing usage of AI to find solutions to everyday problems will lead to a change in the application portfolio of data centers. Unfortunately, the power requirement of these applications is expected to explode due to the availability of better training data sets and tuning processes. Hao [6] states that training a single AI model with 213 M parameters needs about 201 kWh compared to 27 kWh for a model with 65 M parameters. The consumed power increased to 656 MWh when introducing a neural architecture search in first model. Fortunately, such AI training jobs do not require immediate resource provision contrary to interactive jobs. In order to address the power consumption challenges of the future, we must exploit such timing flexibility to maximize the use of renewable power. To this end, we express this timing flexibility by using job deadlines and apply online job scheduling under consideration of those deadlines. In more detail, conventional jobs have rather tight deadlines while more flexible jobs have rather loose deadlines. We express the tightness of a deadline by relating the maximum amount of delay of a job to the processing time of the job. The result is called the slack of the job.

Since present workloads in data centers usually do not include any jobs with explicit deadlines, we must introduce such deadline to execute a job scheduling study in a practical environment that addresses deadline scheduling in data centers. This problem does not occur in theoretical studies. In this domain, Jamalabadi et al. [9] have shown that a threshold based algorithm significantly outperforms a simple greedy acceptance approach when considering online deadline scheduling for load maximization. However, greedy acceptance has practical advantages since it is better able to address a sudden change of resource availability and variability in job processing times. Therefore, we are interested in the performance differences between greedy acceptance and the threshold approach under practical constraints instead of using worst case conditions as in the theoretical studies.

In addition, we want to determine which kind of allocation approach is best suited to complement the chosen acceptance algorithm. The straight forward approaches are either load balancing or load biasing. If the workload includes highly parallel and rigid jobs then we additionally consider an allocation that locally minimizes the idle time when placing a parallel job. Finally, we can exploit such intermediate idle times with the well known backfilling approach.

For our simulation experiments, we must create conditions that represent scenarios of the expected job workload. As already mentioned, we must adapt an existing workload. Then we execute extensive experiments. Due to the limited space available for this paper, we can only present some of the obtained results. To show that these results are representative for the entire suit of experiments, we have provided a generally accessible repository that contains all experiments and additional details of the considered algorithms and the experimental environment.

1.1 Our Methods

This section summarizes our methods that belong to three areas:

1. Scheduling algorithms
2. Input data
3. Experiments

Since large data centers are major consumers of electrical power they must provide in advance an estimate of their power consumption. If they use less power than this estimate they must pay for the estimated power consumption but may sell any excess power on the spot market if there is sufficient demand. Unfortunately, a lack of power demand for a data center often coincides with a generally reduced demand. If the power usage of a data center exceeds its estimate then the data center must buy any additionally required power on the spot market. This situation usually results to high additional costs and must be avoided unless favorable environmental conditions produce an unexpected increase of available power.

The results of the SPEC power benchmarks for modern processors indicate an approximately linear relationship between the power consumption of a rigid parallel job and its resource consumption (processing time times parallelism). Since the power consumption of idle processing resources is relatively high, it is desirable to avoid such idling. Therefore, we use load maximization as our scheduling objective.

As always in data centers, we are facing an online scheduling problem since customers typically submit their job requests over time. Note that in our model, the number of the available active machines in the scheduling problem represents the power estimate and may deviate from the maximal number of physical processing resources in the data center. Therefore, the machine number is fixed within an intermediate time horizon but may be subject to some variation in the long run. Since the underlying system of a workload trace is typically characterized by the number of cores while scheduling algorithms always refer to machines, we use cores and machines interchangeably depending on the context.

Any scheduling algorithm for jobs with deadlines comprises an *acceptance* and an *allocation* component. For the acceptance component, we may use a simple greedy approach that always accepts a new job if there is a schedule that completes the job and all previously accepted jobs on time. This approach is flexible and works for any number of machines. Alternatively, we can use a threshold algorithm that may reject a job although the greedy approach may accept it. As already mentioned, Jamalabadi et al. [9] have shown that the threshold algorithm clearly outperforms any greedy approach in the worst case if the deadlines of the jobs do not allow a large flexibility. We expect that this property holds for most future jobs with time flexibility. Since the thresholds depend on the number of machines, the threshold algorithm is not as flexible as the greedy approach.

Load balancing is the most common allocation approach used by numerous job scheduling algorithms. Kim and Chwa [10] have provided a worst case analysis for load balancing with greedy acceptance and load balancing. Jamalabadi et al. [9] combine the threshold algorithm with an allocation strategy that favors machines with more load, also known as BestFit strategy [4]. For rigid jobs with a high degree of parallelism, we consider an allocation approach that produces the least amount of enclosed idle time for the new job. Many data centers implement a backfilling variant to use some of the enclosed idle time. However, the observance of deadlines requires the computationally expensive conservative backfilling variant instead of EASY backfilling to prevent a deadline violation of a previously accepted job.

Although preemptive scheduling offers more flexibility than non-preemptive scheduling, we only address systems without preemption since preemption of AI training jobs typically generates a large data footprint that increases the power consumption significantly. In addition, Bertogna and Barua [2] state that storing and retrieving the context of the preemptive state contributes significantly to the runtime overhead. This approach does not prohibit the preemption of individual jobs if the preemption is clearly beneficial. Since such decision depends on the characteristic of the preempted job, we do not discuss such modification of the schedule in this study.

Our input data are based on the workload traces from a Google cluster [20]. For each job j, we extract practically relevant request data: its submission time r_j, its consumed processing time p_j, and its degree of parallelism m_j. Since the original workload traces do not include any deadline information, we must artificially generate this information. Instead of directly selecting the deadline d_j of a job, we use the individual slack value $\varepsilon_j = (d_j - r_j)/p_j - 1$. We choose the slack approach since corresponding theoretical evaluations use a minimum slack as an input value. We pick a target slack value ε for the workload and randomly select the individual slack for each job using a lognormal distribution with the geometric mean ε. Then we use the above expression for determining the individual deadline.

We must also determine the number of available cores in the simulated system, that is, the available amount of power. A lower bound of this number is given by the maximum degree of parallelism of any job in the applied input set while the upper bound depends on the smallest number of cores that allows the acceptance of all requests. Therefore, a single input data set is characterized by the geometric mean ε and the geometric standard deviation σ of the slack distribution, the original workload, and the total number of available cores.

We apply discrete event simulation to execute our experiments separately for each input set. Some experiments only consider jobs running on a single core and support a direct comparison with the theoretical reference studies while other experiments also allow jobs with different degrees of parallelism.

1.2 Our Results

We have obtained the following main results.

1. The choice of the acceptance method is dominant for small slack values while the allocation method becomes more important with increasing slack values.
2. Regardless of the allocation method, greedy acceptance outperforms the threshold algorithm for small slack values.
3. BestFit is a better allocation approach than load balancing unless we allow highly parallel requests.
4. For rigid jobs with high parallelism, conservative backfilling and the minimization of idle times for rigid jobs with high parallelism produce slightly better results than the simple allocation methods but require a significantly larger computational effort.

1.3 Related Work

We refrain from the discussion of additional theoretical studies and refer to the corresponding section in the publication by Jamalabadi et al. [9].

For rigid jobs with a high degree of parallel, we can improve the performance of most simple scheduling algorithms, like First-Come-First-Serve (FCFS), by using backfilling, that is, allowing an early start of jobs submitted later if these jobs do not delay previously scheduled jobs, see, for instance, Mu'alem and Feitelson [16]. To reduce the resulting significant computational effort, Lifka [12] proposed a simpler version named EASY backfilling, that only guarantees no delay for the most restrictive job. N'takpé and Suter [17] designed and evaluated Deadline-Based Backfilling algorithm using highly parallel workloads. Compared to conservative backfilling, their results show a significant improvement in average weight time.

While result descriptions with 2d-graphs only allow a single independent parameter, heatmaps help in investigating the difference in performance across two independent parameters in a single representation. Krakov and Feitelson [11] employ them as tools to analyze the performance of simulation logs of parallel job schedulers.

For our experimental evaluation, we use traces from a Google Cluster for a time period of 29 successive days [20]. Dong et al. [5] used these traces for the evaluation of a proposed scheme to minimize energy consumed by data centers. Cavdar et al. [3] studied the task eviction event in these traces and proposed policies for better inclusion of tasks with low priority. Iglesias et al. [8] introduced a methodology based on prediction, monitoring, and scheduling that improves the efficiency of scheduling tasks on machines. Later, the authors supplemented the study with a focus on an eviction policy [7]. Using these traces, Rampersaud and Grosu [18] evaluated the performance of their algorithms that allow sharing of memory pages on same physical server. They also extended their study to understand how their allocation maximizes revenue [19].

2 Scheduling Algorithms

This section describes the scheduling algorithms of our simulation study. We present an intuitive description of most algorithms and a theoretical analysis of greedy acceptance together with BestFit allocation. Detailed descriptions of the algorithms and of their implementation are provided in our repository[1].

For the acceptance of a new job, we distinguish between greedy acceptance and a threshold algorithm. Greedy acceptance only rejects a new job if there is no schedule that completes this job on time without changing the allocation of any previously accepted job. The threshold algorithm uses a deadline threshold and rejects a new job if its deadline is less than the threshold. The calculation of the threshold depends on the number of machines and the load on each machine.

[1] https://github.com/nileshwar-ganesh/simulation-jsspp2022.

For the allocation, the most basic approaches are load balancing and BestFit. Load balancing allocates the new job to the necessary number of least loaded machines while BestFit selects a set of machines with the largest possible total load that still allows a schedule without any deadline violation. For rigid parallel jobs, we can also use a set of jobs that produces the least amount of additionally enclosed idle time in a valid schedule. We use the name MinIdle for the latter algorithm.

We explain the difference between Greedy Balanced, Greedy BestFit and Greedy MinIdle with help of following example. In Fig. 1, the gray area represents allocated requests on the machines. Consider a new request J, with $p_j = 2$, $r_j = 3$, $d_j = 11$ requiring 2 cores. The possible outcomes of all three allocation policies are illustrated in the figure.

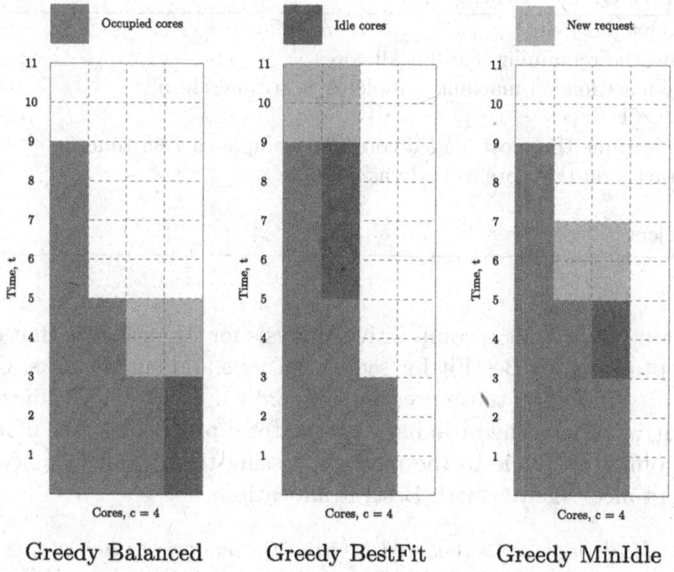

Fig. 1. Allocation pattern of different algorithms

The red area represents idle time on each machine. In our backfilling version of the algorithms, we consider this area first, when a new job arrives and allocate it to such holes in the schedule, wherever possible.

We may be able to apply the well known backfilling approach to exploit some enclosed idle time in the schedule. Since we cannot violate the deadline of any allocated jobs, EASY backfilling is not applicable and we must use the conservative variant of backfilling although it is computationally more demanding.

In theoretical studies, the competitive ratio is the method of choice to evaluate online algorithms. The competitive ratio is the ratio between the value of the objective function obtained by an online algorithm to the value of this objective function produced by the optimal offline algorithm in the worst case. For our problem, the competitive ratio of the combination of the threshold algorithm with BestFit allocation is very close to the best possible competitive ratio for small individual slacks ($\varepsilon \leq 1$) and sequential jobs, see Jamalabadi et al. [9] for details and the analysis of the algorithm. The parameter ε is the minimum individual slack of all jobs as defined in Sect. 1.1. Kim and Chwa [10] have combined greedy acceptance and load balancing. This combination achieves a competitive ratio of $2 + 1/\varepsilon$ for single-core jobs on any number of machines.

2.1 Greedy Acceptance and BestFit Allocation

Algorithm 1. Greedy BestFit

for the next job j **do**
    update the remaining load for all cores
    if the least loaded machine completes j on time **then**
        accept j
        determine the most loaded core that completes j on time
        start j on this core as early as possible
    else
        reject j

In this section, we provide a competitive analysis for Algorithm 1 that combines greedy acceptance with BestFit for sequential jobs and small slacks. Our proof techniques are similar to those used by Jamalabadi et al. [9]. For our problem, the competitive ratio is the ratio between the total processing time of all jobs in an optimal offline schedule to the total processing time of all jobs accepted by greedy acceptance together with BestFit allocation.

Lemma 1. *If all jobs are submitted at time 0 then greedy acceptance with the BestFit allocation strategy guarantees a competitive ratio of* $1 + \frac{1}{m} + \frac{1}{\varepsilon}$ *for the load maximization problem with* m *machines and slack* $\varepsilon \leq 1$.

Proof. Since all jobs have the same submission time, Algorithm 1 does not generate any intermediate idle.

The notation l_i describes the load of machine i. We use decreasing machine load to index the machines: $l_1 \geq l_2 \geq \ldots \geq l_m$. Without loss of generality, we assume a submission sequence of the jobs such that BestFit determines the load on machine i before allocating any job to machine $i+1$.

Due to greedy acceptance, Algorithm 1 does not reject any job j with deadline $d_j \geq l_m \cdot (1+\varepsilon)/\varepsilon$. Therefore, we only consider the interval $[0, t_e = l_m \cdot (1+\varepsilon)/\varepsilon)$. The notation $P(t_e)$ describes the part of the total processing time of all accepted jobs that any schedule must execute in interval $[0, t_e)$ if it includes these jobs.

The competitive ratio $\mathcal{R}$ is upper bounded by

$$\mathcal{R} \leq \frac{\sum_{i=1}^{m} l_i - P(t_e) + m \cdot t_e}{\sum_{i=1}^{m} l_i}$$

If Algorithm 1 allocates a job j to machine i with $i > 1$ then at least load $\min\{p_j, t_e - l_{i-1}\}$ must be executed in interval $[0, t_e)$ in any schedule that includes job j.

We obtain the largest competitive ratio if the load on all machines is l_m. Since we may be able to execute the load on machine 1 after time t_e, the competitive ratio is less than

$$\mathcal{R} \leq \frac{m \cdot l_m - (m-1) \cdot l_m + m \cdot l_m \cdot \frac{1+\varepsilon}{\varepsilon}}{m \cdot l_m} = 1 + \frac{1}{m} + \frac{1}{\varepsilon}.$$

□

If jobs can be submitted at any time then Algorithm 1 may allocate some processing time to an interval $[t_s, t_e)$ although it is possible to execute this processing time before time t_s, that is, the algorithm may produce a delayed execution of some processing time. If the algorithm does not reject any jobs in the interval I preceding interval $[t_s, t_e)$ then the optimal schedule can use the processing resources in I to execute jobs allocated to $[t_s, t_e)$ and may execute some rejected jobs with the additionally available resources in interval $[t_s, t_e)$.

Lemma 2. *Delayed execution caused by Algorithm 1 can increase the competitive ratio of Lemma 1 by at most* 0.3095.

Proof. We assume that delayed execution occurs on $d \leq m$ machines and determine the difference $\Delta(d, m, \mathcal{R})$ between the competitive ratios of a schedule with delayed allocation and a reference schedule without delayed execution using the same value m and generating $\mathcal{R}$. We increase the impact of delayed execution by also allowing delayed execution on machines 1 and m although delayed execution on machine 1 is already included in Lemma 1 and Algorithm 1 prevents such execution on machine l. Since we ignore the restriction of machine 1, the reference schedule has the reduced competitive ratio $1 + 1/\varepsilon$, see the proof of Lemma 1.

We use a continuous extension of the problem and discuss maximization of $\Delta(d, m, \mathcal{R})$. Let intervals $[0, t_s)$ and $[t_s, (1+1/\varepsilon) \cdot (t_l - t_s))$ be the two intervals in succession with Lemma 1 addressing interval $[t_s, (1 + 1/\varepsilon) \cdot (t_l - t_s))$. Therefore, time instance t_l is the last completion time of any job in interval $[t_s, \mathcal{R} \cdot (t_l - t_s))$ in the online schedule on every machine, see the proof of Lemma 1. Further, $t(x) \in [0, t_s)$ with $0 \leq x \leq d$ describes the time instance when machine x becomes busy. To maximize the impact of delayed execution, we require the total processing time in time interval $[0, t_l)$ and machine interval $[0, x)$ with $x \leq d$ to be identical to $t(x) \cdot m$. Then we obtain

$$t(x) \cdot m = \int_0^x t_l - t(z) dz$$

with the solution $t(x) = t_l \cdot (1 - e^{-x/m})$.

Then we have

$$\Delta(d,m,\mathcal{R}) = \frac{m\cdot\mathcal{R}\cdot(t_l-t_s)+m\cdot t_s}{m\cdot t_s+m\cdot(t_l-t_s)\cdot\frac{m-d}{m}} - \mathcal{R} = \frac{\mathcal{R}\cdot e^{-\frac{d}{m}}+1-e^{-\frac{d}{m}}}{1-\frac{d}{m}\cdot e^{-\frac{d}{m}}} - \mathcal{R}$$

To obtain the maximum value, we determine the dependence of $\Delta(m,d,\mathcal{R})$ on d and $\mathcal{R}$ by derivation. Since $\Delta(m,d,\mathcal{R})$ never decreases with decreasing $\mathcal{R}$, we select $\mathcal{R}=2$ and obtain

$$\Delta(d,m,2) = \frac{e^{-\frac{d}{m}}+1}{1-e^{-\frac{d}{m}}} - 2.$$

This function has its maximum value in the permitted range for $\frac{d}{m} = -\ln\frac{d}{m} \approx 0.567$. Then we have

$$\Delta(d,m,\mathcal{R}) \leq \Delta(0.567\cdot m, m, 2) \approx 0.3095.$$

□

Finally, we must combine the results of Lemmas 1 and 2.

Theorem 1. *Algorithm 1 guarantees a competitive ratio of* $1+\frac{1}{m}+\frac{1}{\varepsilon}+0.3095$ *for the load maximization problem with machine number* m *and slack* $\varepsilon \leq 1$.

Proof. An interval in the schedule is open if it is not possible to reject any job with a submission time in this interval. Therefore, at any time instance in this interval, less than m machines are busy. If this property does not hold, we say the interval is closed.

We partition the schedule into open and closed intervals such that no open interval directly precedes or succeeds another open interval. Further we cannot split any closed interval into an open interval and a closed interval.

If there is a chain of closed intervals and no job has a submission time prior to the beginning of the first of these closed intervals then Lemma 1 applies to this chain of intervals since it is not possible to execute any job contributing to this chain of intervals before this chain of intervals. Therefore, it is sufficient to consider an alternating sequence of open and closed intervals. Then the combination of Lemmas 1 and 2 yields the result. □

The proof also shows that MinIdle cannot achieve a better competitive ratio for sequential jobs. It is straight forward to see that the competitive ratio is at least $m\cdot(1+1/\varepsilon)$ for any algorithm if we allow parallel jobs.

3 Workload Generation

Since there are no workload traces that we can apply directly for our experiments, we use a hybrid approach: we select published workload traces, apply some preprocessing steps, and add the missing data using random generation based on a reasonable distribution.

First, we partition the published Google traces [20] into 29 separate days based on the submission times of the recorded jobs. Therefore, we eliminate all jobs that run for more than a day. For further processing, we categorize the jobs using their processing times and the cores required for their execution, see Fig. 2a and Fig. 2b. Figure 2c shows the distribution of jobs based on its resource consumption or total load, that is the product of its run-time and its required number of cores.

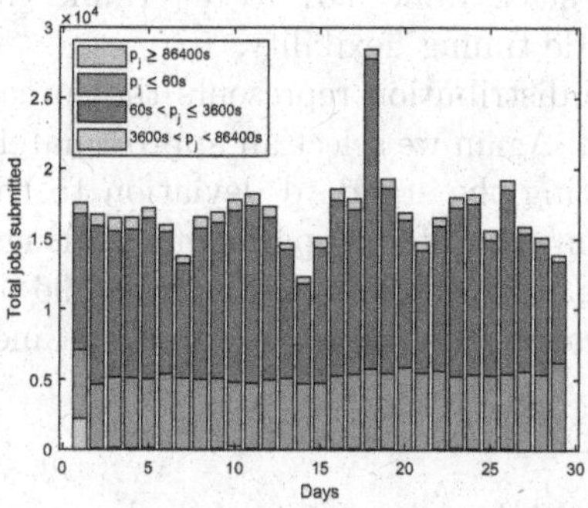

(a) Classification of jobs based on their run-times

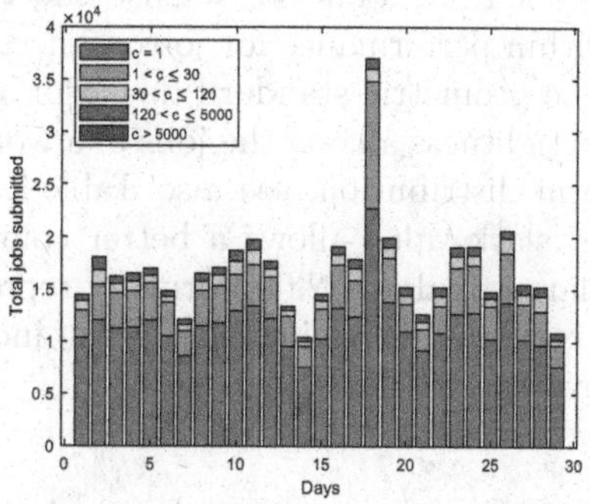

(b) Classification of Jobs based on their core requirements

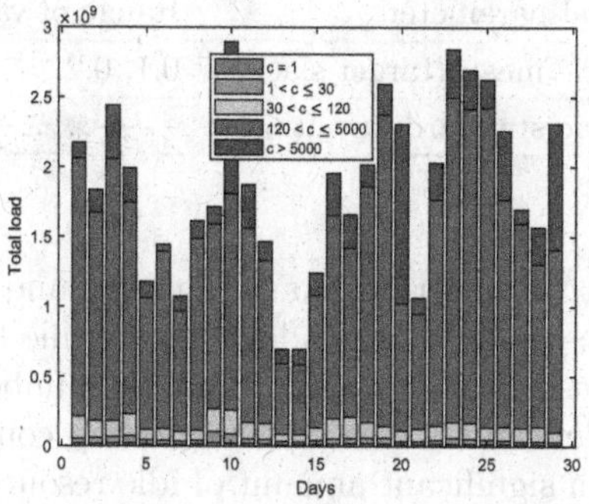

(c) Total load of different groups of jobs

Fig. 2. Workload Profile

It is known from other workload traces that many terminations of jobs briefly after their start-times are caused by programming errors or faulty configurations. In comparison to their run-time, these jobs have a very large slack. Unfortunately, we cannot reliably determine such jobs since the workload data do not specify whether a job has successfully completed. Therefore, we remove all jobs with a processing time of less than 60 s to avoid a misleading parameter selection.

To establish a reasonably good coverage of the practically relevant problem space, we use the parameters target slack value or geometric mean of a suitable distribution, geometric standard deviation of this distribution, and number of available cores.

The target slack value indicates the average flexibility of the job requests. We restrict the target slack value to the range $(0, 1)$. From a practical point of view, this range is reasonable since an individual slack of 1 requires a user to wait for the time of the job processing time before the system starts the job. Since there is no available deadline information from real workloads, we select an approximately uniform distribution of the target slack values within this range, see Table 1. In addition, we use the target slack value 0.01 to determine the algorithm performance for jobs with very little timing flexibility.

The geometric standard deviation of the distribution represents the spread of the tightness among the jobs of a workload. Again we select an approximately uniform distribution, see also Table 1. Relating the standard deviation to the target slack value allows a better comparison for different parameter settings. The largest value $\varepsilon/2.0$ informally represents a spread of approximately $0.96 \cdot \varepsilon$, that is, the additive increase of the individual waiting time is up to 0.71 times the average waiting time.

Table 1. Geometric mean and geometric standard deviation values of the lognormal distribution

Statistical parameter	Range of values
Geometric mean (target slack) ϵ	0.1, 0.2, ..., 0.9
Geometric standard deviation σ	$\frac{\epsilon}{3}, \frac{\epsilon}{2.9}, \ldots, \frac{\epsilon}{2}$

For each configuration of distribution parameters and each workload trace of a day, we generate ten separate input data sets. While the target slack value represents a temporary resource bottleneck, the total number of cores (the power budget in our model) determines the static resource contention. There is no resource contention and a significant amount of idle resources if all requests can start at their submission time. To prevent exclusion of individual requests, the largest number of cores used by any request of the workload is the lower bound of the core number. For a single-core data set, we select this lower bound to be 10. Between the lower and upper limit, we increase the number of cores from one data set to the next by a constant amount.

4 Performance Ratio

To compare the performance of different algorithms for different slack, deviation, and core parameters, we determine an approximate *performance ratio* of an algorithm specified by an acceptance/allocation pair for an input set, that is, the upper load limit over the total accepted load obtained by the approach. The use of this performance ratio is inspired by the competitive ratio obtained by the competitive analysis of online algorithms. The upper load limit is the minimum of the total processing time of all submitted jobs and the total processing time provided by the system in the considered execution time frame.

Example: Consider a scheduling problem with three jobs submitted in the order $J_1 - J_2 - J_3$ as described in Table 2.

Table 2. Three job scheduling problem

Job	p_j	r_j	d_j
J_1	2	0	2
J_2	4	0	4
J_3	4	0	4

We consider two different scheduling scenarios based on availability of resources, a 2-core scenario and a 3-core scenario. We accept jobs on a greedy basis provided every job ends before its deadline. Visual representation of the schedules in both scenarios is provided in Fig. 3.

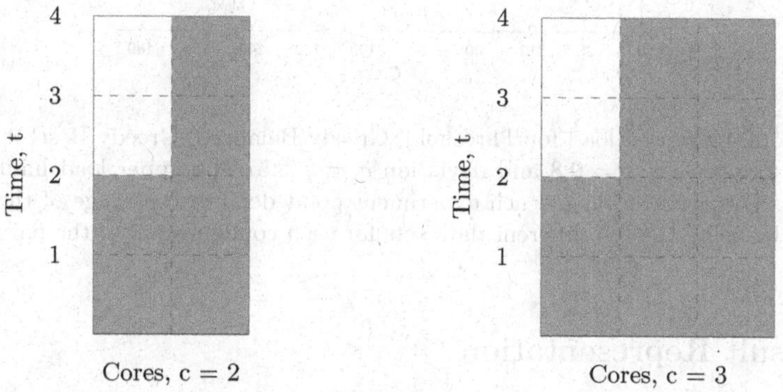

Fig. 3. Schedules obtained with greedy allocation

Since we accept jobs on a greedy basis, we end up rejecting job J_3 when we have only 2 cores available. However, the optimal schedule would have J_3 in it instead of J_1. So, the upper load limit in the optimal scenario is determined by the total processing time provided by the system and would be $c \cdot C_{max} = 2 \cdot 4 = 8$, where as the total load processed by the algorithm is 6.

When 3 cores are available, we end up accepting all three jobs. Even when processing power of $c \cdot C_{max} = 3 \cdot 4 = 12$ is available, we only have request for 10. Hence, the upper load limit in this scenario will take the value of total processing time of all submitted jobs, which is 10.

The best performance ratio has value 1 while an increase of the performance ratio denotes a worse performance. Informally, a performance ratio 2 means that either only 50% of the cores are utilized or only 50% of the submitted job load is accepted. For Day 11, Fig. 4 shows the upper load limit of a data set and the load accepted by various algorithms in relation to the total core number. The vertical bars indicate the range of the results due to executing a simulation with ten different input sets for each set of parameters, see Sect. 3. The size of these bars show the small impact of a specific input set.

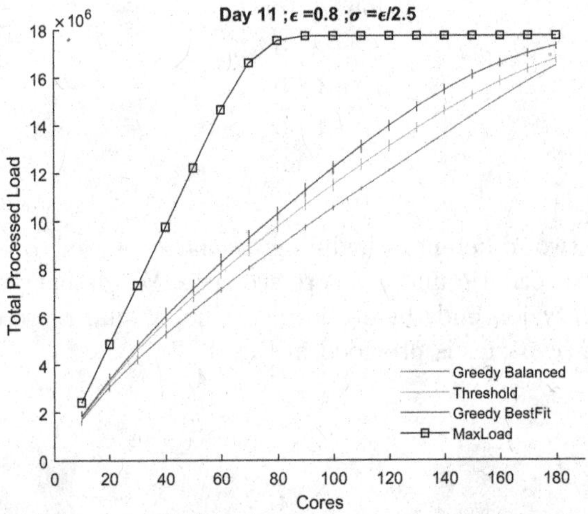

Fig. 4. Total processed load for Threshold, Greedy Balanced, Greedy BestFit on Day 11 using target slack $\varepsilon = 0.8$ and deviation $\sigma = \varepsilon/2.5$. The upper load limit is also displayed. The vertical bar at each experiment point denotes the range of the results obtained by using the ten different data sets for each configuration of the parameters.

5 Result Representation

The number of active cores is our primary independent parameter since it represents the available power. Note that our simulation only produces discrete values. We use the connecting lines to represent the trends between two neighboring values. Our basic result representation displays the performance ratio of different algorithms over the number of cores for a specific workload while the other parameters (target slack and geometric deviation of the slack) remain constant.

In order to show performance differences between two algorithms depending on two parameters, we use the heat map concept. The second parameter stretches along the vertical axis while the number of cores uses the horizontal axis. Then we obtain a mesh of result values. We use colors to represent the performance difference between two algorithms and apply linear interpolation to generate a colored area.

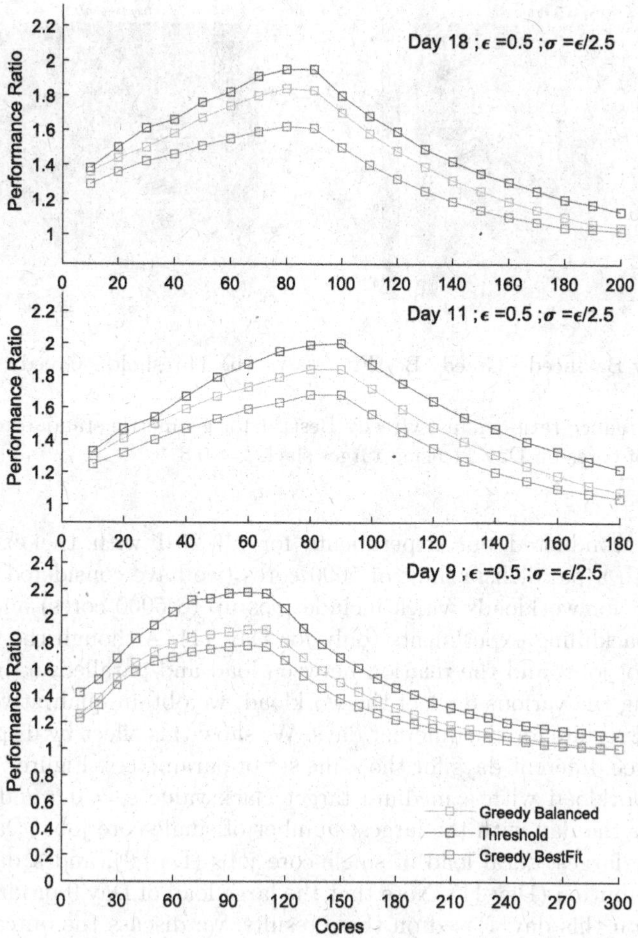

Fig. 5. Performance ratio of Threshold, Greedy Best Fit, and Greedy Balanced for Days 9, 11, and 18 using the same target slack $\varepsilon = 0.5$ and the same deviation $\sigma = \varepsilon/2.5$

6 Simulation Experiments

We have implemented the algorithms in Java and used Eclipse IDE 2019-12 for the simulation. For each configuration of parameters, we execute our algorithms with each of the ten generated data sets. Then we calculate the mean of the results that we obtain for each algorithm. This mean is the final result and depicted in the various representations. As already mentioned, we show the range of the different results using a vertical bar in Fig. 4. Due to the small impact of a specific input set, we omit these deviation ranges in further graphs that represent algorithmic results.

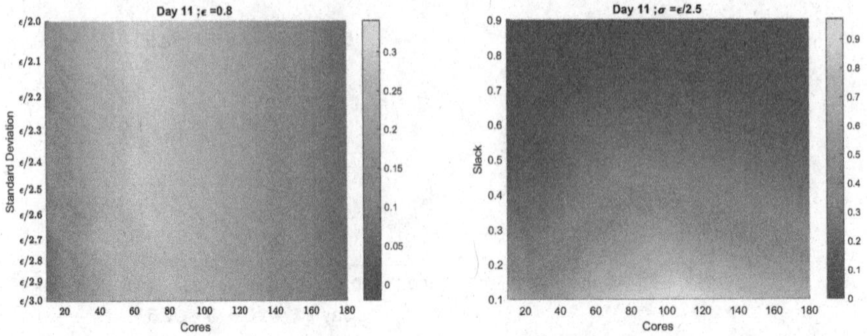

(a) Greedy Balanced - Greedy BestFit (b) Threshold - Greedy BestFit

Fig. 6. Performance ratio against Greedy BestFit for geometric standard deviation σ and number of cores on Day 11 using target slack $\varepsilon = 0.8$

We have conducted our experiments for all 29 d with the exception of instances with a parallelism limit of 5000 cores (we have considered only Days 9, 11, and 18 for workloads which include jobs up to 5000 cores) and the time consuming backfilling experiments (only for Day 11). Although the total load, the number of jobs, and the relation between load and parallelism differ significantly among the various days of the workload, we obtain qualitatively similar experimental results for the different days. We show this effect by displaying the results of three different days for the same set of parameters. Figure 5 shows the single-core workload with a medium target slack value $\varepsilon = 0.5$ and deviation $\sigma = \varepsilon/2.5$ for the day with the largest number of single-core jobs (Day 18), the day with the largest total load of single-core jobs (Day 9), and a day with an average distribution (Day 11). Note that the large load of Day 9 produces a shift of the peak on this day. Based on these results, we discuss the outcome of the experiments using the simulations for a single day (Day 11). Further, we have provided links to the complete results of our simulation in our repository[2].

6.1 Single-Core Results

To eliminate the impact of idle time generated by job allocation, we first consider only workloads with sequential jobs. First we address the impact of deviation σ and discuss heat maps that display the difference of the performance ratio between Greedy BestFit and Greedy Balanced depending on the geometric standard deviation (vertical) and the total number of cores (horizontal), see Fig. 6a for target slack $\varepsilon = 0.8$ as an example. Heat maps for other target slack values look similar. Since the heat map shows vertical features stretching over the whole range of the standard deviation, the standard deviation has no significant impact on the performance difference between both algorithms. Therefore, we ignore parameter σ for evaluating the algorithms.

[2] https://github.com/nileshwar-ganesh/simulation-jsspp2022.

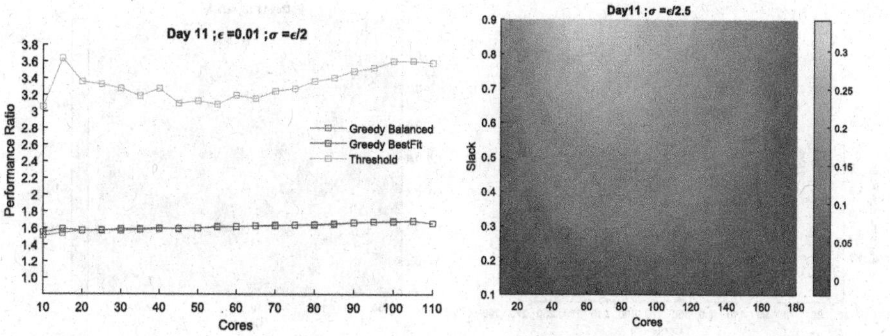

(a) Target slack $\varepsilon = 0.01$ and deviation $\sigma = \varepsilon/2.0$

(b) Greedy Balanced - Greedy BestFit for slack ε and deviation $\sigma = \varepsilon/2.5$

Fig. 7. Performance ratios Threshold, Greedy Balanced, Greedy BestFit on Day 11

Figure 5 shows that Greedy BestFit generally outperforms Threshold and Greedy Balanced. To determine the dependence of this result on the slack, we compare the performance ratios of Threshold and Greedy BestFit since both approaches use the same allocation method. We select a medium value $\sigma = \varepsilon/2.5$ and generate the heat map for the parameters target slack value ε and number of cores, see Fig. 6b. The figure shows that Greedy BestFit clearly outperforms Threshold for small slacks while both algorithms perform similarly for large slacks. This result even holds for a single workload with very small slack $\varepsilon = 0.01$ and small deviation $\sigma = \varepsilon/2.0$, see Fig. 7a.

Therefore, we can state as a first result that for small slacks, greedy acceptance performs very well for practical workloads.

While Greedy BestFit and Greedy Balanced have almost the same performance for small slacks, see Fig. 7a, Greedy BestFit has a better performance ratio for larger target slack values and a certain range of cores, see Fig. 7b. Note that the dependence on the number of cores is more pronounced in Fig. 7b than in Fig. 6b. Both figures combined indicate that for an increasing target slack, the performance ratio difference between Threshold and Greedy Balanced decreases. Taking into account the BestFit allocation strategy of Threshold, this observation supports the claim that the acceptance part of the scheduling algorithm plays a dominant role for small slacks while the allocation part becomes more important for larger slacks. Figure 7b shows that the dominance of BestFit over load balancing disappears for installations with many cores (low resource contention) or for installations with very few cores (very high resource contention). But since BestFit allocation is never worse than load balancing, it is useful to generally prefer BestFit over load balancing.

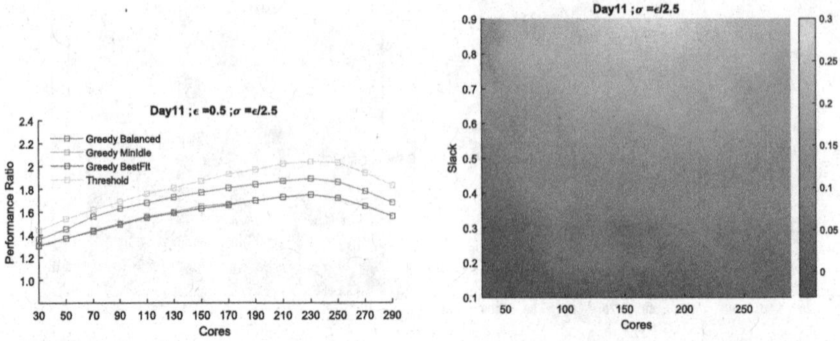

(a) Performance ratio, target slack $\varepsilon = 0.5$, and deviation $\sigma = \varepsilon/2.5$.

(b) Greedy Balanced - Greedy BestFit

Fig. 8. Results with parallelism limit of 30 cores on Day 11 using $\sigma = \varepsilon/2.5$

Next, we discuss the total accepted load in relation to the number of cores. Based on the result of Fig. 7b, we select $\varepsilon = 0.8$ and $\sigma = \varepsilon/2.5$, see Fig. 4. The load gap constantly increases as long as the total number of cores determines the upper load limit (until about 80 cores). Remember that a large number of idle cores represents a low energy efficiency.

6.2 Multi-core Results

Typical workloads in large computer installations contain a large number of parallel jobs. These parallel jobs are usually responsible for most of the system load, see Fig. 2c in Sect. 3. When trying to allocate a rigid parallel request, we may not always find sufficient cores that become idle at exactly the same time. Therefore, we must delay the start of this request and produce some idle time on some cores. Since this problem does not occur for single-core requests, we consider a specific allocation method MinIdle that selects the allocation that generates the minimum amount of this idle time. Our experiments show that Greedy MinIdle is slightly better than Greedy BestFit for a parallelism limit of 30 cores, see, as an example, Fig. 8a that uses target slack $\varepsilon = 0.5$ and deviation $\sigma = \varepsilon/2.5$. For 120 cores, the improvement is a bit larger, see Fig. 10b. However, Greedy MinIdle generates these better results at the expense of a significantly larger run time that further increases with the number of cores.

Since an extension of Threshold to a multi-core environment produces a similar result to that of the single-core simulation, see Fig. 8a, we ignore the Threshold approach for multi-core requests.

We extend our comparison between Greedy BestFit and Greedy Balanced for single core jobs to instances with parallelism limits of 30 cores, 120 cores, and 5000 cores, see Fig. 8b, 9a, and 9b, respectively. We observe that a workload

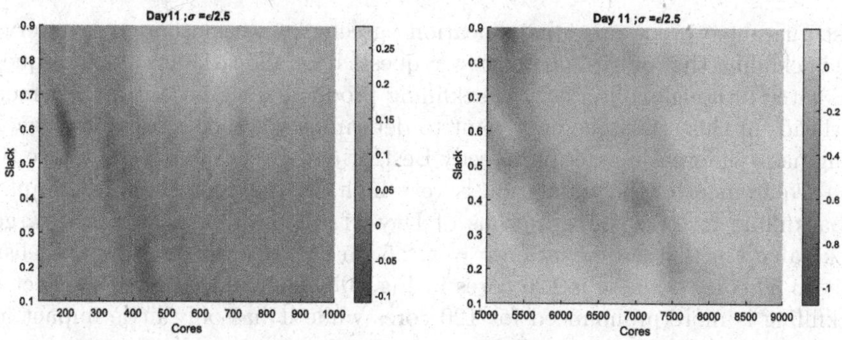

(a) Parallelism limit 120 cores (b) Parallelism limit 5000 cores

Fig. 9. Performance ratio greedy balanced - Greedy BestFit for target slack value ε and number of cores on Day 11, with deviation $\sigma = \varepsilon/2.5$

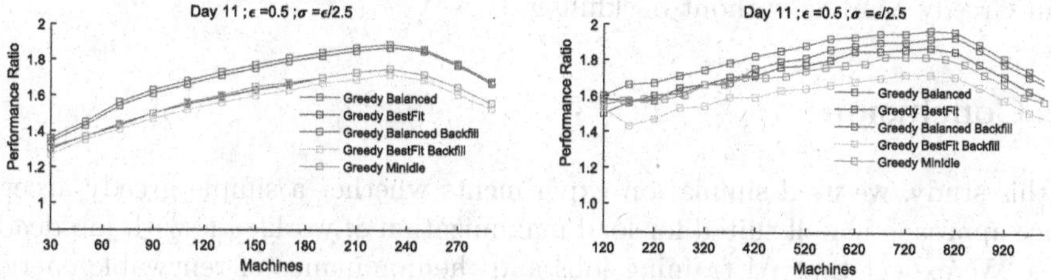

(a) Parallelism limit 30 cores (b) Parallelism limit 120 cores

Fig. 10. Performance ratio of Greedy Best Fit and Greedy Balanced with and without backfilling for Day 11, target slack $\varepsilon = 0.5$, and deviation $\sigma = \varepsilon/2.5$.

with a parallelism limit of 30 cores qualitatively behaves similar to the single-core workload in Fig. 7c. Quantitatively, the difference in the performance ratio is slightly less. For a parallelism limit of 120 cores, we must increase the core range significantly and observe a qualitatively similar behavior but with again less differences in the performance ratio. There are also some configurations for which Greedy Balanced is slightly better than Greedy BestFit. For a parallelism limit of 5000 cores, Greedy Balanced is almost always better than Greedy Best-Fit. However, we must note that the large number of cores forces a sequential execution of all highly parallel requests (almost 5000 cores) roughly dividing the schedule into several layers. It is not surprising that load balancing is the best approach for allocating requests within these layers.

The existence of enclosed periods of idleness in cores due to highly parallel requests generally occurs in large computer installations. Most installations use various forms of backfilling to exploit this idleness for other jobs. Since we must guarantee every previous allocation agreement, we must apply conservative backfilling that only allocates new requests if no allocation of an old request is violated although conservative backfilling produces a significant management overhead. In this study, we only want to determine whether conservative backfilling has a different impact on Greedy BestFit and Greedy Balanced. Since the time requirement of the simulation is very high, we only determine the impact of backfilling for two configurations of Day 11. In both cases, we pick target slack value $\varepsilon = 0.5$ and deviation $\sigma = \varepsilon/2.5$. In Fig. 10a, we set the parallelism limit to 30 cores while it is 120 cores in Fig. 10b. We can see that the effect of backfilling is more pronounced for 120 cores while it has only little impact for 30 cores. Since the larger parallelism limit generates more idle time, there are more opportunities to find an earlier allocation for jobs with less parallelism. Informally, this is the same reason that leads to the already stated superiority of Greedy Balanced over Greedy BestFit for a parallelism limit of 5000 cores. For a parallelism limit of 120 cores, Greedy BestFit with backfilling is clearly better than Greedy MinIdle without backfilling.

7 Conclusion

In this study, we used simulation experiments whether a simple greedy acceptance approach is well suited for load maximization of workloads with job deadlines. We expect that AI training jobs and the dominance of renewable energy sources will lead to such deadlines in future data centers. Our results show that in practically relevant environments, greedy acceptance even outperforms other algorithms with an almost optimal competitive ratio.

For jobs with little parallelism, the BestFit allocation strategy outperforms load balancing thus confirming the theoretical worst case analysis. The allocation strategy is particularly relevant if the jobs have more than just a very small timing flexibility.

For jobs with more parallelism, we can further improve the energy efficiency of data center by using some intermediate allocation approach that minimizes the additional idle time of the allocation. Unfortunately, this approach requires a significant computational overhead and may therefore not be suited for application in practice.

Finally, the well known backfilling allocation may also be not suitable for the load maximization problem. It also produces a better energy efficiency but due to the need of conservative backfilling, again the computational overhead is significant.

Altogether, our experiments show that we can exploit timing flexibility of jobs with very simple job scheduling algorithms that also leaves some room for additional modifications and extensions of the execution model.

References

1. Andrae, A.S.: Projecting the chiaroscuro of the electricity use of communication and computing from 2018 to 2030. Preprint, pp. 1–23 (2019)
2. Bertogna, M., Baruah, S.: Limited preemption edf scheduling of sporadic task systems. IEEE Trans. Industr. Inf. **6**(4), 579–591 (2010). https://doi.org/10.1109/TII.2010.2049654
3. Çavdar, D., Rosà, A., Chen, L., Binder, W., Alagöz, F.: Quantifying the brown side of priority schedulers: Lessons from big clusters. ACM SIGMETRICS Perfor. Evaluat. Rev. **42**(3), 76–81 (2014)
4. Ding, J., Ebenlendr, T., Sgall, J., Zhang, G.: Online scheduling of equal-length jobs on parallel machines. In: Arge, L., Hoffmann, M., Welzl, E. (eds.) ESA 2007. LNCS, vol. 4698, pp. 427–438. Springer, Heidelberg (2007). https://doi.org/10.1007/978-3-540-75520-3_39
5. Dong, Z., Zhuang, W., Rojas-Cessa, R.: Energy-aware scheduling schemes for cloud data centers on google trace data. In: 2014 IEEE Online Conference on Green Communications (OnlineGreenComm), pp. 1–6. IEEE (2014)
6. Hao, K.: Training a single ai model can emit as much carbon as five cars in their lifetimes. Web post on MIT Technology Review (2019)
7. Iglesias, J., De Cauwer, M., Mehta, D., O'Sullivan, B., Murphy, L.: Increasing task consolidation efficiency by using more accurate resource estimations. Futur. Gener. Comput. Syst. **56**, 407–420 (2016)
8. Iglesias, J., Murphy, L., De Cauwer, M., Mehta, D., O'Sullivan, B.: A methodology for online consolidation of tasks through more accurate resource estimations. In: 2014 IEEE/ACM 7th International Conference on Utility and Cloud Computing, pp. 89–98. IEEE (2014)
9. Jamalabadi, S., Schwiegelshohn, C., Schwiegelshohn, U.: Commitment and slack for online load maximization. In: Scheideler, C., Spear, M. (eds.) SPAA 2020: 32nd ACM Symposium on Parallelism in Algorithms and Architectures, Virtual Event, USA, 15–17 July 2020, pp. 339–348. ACM (2020). https://doi.org/10.1145/3350755.3400271
10. Kim, J., Chwa, K.Y.: On-line deadline scheduling on multiple resources. In: Proc. of the 7th Annual International Conference of Computing and Combinatorics, pp. 443–452. COCOON (2001)
11. Krakov, D., Feitelson, D.G.: Comparing performance heatmaps. In: Desai, N., Cirne, W. (eds.) JSSPP 2013. LNCS, vol. 8429, pp. 42–61. Springer, Heidelberg (2014). https://doi.org/10.1007/978-3-662-43779-7_3
12. Lifka, D.A.: The ANL/IBM SP scheduling system. In: Feitelson, D.G., Rudolph, L. (eds.) JSSPP 1995. LNCS, vol. 949, pp. 295–303. Springer, Heidelberg (1995). https://doi.org/10.1007/3-540-60153-8_35
13. Masanet, E., Shehabi, A., Lei, N., Smith, S., Koomey, J.: Recalibrating global data center energy-use estimates. Science **367**(6481), 984–986 (2020)
14. Mastelic, T., Oleksiak, A., Claussen, H., Brandic, I., Pierson, J.M., Vasilakos, A.V.: Cloud computing: survey on energy efficiency. ACM Comput. Surv. **47**(2) (2014). https://doi.org/10.1145/2656204
15. Meulen, R.: What edge computing means for infrastructure and operations leaders. Web post on Infrastructure & Operations, Garner (2018)
16. Mu'alem, A., Feitelson, D.: Utilization, predictability, workloads, and user runtime estimates in scheduling the IBM SP2 with backfilling. IEEE Trans. Parallel Distrib. Syst. **12**(6), 529–543 (2001)

17. N'takpé, T., Suter, F.: Don't hurry be happy: a deadline-based backfilling approach. In: Klusáček, D., Cirne, W., Desai, N. (eds.) JSSPP 2017. LNCS, vol. 10773, pp. 62–82. Springer, Cham (2018). https://doi.org/10.1007/978-3-319-77398-8_4
18. Rampersaud, S., Grosu, D.: Sharing-aware online virtual machine packing in heterogeneous resource clouds. IEEE Trans. Parallel Distrib. Syst. **28**(7), 2046–2059 (2016)
19. Rampersaud, S., Grosu, D.: An approximation algorithm for sharing-aware virtual machine revenue maximization. IEEE Trans. Serv. Comput. **14**, 1–15 (2017)
20. Reiss, C., Wilkes, J., Hellerstein, J.: Obfuscatory obscanturism: making workload traces of commercially-sensitive systems safe to release. In: 3rd International Workshop on Cloud Management (CLOUDMAN), pp. 1279–1286. IEEE, Maui, HI, USA, Apr 2012. https://doi.org/10.1109/NOMS.2012.6212064, http://ieeexplore.ieee.org/xpls/abs_all.jsp?arnumber=6212064

Toward Building a Digital Twin of Job Scheduling and Power Management on an HPC System

Tatsuyoshi Ohmura[1(✉)], Yoichi Shimomura[2], Ryusuke Egawa[2,3], and Hiroyuki Takizawa[2]

[1] Advanced Platform Division, NEC Corporation, Tokyo, Japan
tat-ohmura@nec.com
[2] Cyberscience Center, Tohoku University, Sendai, Japan
{shimomura32,takizawa}@tohoku.ac.jp, egawa@mail.dendai.ac.jp
[3] School of Engineering, Tokyo Denki University, Tokyo, Japan

Abstract. The purpose of this work is to reduce the burden on system administrators by virtually reproducing job scheduling and power management of their target systems and thereby helping them properly configure the system parameters and policies. Specifically, this paper focuses on a real computing system, named Supercomputer AOBA, as an example to discuss the importance of accurately reproducing the behaviors of job scheduling in the simulation. Since AOBA uses some special power saving features that are not supported by any existing job scheduling simulators, we have first implemented a component for a job scheduling simulator to support the special features, and thus to build a"Digital Twin" of AOBA's job scheduler. By using the Digital Twin with actual operation data, a system administrator can check if the system is efficiently used in terms of computational performance and power efficiency. This paper shows a use case of exploring appropriate scheduling and power saving parameters. In the use case, we found that there are more appropriate parameter configurations, which can reduce the job waiting time by 70% at most and the energy consumption by 1.2% at most when the system is busy. By exploiting such a Digital Twin, therefore, it is demonstrated the feasibility that a system administrator can properly adjust various parameters without disturbing the system operation.

Keywords: Job scheduling · Simulator · Power saving · HPC · Parameter survey

1 Introduction

In recent years, large amounts of computing resources have become required for a diverse range of applications such as emerging Artificial Intelligence applications, and traditional numerical simulations in the High Performance Computing (HPC) field. As a result, the operation of a real-world HPC system with a

D. Klusáček et al. (Eds.): JSSPP 2022, LNCS 13592, pp. 47–67, 2023.
https://doi.org/10.1007/978-3-031-22698-4_3

large number of users is required to simultaneously satisfy various requirements such as users' satisfaction, system utilization, and power consumption. To meet the requirements, a key component is a job scheduler, such as SLURM [26], LSF [10], and Open PBS [21].

In general, job schedulers have many scheduling algorithms and functions to increase users' satisfaction and system utilization, and hence require the system administrators to make various decisions usually in advance of system operation. Typical examples are as follows.

- Backfill Scheduling
  Backfill scheduling algorithms such as EASY backfilling [18] have been studied extensively. A system administrator needs to properly decide the algorithm, parameters and policy for efficient backfill scheduling without knowing the statistical information about future job submissions.
- Multi Queue Scheduling
  Computing resources are virtually divided into several partitions, each of which is associated with a different job queue. For example, A queue can be created for jobs whose sizes are in a certain range. It is not trivial to decide how much computing resources should be allocated to each queue. When a queue is busy, a system administrator may dynamically allocate more computing resource to the queue. However, such a dynamic adjustment further complicates the resource allocation problem.
- Power Saving Scheduling
  Job schedulers can work together with power management mechanisms that turn off some computing resources to reduce the power consumption. However, power management always requires some overheads, and there is a risk of degrading users' satisfaction and system utilization especially if it is inappropriately configured.

System administrators need to understand and use various functions of job schedulers, to fully exploit their HPC systems. To properly configure a job scheduler, they need to analyze a large amount of data, such as user-submitted jobs, node status, and utilization, and keep monitoring whether their HPC systems are being operated efficiently. Moreover, even if they find that the system is being inefficiently used, they cannot easily change the parameters and policies of job scheduling because it is difficult to predict how the changes affect the system operation efficiency, i.e., users' satisfaction, system utilization, and power consumption.

The purpose of this work is to reduce the burden on the system administrators by building a Digital Twin of job scheduling and power management of an HPC system. Our approach is to compare the simulated results of job scheduling and power management to the observed ones on a real-world HPC system, and improve the power-aware job scheduling simulator as the core of the Digital Twin. By using the Digital Twin, system administrators can check if the system operation efficiency is as expected. They can also estimate the system operation efficiency under different parameter configurations to find a better configuration. Moreover, since the Digital Twin enables to estimate how parameter adjustment will affect the system operation efficiency, it will also be helpful to automate dynamic adjustment of parameters and policies so as to improve the system operation efficiency.

In this paper, we focus on the AOBA system installed at Tohoku University Cyberscience Center as an example of real-world HPC systems, and show the feasibility of building its Digital Twin so as to discuss how such a Digital Twin is helpful to improve the system operation efficiency. First, we describe the real-world target HPC system and its operation. Then, we present extensions of an existing job scheduling simulator to reproduce the behaviors of the AOBA system. Finally, using the simulator, we perform a parameter survey to find appropriate parameters that can maximize the system operation efficiency while minimizing the power consumption of the AOBA system.

The main contributions of this paper are as follows:

- Showing the feasibility of implementing a commercial job scheduler simulation by extending an existing simulator, SLURM Simulator.
- Discussing how helpful the accurate simulation of job scheduling and power management, refereed to as a Digital Twin of HPC systems, is for parameter survey to improve the operation efficiency of a real-world HPC system.

2 Related Work

The most important part of the Digital Twin discussed in this paper is to fully simulate the behavior of the HPC system's job scheduler. Job scheduling simulators have actively been developed, and typical examples of such simulators are ALENA [11] and GridSim [27]. Among the examples, Batsim [5] is a simulator suited for comparison among job scheduling algorithm. In general, HPC system's job scheduler has functions that could affect job scheduling, such as Burst Buffer and heterogeneous jobs. Building a Digital Twin needs to simulate these functions, and thus a simulator must be extended to support those functions. More recently, SLURM Simulator [25], a job simulator that reproduces the job scheduling of a real-world HPC system, has been introduced. SLURM Simulator is designed based on SLURM [26], which is used in various systems registered in the Top 500 list [29], and has functions to simulate job operations similar to those in real systems, such as priority, partition (queue), and scheduling parameters. Using SLURM Simulator, it is also possible to estimate Quality of Service (QoS) such as the average waiting time of jobs and system utilization with a given parameter configuration. In addition, since the functions that affect job scheduling are already supported by SLURM, SLRUM Simulator can implement the functions more easily than other simulators.

Maiterth et al. [15] have reported that real-world HPC systems are operated with Power Saving Scheduling. Although the power saving features of SLURM can be simulated in SLURM Simulator, commercial job schedulers often provide some other advanced features that are not supported by the simulator. SLURM's Power Saving Scheduling is controlled mainly by two parameters. One is the idle time until turning off a node, and the other is the number of nodes allowed to start up per minute. On the other hand, other job schedulers could have more parameters than SLURM. For example, a proprietary job scheduler named NQSV [19] has an additional parameter that limits the number of times a node could be turned off in a day to prevent frequent node starts. This could be effective to alleviate the risk of hardware failures caused by frequently stopping and starting a node. Moreover, NQSV is capable of scheduling jobs with considering the startup time of a stopped node. If there is a running job whose remaining elapsed time is shorter than the startup time, NQSV does not start up a stopped node and waits for the running job to end. As a result, it can avoid from excessively starting up a stopped node. System administrators can control such behaviors by adjusting NQSV's configuration parameters, based on the statistical behaviors of recent job requests.

There are many studies for reducing the operational burden of HPC systems. Recently, scheduling algorithms [2,4,7,16,17,22,24,30] based on reinforcement learning have been proposed. Fan et al. [7] proposed an automated HPC job scheduling agent named DRAS (Deep Reinforcement Agent for Scheduling). DRAS realized HPC job scheduling features such as resource reservation and backfilling with a hierarchical neural network. DRAS performs 45% better than the algorithm used in the conventional job scheduler. However, to the best of our knowledge, there is no practical AI scheduler that can fully support Power Saving Scheduling.

Several studies such as in [3,9,13,14,23] have discussed the optimization of job scheduling parameters for maximizing QoS and system utilization. Powers [23] proposed a tool for exploring system scheduler parameters such as scheduling intervals. Kondameedi et al. [13] presented that the waiting time for jobs can be reduced by dynamically changing the queue settings. Chahal et al. [3] introduced a simulation-based scheduling method for workflow jobs. However, these studies focus only on Backfill Scheduling or Multi Queue Scheduling, and not on Power Saving Scheduling.

In this work, we develop a simulator of Power Saving Scheduling on a real-world HPC system, AOBA. Then, we survey scheduling parameters for Power Saving Scheduling and Multi Queue Scheduling to improve the system operation efficiency while reducing power consumption.

3 A Real-World HPC System and Its Operation

3.1 Overall System Configuration

In this paper, we show a case study of building a Digtal Twin of an HPC system, taking the AOBA system [6] as a concrete example. Therefore, this section describes the AOBA system and its operation.

AOBA is an HPC system consisting of two subsystems. One is a vector-type computing system called AOBA-A, which consists of 72 nodes of SX-Aurora

TSUBASA [12,20]. The other is a scalar computing system called AOBA-B. In this paper, we target the job simulation of the AOBA-A system.

SX-Aurora TSUBASA is equipped with Vector Engines (VEs) for executing user applications and Vector Hosts (VHs) for running OS and hosting VEs. A collection of one or more VHs, VEs hosted by those VHs, and InfiniBand HCAs is called a Vector Island (VI) [28]. In the case of the AOBA system, one VI has one VH, eight VEs, and two InfiniBand HCAs. In this paper, a VI is referred to as a *node*.

3.2 Queue Configurations

The AOBA-A system provides six job queues listed in Table 1. To maximize job throughput, job queues are classified into two types. One is for jobs of using only one VE, and the other is for jobs of using multiple VEs. A job submitted to the free queue can run for one hour at a maximum. Users are supposed to select a job queue, considering the expected job execution time and the job size, which is defined by the number of VEs requested by the job. The system administrator could manually reallocate the resources to each queue. In practice, when a medium-sized job queue (sx_m in Table 1) is busy, the system administrator will allocate more resources to that queue by reducing resources of other queues.

Table 1. Queue Configurations

Usage Type	Queue name	Number of VEs per job	Allocated resources
Free	sxf	1 VE	4 VHs
Paid use	sxl	1 VE	58 VHs
	sxmix_s	1 VE	
	sx_s	2-8 VEs (1 VH)	
	sx_m	9-64 VEs (2-8 VHs)	
	sx_l	65-256 VEs (9-32 VHs)	
Reserved for specific users	–	–	10 VHs
Urgent	–	–	4 VHs or 24 VHs. Shared with paid use queues

3.3 Job Scheduling and Parameters

The AOBA system uses a proprietary scheduler, NQSV [19], developed by NEC. In this section, we describe the job scheduling and parameters.

Basic Job Scheduling. NQSV's job scheduling adopts an extended algorithm of EASY backfilling [18]. Based on the resource information (the number of CPU cores, the number of VEs, estimated execution time, etc.) specified at job submission, the algorithm determines where and when to execute each job.

The nodes for executing a job are selected from the resources allocated to the queue, to which the job has been submitted. NQSV has some advanced features to improve system utilization, such as the feature of starting subsequent jobs when a job finishes earlier than estimated. System administrators can adjust the following parameters and options to control EASY backfilling (the descriptions in () indicate the parameter values and options adopted in the AOBA system).

- Map Size: how far ahead in the future a job can be scheduled (one month).
- Scheduling Interval: the interval at which job scheduling is performed (30 s).
- Reordering Policy: a policy to determine the execution order of jobs in a queue. The supported policies are First Come First Serve (FCFS), Smallest Job First, Largest Job First, etc. (the FCFS policy).
- Resource Allocation Policy: a policy to determine how to allocate nodes to jobs. There are two options; whether jobs are concentrated on as few nodes as possible, or not (the concentration policy).

Multi Queue Scheduling. NQSV can virtually separate computing resources by linking each queue with a particular set of resources. NQSV considers the inter-queue priority and linked resources at job scheduling. Multi Queue Scheduling can be tuned by mainly adjusting the following parameters and options.

- Allocated Resources: the resources on which jobs in the queue are executed. In the case of the AOBA system, the resource allocation is as described in Table 1.
- Queue Type: whether a job is urgent or not. An urgent job can be executed as early as possible on the AOBA system [1].

NQSV also has some other advanced features such as limiting the number of jobs in each queue that are being executed by one user at the same time.

Power Saving Scheduling. A node of the AOBA system can be in either of two states, "active state" and "power-saving state." A job can be assigned only to nodes in the active state because the power supply to nodes in the power-saving state is stopped for power saving. If no job is assigned to a node for a certain period, the power supply to the node is stopped, and the node is transiting to the power-saving state. The state transition takes a certain time period as the overhead.

Power Saving Scheduling of NQSV has two functions. The first function is to detect an idle node and change its state from active state to power-saving state. The second function is to systematically schedule a job considering the timing overhead of waking up a power-saving state node. Suppose that a job is submitted and a node to be allocated is in the power-saving state. Then, NQSV

Table 2. Configurable parameters for power saving

Item	Description	Setting value
Min idle time	When the idle state continues for a certain period of time, the node is shutdown	7200 s
Margin for stop host	Time needed to stop a node	600 s
Margin for start host	Time needed to start a node	1200 s
Dcoff limit	Maximum number of times to stop nodes per day	5
Min operation hosts	Number of nodes that should always be running	0
Estimated dcoff time	If the execution start time of a subsequent job is longer than this parameter, the node enters the power-saving state	3600 s

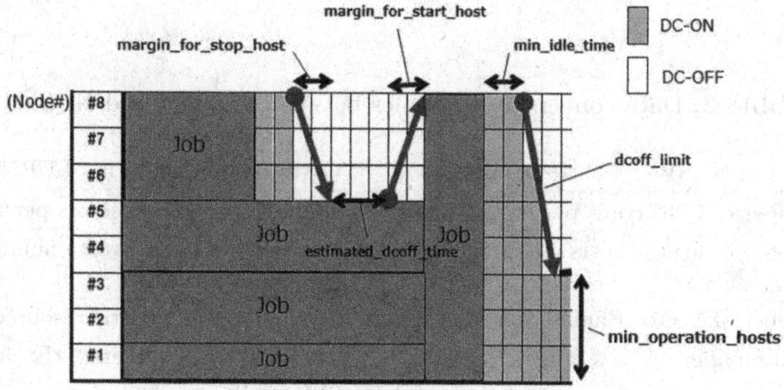

Fig. 1. Parameters of power saving scheduling.

can decide the execution start time of a job by estimating how long it takes for the node to transit to the active state and thus become ready for the job execution. Power Saving Scheduling can be tuned by adjusting the parameters shown in Fig. 1 and Table 2.

4 Job Scheduling Simulation of a Real-World HPC System

In this section, we first show an overview of the job scheduling simulator, which is an extension of SLURM Simulator to accurately simulate job scheduling and power management on a real-world HPC system, AOBA-A. Then, we describe the implementation details of the simulator.

4.1 Extended SLURM Simulator

SLURM is an extensible job scheduler by using plug-ins. The scheduler used in SLURM Simulator can be replaced with a custom scheduler that uses the same scheduling algorithm as NQSV for simulating AOBA-A's job scheduling. Job scheduling policies and features of SLURM and NQSV are significantly different. For example, in SLURM, task based resources (i.e., the number of processors per task) assigned to a job can be specified at its submission. On the other hand, in NQSV, logical hosts which are a set of resources virtually divided into execution hosts can be specified by users, i.e., the number of CPU cores per logical host. Therefore, a SLURM plug-in needs to be developed with considering all the differences.

In this work, we develop a SLURM plug-in named NQSV Plug-in, which implements NQSV's job scheduling algorithm, and also a translator to convert the job and partition (queue) information of SLURM to those of NQSV and vice versa. Examples of data conversion between SLURM and NQSV are shown in Table 3. Job data for NQSV are converted from their corresponding data in SLURM.

Table 3. Data conversion examples between SLURM and NQSV.

Definition in NQSV	Corresponding data in SLURM
The number of CPU cores per logical host	The number of processors per task
The number of logical hosts	The number of tasks/the number of processors per task
The number of Vector Engines per logical host	The number of generic resources
The total number of CPU cores	The number of sockets * the number of cores per socket

4.2 Node State Control

SLURM manages the node operation state by a power management thread. At a certain interval, the thread decides whether a node is turned on or off. On the other hand, power management of NQSV works together with job scheduling to determine when a node is turned on or off. Due to the differences above, SLURM's power management thread is not able to simulate the power management of NQSV. Therefore, we develop *Node State Simulator* for SLURM Simulator to implement the transition between the active and power-saving states in NQSV. Node State Simulator can also consider the timing overheads for starting and stopping a node due to the state transition. The extended SLURM Simulator developed in this work is called AOBA-A Job Simulator, because it is developed to be used as a Digital Twin of the AOBA-A system.

Figure 2 shows an overview of our simulator. "Simulator" in the SLURM daemon (slurmctd) is a component provided by the original SLURM Simulator

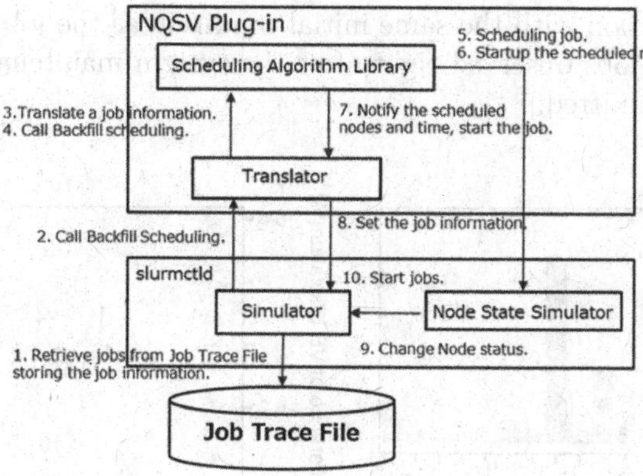

Fig. 2. Overview of AOBA-a job scheduler.

to manage time, nodes, partitions, and jobs of the simulation. Collaborating with the Simulator component, AOBA-A Job Simulator works as follows.

1. Simulator retrieves jobs from Job Trace File, storing the job information.
2. When the scheduling interval is expired, Simulator calls Backfill Scheduling.
3. Translator in NQSV Plug-in converts the job information for SLURM to that for NQSV.
4. Translator calls Scheduling Algorithm Library in NQSV Plug-in.
5. Scheduling Algorithm Library schedules each job by determining its execution start time and nodes which is equipped with VEs to be allocated for the execution.
6. If an allocated node is in the power-saving state, the startup time of the node is calculated, and the execution start time is delayed.
7. Scheduling Algorithm Library reports the execution start time and allocated nodes to Translator.
8. Translator converts and sends the reported information to Simulator.
9. When the startup time of the sleeping node is expired, Node State Simulator changes the node state to active.
10. Simulator starts each job at its execution start time.

The above steps are repeated to simulate the job scheduling with power management for the given job traces.

5 Simulation Accuracy of AOBA-A Job Simulator

In this section, we evaluate the accuracy of the job scheduling simulation with AOBA-A Job Simulator described in Sect. 4. In the evaluation, the simulation is performed using job traces, i.e., the information about actual jobs executed at the AOBA-A system. Then, the simulation results are compared with the observed job scheduling results. Initially, all the job queues are empty in the simulation.

To start the simulation with the same initial condition as the job traces, we use the data of 10,000 jobs observed right after the system maintenance period, in which no job is submitted.

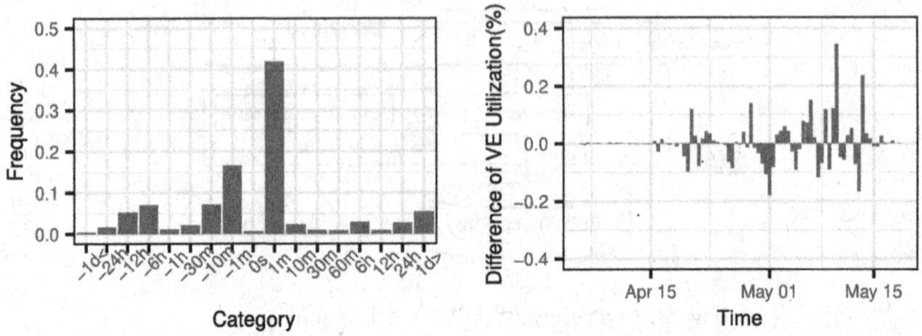

(a) Differences of start time. (b) Differences of VE utilization.

Fig. 3. Simulation with original job traces.

Figure 3 shows the simulation results. Figure 3(a) shows the histogram of differences in start time between the observed and simulation results. The vertical axis shows the frequency, and the horizontal axis shows the class of the difference in starting time. A negative difference means that the job execution has been delayed in the simulation. For example, the frequency of class "-1m" means the number of jobs, for which the time difference between the observation and simulation is in between one second to one minute. We can see that about 60% of the jobs are in the classes of "-1m," "0," and "1m." Therefore, the simulator can accurately simulate the majority of jobs recorded in the job traces. Figure 3(b) shows the differences between the observed utilization ratio of VEs and the corresponding simulated ratio. The vertical axis indicates the utilization ratio, which is calculated by subtracting the simulation data from the original data, and the horizontal axis shows the time sequence. We can see that there is no difference in the VE utilization rate at first, and the difference gradually becomes visible for the job scheduling on April 15 and later. In practice, the simulation results are reasonably accurate except for some cases described below.

The current implementation of AOBA-A Job Simulator supports only the core scheduling algorithm of NQSV, and does not support some features to strictly simulate the AOBA-A system operation. One example of unsupported features is that NQSV allows users to specify the execution start time at job submission. Another example is the workflow support to guarantee that one job is executed after another job. The difference in waiting time between observed and simulated results becomes large for some jobs, and exceeds one day for about

5% of jobs in Fig. 3(a). This is because the workflow management feature delayed to start executing the job until the execution of its preceding job is finished. The information about use of such unsupported features is not recorded in the job traces. Therefore, we do not implement the features in AOBA-A Job Simulator at present.

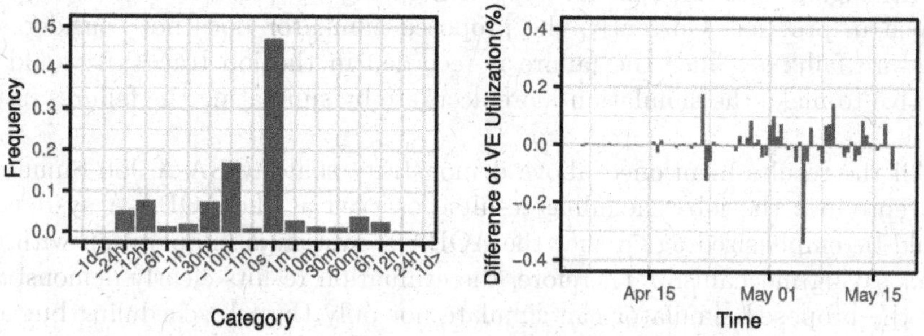

(a) Differences of start time. (b) Differences of VE utilization.

Fig. 4. Simulation with corrected job traces.

For considering the workflow management, job traces are modified. Specifically, the submission time of a job is replaced with the execution start time recorded in the job traces if the difference between the submission time and the execution start time is longer than 12 h. The simulation results using the corrected job trace are shown in Fig. 4. Comparing Fig. 3(a) and Fig. 4(a), the frequencies of jobs with larger time differences are reduced. The frequency of the "1d>" class decreased from 0.055 to 0 and the frequency of the "24h" class decreased from 0.027 to 0.01. Similar results can be seen in Fig. 3 (b) and Fig. 4 (b). Therefore, these results indicate that data correction under a simple assumption allows the proposed simulator to simulate the job scheduling more accurately, even though the workflow management information is not recorded in the job traces.

In Fig. 4(b), there is a time period in which the differences between the observed utilization ratio and the simulated one is -0.3%. This is due to the execution of urgent jobs [1]. The urgent job suspends some running jobs with a lower priority. However, both regular and urgent jobs are kept running in the observed results. As a result, the utilization ratio appears to be large in the observed job traces.

In Fig. 3(a), there are jobs whose simulation results are 10+ minutes faster than the observed results. This is because another feature of NQSV is not supported by the proposed simulator. NQSV limits the number of concurrently running jobs of each user to avoid the computing resource from being occupied by specific users. The execution of some jobs of a user would be delayed at the AOBA system if the user has submitted too many jobs. However, the proposed simulator does not support this feature, and excessively submitted jobs are not delayed in the simulation. AOBA is a production system and thus job traces include actual personal information. However, since it is not allowed to identify individuals, user information in the job traces is anonymized, and thus we do not implement the feature that needs to use each user's activity. As a result, there is the difference between the observation and simulation.

Although no hardware failure happened during the simulated period, it could happen in practice. Currently, the proposed simulator does not consider any hardware failures. Since the failure is recorded in the job traces, it would be effective to make the simulation more accurate by simulating the failures in the future.

All the results mentioned above demonstrate that AOBA-A Job Simulator can reproduce the job scheduling results observed at the AOBA-A system. It should be emphasized again that the AOBA-A system is in operation with the power saving mechanism. Therefore, the evaluation results clearly demonstrate that the proposed simulator can simulate not only the job scheduling but also the power saving mechanism of a real-world HPC system. With the simulator, we can explore the optimal configuration of scheduling and power saving parameters as discussed in Sect. 6.

6 Survey of Scheduling and Power Saving Parameters

6.1 Parameter Settings and Job Submission Behaviors

Scheduling policies and parameters related to scheduling and power saving would usually be decided at the system design. The same applies to the allocation of resources to the job queues. When a queue is extremely busy, the system administrators may manually change the resource allocation to increase the resource for the busy queue. However, changes in scheduling and power saving parameters could have a significant impact on the QoS visible from users, and thus the system administrators are generally conservative to change the parameters during the system operation. Those parameters would empirically be configured based on past operation experience, such as the job submission history, and thus the parameter configuration is not necessarily optimal for the system. Therefore, a parameter survey with an accurate job scheduling simulator is helpful to check whether the current parameter configuration is appropriate for the system operation that could change dynamically. In this section, we describe a parameter survey of scheduling and power saving parameters.

First, we describe the statistical analysis of job submissions observed in a real-world system. Figure 5 shows the job submission times, elapsed times, and sizes of jobs submitted to the AOBA-A system in April and May, 2021. The vertical axis indicates the elapsed time of each job, the horizontal axis shows the time sequence, and the circle size represents the number of VEs requested by the job. Overall, more jobs were submitted and executed in the second half

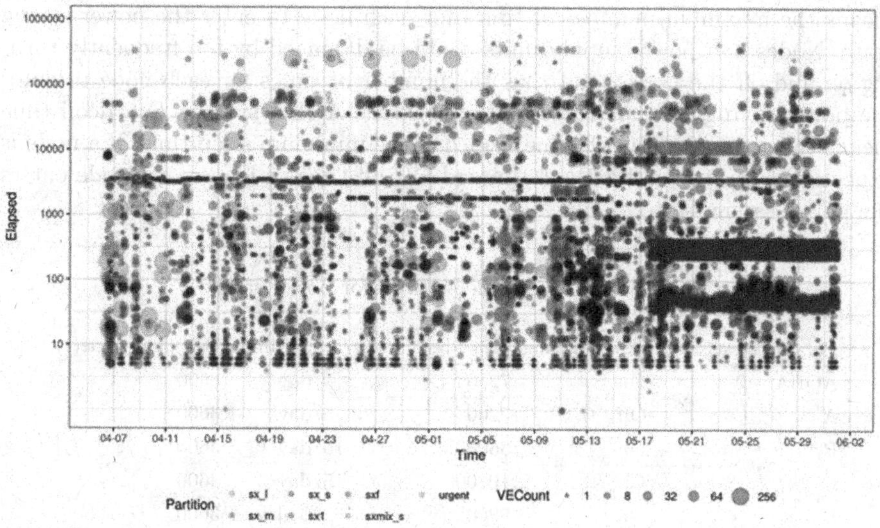

Fig. 5. Submission times, elapsed times and sizes of jobs.

of May. There is a trend that users are likely to submit short-running jobs to the free queue in the daytime but not on holidays. In addition, some users keep submitting jobs at a regular interval by probably running a job submission script, and hence their jobs are constantly executed on the system regardless of the date and time. Since a single parameter configuration cannot be optimal for all job submission patterns, we explore an appropriate parameter configuration for each pattern.

In this paper, the data in Fig. 5 are split into two, off period and busy period data. The data from April to mid-May can be seen as the off period job submission data, while the data in late-May are the busy period ones. Since the system is not so busy in the off period, some of compute nodes could be turned off for power saving. With the off period job data, hence, we can discuss the effect of power saving on the system operation efficiency by adjusting relevant parameters in the simulation. On the other hand, with the busy period data, we can discuss if the power saving mechanism has a negative effect on the system operation efficiency when the system is keeping busy.

6.2 Parameter Survey of Job Scheduling in Off Period

Using the data of 10,000 jobs submitted from April 6 to May 17, we investigate the effects of changing power saving parameters on the system operation efficiency. The parameter configurations used in the evaluation are listed in Table 4. In the table, Min Idle Time means the minimum idle time, and a node enters the power-saving state if the node is idle for the minimum idle time. Dcoff limit means the maximum number of times for each node to enter the power-saving state. Nodes and power supply units could be damaged by too frequently turning on and off the nodes, and thus the number of times for each node to enter the power-saving state per day is limited at the AOBA system. Est. dcoff time means the estimated DC off time, which is the minimum sleep time. If a node is expected to be unused for the estimated DC off time or longer, the node enters the power-saving state.

Table 4. Configurable settings for power saving

Parameter settings	Power saving	Min Idle Time(s)	Dcoff limit	Est. dcoff time(s)
AOBA	On	7200	5/day	3600
A	Off	7200	5/day	3600
B	On	3600	5/day	3600
C	On	10800	5/day	3600
D	On	7200	200/day	3600
E	On	7200	5/day	1800
F	On	7200	5/day	7200

The power consumption of a node has been measured during the job execution, and is not equal to the value shown in the specification sheet of SX-Aurora TSUBASA. Specifically, the power consumption of an idle node is about 600W, while the power consumption reaches about 2100W when the node runs a well-vectorized job. In addition, the startup time and shutdown time of a node are set to be 60 s and 120 s, respectively. These values are decided based on the actual measurement, instead of using not the scheduler parameters "Margin for start host" and "Margin for stop host" in Table 2.

The simulation results with different parameter configurations are shown in Fig. 6. The left vertical axis indicates the average waiting time of a job, the right vertical axis indicates the total energy consumption, and the horizontal axis shows parameter configurations. In the figure, the differences between AOBA and Condition A shows the effects of enabling the power saving mechanism, meaning that the mechanism can save about 11 MWh without increasing the average waiting time. The results with Condition B show that if the minimum idle time is decreased, the energy consumption is further reduced by 1.2 MWh, but the average waiting time becomes longer, degrading the system operation efficiency. The results with Condition D show that increasing the maximum number of times for each node to enter the power-saving state has no effect on the system operation efficiency including the energy consumption. The results with Condition E show that decreasing the minimum sleep time by 30 min has no effect. On the other hand, the results with Condition F show that increasing the minimum sleep time by 1 h makes the average waiting time longer. This is because the nodes that have a running single-node job and a multi-node job scheduled for subsequent time periods can enter the power-saving state less frequently. The other jobs are scheduled before the multi-node job. If the single-node job finishes earlier than estimated, the execution of the multi-node job is inhibited by the newly scheduled jobs. Using these results, the system administrator can estimate the effectiveness of the power saving function and decide to change the parameters considering the variations of the energy consumption and the average waiting time.

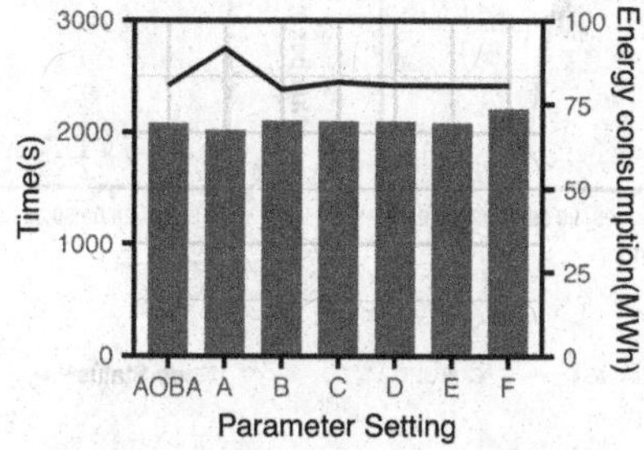

Fig. 6. Results of off-period simulation. The bars indicate the average waiting time of a job, and the line indicates the total energy consumption.

6.3 Parameter Survey of Job Scheduling in Busy Period

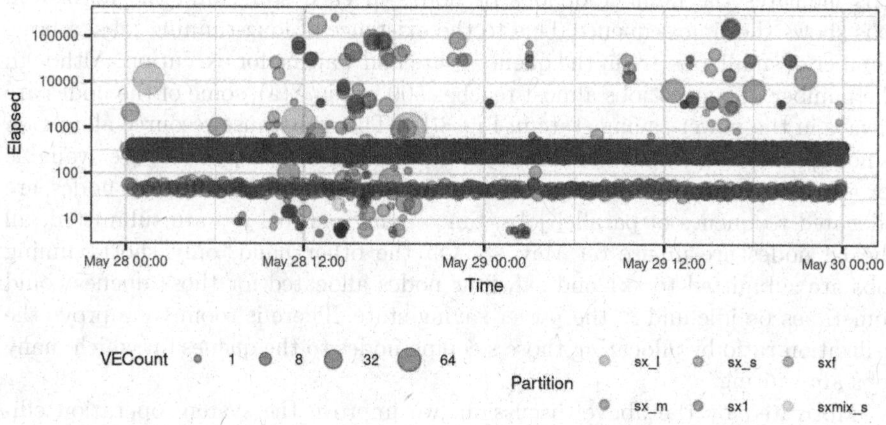

Fig. 7. Job pattern of May 28 to 29.

The job traces from May 28 to 29 are shown in Fig. 7. The meanings of the vertical axis, the horizontal axis, and the circle size are the same as in Fig. 5. The figure shows that various jobs were intensively submitted in the daytime on May 28. Another characteristic point is that small jobs are submitted to the sx_s queue continuously the whole day. In addition, long-running jobs of small and medium sizes were submitted on May 28.

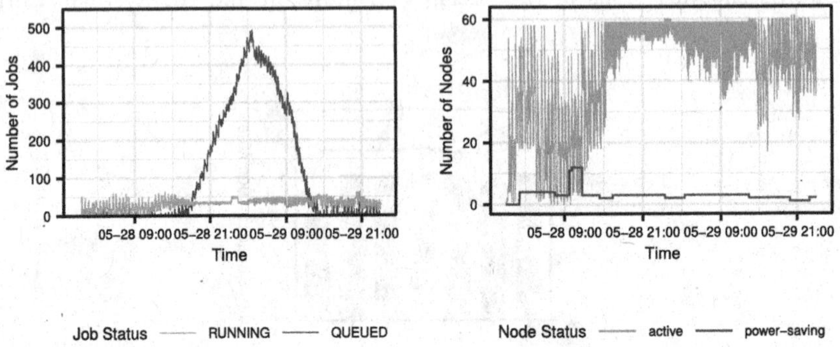

(a) Job status. (b) Node status.

Fig. 8. Transition of the numbers of running and waiting jobs, and the number of nodes in each power state.

A submitted job can be in either of running or queued state, while a node can be in either of active or power-saving state. The state changes of jobs and nodes simulated with AOBA's parameter configuration are shown in Fig. 8. The vertical axis indicates the number of jobs or nodes in each state, and the horizontal axis shows the time sequence. Due to the existence of long-running jobs, a large number of small jobs are in the queued state and waiting for execution. Although the number of queued jobs almost reaches 500 in Fig. 8(a), some of the nodes are always in the power-saving state in Fig. 8(b). This is because resource allocation is not appropriate for the situation. As shown in Table 1, four nodes are available for jobs in the sxf and sx1 queues at the AOBA system, while 58 nodes are allocated to queues of parallel jobs. Since many parallel job are submitted, all the 58 nodes are in use on May 28. On the other hand, only short-running jobs are submitted to sx1 and sxf, four nodes allocated for those queues could sometimes be idle and in the power-saving state. There is room to improve the utilization ratio by allocating those sleeping nodes to the queues, in which many jobs are waiting.

Motivated by the above discussion, we improve the system operation efficiency by adjusting the resource balance among queues as shown in Table 5. In the table, "Move 2 nodes" means that two nodes out of four are moved from sx1 and sxf to queues of parallel tasks in Table 1. "Share 2 nodes" means that two nodes out of four are shared by all the queues, and the other two nodes remain dedicated to sx1 and sxf. "Share all nodes" means that all the four nodes originally allocated to sx1 and sxf are shared by all queues.

Table 5. Resource Balancing in the Simulation

Item	Description
(1) Move 2 nodes (2) Move 3 nodes	Move 2 or 3 nodes of sx1 and sxf to sx_s, sx_m and sx_l queue
(3) Share 2 nodes (4) Share 3 nodes	Share 2 or 3 nodes of sx1 and sxf to all queues
(5) Share all nodes	Paid use queue and free queue uses all nodes

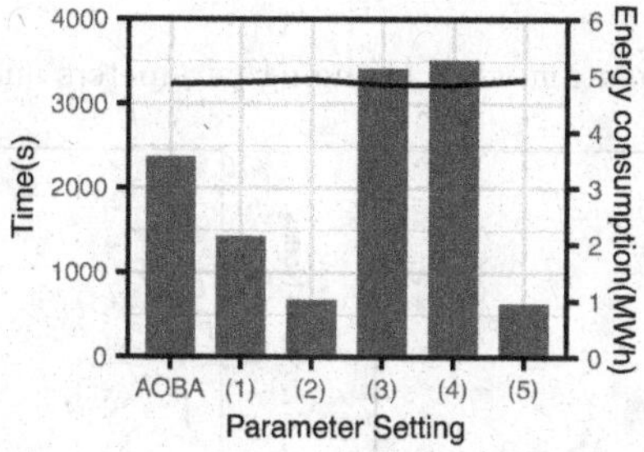

Fig. 9. Results of busy-period simulation.

The results of scheduling parameter tuning are shown in Fig. 9. The left vertical axis indicates the average waiting time of a job, the right vertical axis indicates the energy consumption, and the horizontal axis shows the resource allocation. The average waiting time decreases as the number of nodes increases by moving nodes from the sx1 and sxf queues to the others. On the other hand, the average waiting time increases if two or three nodes are shared by multiple queues, worsening the system operation efficiency. The average waiting time is minimized if all the nodes are shared by queues. In this simulation, we can see that the average waiting time is significantly reduced with a little increase in the energy consumption in 11Move 3 nodes" and "Share all nodes" cases. In the following discussion, we focus on the "Move 3 nodes" case because system administrators will likely avoid using "Share all nodes" to ensure the QoS of paid use by limiting resources for the free queue.

Considering the results in Fig. 6, we simulate the job scheduling by changing the minimum idle time in the case, as shown in Fig. 10. The vertical and horizontal axes are the same as those in Fig. 9. We can see that the energy consumption is smaller than that with the minimum idle time of 7200 s. The scheduling parameter tuning of the minimum idle time is possible even when the resource balance is adjusted.

The status changes in jobs and nodes in the case with the minimum idle time of 1800 s seconds are shown in Fig. 11. The vertical and horizontal axes are the same as those in Fig. 8. In Fig. 11(a), the number of jobs in the queued status is decreased compared to that in Fig. 8(a), indicating that this resource allocation can start jobs earlier than that in the AOBA-A system. In Fig. 11(b),

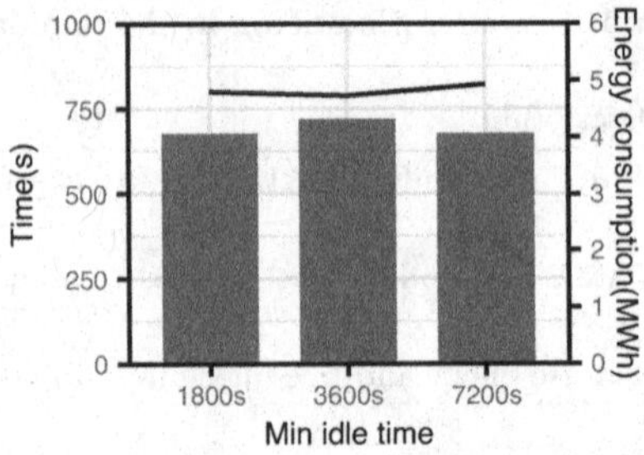

Fig. 10. Results of simulation when changing parameters and resource allocation.

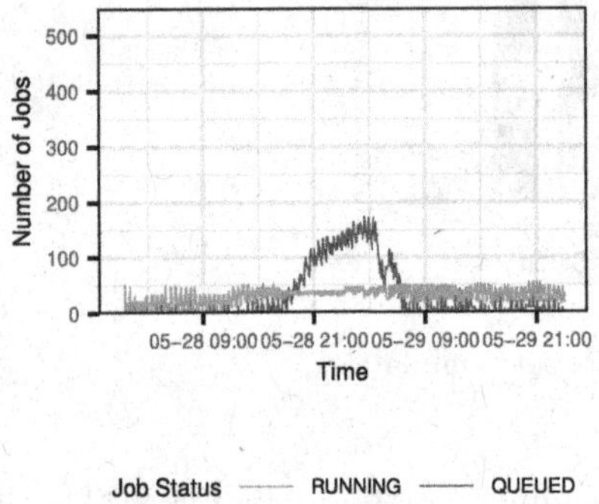

(a) Job status.

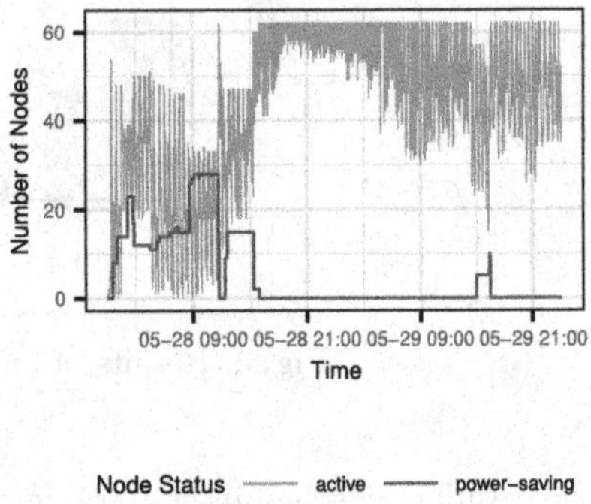

(b) Node status.

Fig. 11. Status transition of jobs and nodes when resource balance and power saving parameter is changed.

we can see that the number of nodes in the power-saving status has increased compared to that in Fig. 8(b). Even in the busy period, the average waiting time can be reduced from 2370 s to 678 s, while reducing the energy consumption from 4.85 MWh to 4.80 MWh in comparison with the parameter settings adopted by the AOBA-A system in Table 4. These results clearly indicate that we are able to achieve better efficiency with less energy consumption than the current parameter settings of the AOBA system in those two days if the resource balance and parameter configurations can properly be adjusted. In this way, the proposed simulator is helpful for system administrators to adjust the scheduling and power saving parameter configuration to achieve better system operation efficiency and/or less energy consumption. Furthermore, these results show the effectiveness of a Digital Twin of a real-world HPC system because it predicts daily, weekly, and monthly data and suggests suitable parameters to system administrators.

7 Conclusions

In this paper, we have first implemented a component for a job scheduling simulator to support the necessary features for building a "Digital Twin" of a real-world HPC system, named AOBA. By using the Digital Twin with actual job traces, a system administrator can check whether the system is being efficiently operated as expected. Although we have implemented only the core algorithm of NQSV, the simulation results are reasonably accurate except for some cases such as hardware failures, and hence the proposed simulator is useful to explore the optimal parameter configurations for individual situations.

This paper has shown a use case of exploring appropriate scheduling and power saving parameters. In the use case, we found that there are more appropriate parameter configurations, which can reduce the job waiting time by 70% at most and the energy consumption by 1.2% at most when the system is busy. By exploiting such a Digital Twin, therefore, it is demonstrated the feasibility that a system administrator can properly adjust various parameters without disturbing the system operation.

Feitelson [8] has reported on the limitations of simulation with job traces. In this paper, we assume that every node has the same performance at executing a job. The execution time of a parallel job could be affected by the physical placement of parallel tasks. In addition, since AOBA consists of a vector-type computing system and a scalar computing system, a user can select one of those two systems suited for each job. To build a "Digital twin" of a real-world HPC system more accurately, we will model the execution time and power consumption of individual jobs, and also predict user behaviors. Moreover, we will consider how to identify underlying job patterns in a short period of time and find an appropriate parameter configuration for the patterns by using machine learning. These will be further discussed in our future work.

Acknowledgements. This work is partially supported by MEXT Next-Generation High-Performance Computing Infrastructures and Applications R&D Program R&D of a Quantum-Annealing-Assisted Next Generation HPC Infrastructure and its Applications and Grant-in-Aid for Scientific Research(B) #21H03449.

References

1. Agung, M., Watanabe, Y., Weber, H., Egawa, R., Takizawa, H.: Preemptive parallel job scheduling for heterogeneous systems supporting urgent computing. IEEE Access **9**, 17557–17571 (2021). https://doi.org/10.1109/ACCESS.2021.3053162
2. Baheri, B., Guan, Q.: Mars: Multi-scalable actor-critic reinforcement learning scheduler. ArXiv abs/ arXiv: 2005.01584 (2020)
3. Chahal, D., Mathew, B., Nambiar, M.: Simulation based job scheduling optimization for batch workloads. In: Proceedings of the 2019 ACM/SPEC International Conference on Performance Engineering, ICPE 201, pp. 313–320. Association for Computing Machinery, New York (2019). https://doi.org/10.1145/3297663.3310312

4. Cunha, R.L.F., Chaimowicz, L.: Towards a common environment for learning scheduling algorithms. 2020 28th International Symposium on Modeling, Analysis, and Simulation of Computer and Telecommunication Systems (MASCOTS), pp. 1–8 (2020)
5. Dutot, P.F., Mercier, M., Poquet, M., Richard, O.: Batsim: A realistic language-independent resources and jobs management systems simulator. In: Desai, N., Cirne, W. (eds.) Job Scheduling Strategies for Parallel Processing, pp. 178–197. Springer International Publishing, Cham (2017)
6. Egawa, R., et al.: Exploiting the potentials of the second generation sx-aurora tsubasa. In: 2020 IEEE/ACM Performance Modeling, Benchmarking and Simulation of High Performance Computer Systems (PMBS)m pp. 39–49 (2020). https://doi.org/10.1109/PMBS51919.2020.00010
7. Fan, Y., Lan, Z., Childers, T., Rich, P., Allcock, W., Papka, M.E.: Deep reinforcement agent for scheduling in hpc (2021)
8. Feitelson, D.G.: The forgotten factor: facts on performance evaluation and its dependence on workloads. In: Monien, B., Feldmann, R. (eds.) Euro-Par 2002. LNCS, vol. 2400, pp. 49–60. Springer, Heidelberg (2002). https://doi.org/10.1007/3-540-45706-2_4
9. Gaussier, E., Lelong, J., Reis, V., Trystram, D.: Online tuning of easy-backfilling using queue reordering policies. IEEE Trans. Parallel Distrib. Syst. **29**(10), 2304–2316 (2018). https://doi.org/10.1109/TPDS.2018.2820699
10. IBM Spectrum LSF Suites: https://www.ibm.com/products/hpc-workload-management
11. Klusâček, D., Rudovà, H.: Alea 2 - job scheduling simulator. SIMUTools 2010–3rd International ICST Conference on Simulation Tools and Techniques, p. 61 (01 2010). https://doi.org/10.4108/ICST.SIMUTOOLS2010.8722
12. Komatsu, K., et al.: Performance evaluation of a vector supercomputer sx-aurora tsubasa. In: SC18: International Conference for High Performance Computing, Networking, Storage and Analysis, pp. 685–696 (2018). https://doi.org/10.1109/SC.2018.00057
13. Kondameedi, V., Vadhiyar, S.S.: Adaptive hybrid queue configuration for supercomputer systems. In: 2017 17th IEEE/ACM International Symposium on Cluster, Cloud and Grid Computing (CCGRID), pp. 90–99 (2017)
14. Krishnamurthy, D., Alemzadeh, M., Moussavi, M.: Towards automated hpc scheduler configuration tuning. In: Concurrency and Computation: Practice and Experience 23 (2011)
15. Maiterth, M., et al.: Energy and power aware job scheduling and resource management: Global survey - initial analysis. In: 2018 IEEE International Parallel and Distributed Processing Symposium Workshops (IPDPSW), pp. 685–693 (2018). https://doi.org/10.1109/IPDPSW.2018.00111
16. Mao, H., Alizadeh, M., Menache, I., Kandula, S.: Resource management with deep reinforcement learning. In: Proceedings of the 15th ACM Workshop on Hot Topics in Networks, HotNets 2016, pp. 50–56. Association for Computing Machinery, New York (2016). https://doi.org/10.1145/3005745.3005750
17. Mao, H., Schwarzkopf, M., Venkatakrishnan, S.B., Meng, Z., Alizadeh, M.: Learning scheduling algorithms for data processing clusters. In: Proceedings of the ACM Special Interest Group on Data Communication, SIGCOMM 2019, pp. 270–288. Association for Computing Machinery (2019). https://doi.org/10.1145/3341302.3342080,https://doi.org/10.1145/3341302.3342080

18. Mu'alem, A., Feitelson, D.: Utilization, predictability, workloads, and user runtime estimates in scheduling the ibm sp2 with backfilling. IEEE Trans. Paral. Distrib. Syst. **12**, 529–543 (2001). https://doi.org/10.1109/71.932708
19. NEC Network Queuing System V (NQSV) User's Guide [Introduction]. https://www.hpc.nec/documents/nqsv/pdfs/g2ad01e-NQSVUG-Introduction.pdf
20. NEC SX-Aurora TSUBASA. https://www.nec.com/en/global/solutions/hpc/sx
21. OpenPBS. https://www.openpbs.org/
22. Peng, Y., Bao, Y., Chen, Y., wu, C., Meng, C., Lin, W.: Dl2: A deep learning-driven scheduler for deep learning clusters. IEEE Trans. Paral. Distri. Syst. 1–1 (2021). https://doi.org/10.1109/TPDS.2021.3052895
23. Powers, S.: A study of the impact of scheduling parameters in heterogeneous computing environments. In: Proceedings - Winter Simulation Conference, vol. 2015, pp. 933–942, Jan 2015. https://doi.org/10.1109/WSC.2014.7019953
24. Ryu, B., An, A., Rashidi, Z., Liu, J., Hu, Y.: Towards topology aware pre-emptive job scheduling with deep reinforcement learning. In: Proceedings of the 30th Annual International Conference on Computer Science and Software Engineering, CASCON 2020, pp. 83–92. IBM Corp., USA (2020)
25. Simakov, N., et al.: A slurm simulator: implementation and parametric analysis, pp. 197–217. In: High Performance Computing Systems. Performance Modeling, Benchmarking, and Simulation, Jan 2018. https://doi.org/10.1007/978-3-319-72971-8_10
26. SLURM. https://www.schedmd.com/
27. Sulistio, A., Cibej, U., Venugopal, S., Robic, B., Buyya, R.: A toolkit for modelling and simulating data grids: An extension to gridsim. Concur. Comput. Pract. Exp. **20**, 1591–1609 (2008). https://doi.org/10.1002/cpe.1307
28. SX-Aurora TSUBASA Architecture Guide Revision 1.1. https://www.hpc.nec/documents/guide/pdfs/Aurora_ISA_guide.pdf
29. Top500. https://www.top500.org/
30. Zhang, D., Dai, D., He, Y., Bao, F.S., Xie, B.: Rlscheduler: An automated hpc batch job scheduler using reinforcement learning. In: Proceedings of the International Conference for High Performance Computing, Networking, Storage and Analysis, SC 2020. IEEE Press (2020)

Encoding for Reinforcement Learning Driven Scheduling

Boyang Li[1(✉)], Yuping Fan[1], Michael E. Papka[2,3], and Zhiling Lan[1]

[1] Illinois Institute of Technology, Chicago, IL 60616, USA
{bli70,yfan22}@hawk.iit.edu, lan@iit.edu

[2] Argonne National Laboratory, 9700 S S Cass Ave, Lemont, IL 60439, USA
papka@anl.gov

[3] Northern Illinois University, 1425 W Lincoln Hwy, DeKalb, IL 60115, USA

Abstract. Reinforcement learning (RL) is exploited for cluster scheduling in the field of high-performance computing (HPC). One of the key challenges for RL driven scheduling is state representation for RL agent (i.e., capturing essential features of dynamic scheduling environment for decision making). Existing state encoding approaches either lack critical scheduling information or suffer from poor scalability. In this study, we present SEM (Scalable and Efficient encoding Model) for general RL driven scheduling in HPC. It captures system resource and waiting job state, both being critical information for scheduling. It encodes these pieces of information into a fixed-sized vector as an input to the agent. A typical agent is built on deep neural network, and its training/inference cost grows exponentially with the size of its input. Production HPC systems contain a large number of computer nodes. As such, a direct encoding of each of the system resources would lead to poor scalability of the RL agent. SEM uses two techniques to transform the system resource state into a small-sized vector, hence being capable of representing a large number of system resources in a vector of 100–200. Our trace-based simulations demonstrate that compared to the existing state encoding methods, SEM can achieve 9X training speedup and 6X inference speedup while maintaining comparable scheduling performance.

Keywords: Batch scheduling · Reinforcement learning · Scalability · High-performance computing

1 Introduction

Cluster scheduler, also known as batch scheduler, plays a very critical role in high-performance computing (HPC). It is responsible for determining the order in which jobs are executed on a HPC system. Heuristic approaches are typically used for HPC cluster scheduling [8,22,26]. For instance, first come, first served (FCFS) is a well-known scheduling policy deployed on production HPC systems [22]. Backfilling is commonly used to enhance job scheduling by improving system utilization, where subsequent jobs are moved ahead to utilize free resources [22].

D. Klusáček et al. (Eds.): JSSPP 2022, LNCS 13592, pp. 68–87, 2023.
https://doi.org/10.1007/978-3-031-22698-4_4

Recently, reinforcement learning (RL) is exploited to enhance cluster scheduling in HPC. In RL driven scheduling, the agent is trained to learn a proper scheduling policy according to a specific scheduling objective (e.g., reward) provided by system managers. Once trained, the agent can automatically interact with the scheduling environment and dynamically adjust its policy as workload changes. The application of reinforcement learning to the scheduling problem has yielded a number of promising results for cluster scheduling [10–12, 14, 19, 20, 23, 25, 30]. One of the key challenges for RL driven scheduling is *state representation (i.e., encoding)* for RL agent. Encoding must be *efficient* and *scalable*. An efficient encoding must capture critical system resource and waiting job information. These pieces of information must be represented as a fixed-sized input to the agent. RL agent is commonly built on deep neural network, and its computational cost grows exponentially with the size of its input. Production HPC systems typically contain a large number of computing resources. Hence, a direct encoding of each of the system resources leads to poor scalability of the RL agent. The training and inference time would increase drastically with the system size growing.

Existing encoding approaches can be broadly classified as *image-based* or *vector-based*. Image-based state representation uses a fixed-sized 2D image to represent waiting jobs and system resources: one dimension for resource availability and the other dimension for time duration [10, 11, 14, 19, 25]. Image-based state representation has two limitations. First, for HPC scheduling, although system resource has a fixed size, time duration could be infinite as a job may take seconds to days or even weeks to complete. As such, image-based state representation cannot effectively address the wide range of or even infinite time duration issue. Second, while image-based representation can capture resource requirement per job, it lacks the encoding of job information such as job priority or job waiting time [10, 11, 14, 19, 25]. In order to overcome the aforementioned issues of image-based encoding, vector-based encoding is widely adopted [12, 20, 23, 30], in which the resource information and the job information are represented by vectors and concatenated into a fixed-sized vector input to the agent. Unfortunately, existing vector-based encoding methods suffer from two major shortcomings. First, prior vector-based encoding methods are mainly designed for directed acyclic graph (DAG) or malleable jobs, which are very different from rigid parallel jobs dominating in HPC with fixed resource requirements [20, 23]. Second, while several vector-based encoding methods are presented for HPC scheduling [12, 30], they either miss essential resource information [30], or lead to a huge state space, hence causing a scalability concern [12].

This work aims to tackle the aforementioned encoding problems. Specifically, we present SEM, a new **S**calable and **E**fficient state representation **M**odel for general RL driven scheduling in HPC. SEM adopts a vector-based encoding approach. It is designed to be *efficient* as it encodes system resources and waiting jobs, both being critical for efficient scheduling. It is also *scalable* such that it is capable of representing the scheduling state of a large-scale system in a small-sized vector (e.g., with 100–200 elements). RL agent typically uses deep neural network for decision making, and the computational cost of the neural work grows exponentially with the input size. The significant reduction of input size via SEM encoding means dramatic scaling improvement of the agent.

In SEM, each waiting job is encoded into a 4-element vector to capture its state (i.e., job size, job estimated runtime, priority, and job waiting time). Rather than encoding each system resource individually as a vector, SEM encodes the system resources through the viewpoint of running jobs. We represent system resources by a concatenated vector of the resources used by a fixed number of running jobs. Resources used per running job is encoded as a 2-element vector (i.e. job size, estimated remaining time). This design is based on a *key observation*, that is, the resources belonging to the same job have the same system status (e.g., the same start and end time). Furthermore, parallel jobs occupying multiple computing resources are common in HPC. Hence, the number of running jobs is significantly less than the amount of system resources. In order to encode both system resources and waiting jobs into a small fixed-sized vector, we develop two solutions, one for systems with minimum job size requirement and the other for systems without such a requirement.

We compare SEM with existing encoding method under various configurations by using trace-based, event-driven scheduling simulation. Experimental results show that the use of SEM encoding can lead to a significant reduction in RL agent training and inference (or testing) time while maintaining comparable scheduling performance. Specifically, this paper makes three major contributions:

- We propose a novel encoding model for RL driven scheduler by leveraging the fact that the resources belonging to the same running job have the same system status and the number of running jobs is significantly less than the amount of system resources in parallel computing.
- We develop two methods to address the challenge that a fixed-sized state representation is required for RL agent even though the number of running jobs dynamically changes in a realistic environment.
- Extensive trace-driven experiments show that compared to existing state encoding models, our proposed method has a faster convergence speed. It allows the RL agent to achieve 9X training speedup and 6X inference speedup while maintaining comparable scheduling performance. Moreover, SEM can scale well as the system size increases.

The remainder of this paper is organized as follows. We start by introducing background and related work in Sect. 2. In Sect. 3, we describe SEM design. We present workload trace, comparison method, experiment setup and evaluation metrics in Sect. 4. The experimental results are presented in Sect. 5. Finally, we conclude the paper in Sect. 6.

2 Background and Related Work

2.1 Cluster Scheduling

A cluster scheduler is responsible for allocating resources and for determining the order in which jobs are executed on a HPC system. When submitting a job, a user is required to provide two pieces of information: number of compute resources required for the job (i.e., job size) and job runtime estimate (i.e., walltime). The scheduler determines when and where to execute the job. The jobs are stored and sorted in the waiting queue based on a site's policy. Once a new job is submitted, job scheduler sorts all the jobs in the waiting queue based on a job prioritizing policy. A number of popular job prioritizing policies have been proposed, and a widely used policy is FCFS [22], which sorts jobs in the order of job arrivals.

In addition, backfilling is a commonly used approach to enhance job scheduling by improving system utilization, where subsequent jobs are moved ahead to utilize free resources. A widely used strategy is EASY backfilling which allows short jobs to skip ahead under the condition that they do not delay the job at the head of the queue [22].

2.2 Reinforcement Learning Driven Scheduling

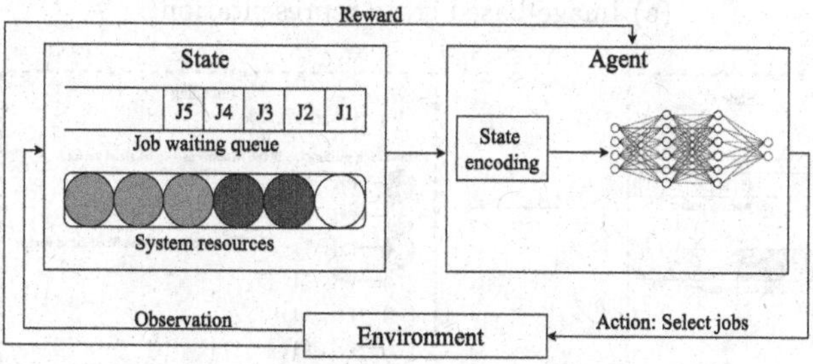

Fig. 1. Overview of RL driven scheduling. In the state, each system resource is represented by a circle. The circles sharing the same color indicate these system resources are allocated to the same running job; blank circles mean free/available system resources.

Reinforcement learning is an area of machine learning that is primarily focused on dynamic decision making where an intelligent agent takes actions in an environment with the goal of maximizing some reward [28]. The environment is captured by its state information. When the agent performs an action, it will be provided with the environment's response to that action as feedback (i.e., reward) and be taken to another state within the environment. These feedback and reward mechanisms allow the agent to learn, by trials and errors, how to act in order to maximize its reward [17].

Pioneering studies have explored RL for cluster scheduling with encouraging results [10–12,14,19,20,23,25,30]. In RL driven scheduling, the agent is trained to learn a proper scheduling policy according to a specific scheduling objective (e.g., reward) provided by system managers. Once trained, the agent can automatically interact with the scheduling environment and dynamically adjust its policy as workload changes. Since the state space is typically enormous, memorizing all states becomes infeasible. RL driven scheduling uses deep neural network for approximation [21]. Figure 1 shows an overview of a typical RL driven scheduling. At each step, state is observed and fed to the scheduling agent. The agent provides job selection and receives the reward as the feedback. It is obvious that state representation plays a critical role in RL driven scheduling.

2.3 Encoding Approaches

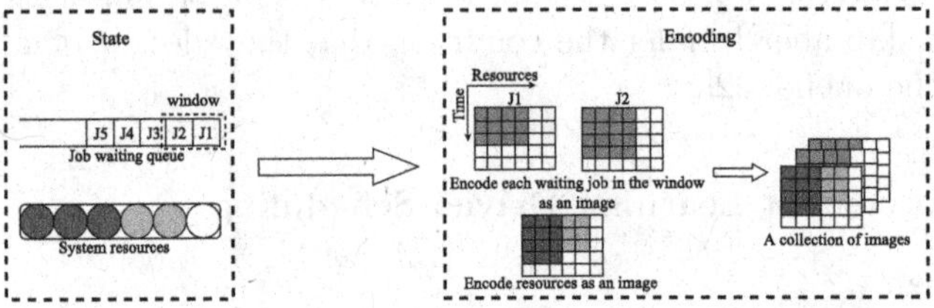

(a) Image-based state representation

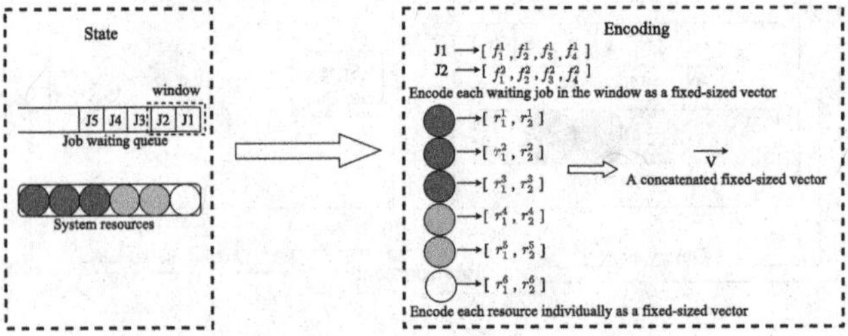

(b) Vector-based state representation

Fig. 2. Overview of existing state representation approaches.

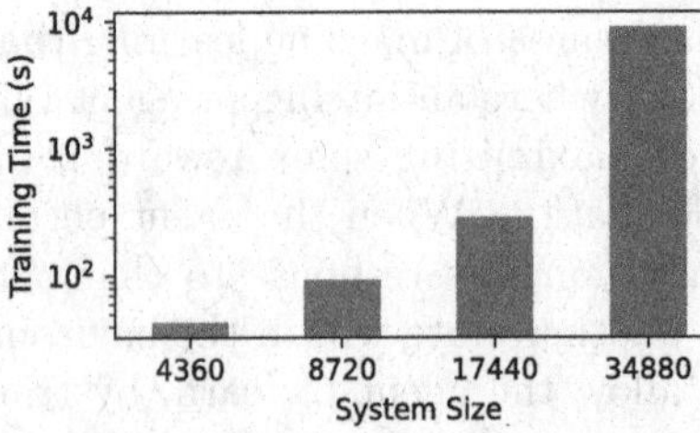

Fig. 3. Analysis of training costs with growing system size when using the vector-based encoding from the literature [12].

A key challenge of designing reinforcement learning driven scheduler is how to represent a dynamic scheduling state. Existing state representation models can be broadly divided into two classes: image-based state representation [10,11,14, 19,25] and vector-based state representation [12,20,23,30].

Figure 2(a) illustrates image-based state representation. Image-based state representation typically represents the waiting job information and resource information by a fixed-sized 2D image: one dimension for resource availability and the other dimension for time duration [10,11,14,19,25]. The images for the first W waiting jobs are maintained for constraining the action space. Image-based representation has limitations of limited time duration and lack of the encoding of other critical job information as mentioned in Sect. 1 [10,11,14,19,25].

To overcome aforementioned issues, vector-based state representation methods are proposed [12,20,23,30]. Figure 2(b) illustrates vector-based state representation. The waiting job information and resource information are represented by vectors and concatenated into a fixed-sized vector as the input to the neural network. Specifically, the first W jobs in the waiting queue are encoded for constraining the action space and each resource is also encoded as a vector. However, these proposed approaches still have their own limitations. In Decima and DL2, all the jobs were DAG jobs and could be decomposed into malleable tasks, whereas HPC was dominated by single rigid jobs that could not be decomposed [20,23]. RLScheduler didn't capture the allocated resource state information in its state representation, hence missing essential resource information in the model building [30]. DRAS overcame these issues; however, the state encoding adopted in DRAS may lead to poor scalability [12]. DRAS used a vector to capture each system resource (e.g, compute node). As a production system may contain thousands of compute nodes, such an encoding results in an input vector in the size of thousands of elements and consequently leads to nontrivial training cost. As an example, we examine the potential training time when applying the vector-based state representation used in [12]. As shown in Fig. 3, the cost exponentially increases with growing system size. The SEM model is designed to address these encoding issues for RL driven scheduling.

3 SEM Design

SEM, shown in Fig. 4, is developed to provide a scalable and efficient state encoding for general RL driven scheduling in HPC. It encodes waiting jobs and system resources as vectors and concatenates them into a fixed-sized vector input to the agent. The design of SEM is based on the two key observation: (1) the resources belonging to the same job have the same system status and (2) the number of running jobs is significantly less than the amount of system resources. Rather than encoding each system resource individually as a vector, SEM encodes the system resources through the viewpoint of running jobs. We represent system resources by a concatenated vector of the resources used by a fixed number of running jobs. Such a resource encoding can significantly reduce vector size.

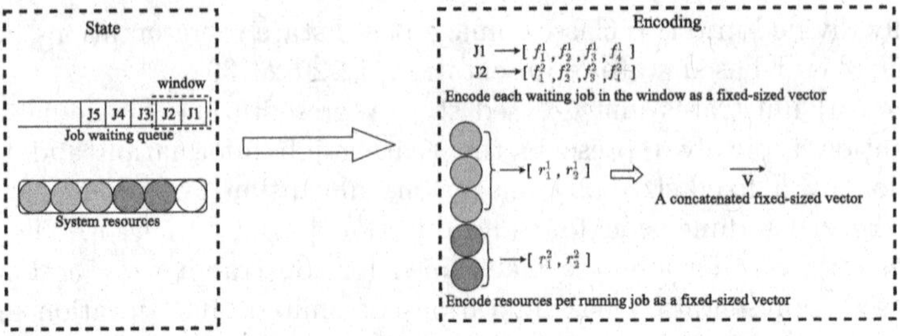

Fig. 4. SEM state representation. It captures system resources and user jobs as a fixed-size input to the RL agent depicted in the general RL driven scheduling shown in Fig. 1.

We start by introducing the key observation through trace analysis in Sect. 3.1. In Sect. 3.2, we present the encoding of waiting jobs. We describe the resource encoding, including two methods to address the challenge that RL agent requires a fixed-sized input whereas the number of running jobs dynamically changes in a realistic environment, in Sect. 3.3. Finally, we analyze computational complexity of SEM in Sect. 3.4.

3.1 Observations

Table 1. Workload trace

Workload	Site	System size	Period
Theta [7]	Argonne	4,360	Jan.2018-Dec.2019
Mira [4]	Argonne	49,152	Jan.2014-Dec.2014
Atlas [6]	LLNL	9,216	Nov.2006-Jun.2007
DataStar [6]	SDSC	1,664	Mar.2004-Apr.2005

For rigid jobs in HPC, the resources requested by the same job will be allocated to start the job and released after job completion as a whole (i.e. the same start and end time). Thus, *the resources belonging to the same job have the same system status.*

To validate the assumption that the number of running jobs is much less than the system size, we analyze a number of workload traces from production supercomputers and four representative traces are presented in Table 1. Among them, Mira and Theta represent the HPC systems that have a minimum job size requirement, whereas Atlas and DataStar represent the systems without such a job requirement. Note that for DataStar and Atlas, their resources are expressed in the number of cores, hence the system size is set to the total number of cores for these systems [13].

We analyze these traces and present our data analysis in Fig. 5. It plots the cumulative distribution function (CDF) of the number of running jobs. For example, while Theta has 4,360 compute nodes for default queue, the number of running jobs is no more than 32. Even for the larger system Mira with about 50K nodes, the number of running jobs is typically less than 50. In other words, we observe that *the number of running jobs is significantly less than the system size on production supercomputers.* Table 2 summarizes the maximum number of running jobs for each trace. There are two reasons for this phenomenon. First, a system is rarely fully occupied due to external and/or internal fragmentations [24,29]. Second, parallel jobs using multiple system resources are common in HPC systems. Many capability computing systems such as those deployed for capability computing have a minimum job size requirement [1,3,5]. For instance, the minimum job size on Theta is 128.

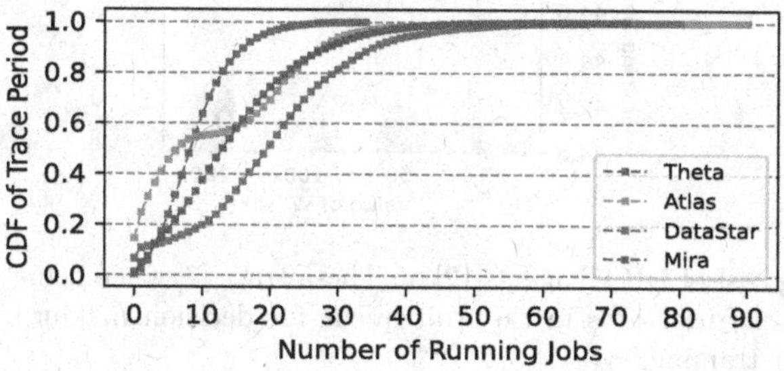

Fig. 5. The relationship between the number of running jobs and cumulative distribution function of trace period.

Table 2. Maximum number of running jobs

Workload	System Size	Maximum Number of Jobs
Theta	4,360	32
Mira	49,152	71
Atlas	9,216	90
DataStar	1,664	81

3.2 Encoding of Waiting Jobs

SEM adopts a vector-based state representation. It encodes the scheduling environment by capturing the state of both waiting jobs and system resources. In practice, the number of waiting jobs in job queue dynamically changes. When scheduling the queued jobs, since the available system resources are limited, usually only front jobs have chance to be selected for execution. As the RL agent requires a fixed-sized input, the first W jobs in the queue are encoded in previous vector-based methods [12,30]. Take an example, we investigate the training cost of DRAS agent under different W values [12], and the results are shown in Fig. 6. In order to perform such an analysis, we purposely adjust the job density in the original trace to ensure there are sufficient waiting jobs in the queue. The results show that the training time increase is negligible (within 1s). One key reason is that compared to the system state, the waiting job representation accounts for a smaller percentage.

In this work, we use the same window based design. We choose to encode the first W jobs in the queue. For each waiting job, we encode it as a vector of four elements: job size, job estimated runtime, priority (1 means high priority; 0 means low priority), and job waiting time (time elapsed since submission). Job size is expressed by the percentage of system size.

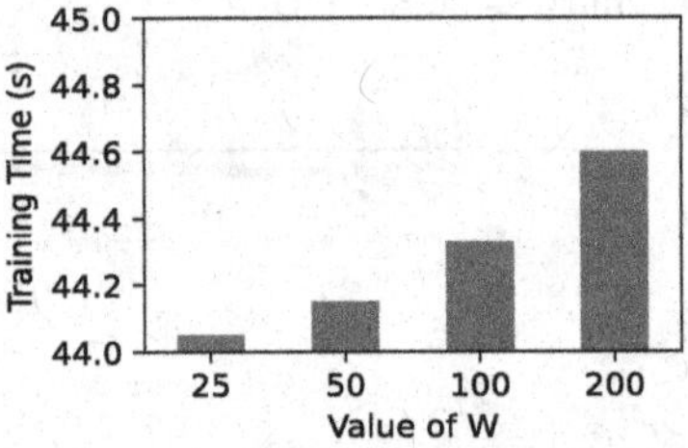

Fig. 6. Training cost of DRAS agent [12] on Theta trace [7] when using different values of W (a window of user jobs in the wait queue for decision making). One thousand jobs are used for training.

In general, W can be chosen by the system administrator. For typical HPC systems, W is set in the range of 10–100 [12,30].

3.3 Encoding of System Resources

SEM encodes the system resources through the viewpoint of running jobs rather than encoding each system resource individually based on the key observations in Sect. 3.1.

Specifically, we separate the system resources into two groups: the resources occupied by running jobs, and the rest. For the former, SEM encodes them by the viewpoint of the running jobs. For instance, if a job is executed on c compute nodes, SEM encodes these c nodes by one vector: the group size (i.e., job size normalized by the system size) and the remaining occupancy time (i.e., the time difference between the job estimated end time and the current time). For the latter, SEM does not encode it because it is a redundant feature (which can be calculated by the system size minus the total allocated resources). Existing research indicates that redundant features add no useful information for model training [9]. By using such a resource encoding, SEM is capable of significantly reducing the input size. For example, for the 4,360-node Theta, instead of having an input of over 4K features, SEM only needs to encode dozens of features — a reduction of two orders of magnitude.

A remaining issue is how many running jobs K should be encoded for representing the system state. RL agent requires a fixed-sized input whereas the number of running jobs dynamically changes. To attack this issue, we propose two methods. Note that production supercomputers can be broadly classified as systems with minimum job size requirement and systems without such a requirement. For the former systems, we propose a method named *zero-padding*. More specifically, we set K to the maximum number of running jobs which is calculated by dividing the system size over the minimum job size requirement. This number reflects the maximum number of concurrent running jobs on the system. For instance, Theta has 4,360 nodes for default queue and the minimum job size requirement in default queue is 128 nodes. Hence the maximum number of running jobs is 34 (4,360/128) on Theta. When the number of existing running jobs is less than K, we pad the rest of the vectors with zeros. Algorithm 1 shows the pseudo code of this zero-padding algorithm.

Algorithm 1. The zero-padding method

procedure SYSTEM RESOURCES ENCODING(K)
    Read system state
    $R \leftarrow$ number of running jobs
    Encode each running job as a vector
    if $R < K$ **then**
        Pad the rest $(K - R)$ vectors with zeros
    end if
end procedure

For the systems without minimum job size requirement such as Atlas and DataStar, the number of running jobs in practice is much less than the system size as shown in Table 2. We propose *K-largest-job* method. In the fields of natural language processing (NLP) and computer vision (CV), spatial pyramid pooling [15] and K max pooling [18] are shown to preserve the important information for variable size inputs. However, encoding for RL driven scheduling is different from that in the problems in NLP and CV. In NLP and CV, we cannot tell what information is important in advance. Fortunately, we can in RL driven scheduling. With respect to resource allocation, a large-sized job weights more than a small-sized job because the large-sized job requires a large amount of the system resources. Hence, when the number of running jobs is greater than K, SEM chooses to use the K largest jobs for encoding the system resources. Algorithm 2 shows the pseudo code of K-largest-job algorithm. K can be chosen by the administrator via experience or trace analysis.

To validate that the K-largest-job method can preserve system state with negligible information loss, we examine the percentage of total node-hour loss for each workload in Table 3. Node-hour is defined as the product of number of nodes and time duration. For example, using one node for an hour is one node-hour. Node-hour is a commonly used resource allocation unit at supercomputing

Algorithm 2. The K-largest-job method

```
procedure SYSTEM RESOURCES ENCODING(K)
    Read system state
    R ← number of running jobs
    if R > K then
        sort running jobs by job size
        Encode the first K largest jobs as vectors
    else
        Encode each running job as a vector
        Pad the rest (K − R) vectors with zeros
    end if
end procedure
```

facilities [1,5]. The table shows the amount of node-hour losses by using different K values. It clearly indicates that total node-hour loss percentage is extreme trivial (within 1.3%), no matter when K is set to 30, 40 or 50 for both DataStar and Atlas workloads.

Table 3. Information loss when using the K-largest-job method

Workload	Information loss (node-hour loss %)		
	K = 30	K = 40	K = 50
DataStar	1.22%	0.36%	0.01%
Atlas	0.23%	0.03%	9e-05

In addition, we also expect to ensure that the K-largest-job method can cover the majority of resources nearly all the time. Figure 7 shows the amounts of trace period that is covered by using different K values. Two plots are presented here, one for covering 90% of the allocated nodes and the other for 95%. When K is set to 30, for DataStar, out of thirteen months, it covers 90% of the allocated nodes for about 97% of the time and covers 95% of the allocated nodes for about 93% of the time. For Atlas, it covers 90% of the allocated nodes for about 99% of the time and covers 95% of the allocated nodes for more than 98% of the time. When K is set to 40, for DataStar, 90% of the allocated nodes are covered for about 99% of the time and 95% of the allocated nodes are covered for about 97% of the time. For Atlas, it can cover 95% of the allocated nodes for more than 99% of the time. When K is set to 50, for more than 99% of the time, 95% of the allocated nodes are covered for DataStar. For 100% of the time, 95% of the allocated nodes are covered for Atlas. This clearly demonstrates we can encode K largest running jobs to represent the system state with negligible information loss.

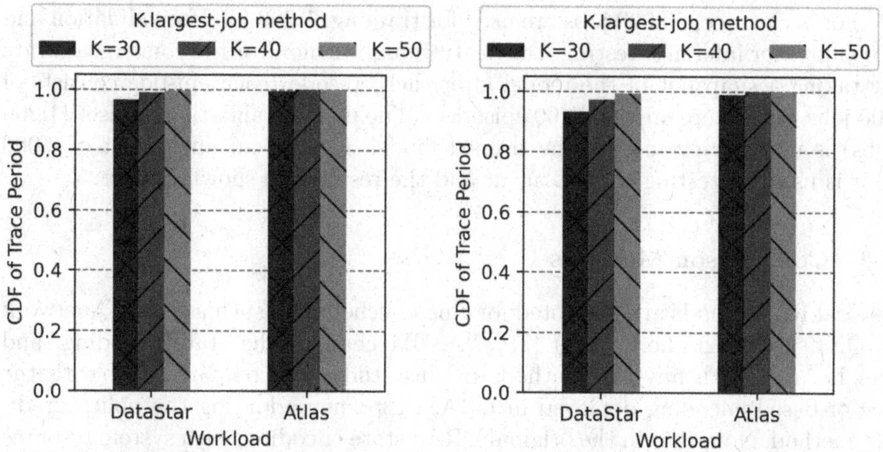

(a) 90% of the allocated nodes (b) 95% of the allocated nodes

Fig. 7. Trace coverage by using different K values

3.4 Complexity Analysis

For the existing vector-based encoding such as [12], the input vector is $O(W+N)$, where W is the number of waiting jobs and N is the size of the system. When adopting SEM, the input vector is reduced to $O(W+K)$, where K is the number of running jobs used for representing the system resources. As discussed in Sect. 3.1, K is greatly smaller than N. As shown in Fig. 1, the number of neurons, hence the computational complexity of the agent, grow exponentially with the input size [16]. As a result, a significantly reduced-size state representation can lead to a great reduction of the corresponding RL model.

4 Evaluation

We describe how we evaluate our SEM design through extensive trace-based simulation using real workload traces collected from several supercomputers, and the results are listed in the next section.

4.1 Workload Trace

We implement SEM in the event driven scheduling simulator CQSim [2] and use it in our evaluation. We use two workload traces, Theta and DataStar, for evaluation. They are chosen to represent two HPC systems, where Theta stands for the computing system with minimum job size of 128 nodes and DataStar represents the computing system with no minimum job size requirement. All experiments were conducted on a personal computer configured with Intel 2 GHz quad-core CPU with 16 GB memory.

For each trace, 60,000 jobs are used for training, 1,200 jobs for validation and 6,000 jobs for inference testing. During training, we monitor the convergence rate by taking a snapshot of the model after each episode (each episode consists of 600 jobs, thus there are total 100 episodes). The unseen validation dataset (1,200 jobs) is used for evaluating the trained model. Finally, an unseen set of 6,000 jobs is used for testing the RL agent and the results are shown in Sect. 5.

4.2 Comparison Methods

Several RL methods are presented for cluster scheduling such as deep Q-network (DQN), policy gradient (PG) [21,27]. SEM changes the state encoding, and can be used with any RL method. In this study, we compare SEM with the vector-based encoding deployed in DRAS [12] when adopting the policy gradient method. Note that in the original DRAS state encoding, each system resource (i.e., compute node) is captured by a 2-element vector and the entire state encoding grows linearly with the system size. In the rest of the paper, we use SEM to denote the new state encoding presented in this work and DRAS to denote a general vector-based state encoding.

Table 4. RL agent configurations under SEM and DRAS

Configuration	Theta		DataStar	
	SEM	DRAS	SEM	DRAS
State vector size	268	8,920	280	3,528
Convolutional layer	134	4,460	140	1,764
Fully connected layer 1	200	4,000	200	1,000
Fully connected layer 2	100	1,000	100	250
Output	50	50	50	50

4.3 Experiment Setup

For Theta, DRAS encodes the scheduling state in a 8,920-element vector where the 4,360-node machine is captured by 8,720 elements and the rest captures a window of W (=50) waiting jobs. When using SEM, K is set to 34 which is determined by the system size divided by the minimum job size requirement (i.e., 4,360/128). SEM uses the same sized window for waiting jobs. Following the reward deployed in DRAS [12], the reward is set to $w_1 \times \frac{\overline{t_i}}{t_{max}} + w_2 \times \frac{\overline{n_i}}{N} + w_3 \times \frac{N_{used}}{N}$, where $\overline{t_i}$ denotes the average wait time of selected jobs; t_{max} is the maximum wait time of jobs in the queue. Similarly, $\overline{n_i}$ is the average job size of the selected jobs; N is the total number of nodes in the system; N_{used} is the number of occupied nodes. This reward function intends to balance three factors: to prevent job starvation, to promote capability (large) jobs, and to improve system utilization. The weights are equally set to 1/3.

For DataStar, DRAS encodes the scheduling state in a 3,528-element vector where the 1,664-node machine is captured by 3,328 elements and the rest captures a window of W (=50) waiting jobs. When using SEM, K is set to 40 according to the trace analysis in Fig. 7. SEM uses the same sized window for waiting jobs. The reward is set to $\sum_{j \in J} -1/t_j$ [19], where J is the set of jobs currently in the system, t_j is the (ideal) duration of the job. This reward function aims to minimize the average job slowdown.

The details of SEM and DRAS neural networks for Theta and DataStar are listed in Table 4. For instance, on Theta, when using SEM, we use a convolutional layer with 134 neurons and two fully-connected layers with 200 and 100 neurons respectively. The output layer contains 50 neurons representing jobs in the window. When using the existing vector encoding [12], we use a convolution layer with 4,460 neurons, two fully-connected layers with 4,000 and 1,000 neurons respectively. The output layer contains 50 neurons representing waiting jobs in the window.

4.4 Evaluation Metrics

When evaluating different encoding methods, we use three quantitative metrics: *(1) agent convergence rate, (2) agent training/inference time, and (3) scheduling performance.*

Following the common practice, we use the following metrics to quantify scheduling performance. *Node utilization* measures the ratio of the used node-hours for useful job execution to the elapsed node-hours. *Job wait time* measures the interval between job submission to job start time. We analyze both average job wait time and maximum job wait time. *Job slowdown* denotes the ratio of the job response time (job runtime plus wait time) to its actual runtime. It is used to gauge the responsiveness of a system.

5 Results

In this section, we present the experimental results of comparing SEM with DRAS. Our analysis centers upon four questions:

1) Does SEM lead to a faster convergence rate for training RL agent? (Sect. 5.1)
2) Does SEM lead to comparable scheduling performance? (Sect. 5.2)
3) How much are RL agent training and inference costs when adopting SEM? (Sect. 5.3)
4) How scalable is SEM-enabled RL driven scheduling? (Sect. 5.4)

5.1 Convergence Rate

Convergence rate reflects how fast the scheduling agent can converge. We monitor the progress of the training by taking a snapshot of the model after each episode. We validate the trained SEM and DRAS enabled agent with an unseen validation dataset.

Figure 8 compares the convergence rates of the scheduling agents by using SEM and DRAS state representations separately. For Theta, SEM converges after 60 episodes while DRAS converges after 86 episodes. For DataStar, SEM converges after 53 episodes whereas DRAS converges after 74 episodes. It is clear that SEM leads to a faster convergence rate than DRAS. As shown in Table 4, SEM results in a much smaller sized neural network and consequently leads to faster convergence.

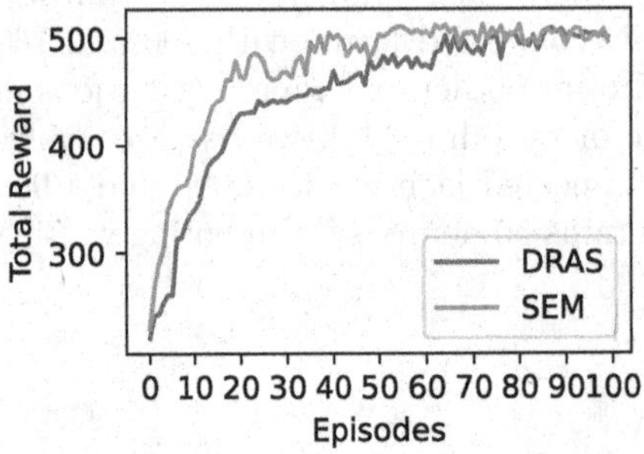

(a) Theta

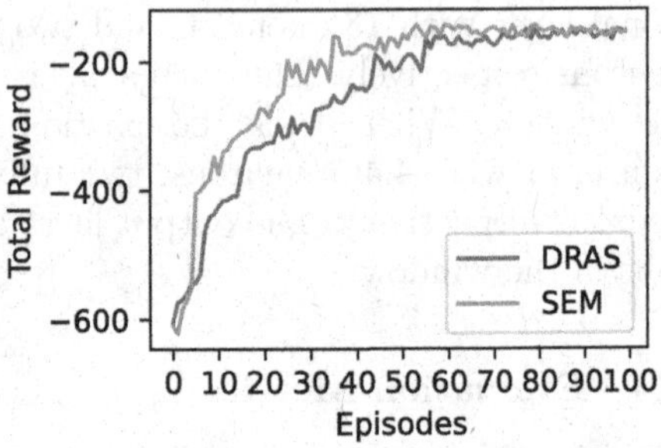

(b) DataStar

Fig. 8. Convergence rate of RL agent using different state encodings.

5.2 Scheduling Performance

Figure 9 presents the overall scheduling performance obtained by SEM and DRAS state representations with Kiviat graphs. We use node utilization, the reciprocal of average job wait time, the reciprocal of maximum job wait time and the reciprocal of average slowdown in the plots. All metrics are normalized within the range of 1. 1 means a method achieves the best performance among all methods. For all metrics, the larger the area is, the better the overall performance is.

We observe that the Kiviat graphs of SEM and DRAS almost overlap both on Theta and DataStar. On Theta, SEM performs slightly better than DRAS in utilization, maximum job wait time, average job wait time while DRAS performs a little better in average job slowdown. The difference of all these metrics are within 4%. On DataStar, SEM achieves a better performance than DRAS in utilization, average slowdown, average wait time whereas DRAS achieves a smaller maximum job wait time. The difference of all these metrics are within 6%. The results demonstrate that SEM can achieve comparable scheduling performance compared with DRAS and SEM can capture all the necessary system state information.

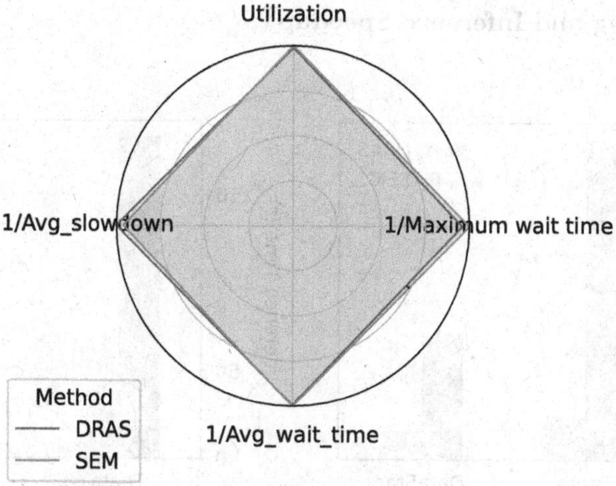

(a) Theta

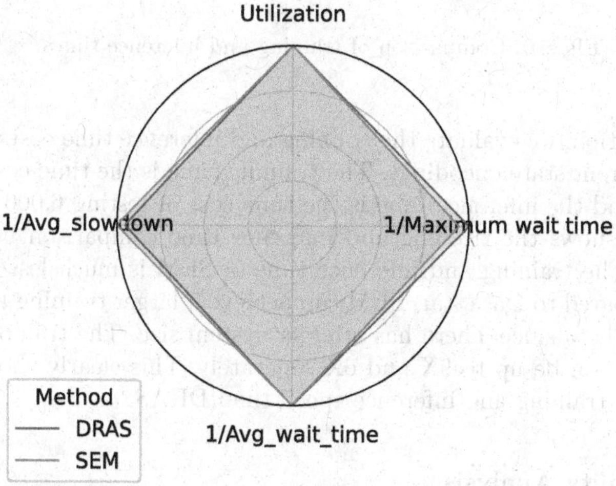

(b) DataStar

Fig. 9. Scheduling performance by using different state encodings. The plots use Kiviat graphs to provide a comprehensive view of scheduling performance. The larger the area is, the better the overall performance is. It indicates that SEM can achieve comparable scheduling performance as those obtained by the existing state encoding.

5.3 Training and Inference Speedup

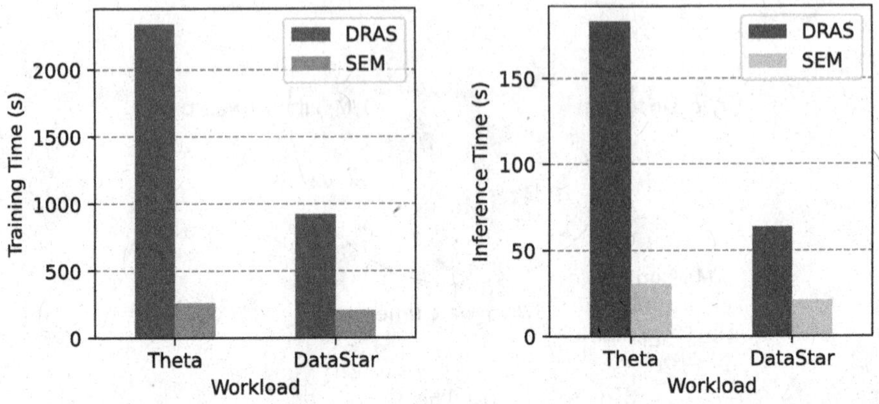

(a) Training time (b) Inference time

Fig. 10. Comparison of training and inference times.

In this subsection, we evaluate the training and inference time costs of RL agent by using different state encodings. The training time is the time cost of training 60,000 jobs and the inference time is the time cost of testing 6,000 jobs.

Figure 10 shows the training and inference time comparison between SEM and DRAS. The training and inference time of SEM is much less than that of DRAS. Compared to DataStar, SEM can achieve a larger training and inference speedup on Theta since Theta has a larger system size. The training and inference speedup can be up to 9X and 6X separately. This clearly shows SEM has a much faster training and inference speed than DRAS.

5.4 Scalability Analysis

As described in Sect. 2.3, existing vector-based encoding captures system resources individually. Since production supercomputers may contain a large number of resources to meet the ever-increasing demand of workloads, the use of existing vector-based encoding may lead to a neural network with millions or even billions of parameters. In contrast, SEM captures system state through a viewpoint of running jobs and is capable of capturing environment state using a fixed-sized vector of dozens of elements. Such a significant reduction of input size via SEM encoding means dramatic scaling improvement of the agent.

In this set of experiments, we examine training and inference time when increasing system size by using SEM and DRAS state encodings. The results are presented in Fig. 11. In this figure, system size is increased from 4,360 to 34,880. As system size increases, number of jobs and vector input also grow

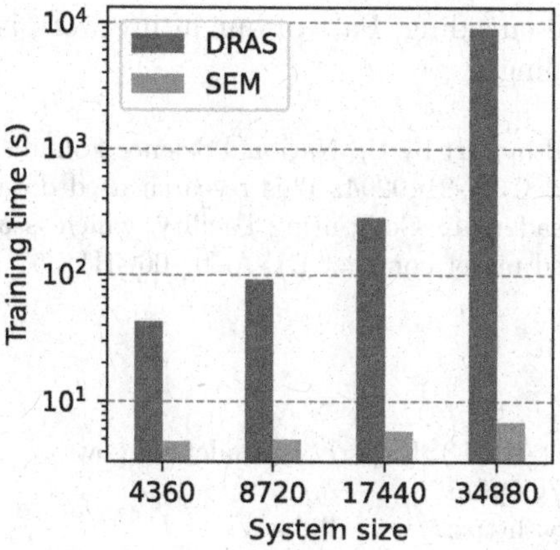

(a) Training time

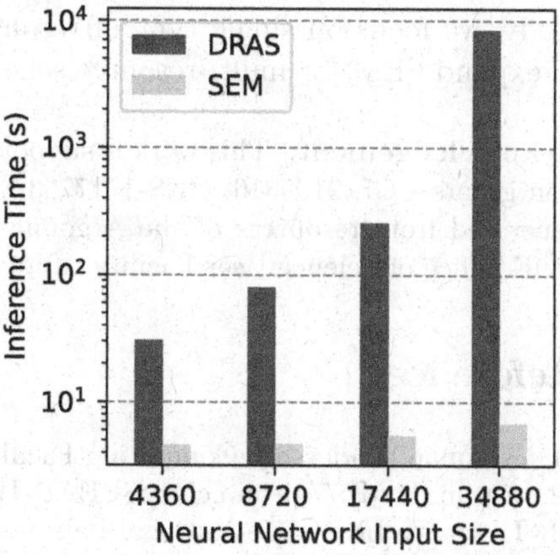

(b) Inference time

Fig. 11. Analysis of training and inference times when system size increases. One thousand jobs are used for training and inference testing separately.

proportionally in this experiment. The plots show that the training and inference time of SEM increases very slowly while the training and inference time of DRAS increases drastically with the system size increasing. When the system size is set to 34,880, the use of existing vector-based encoding leads to a training cost of over 8,000 s, whereas SEM results in a training cost of only 7 s. This means over 1000X improvement compared to DRAS state encoding.

6 Conclusions

Reinforcement learning driven scheduling is a promising approach for cluster scheduling. Prior RL driven scheduling studies mainly focus on exploiting different RL methods with little attention to state representation. Existing state representation approaches either lack sufficient scheduling information or suffer from poor scalability. In this work, we have presented a new and generic state representation called SEM for general RL driven scheduling. SEM captures the state of scheduling environment in a fixed-sized vector. It is efficient as it captures both waiting jobs and system resources for scheduling environment. It is also scalable as it utilizes a new method to capture system state through a viewpoint of running jobs. In this study, two methods are presented to encode scheduling environment into a fixed-sized vector, i.e., zero-padding and K-largest-job. Experimental results show that SEM can lead to a faster convergence speed, up to 9X training/inference time reduction, and high scalability as compared to the existing encoding methods.

The proposed SEM encoding is generally applicable to a variety of RL driven scheduling methods that use deep neural network for decision making. In this study, we focus on single type of resource encoding. Part of our future work is to expand SEM for multi-resource scheduling.

Acknowledgement. This work is supported in part by US National Science Foundation grants CCF-2109316, CNS-1717763, and CCF-2119294. This research used data generated from resources of the Argonne Leadership Computing Facility, which is a DOE Office of Science User Facility supported under contract DE-AC02-06CH11357.

References

1. Argonne Leadership Computing Facility (ALCF). https://www.alcf.anl.gov
2. Cqsim. https://github.com/SPEAR-IIT/CQSim
3. Lawrence Livermore National Laboratory. https://www.llnl.gov/
4. Mira. https://www.alcf.anl.gov/alcf-resources/mira
5. Oak Ridge Leadership Computing Facility (OLCF). https://www.olcf.ornl.gov/
6. PWA. https://www.cs.huji.ac.il/labs/parallel/workload/
7. Theta. https://www.alcf.anl.gov/theta
8. Allcock, W., Rich, P., Fan, Y., Lan, Z.: Experience and practice of batch scheduling on leadership supercomputers at argonne. In: Workshop on Job Scheduling Strategies for Parallel Processing (JSSPP), IEEE (2017)
9. Appice, A., Ceci, M., Rawles, S., Flach, P.: Redundant feature elimination for multi-class problems. In: Proceedings of the 21st International Conference on Machine Learning, p. 5 (2004)
10. Baheri, B., Guan, Q.: Mars: multi-scalable actor-critic reinforcement learning scheduler. arXiv preprint arXiv:2005.01584 (2020)
11. Domeniconi, G., Lee, E.K., Venkataswamy, V., Dola, S.: Cush: cognitive scheduler for heterogeneous high performance computing system. In: DRL4KDD 19: Workshop on Deep Reinforcement Learning for Knowledge Discover, vol. 7 (2019)
12. Fan, Y., Lan, Z., Childers, T., Rich, P., Allcock, W., Papka, M.E.: Deep reinforcement agent for scheduling in HPC. In: Proceedings of the 35th International Parallel and Distributed Processing Symposium, IEEE (2021)
13. Feitelson, D.G., Tsafrir, D., Krakov, D.: Experience with using the parallel workloads archive. J. Parallel Distrib. Comput. **74**(10), 2967–2982 (2014)
14. de Freitas Cunha, R.L., Chaimowicz, L.: Towards a common environment for learning scheduling algorithms. In: 2020 28th International Symposium on Modeling, Analysis, and Simulation of Computer and Telecommunication Systems (MASCOTS). pp. 1–8. IEEE (2020)
15. He, K., Zhang, X., Ren, S., Sun, J.: Spatial pyramid pooling in deep convolutional networks for visual recognition. IEEE Trans. Pattern Anal. Mach. Intell. **37**(9), 1904–1916 (2015)
16. Heaton, J.: Introduction to neural networks with Java. Heaton Research, Inc. (2008)
17. Kaelbling, L.P., Littman, M.L., Moore, A.W.: Reinforcement learning: a survey. J. Artif. Intell. Res. **4**, 237–285 (1996)
18. Kalchbrenner, N., Grefenstette, E., Blunsom, P.: A convolutional neural network for modelling sentences. arXiv preprint arXiv:1404.2188 (2014)
19. Mao, H., Alizadeh, M., Menache, I., Kandula, S.: Resource management with deep reinforcement learning. In: Proceedings of the 15th ACM Workshop on Hot Topics in Networks (2016)

20. Mao, H., Schwarzkopf, M., Venkatakrishnan, S.B., Meng, Z., Alizadeh, M.: Learning scheduling algorithms for data processing clusters. In: Proceedings of the ACM Special Interest Group on Data Communication, pp. 270–288 (2019)
21. Mnih, V., et al.: Playing atari with deep reinforcement learning. arXiv preprint arXiv:1312.5602 (2013)
22. Mu'alem, A.W., Feitelson, D.G.: Utilization, predictability, workloads, and user runtime estimates in scheduling the IBM SP2 with backfilling. IEEE Trans. Parallel Distrib. Syst. **12**(6), 529–543 (2001)
23. Peng, Y., Bao, Y., Chen, Y., Wu, C., Meng, C., Lin, W.: Dl2: a deep learning-driven scheduler for deep learning clusters. IEEE Trans. Parallel Distrib. Syst. **32**(8), 1947–1960 (2021)
24. Pinto, F.A.P., de Moura, L.G.L., Barroso, G.C., Aguilar, M.M.F.: Algorithms scheduling with migration strategies for reducing fragmentation in distributed systems. IEEE Lat. Am. Trans. **13**(3), 762–768 (2015)
25. Ryu, B., An, A., Rashidi, Z., Liu, J., Hu, Y.: Towards topology aware pre-emptive job scheduling with deep reinforcement learning. In: Proceedings of the 30th Annual International Conference on Computer Science and Software Engineering, pp. 83–92 (2020)
26. Shahzad, B., Afzal, M.T.: Optimized solution to shortest job first by eliminating the starvation. In: The 6th Jordanian International Electrical and Electronics Engineering Conference (JIEEEC 2006), Jordan (2006)
27. Silver, D., Lever, G., Heess, N., Degris, T., Wierstra, D., Riedmiller, M.: Deterministic policy gradient algorithms. In: International Conference on Machine Learning, pp. 387–395 PMLR (2014)
28. Sutton, R.S., Barto, A.G.: Reinforcement learning: an introduction. MIT press (2018)
29. Tang, W., Lan, Z., Desai, N., Buettner, D., Yu, Y.: Reducing fragmentation on torus-connected supercomputers. In: 2011 IEEE International Parallel Distributed Processing Symposium, pp. 828–839 IEEE (2011)
30. Zhang, D., Dai, D., He, Y., Bao, F.S., Xie, B.: RLScheduler: an automated HPC batch job scheduler using reinforcement learning. In: SC'20: International Conference for High Performance Computing, Networking, Storage and Analysis, IEEE/ACM (2020)

RADICAL-Pilot and PMIx/PRRTE: Executing Heterogeneous Workloads at Large Scale on Partitioned HPC Resources

Mikhail Titov[1(✉)], Matteo Turilli[1,2], Andre Merzky[2], Thomas Naughton[3], Wael Elwasif[3], and Shantenu Jha[1,2]

[1] Brookhaven National Laboratory, Upton, NY 11973, USA
{titov,mturilli,shantenu}@bnl.gov

[2] Rutgers, The State University of New Jersey, Piscataway, NJ 08854, USA
andre@merzky.net

[3] Oak Ridge National Laboratory, Oak Ridge, TN 37830, USA
{naughtont,elwasifwr}@ornl.gov

Abstract. Execution of heterogeneous workflows on high-performance computing (HPC) platforms present unprecedented resource management and execution coordination challenges for runtime systems. Task heterogeneity increases the complexity of resource and execution management, limiting the scalability and efficiency of workflow execution. Resource partitioning and distribution of tasks execution over portioned resources promises to address those problems but we lack an experimental evaluation of its performance at scale. This paper provides a performance evaluation of the Process Management Interface for Exascale (PMIx) and its reference implementation PRRTE on the leadership-class HPC platform Summit, when integrated into a pilot-based runtime system called RADICAL-Pilot. We partition resources across multiple PRRTE Distributed Virtual Machine (DVM) environments, responsible for launching tasks via the PMIx interface. We experimentally measure the workload execution performance in terms of task scheduling/launching rate and distribution of DVM task placement times, DVM startup and termination overheads on the Summit leadership-class HPC platform. Integrated solution with PMIx/PRRTE enables using an abstracted, standardized set of interfaces for orchestrating the launch process, dynamic process management and monitoring capabilities. It extends scaling capabilities allowing to overcome a limitation of other launching mechanisms (e.g., JSM/LSF). Explored different DVM setup configurations provide insights on DVM performance and a layout to leverage it. Our experimental results show that heterogeneous workload of 65,500 tasks on 2048 nodes, and partitioned across 32 DVMs, runs steady with resource utilization not lower than 52%. While having less concurrently executed tasks resource utilization is able to reach up to 85%, based on results of heterogeneous workload of 8200 tasks on 256 nodes and 2 DVMs.

D. Klusáček et al. (Eds.): JSSPP 2022, LNCS 13592, pp. 88–107, 2023.
https://doi.org/10.1007/978-3-031-22698-4_5

Keywords: High performance computing · Resource management · Middleware · Runtime system · Runtime environment

1 Introduction

Workflows are increasingly necessary for scientific discovery, and represent a fast growing class of applications [11] that require efficient and effective scalability on computing resources. Workflow-based applications are increasing in number, are often diverse and highly complex. This trend is driven by the coupling of traditional high performance computing (HPC) with new simulation, analysis, and data science approaches. Several workflows of the Exascale Computing Project, the winners and contestants of the special Gordon Bell Prize for COVID-19 research of the last two years, and of multiple INCITE awards exemplify this new reality [14,15,34]: a heterogeneous combination of applications, machine learning models, and "glue" code, running on heterogeneous computers, orchestrated by a scalable workflow system.

Executing workflows on leadership-class HPC platforms at scale poses unprecedented challenges in terms of capability and performance requirements. Departing from traditional monolithic MPI applications, modern workflows applications require executing tens of thousand heterogeneous tasks on heterogeneous computing supports. Tasks may have different for runtime and I/O properties, execute on CPU and/or GPU, utilize MPI across few or large amount of nodes, and run as standalone executables, functions written in diverse languages or services exposing dedicated interfaces. Workflow applications require middleware capable of prioritizing, scheduling, placing and launching heterogeneous workflow tasks across entire HPC platforms while maintaining high resource utilization and low management overheads.

Addressing those challenges requires the development of new middleware components specifically designed for modern HPC platforms. Among these, pilot systems have played a major role in enabling the execution of many tasks applications on HPC resources. By decoupling resource acquisition performance via a single job submission to the HPC platform's batch system, and task scheduling performed via a dedicated scheduler on the acquired resources, pilot systems have made possible to execute hundreds of thousand tasks on resources otherwise designed to execute a single large job. Pilot systems are relying on lower-level middleware to place and launch those tasks across the nodes of the HPC platforms. Often, that middleware is not designed specifically for high-throughput task launching and poses bottlenecks both in terms of performance and reliability. The Process Management Interface for Exascale (PMIx), focused on support exascale environments, provides abstracted and standardized interfaces used as building blocks for the implementation of distributed asynchronous runtimes. PMIx-based Reference RunTime Environment (PRRTE) is a corresponding reference implementation with capabilities to launch and monitor MPI jobs.

In this paper, we offer a performance evaluation of PMIx/PRRTE when used to execute up to 65,600 heterogeneous tasks on up to 2048 compute nodes of Summit, the leadership class HPC platform hosted at the Oak Ridge National Laboratory. We couple our pilot system—RADICAL-Pilot—with PMIx/PRRTE to enable task scheduling, placement and launching. We confirm that RADICAL-Pilot and PMIx/PRRTE can be efficiently and effectively coupled, without introducing mutual bottlenecks. Further, while PMIx/PRRTE was not originally designed to support this use case, we show its ability to scale the provided workload, reaching a peak of concurrently executed tasks up to 25K with resource utilization not lower than 52%. Having workload with smaller number of concurrently executed tasks allows reaching a peak of resource utilization up to 85%.

Our analysis focuses on resource partitioning via multiple PRRTE Distributed Virtual Machines (DVMs). Resource partitioning is fundamental for scalability as the overheads of task placement and launching grows with the number of managed resources per DVM. Without partitioning, the cost of bookkeeping and concurrent communication becomes dominant at petascale [31] and unpractical at the upcoming exascale. By utilizing multiple DVMs, we partition the costs of task placement and launching across multiple concurrent and independent processes, limiting the impact of global overheads. While this approach is generally considered promising, we are still missing a detailed performance analysis on a production leadership class machine and with realistic workload parameters. This paper fills this gap.

In the next section we introduce PMIx, PRRTE, DVM and RADICAL-Pilot, detailing their architectures and integration, and explain how they support the execution of heterogeneous tasks on Summit. In Sect. 3 we review related work, outlining the gaps that this paper address in the current state of the art. In Sect. 4 we describe our experimental design and setup, show how we have parameterized our workloads to be consistent with the workflow applications that are currently supported on Summit, and discuss the results of our performance evaluation across diverse scales and configurations. Finally, in Sect. 5 we summarize the contributions of this paper and suggest some future lines of research supported by our results.

2 Background

2.1 Process Management Interface for Exascale

The Process Management Interface for Exascale (PMIx) [5] is an open source standard that extends the prior PMI v1 & v2 interfaces used to launch tasks on compute resources. PMIx provides a method for tools and applications to interact with system-level resource managers and process launch mechanisms. PMIx provides a bridge between such clients and underlying execution services, e.g., process launch, signaling, event notification. The clients communicate with PMIx enabled servers, which may support different versions of the standard. PMIx can also be used as a coordination and resource discovery mechanism for, e.g., machine topology information. An implementation of the PMIx standard is provided by the OpenPMIx project [4] as a software library that contains the programming interfaces needed to use the standard. The OpenPMIx project also provides a reference implementation of a PMIx enabled runtime: PRRTE.

2.2 PMIx Reference RunTime Environment

A reference implementation of the PMIx server-side capabilities is available via the PMIx Reference RunTime Environment (PRRTE) [16]. PRRTE leverages the modular component architecture (MCA) that was developed for Open MPI [19], which enables execution time customization of its runtime capabilities. The PRRTE implementation provides a portable runtime layer that users can leverage to launch a PMIx server.

PRRTE includes a persistent Distributed Virtual Machine (DVM), which uses system-native launch mechanisms to bootstrap an overlay runtime environment that can then be used to launch tasks via the PMIx interface. This removes the need to bootstrap the runtime layer on each individual task launch. Instead, after the launch of the DVM, a tool connects and sends a request to start a task. The task is processed and then generates a launch message that is sent to the PRRTE daemons. These daemons then launch the task. Internally, this task is referred to as a *PRRTE job*, not to be confused with the batch job managed by the system-wide scheduler. The stages of each PRRTE job are tracked from initialization through completion. DVM is teared down after the user session is completed.

The lifetime of a PRRTE job could be roughly divided into the following stages (marked by internal PRRTE state change events): (i) from `init_complete` to `pending_app_launch`—time to setup the task and prepare launch details; (ii) from `sending_launch_msg` to `running`—time to send the process launch request to PRRTE daemons and to enact them on the target nodes; and (iii) from `running` to `notify_complete`—duration of the application's execution plus time to collect task completion notification. First two stages are usually combined into a generalized metric and we will refer to it as a task setup time, i.e., the time between when the PRRTE job has started and when the job's application payload starts running.

In our experiments, we use multiple DVMs (i.e., multi-DVM) to partition available resources for heterogeneous task execution, measuring task setup time, DVM startup and termination times, and overall resource utilization. Together, our experiments allow to understand how to configure PRRTE and DVMs to support the execution of workloads with heterogeneous tasks at scale on Summit.

2.3 RADICAL-Pilot

RADICAL-Pilot (RP) [23] is a runtime system designed to decouple resource acquisition from task execution. As every pilot system, RP acquires resources by submitting a batch job, then bootstraps dedicated software components on those resources to schedule, place and launch application tasks, independent from the machine batch system [32]. Scheduling, placing and launching capabilities are specific to each HPC platform, which makes supporting diverse platforms with the same code base challenging. RP can execute single or multi core/GPU tasks within a single compute node, or across multiple nodes. RP isolates the execution of each tasks into a dedicated process, enabling concurrent and sequential execution of heterogeneous tasks by design.

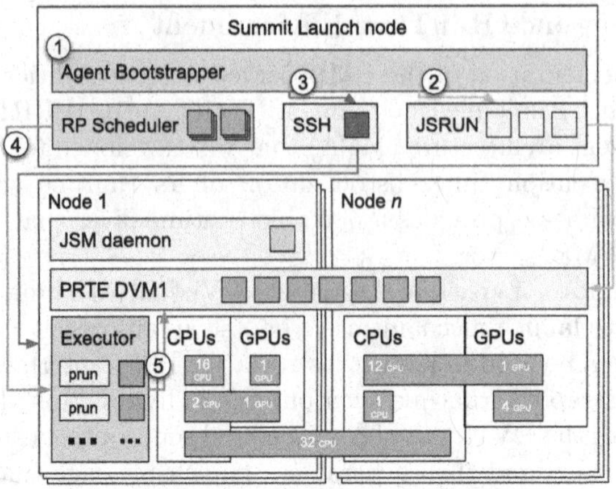

Fig. 1. Deployment of RP on Summit with PRRTE/DVM.

RP is a distributed system designed to instantiate its components across available resources, depending on the platform specifics. Each components can be individually configured so as to enable further tailoring while minimizing code refactoring. RP uses RADICAL-SAGA [24] to support all the major batch systems, including Slurm, PBSPro, Torque and LSF. RP also supports many methods to perform node and core/GPU placement, process pinning and task launching like, for example, `aprun`, `jsrun`, `srun`, `prun` (PRRTE), `mpirun`, `mpiexec` and `ssh`.

RP is composed of two main components: Client and Agent. Client executes on any machine, while Agent bootstraps on one of Summit's batch nodes. Agent is launched by a batch job submitted to Summit's LSF batch system via RADICAL-SAGA. After bootstrapping, Agent pulls bundles of tasks from Client, manages the tasks' data staging if needed, and then schedules tasks for execution via either JSM/LSF or PRRTE/DVM on Summit.

How Agent deploys on Summit depends on several configurable parameters like, for example, number of sub-agents, number of schedulers and executors per sub-agent, method of communication between agent and sub-agents, and method of placing and launching tasks for each executor of each sub-agent. A default deployment of Agent instantiates a single sub-agent, scheduler and executor on a batch node of Summit. In case of JSM/LSF, the executor calls one `jsrun` command for each task, and each `jsrun` uses the JSMD daemon to place and launch the task on work nodes resources (thread, core, GPU).

An architecture block diagram describing the integration between RP and PRRTE (Fig. 1) shows the deployment of RP/PRRTE Agent on a batch node and one sub-agent on a compute node. In this configuration, RP uses SSH to launch sub-agents on compute nodes and then PRRTE/DVM to place and launch tasks across compute nodes. This configuration enables the sub-agent to use more resources and, as shown in the next section, improves scalability and performance of task execution. Note that, independent from the configuration and methods used, RP can concurrently place and launch different types of tasks that use different amount and types of resources.

The RP resource manager is responsible to collect and manage information about acquired nodes and to start related services if required. In case of PRRTE, RP allows to configure the number of DVMs to be started and resource manager distributes available compute nodes among all that DVMs. The command to start a corresponding PRRTE process is `prte`, which does setup a DVM environment and provides a list of compute nodes, which will be managed by the DVM. In RP, it is configured to set a flat routing tree, i.e., *a high connectivity mode* (all daemons directly connect to the DVM controller), to eliminate relay times in the tree impacting startup time. Such mode is set due to PRRTE uses a single progress thread, so communication competes with mapping and local process start, thus the notion is to take out the time a daemon spent relaying launch messages by having it directly connect to the DVM controller. Related to it, a task placement mechanism uses `prun` command to invoke each application/task as opposed to using `PMIx_Spawn`. DVM controller is responsible for handling `prun` connection requests, doing the initial mapping of each PRRTE job, etc. `prun` command is configured to allow oversubscription (i.e., running more tasks than available slots per node), but RP schedules tasks based on availability of slots without oversubscribing.

There are several tracing events produced by RP for measuring performance characteristics regarding PRRTE/DVM: DVM startup events `dvm_start` and `dvm_ready`, DVM termination event `dvm_stop`, task execution (DVM placement) events `task_exec_start` and `task_exec_stop`, and application running events `app_start` and `app_stop`. Thus, task setup time is measured from the time `prun` call is executed (`task_exec_start`) until the time application starts running (i.e., to the time when process reports in, `app_start`).

3 Related Work

Pilot systems like GlideinWMS [28], PanDA [29] and DIRAC [30] are used to implement late binding and multi-level scheduling on a variety of platforms. While these systems have been successfully used on HPC machines [18,21,22], including on the former ORNL leadership class machine Titan [25], they are currently not available on Summit and do not support PRRTE.

PRRTE [16] relies on PMIx to place and launch processes on Summit's nodes. Many applications are actively working to directly use PMIx to interface with the system management stack to benefit from portable process and resource management capabilities [33]. While PMIx explicitly supports interfacing with command line tools, there are no other pilot systems using PMIx via PRRTE. MPICH and Hydra [10] offer capabilities similar to PRRTE but are not supported on Summit.

Pilot systems are not the only way to execute many-task applications on HPC machines. JSM and LSF natively support this capability but, as seen in [31], in their current deployment on Summit they cannot scale beyond 1000 concurrent task executions. Flux [7] is a resource manager that provides users with private schedulers on pools of dedicated resources. This enables the task scheduling capabilities of a pilot system, including RP, but requires to be either adopted as the main job manager of the machine or be deployed as part of a pilot system.

METAQ [13] are a set of shell scripts that forms a "middle layer" between the batch scheduler and the user's computational job scripts and supports task packing. METAQ requires a separate invocation of mpirun (or equivalent) for each task. METAQ has been superseded by `mpi_jm` [12]—a Python library that is linked to applications. In addition to intelligent backfilling and task packing, `mpi_jm` allows the executable to be launched based upon an affinity with the hardware but requires the be coded into task executables and the overall workflow application.

TaskWorks—a task execution engine built using the PMIx interface—is designed as a high-level, light-weight and portable task execution engine for HPC applications [20]. It enables defining tasks and resolving their dependencies within an application, and it supports MPI tasks. PMIx is used as an interface to coordinates thread/task execution packages, such as OpenMP or MPI, and to manage resource usage.

In Reference [23,27] we investigated the performance of RP on ORTE—a precursor to PRRTE. Using ORTE, RP was capable of spawning more than 100 tasks/second and the steady-state execution of up to 16K concurrent tasks. Resource utilization was significant lower than with PRRTE and more sensitive to the number of tasks and tasks duration.

There is no other available solution with integration of PMIx/PRRTE using multi-DVM approach. There is an ongoing development effort to introduce resource partitioning in RP, which includes such multi-DVM approach as part of RP scaling capabilities.

4 Experiments

The performance space of RP is vast, including the execution of both homogeneous and heterogeneous tasks with resolved dependencies beforehand at both small and large scales. In Reference [31] we presented a baseline characterization of executing homogeneous workloads on Summit, comparing the performances of `jsrun` and `prun` (PRRTE). In this paper, we build upon those results, focusing on the execution of heterogeneous workloads consistent with the requirements of the INCITE program [3]. Specifically, we consider two types of task heterogeneity: spatial and temporal. We execute workloads with multi-core tasks of different duration, requiring both CPUs and GPUs, within the boundaries of Summit's compute nodes. Further, we adjust configuration for DVMs setup, significantly extending upon our previous characterization by scaling the concurrent execution of heterogeneous tasks and optimizing baseline performance for real-life workloads.

4.1 Use Cases

We consider the use cases from five DOE INCITE allocation awards [3] on Summit. We elicited the computing requirements of their workflows, deriving size and duration of each type of task alongside their I/O requirements. All workflows require to scale on Summit's CPUs and GPUs, executing a variety of workloads with MPI and single/multi-threaded tasks. We focus our experiments on PRRTE/DVM, and on how they support the placement and execution of those tasks at scale. As such, we evaluate the upper and lower boundary requirements of each workload, executing synthetic tasks consistent with those boundaries. Note that for PRRTE/DVM, it makes no different what type of executable each task launches or their I/O requirements, only how many CPUs/GPUs each task requires and for how long.

Future studies will build upon our results to evaluate the actual workflows in collaboration with the domain scientists. Without understanding the scalability of PMIx/PRRTE with heterogeneous workloads, those studies would be premature.

Overall, the workloads of the use cases we considered have the following types of tasks: (i) up to 15 million single core tasks (no GPUs) with runtime from a range 10..60 seconds for high-throughput ensemble docking to identify small molecules (MD docking scans); (ii) an ensemble of about 120 MD simulation tasks using GPUs with runtime of several hours for modeling specific binding regions and understanding mechanistic changes in drug discovery (AI-driven Molecular Dynamics); (iii) one large MPI task with many GPUs over several nodes and many CPU tasks with one core requirement (Earth Sciences domain, PrincetonU); (iv) many OpenMM [17] simulation tasks with one GPU requirement over 1000 nodes (OpenMM Ensemble, Cornell Medical Center); (v) many NAMD [26] simulation tasks with CPUs requirement only, one task per node over 1024 nodes (MDFF Error Analysis, ASU).

The first two use cases among selected are highlighted the most, due to their tasks configurations, which cover all significant heterogeneity characteristics. Both workloads are part of a multi stage campaign for a drug discovery, namely IMPECCABLE (Integrated Modeling PipelinE for COVID Cure by Assessing Better LEads) [9].

Based on the assessment of the considered workloads, we determined the following setup for experiments: (i) we group compute nodes in multiple of 256 for all experiments, and every group of nodes process 8K tasks (weak scaling up to 2048 nodes and 65K tasks); (ii) there are two types of tasks: 90% of all tasks are small and short, which represent the small CPU tasks of the use cases, and 10% of all tasks are large and long, including tasks with GPUs, which represent a dedicated group of larger tasks (e.g., simulation tasks) in the use cases. Important to note that we didn't map MPI task over several nodes into our experiment setup—larger tasks are easier to handle for RP and PRRTE and thus essentially decreasing the load we test the system under.

4.2 Experiments Design

Our experiments measure the performance of PRRTE/DVM in addition to the performance of RP with PRRTE, when concurrently and sequentially executing workloads with heterogeneous tasks on Summit. Task execution requires assigning suitable resources to the tasks, placing them on resources (i.e., a specific compute node, core, GPU or hardware thread) and then launching the execution of those tasks. RP tracks both tasks and available resources, scheduling the former onto the latter; PRRTE enacts task placement and launching.

Combining experiments with different configurations (different number of DVMs and number of nodes each DVM manages) helps to study how well PRRTE/DVMs perform when managing nodes and tasks execution, as well as the potential interference among DVMs. The number of nodes will vary from 256 up to 2048 nodes on Summit, doubling at every experiment configuration. The experiment with 2048 nodes will demonstrate the performance of RP using multi-DVM approach with configuration setup based on gained knowledge from the previous experiments with lower number of nodes. Experiments setup parameters are collected in Table 2.

Our experiment tasks are self-contained executables, which carry a synthetic payload (calls for environment variables to check the correctness of allocated resources) and imitates task runtime with defined "sleep" time by suspending the calling process. All tasks are heterogeneous, regarding their runtime, type of using resources, CPU and/or GPU, and the amount of resources. For the tasks parameters setup, it is important to note that the number of *slots* per node on Summit [6] with simultaneous multithreading (SMT) level set to 4 is equal to 168 hardware threads (44 physical cores minus 2 reserved cores).

We elicit the task sizes from our use cases. First we define the min and max for every type of task to have a better understanding of their possible layouts on each compute node. Then we estimate a range of values between each min and max, so to guarantee a wide heterogeneity. The size of "small" tasks will be less than 21 slots (1/8th of compute node), while the size of "large" tasks will be in a range of 42..84 slots (from 1/4th up to half of compute node), so as to have two "large" tasks per node on average. Duration for tasks will be generated randomly as well, and "small" tasks will be twice shorter than "large" tasks with ranges 8..10 min and 16..20 min respectively.

Estimation of the number of compute nodes to be filled avoids task execution "tailing", i.e., having a small number of tasks launched after the anticipated termination time of the run (i.e., walltime), due to a not precise scheduling (since RP scheduler processes tasks as soon as a block of tasks arrived and not waiting for all submitted tasks to perform scheduling). Thus we set to use 97% of all allocated resources (i.e., provided slots) to generate task sizes, and considering 3% of resources as supplementary to avoid "tailing".

Refined ranges for task sizes are calculated during the startup of RP application as following: $N_{slots} >= (N_{tasks}/N_{gen}) \times avg(N_{task\_slots})$, where N_{slots} is a number of provided slots, N_{tasks} is a total number of tasks of a particular type, N_{gen} is a number of generations for tasks of a defined type, i.e., an approximate number of task groups, in which all tasks could be executed concurrently, and N_{task_slots} is a number of slots per task.

For 256 nodes (including 8 "supplementary" nodes) and 8200 tasks, we have 7380 "small" tasks (4 generations) with average N_{task_slots} equals to 5 (slots range in 1..9) and 820 "large" tasks (2 generations) with average N_{task_slots} equals to 76 (slots range in 68..84). Having many "small" tasks will let us to stress the runtime for comparing RTE capabilities.

Experiments Approbation. As part of the experiments design, we performed an approbation stage, which confirmed the expected behavior of RP components without any overhead, and expected nodes load level. Approbation of designed experiments was made using a Docker container produced by the ExaWorks project's SDK [1,8]. RP allows to run an application locally with an arbitrary defined resource characteristics, such as number of cores, GPUs, memory, and it also allows to imitate any number of requested nodes (`fake_resources=true`). In case of Summit, resource description includes 168 cores (SMT=4) and 6 GPUs per node. Docker file and resource description are provided in the GitHub repository [2] as part of the experiments setup.

Runs within Docker container also included usage of sub-agents (as described in Sect. 2.3) for such components as RP scheduler and executor and running each sub-agent on a dedicated node: one node for scheduler component and three nodes for three instances of executor. Usage of sub-agents on a real resource is necessary, because running all RP components on a batch node and having many tasks $O(10^4)$ hits the limitation of concurrent system processes calls per node.

4.3 Experiments on Summit

We used PRRTE release `2.0a1psrvr-v2.0.0rc1-3912-gff83b55e2e` to conduct experiments on Summit, which is referred as a master release for production. Note that a recommended delay of 10 sec was added after resource allocation and before starting any DVM to ensure that resources were ready to be mapped to DVM(s).

In this section we present key studies, which reveal limitations of examined approach and allow to determine experiment configuration for exercising scaling capabilities. We highlight metrics used to estimate the performance and evaluate results.

PRRTE/DVM Size Estimation. PRRTE management capabilities depend on both the number of managed nodes as well as the number of launched tasks (i.e., the size of assigned workload to be executed). We experimentally determined the maximum number of nodes that can be successfully managed by a single DVM in further experiments. At first we tried to run RP with PRRTE without a payload (we submitted only one task with one core and without any `sleep` time that let RP started without providing any task to the most of acquired compute nodes), thus to confirm that DVM has started and then terminated successfully with a list of provided nodes. Then we tried the same configurations, but with our designed workload.

Those experiments showed that, without a payload, the maximum number of managed nodes is 512, but, with a payload of 8200 tasks for every 256 nodes (as described in Sect. 4.2), the maximum number reduces to 256. Experiment without a payload is not presented in the experiments listing, but experiment with 256 nodes per one DVM is the first in Table 1, 2. Note that we disregard possible cases when the number of nodes is in between 256 and 512, since we double the number of nodes in each experiment, starting from 256, and this paper is not focused on finding an exact maximum number of nodes per DVM.

Beyond that observed numbers, DVM either wasn't able to start successfully (i.e., never reached a confirmation status `DVM ready`) or started having "connection lost" errors regarding communication with its managed nodes. We were not able to localize the cause of such limitation (e.g., high connectivity mode and/or Ethernet problems, socket timeouts, etc.), which is to be investigated, but therefore chose to constrain the following experiments to 256 nodes, and to explore the trade-offs of using multiple parallel DVMs instead of one large DVM.

PRRTE/DVM Startup and Termination Processes. The next set of experiments measured the start and termination overheads of one or more DVM, and the possible interference among concurrent DVMs. DVM startup and termination processes depend only on the number of nodes assigned to each DVM, since these processes are responsible for establishing and managing a communication between DVM and PRRTE daemons `prted` on compute nodes.

In this study, we run three experiments with 256 nodes and 8200 tasks, and different number of DVMs (#1,2,3 in Table 2). Table 1 shows the resulted average startup and termination times for DVMs, and the total overhead (OVH) per experiment (including DVMs OVH). All DVMs started and terminated sequentially, which is done to reduce the network load, i.e., it decreases the possibility of DVMs interference and errors related to losing connection. Increasing the number of DVMs decreases both startup and termination times for each DVM, but increases the total OVH from all DVMs on average. Thus, changing the number of DVMs from 1 to 256 decreases resource utilization (RU) from 85% to 65%. This should be considered, while planning runs with many DVMs for RU improvement.

Table 1. Average DVM startup and termination times per each instance and the total overhead for experiments with 256 nodes.

#	Nodes	DVMs	DVM Nodes	Avg DVM Startup (s)	Avg DVM Termination (s)	Total OVH (s)
1	256	1	256	6.48	4.63	51.59
2	256	2	128	2.66	4.55	51.63
3	256	256	1	1.96	1.04	829.57

PRRTE Task Placement. Earlier mentioned three experiments with 256 nodes also showed that decreasing the number of nodes per DVM decreases the task setup time. Figure 2 shows the impact of the size of payload per DVM on the task setup time. Having less tasks per DVM not just improves the average or median of task setup time, but also shrinks the range of its distribution (especially interquartile range). Descriptions of these experiments along with collected metrics, such as mean, median and third quartile, are provided in Table 2.

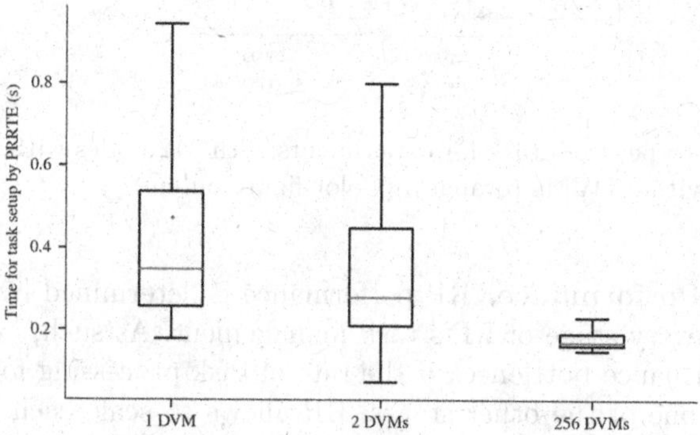

Fig. 2. Distribution of tasks setup time managed by PRRTE for experiments with 256 nodes and 8200 tasks: 1 DVM, which manages 256 nodes; 2 DVMs, each manages 128 nodes; 256 DVMs, each manages 1 node.

With a weak scaling, besides increasing the volume of resources and payload, we increase the number of DVMs per experiment in a way to decrease the load on average per each DVM. The next two experiments (#4,5 in Table 2) are as following: (1) experiment with 512 compute nodes and 2 DVMs, thus each DVM manages 256 nodes; and (2) experiment with 1024 compute nodes and 8 DVMs, thus each DVM manages 128 nodes. Figure 3 shows task setup times for these experiments, and experiment with smaller number of nodes per DVM has smaller task setup time on average. This observation helps to distinguish a pattern - while scaling a heterogeneous workload for processing, the load per DVM should be lowered.

Due to RP's scheduling algorithm to use all available slots with attempting to assign large tasks first, most of the large tasks were placed during the first half of the experiments run, and most of the small tasks were placed during the second half of the experiments run. This explains the two distinct phases visible in Fig. 3 at the begin and middle of both runs: the first peak(s) is caused by starting all large and a few small tasks, the second, larger peak, is caused by launching all remaining small tasks (see Fig. 6 for a detailed comparison).

Note that experiment with 1024 nodes has some tasks with exceptionally large setup times (up to 60 min), which were never executed due to the walltime limit, and that values fall outside of the third sigma and we don't present them on the plot.

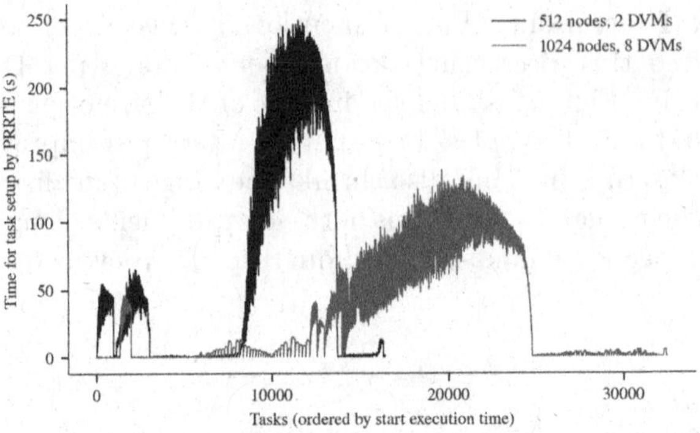

Fig. 3. Setup times per each task for experiments with 512 nodes with 2 DVMs (blue) and 1024 nodes with 8 DVMs (orange). (Color figure online)

Study of RP Performance. RP performance is determined by the task processing rate at every stage of RP's task management. As such, every stage can become a performance bottleneck if the rate of task processing for that stage is lower than the one of the other stages. RP allows to scale each component to improve their performance (e.g., multiple instances of Agent's Scheduler component and use of sub-agents), but has limited options over the execution layer, which depends on third party middleware. When using PRRTE, using multiple DVMs allows to increase task execution rate and match it to the task scheduling rate, avoiding performance bottlenecks. Scheduling rate depends on the number of tasks and the number of nodes, and when using PRRTE as launching method, it is also affected by the number of DVMs. With PRRTE, when a task is assigned to a particular node, the scheduler is also responsible to map it to the DVM, which manages that node. Execution rate consists of RP launching rate and PRRTE/DVM task placement rate, including task setup time and running time.

Experiments with 256 nodes partitioned across 1 and 256 DVMs demonstrate that the increase in amount of DVMs improves the execution rate, since it decreases task setup times, and we got 3% improvement in the total task execution time (TTX). Figure 4 shows that using the same total number of nodes, but changing the number of DVMs, does not significantly change the scheduling and launching rates (plot slopes on a figure). That indicates the number of DVMs should be estimated with consideration of DVMs OVH and achieved tasks TTX.

RP with PRRTE at Scale. Based on the results of our previous experiments, we use 32 DVMs for our final experiment to measure weak scaling of PRRTE/DVM with up to 2048 compute nodes (#6 in Table 2). We increase the number of nodes and tasks proportionally and, as a consequence, we also increase the number of concurrent system processes calls (e.g., *subprocess.Popen*) in the Agent's Scheduler and Executor components. This creates a bottleneck in those

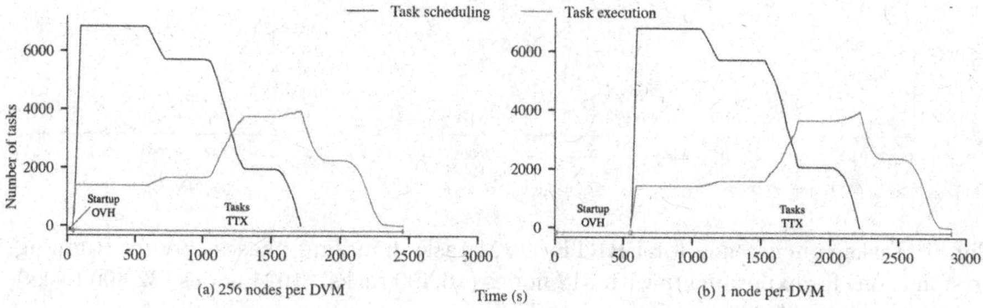

Fig. 4. Tasks concurrency for scheduling and executing processes for experiments with 256 nodes and 8200 tasks.

components, which run out of available processes at the operating system level. For such cases, RP allows using sub-agents to run both Scheduler and Executor on dedicated compute nodes (as discussed in Sect. 4.2). When using sub-agents, we add 4 extra nodes to the experiment resource allocation. RP does not use these service nodes for tasks execution and, as such, we do not count them as available nodes in our experiments.

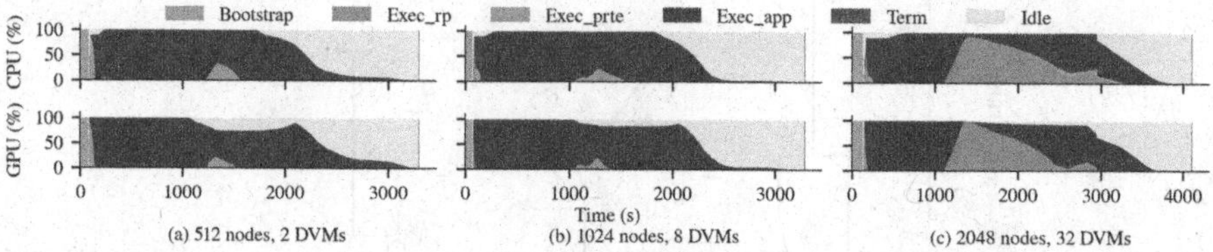

Fig. 5. Resource utilization for experiments with 512 nodes (16,400 tasks), 1024 nodes (32,800 tasks), and 2048 nodes (65,600 tasks), CPU and GPU resources per experiment. The tasks' actual execution is presented as *exec_app*.

As Fig. 5 shows that the resource utilization decreased for experiment with 2048 nodes due to overhead related with RP task preparation stage, which could be caused by shared file system (at this stage RP prepares startup scripts for each task). Our focus in Fig. 5 is on tasks being in stages *exec_prte* (DVM task setup and termination) and *exec_app* (DVM task running). For experiment with 512 nodes, there is a time period when DVM task preparation (setup and termination) slowed down the execution process (i.e., temporary decrease of resource utilization). We assume that such behavior reflects the higher load per each DVM compare to experiments with 1024 and 2048 nodes, where the RP overheads dominate.

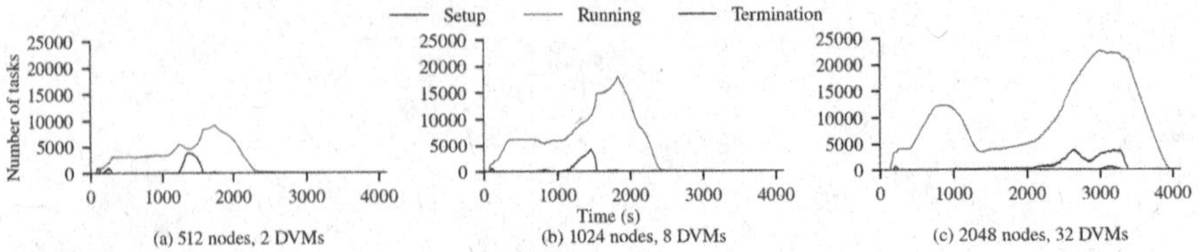

Fig. 6. Tasks concurrency for PRRTE/DVM tasks handling phases (Setup, Running, Termination) for experiments with 512 nodes (16,400 tasks), 1024 nodes (32,800 tasks), and 2048 nodes (65,600 tasks).

Further, we compare the scale of concurrently executed tasks in three DVM stages (setup, running and termination) on Fig. 6. Peak values for the concurrent number of tasks for experiments with 512, 1024 and 2048 nodes are the following: (i) for the *setup* stage: 3.8 K, 4.3 K and 3.9 K; and (ii) for the *running* stage: 9.1 K, 17.9 K and 22.5 K. The *termination* stage is mostly passed by tasks unnoticed, and only for experiment with 2048 nodes there is one peak of ~ 600 tasks finalizing their state in DVMs during the same time.

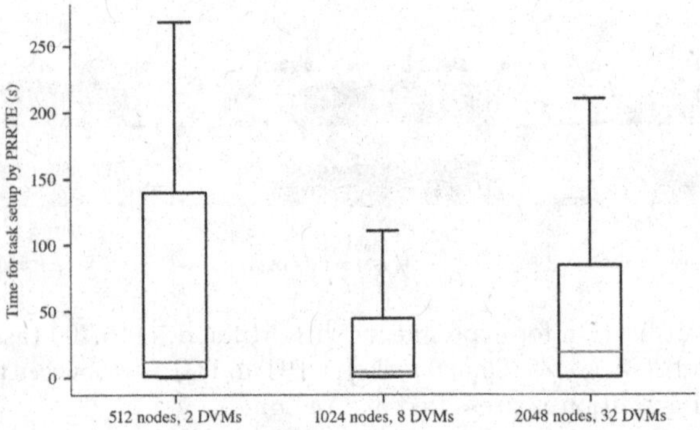

Fig. 7. Distribution of tasks setup time managed by PRRTE for experiments with 512 nodes (16,400 tasks), 1024 nodes (32,800 tasks), and 2048 nodes (65,600 tasks).

For all these cases, RP distributes tasks among nodes not equally, and each DVM processes different amount of tasks (i.e., having some fluctuation in number of tasks per DVM). Further, RP places tasks of different types not evenly in time—most large tasks are scheduled first for better resource utilization. These factors affect the number of concurrently executed tasks, which creates a load on each DVM and DVM task setup time changes accordingly. As mentioned earlier, such designed workload let us to stress the runtime, since RTE is constantly cleaning up completed tasks (*PRRTE jobs*) while trying to start new ones, causing a lot of resource contention within the RTE.

Figure 7 allows to compare the distribution of DVM tasks setup time for experiments with 512, 1024 and 2048 nodes. For experiment with 2048 nodes distribution of task setup times is higher than for experiment with 1024 nodes. This is affected by the high load of DVMs in conjunction with task placement command prun as a high overhead method for invoking a PRRTE job—prun and the DVM have to execute a multi-step handshake to resolve security and communication protocols. The prun connection starts to become significant at these load levels since it flows through a single progress event thread, so each connection has to wait its turn.

Nonetheless, the experiment also shows the possibility to scale the execution of 65,600 heterogeneous tasks on 2048 nodes (+ 4 nodes for sub-agents), which demonstrates a worst-case scenario, considering the type of tasks and their distribution over DVMs.

Table 2. Descriptions and discovered metrics for conducted experiments.

#	Nodes	DVMs	DVM Nodes	Tasks	Startup OVH (s)	Tasks TTX (s)	Task setup time (s)		
							Mean	Median	Q3
1	256	1	256	8200	41.18	2417	9.54	0.35	0.54
2	256	2	128	8200	38.02	2414	9.13	0.28	0.45
3	256	256	1	8200	555.39	2340	0.21	0.17	0.19
4	512	2	256	16,400	64.1 ± 16.4	3208 ± 5	63.5	11.9	139.7
5	1024	8	128	32,800	69.5 ± 9.2	3169 ± 12	44.3	3.9	44.4
6	2048	32	64	65,600	129.5 ± 6.6	3823 ± 53	46.7	18.6	83.9

5 Conclusions

We explored the capabilities and limitations of using PMIx/PRRTE as an execution layer within a pilot-based runtime system (RADICAL-Pilot), executing heterogeneous multi-core CPU/GPU tasks on the leadership-class HPC platform Summit. We identified a set of metrics that we used to characterize the performance of PRRTE and its DVM under different configurations and payloads. Our experiments offer a quantitative understanding of the factors that impact PRRTE/DVM performance at scale.

We introduced several use cases with workflows that require the execution of heterogeneous workloads. We used cumulative characteristics of those workloads to build a synthetic workload of 8200 heterogeneous tasks per 256 compute nodes, focused on spatial and temporal heterogeneity. With many small tasks and non-uniform load on DVMs, it lets to stress the RTE.

We found no interference among DVMs while having 256 concurrently running DVMs and determined that DVM could have a limitation on the number of nodes it can manage in conjunction with the placed payload. In case of our synthetic payload, each DVM was constrained by 256 nodes.

Examination of introduced DVM overhead, as one of the important characteristics, showed that, while changing number of DVMs from 1 to 256 (maximum tested value; DVMs were started and terminated sequentially) for 256 total allocated compute nodes, the RP total overhead has increased by 16 times (from $52s$ to $830s$), even though individual DVM overhead was decreased (from $11s$ to $3s$). This affected resource utilization by dropping it from 85% down to 65%.

The main focus of our experiments is DVM performance evaluation, thus we conducted analysis of DVM task launching process, and particularly DVM task setup time. We investigated the case of changing only the number of DVMs for 256 total allocated nodes, which showed that it is possible to reach only 3% improvement in task TTX (increased OVH is mentioned earlier). Thus, the DVM configuration assumes to have minimal number of DVMs, which will keep OVH low, but allow to partition the payload. The case of weak scaling in amount of resources, payload and DVMs (experiments with 256/8200 and 512/16,400 nodes/tasks, and each DVM manages 256 compute nodes) leads to increase in the average DVM task setup time.

Also, weak scaling experiments showed that increasing the number of allocated compute nodes from 512 to 2048 (executing from 8200 up to 65,600 tasks respectively) requires to have at least 2^2 times more DVMs every time that the total number of compute nodes is doubled. Having a small number of concurrently executed tasks, up to 5000 tasks (experiments with 256 nodes), allowed to have $\sim$ 85% resource utilization, but with up to 25,000 tasks concurrently executed (experiment with 2048 nodes), resource utilization dropped down to $\sim$ 52%. Increased number of concurrently executed tasks affected RP overhead and along with increased DVM load has affected tasks TTX, which was increased from its minimum 2340 s (experiment with 256 nodes and 256 DVMs) to the maximum $\sim$ 3823 s (experiment with 2048 nodes and 32 DVMs).

This approach is not applicable for workloads with many one-core or small multi-core non-GPU tasks, since it will bring a large overhead and could cause execution process being unstable. Thus, for example, such workload as MD docking scans from IMPECCABLE will not benefit from it, workloads with larger tasks will.

This study gives an understanding of the PMIx/PRRTE scalability capabilities with heterogeneous workloads, and highlights corresponding characteristics. Better control over a certain processes will let to redistribute DVMs load, which will help to increase the overall performance.

Observed behaviour of PMIx/PRRTE tools and collected data can be used by the PMIx community for future development, particularly considering breaking down long times for DVM task setup and `prun` connecting states (e.g., allocation, mapping, launching, etc.) for insights, which would assist in improving the total launch time.

Early experiments with the new release of PRRTE `2.0.2v2.0.1-8-gaa5 7929` have demonstrated significant improvements in DVM task setup times (e.g., new numbers for experiment with 512 nodes, #4 in Table 2, are: mean is 0.03 s, median is 0.02 s and q3 is 0.03 s) and increased the stability of overall execution process. Coming RP releases (> 1.14) will support this PRRTE release and will be used in further experiments.

Acknowledgments. We would like to thank other members of the PMIx community, and Ralph Castain in particular, for the excellent work that we build upon. This research used resources of the Oak Ridge Leadership Computing Facility at the Oak Ridge National Laboratory, which is supported by the Office of Science of the U.S. Department of Energy under Contract No. DE-AC05-00OR22725. This work is also supported by the ExaWorks project (part of the Exascale Computing Project (ECP)) under DOE Contract No. DE-SC0012704 and by the DOE HEP Center for Computational Excellence at Brookhaven National Laboratory under B&R KA2401045. We also acknowledge DOE INCITE awards for allocations on Summit.

References

1. Exaworks: Software development kit. https://github.com/ExaWorks/SDK. Accessed 10 Feb 2022
2. Github repository with experiments data. https://github.com/radical-experiments/summit_prrte_multi_dvm
3. INCITE innovative and novel computational impact on theory and experiment program, https://www.doeleadershipcomputing.org. Accessed 10 Feb 2022
4. OpenPMIx, reference implementation of the process management interface exascale (PMIx) standard. https://openpmix.github.io. Accessed 10 Feb 2022
5. Process management interface for exascale (PMIx) standard. https://pmix.github.io/pmix-standard/. Accessed 10 Feb 2022
6. User guide for leadership-class supercomputer summit at ornl oak ridge leadership computing facility. https://docs.olcf.ornl.gov/systems/summit_user_guide.html. Accessed 10 Feb 2022
7. Ahn, D.H., et al.: Flux: overcoming scheduling challenges for exascale workflows. Future Gener. Comput. Syst. **110**, 202–213 (2020). https://doi.org/10.1016/j.future.2020.04.006
8. Al-Saadi, A., et al.: Exaworks: Workflows for exascale. 16th Workshop on Workflows in Support of Large-Scale Science. SC (2021). https://arxiv.org/abs/2108.13521
9. Al-Saadi, A., et al.: IMPECCABLE: Integrated modeling pipeline for covid cure by assessing better leads. In: 50th International Conference on Parallel Processing. ICPP 2021, Association for Computing Machinery, New York, NY, USA (2021). https://doi.org/10.1145/3472456.3473524
10. Balaji, P., et al: Mpich user's guide. Argonne National Laboratory (2014)
11. Ben-Nun, T., Gamblin, T., Hollman, D., Krishnan, H., Newburn, C.J.: Workflows are the new applications: Challenges in performance, portability, and productivity. In: 2020 IEEE/ACM International Workshop on Performance, Portability and Productivity in HPC (P3HPC), pp. 57–69. IEEE (2020)
12. Berkowitz, E., Jansen, G., McElvain, K., Walker-Loud, A.: Job management with mpi_jm. In: International Conference on High Performance Computing, pp. 432–439. Springer (2018)
13. Berkowitz, E., Jansen, G.R., McElvain, K., Walker-Loud, A.: Job management and task bundling. EPJ Web Conf. **175**, 09007 (2018). https://doi.org/10.1051/epjconf/201817509007
14. Bhatia, H., et al.: Generalizable coordination of large multiscale workflows: Challenges and learnings at scale. In: Proceedings of the International Conference for High Performance Computing, Networking, Storage and Analysis. SC '21, Association for Computing Machinery, New York, NY, USA (2021). https://doi.org/10.1145/3458817.3476210

15. Casalino, L., et al.: Ai-driven multiscale simulations illuminate mechanisms of sars-cov-2 spike dynamics. The Int. J. High Performance Comput. Appl. **35**(5), 432–451 (2021)
16. Castain, R.H., Hursey, J., Bouteiller, A., Solt, D.: PMIx: process management for exascale environments. Parallel Comput. **79**, 9–29 (2018)
17. Eastman, P., et al: OpenMM 7: Rapid development of high performance algorithms for molecular dynamics. PLOS Comput. Biol. **13**(7), 1–17 (2017). https://doi.org/10.1371/journal.pcbi.1005659
18. Fifield, T., Carmona, A., Casajús, A., Graciani, R., Sevior, M.: Integration of cloud, grid and local cluster resources with dirac. In: Journal of Physics: Conference Series. vol. 331, p. 062009. IOP Publishing (2011)
19. Gabriel, E., et al.: Open MPI: Goals, concept, and design of a next generation MPI implementation. In: Proceedings. 11th European PVM/MPI Users' Group Meeting, pp. 97–104. Budapest, Hungary (2004)
20. Hou, K., Koziol, Q., Byna, S.: Taskworks: A task engine for empowering asynchronous operations in hpc applications. In: Proceedings of the International Conference for High Performance Computing, Networking, Storage, and Analysis (2020)
21. Hufnagel, D.: Cms use of allocation based hpc resources. In: J. Phys. Conf. Ser. **898** 092050 (2017)
22. Maeno, T., et al.: Evolution of the ATLAS PanDA workload management system for exascale computational science. In: Proceedings of the 20th International Conference on Computing in High Energy and Nuclear Physics (CHEP2013), J. Phys.: Conf. Ser. **513**(3) 032062 IOP Publishing (2014)
23. Merzky, A., Turilli, M., Maldonado, M., Santcroos, M., Jha, S.: Using pilot systems to execute many task workloads on supercomputers. In: Workshop on Job Scheduling Strategies for Parallel Processing. pp. 61–82. Springer (2018). https://doi.org/10.1007/978-3-030-10632-4_4
24. Merzky, A., Weidner, O., Jha, S.: SAGA: A standardized access layer to heterogeneous distributed computing infrastructure. Software-X (2015). http://dx.doi.org/10.1016/j.softx.2015.03.001
25. Oleynik, D., Panitkin, S., Turilli, M., Angius, A., Oral, S., De, K., Klimentov, A., Wells, J.C., Jha, S.: High-throughput computing on high-performance platforms: A case study. In: 2017 IEEE 13th International Conference on e-Science (e-Science), pp. 295–304. IEEE (2017)
26. Phillips, J.C., et al.: Scalable molecular dynamics on cpu and gpu architectures with NAMD. J. Chem. Phys. **153**(4), 044130 (2020). https://doi.org/10.1063/5.0014475
27. Santcroos, M., Castain, R., Merzky, A., Bethune, I., Jha, S.: Executing dynamic heterogeneous workloads on blue waters with radical-pilot. Cray User Group 2016 (2016)
28. Sfiligoi, I.: glideinWMS-a generic pilot-based workload management system. In: Proceedings of the International Conference on Computing in High Energy and Nuclear Physics (CHEP2007). J. Phys.: Conf. Series. **119**(6), 062044. IOP Publishing (2008)
29. Svirin, P., et al.: BigPanDA: panda workload management system and its applications beyond ATLAS. EPJ Web Conf. **214**, 03050 (2019). https://doi.org/10.1051/epjconf/201921403050
30. Tsaregorodtsev, A., Garonne, V., Stokes-Rees, I.: DIRAC: A scalable lightweight architecture for high throughput computing. In: Proceedings of the 5th IEEE/ACM International Workshop on Grid Computing, pp. 19–25 (2004)

31. Turilli, M., Merzky, A., Naughton, T.J., Elwasif, W., Jha, S.: Characterizing the performance of executing many-tasks on summit. In: IPDRM 2019 (2019)
32. Turilli, M., Santcroos, M., Jha, S.: A comprehensive perspective on pilot-job systems. ACM Comput. Surv. (CSUR) **51**(2), 43 (2018)
33. Vallée, G.R., Bernholdt, D.: Improving support of MPI+OpenMP applications. In: Proceedings of the EuroMPI 2018 Conference (2018)
34. Ward, L., et al.: Colmena: Scalable machine-learning-based steering of ensemble simulations for high performance computing. In: 2021 IEEE/ACM Workshop on Machine Learning in High Performance Computing Environments (MLHPC), pp. 9–20. IEEE (2021)

RARE: Renewable Energy Aware Resource Management in Datacenters

Vanamala Venkataswamy[1](✉), Jake Grigsby[1], Andrew Grimshaw[2], and Yanjun Qi[1]

[1] University of Virginia, Charlottesville, VA 22903, USA
{vv3xu,jcg6dn,yanjun}@virginia.edu

[2] Lancium Compute, 6006 Thomas Rd Houston, The Woodlands, TX 77401, USA
andrew.grimshaw@lancium.com

Abstract. The exponential growth in demand for digital services drives massive datacenter energy consumption and negative environmental impacts. Promoting sustainable solutions to pressing energy and digital infrastructure challenges is crucial. Several hyperscale cloud providers have announced plans to power their datacenters using renewable energy. However, integrating renewables to power the datacenters is challenging because the power generation is intermittent, necessitating approaches to tackle power supply variability. Hand engineering domain-specific heuristics-based schedulers to meet specific objective functions in such complex dynamic green datacenter environments is time-consuming, expensive, and requires extensive tuning by domain experts. The green datacenters need smart systems and system software to employ multiple renewable energy sources (wind and solar) by intelligently adapting computing to renewable energy generation. We present RARE (**R**enewable energy **A**ware **Re**source management), a Deep Reinforcement Learning (DRL) job scheduler that automatically learns effective job scheduling policies while continually adapting to datacenters' complex dynamic environment. The resulting DRL scheduler performs better than heuristic scheduling policies with different workloads and adapts to the intermittent power supply from renewables. We demonstrate DRL scheduler system design parameters that, when tuned correctly, produce better performance. Finally, we demonstrate that the DRL scheduler can learn from and improve upon existing heuristic policies using Offline Learning.

Keywords: Renewable energy · Datacenters · Job scheduling · Deep reinforcement learning

1 Introduction

The sustained demand for digital services has led to record datacenter build-outs and increased energy consumption. Conservative estimates suggest that global datacenter energy consumption between 2010 and 2018 went up by 6%, totaling 205 TWh in 2018. Further research [7] implies that the datacenter energy consumption is an order of magnitude higher than the estimated 6%, considering

D. Klusáček et al. (Eds.): JSSPP 2022, LNCS 13592, pp. 108–130, 2023.
https://doi.org/10.1007/978-3-031-22698-4_6

numerous unaccounted small-to-medium scale datacenters and datacenters that cater to new technologies (e.g., blockchain, cryptocurrency mining). Datacenters in the U.S consume 1.8% of the total electricity; electricity predominantly generated using non-renewable sources emitting an estimated $\sim$ 230 Million Metric tons of greenhouse gases every year.

Given high carbon emissions and growing societal awareness of climate change, government agencies, non-profits, and the general public demand cleaner (greener) goods and services. Consequently, cloud service providers are investing in green datacenters, i.e., datacenters partially or entirely powered by renewable energy. While some cloud service providers [9,14] buy carbon offsets, others [2,29] are shifting towards datacenters entirely powered by renewables. These datacenters either generate their own renewable energy (self-generation) or draw from an existing carbon-free (e.g., wind, solar) power generation plant (co-location).

The difficulty with renewables is that power generation is intermittent and subject to frequent fluctuations, making co-location and self-generation interesting from a research perspective. Solar energy generation has a diurnal pattern with maximum energy generation at mid-day, while wind energy generation is higher late in the night (Sect. 3.3, Fig. 3b). By combining the solar and wind sources, the energy generation typically complements each other.

Traditional heuristics-based job schedulers [16,30,33] use hand-crafted scheduling policies suitable for datacenters with constant power supply. Hand-engineering domain-specific heuristics-based schedulers to meet specific objective functions of highly dynamic green datacenters is time-consuming, error-prone, expensive, and requires domain expertise. A Reinforcement Learning (RL) based job scheduler automatically learns scheduling policies from trial-and-error. The growing body of research [12,26,34] has shown that RL schedulers can learn effective job scheduling policies in traditional datacenter environments with constant power supply. Although the results presented in these works are convincing, they do not examine the complex dynamic green datacenter environments. Furthermore, the existing works treat the RL scheduler as a black box without exploring the design choices (Sect. 2.2) that further improve performance.

Scheduling in a green datacenter encounters additional complexity as the resource pool expands and contracts based on the intermittent and varying power supply. In our previous work [31], we demonstrated that the DRL scheduler generates effective scheduling policies, with synthetic power and workload traces, for a cluster of 10 resources. This paper makes the following contributions:

- We present a unified green datacenter DRL scheduler, **RARE**, that allows experimenting with synthetic and real workloads, integrating multiple renewable energy sources and batteries (Sect. 3) to power the datacenter. We show that the DRL scheduler learns effective scheduling policies using synthetic and real HPC workload traces in small and medium scale datacenter environments (Sect. 5.4.1). We demonstrate the DRL scheduler's adaptability to power fluctuations using real power prediction data from renewables (solar and wind) (Sect. 5.4.2).

- We identified four critical challenges in the existing work (Sect. 2.2) and demonstrated performance improvements by appropriately calibrating the DRL scheduler design parameters.
- We explore the impact of various DRL scheduler design choices that lead to better performance. Specifically, we demonstrate that the DRL scheduler performs better with a longer planning horizon (in Sect. 5.4.3) and show the performance implications of choosing the DRL scheduler's neural network configurations (Sect. 5.4.4).
- We show that the DRL scheduler can learn from and improve upon existing heuristic scheduling policies with Offline Learning techniques (Sect. 5.4.5).

2 Background and Challenges

Job scheduling is deciding when and where to run a set of jobs on a set of resources in order to optimize an objective function. Objective functions define the goal of scheduler optimization. Typical objective functions for schedulers include maximizing revenue for the cloud service provider, maximizing utilization, and minimizing the makespan. The efficient utilization of computing resources leads to millions of dollars in savings for the service providers.

2.1 Reinforcement Learning (RL) and Job Scheduling

RL is formalized by a Markov Decision Process (MDP) $\mathcal{M} := (\mathcal{S}, \mathcal{A}, \mathbf{R}, \mathbf{T}, \gamma)$. $\mathcal{S}$ is the set of states, which are representations of information about the environment. $\mathcal{A}$ is the set of available actions that can be taken at each state. $\mathbf{R}$ is the reward function $\mathcal{S} \times \mathcal{A} \times \mathcal{S} \rightarrow \mathbb{R}$. $\mathbf{T}$ is the transition function $\mathcal{S} \times \mathcal{A} \rightarrow \mathcal{S}$ that describes the way actions impact the environment and alter its state. An agent is defined by a stochastic policy π that maps states to a distribution over actions in $\mathcal{A}$. A trajectory is a sequence of the states encountered at each timestep, the action taken in those states, and the rewards received $\tau := (s_0, a_0, r_0, \ldots, s_T, a_T, r_T)$. The goal of RL is to find a policy that maximizes the discounted sum of rewards over trajectories of experience, denoted $\eta_{\mathcal{M}}(\pi) = \mathbb{E}_{\tau \sim \pi}[\sum_{t=0}^{t=\infty} \gamma^t r_t]$ where $\gamma \in [0, 1)$ is a discount factor that determines the agent's emphasis on long-term rewards instead of short-term outcomes.

A Deep Neural Network (DNN) is a function approximator that uses layers of nonlinear transformations to learn a mapping between inputs and outputs. The coefficients of a DNN's matrices and vectors are called its weights or parameters. Learning involves finding accurate weights by taking iterative optimization steps along gradient directions that minimize a loss function. Let π_θ be a policy parameterized by a neural network with a set of weights θ. π_θ takes the current state as input and outputs a distribution over the action space, which can be sampled to make decisions in the environment.

In this work, we utilize a custom variant of the model-free off-policy actor-critic framework with discrete actions [8,15]. The agent interacts with the environment, sampling actions from π_θ in state s, transitioning to a new state s' and receiving a reward r. This experience is saved in a replay buffer $\mathcal{D}$ for later use. In addition to the "actor network", we initialize a neural network ϕ to represent the Q-function, denoted Q_ϕ, which takes state and action vectors as input and outputs an estimate of the expected return when taking action a in state s and following π thereafter. We can use our critic network to train the actor network to output higher-value actions. The improved actor is then used to improve the critic network's value estimates, and this process is repeated until performance converges. This technique is "model-free" because it does not attempt to directly model changes in the environment and "off-policy" because it recycles data collected from past decisions of the actor network. Further technical details of the implementation are provided in (Sect. 4).

2.2 Challenges

First, the environment plays a crucial role in RL by providing suitable reinforcement and encouraging the agent to execute the positive actions repetitively. The specially constrained environment rewards or penalizes the agent for correct or incorrect behavior (action). Although existing work [12,26,27,34] has shown RL schedulers learn effective job scheduling policies in datacenter environments (with constant power supply), they do not capture the complex dynamic green datacenters environments where the resource pool expands and contracts (intermittent power from renewables). Additionally, dissimilarities in their environments make it nearly impossible to make a one-to-one comparison among these implementations.

Second, the existing work does not discuss the implications of system design choices, making it difficult to analyze why the RL schedulers perform better than heuristic policies. One such design choice is the size of the planning horizon. The RL scheduler seeks to maximize the future cumulative rewards over some predefined planning horizon. Typically, renewable energy predictions are generated for a 24-h while others may influence training (day ahead) window. The RL schedulers can make better scheduling decisions with a longer planning horizon, whereas greedy heuristic policies cannot plan for future events. Therefore, studying the DRL scheduler's performance over longer planning horizons is crucial for green datacenters (Sect. 5.4.3).

Third, the current implementations, discussed in Sect. 6, treat the RL schedulers as a black box. These works do not explore RL specific configurations that may significantly contribute to the success of RL schedulers. These configurations may include the neural network size (number of neurons in input, hidden, and output layers) and the state representation (jobs, resources, and power supply). Additionally, following a one-size-fits-all approach while evaluating the RL scheduler with different workloads (with different job properties and size distributions) might diminish the performance. Some of these configuration decisions have performance implications (Sect. 5.4.4), while others may influence training time or system memory consumption (not explored in this paper).

Finally, existing RL schedulers overlook the importance of learning and improving upon existing heuristic policies. For instance, designing reward functions that elicit desired behaviors in complex environments is challenging.

Instead, the RL schedulers can leverage the behavior of custom heuristic schedulers' designed specifically for unique workloads or environments to learn and improve the overall performance. That is, the heuristic schedulers generate expert demonstrations, and the RL schedulers learn from these demonstrations to improve upon the heuristic policies (Sect. 5.4.5).

3 Renewable Energy Datacenter Environment

The green datacenter is a datacenter co-located at or near renewable energy sources. Various renewable sources can power the datacenter with the provision to store (battery) excess energy from renewables. Additionally, the datacenter is connected to the electric grid to support critical infrastructure when energy from renewables and batteries cannot sustain the load. We aim to design a green datacenter environment that can be controlled by heuristic and DRL-based scheduling policies. In order to train the DRL scheduler agent, we convert the renewable datacenter scheduling problem into an MDP (Sect. 2.1) with a state space $\mathcal{S}$ describing the current status of the cluster resources, an action space $\mathcal{A}$ of new jobs, and a reward function $\mathbf{R}$ to be optimized. The operation of the datacenter - including receiving new jobs and placing scheduled jobs on available resources - becomes the MDP transition function, $\mathbf{T}$. Figure 1 provides an overview of a DRL scheduler agent interacting with the green datacenter environment.

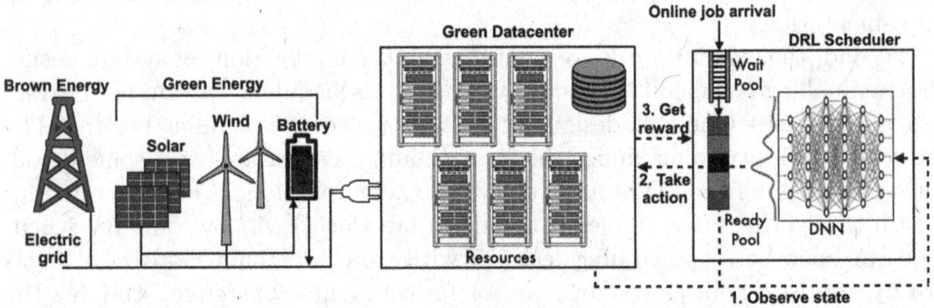

Fig. 1. DRL scheduler agent interacting with the green datacenter powered by renewables, battery and electric grid. (Color figure online)

3.1 State Space, Action Space, and Reward Function

The state space, $\mathcal{S}$, includes information about jobs, resources, and resource availability (based on power generation predictions).

3.1.1 Resources

Resource availability is represented in an image format of shape (time_horizon, resource_types × max_resources), with grey pixels indicating free resources. As jobs are scheduled on the resource pool, segments of the image are occupied by colored rectangles representing jobs' resource requirements and duration. Figure 2 illustrates the cluster image (10 CPUs, 10 GPUs for 24-time units) and the allocation of each resource to jobs scheduled for service, starting from the current timestep and looking ahead 24-time units into the future. Our simulator models a "pool of resources" (CPUs and GPUs), allowing the scheduler to make granular per resource scheduling decisions. The available resources are allocated contiguously to the jobs (e.g., 8 CPUs and 4 GPUs are allocated to the blue job for three time units).

The power availability feedback is not directly provided to the scheduler agent. Instead, the resource pool expands and contracts based on the power available to the datacenter at any given time. The power availability decides when and how many resources are turned on or off. Therefore, power prediction data is an integral part of the state space, i.e., as power availability changes, the corresponding resource availability is reflected in the state information supplied to the scheduler agent. Resources unavailable due to power constraints are marked black in the resource image. For instance, at timestep 22 (Fig. 2), 70% of power is available, so 70% of the resources are on, and 30% are shut down. Similarly, at timestep 23, 80% of power is available, meaning 80% resources are on and 20% are shut down.

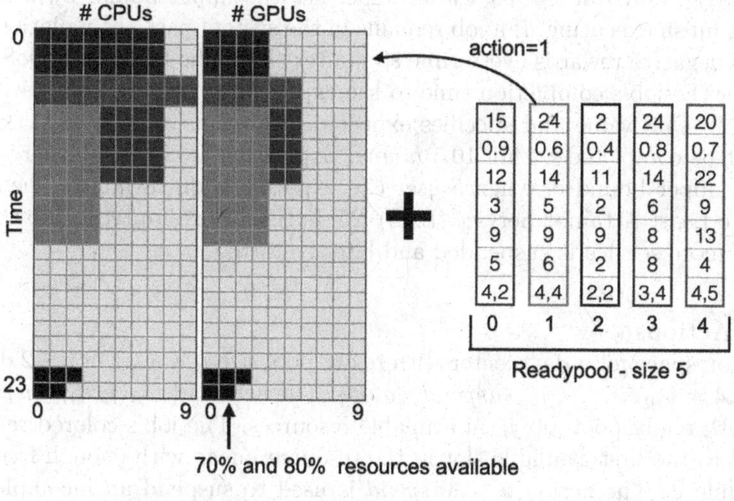

Fig. 2. Resource state: A 10 CPUs, 10 GPUs cluster, time-horizon=24, and readypool size=5.

3.1.2 Jobs

In our system, jobs can be in one of three locations: 1) wait_pool, 2) ready_pool, or 3) scheduled on the resources. The wait_pool is where jobs first arrive. The jobs from wait_pool are moved (in FIFO order) to the ready_pool where they can then be scheduled on the resources. Jobs have meta-data, including the job's id, value, and resource requirements. The jobs in the ready_pool are represented as vectors, each job's vector consists of *job_value, qos, qos_violation_time, enter_time, expected_finish_time, duration* and *resource_requirement.* Additional meta-data for each job is calculated after the job is admitted, e.g., remianing_runtime (if a job gets suspended) and qos_violation_time.

In Fig. 2, the ready_pool size is 5 (with job indices 0 – 4) and has 5 jobs. The yellow job (at ready_pool[1]) requires 4 CPU and 4 GPU units for the next six timesteps, and the job's value is 24. The jobs are processed over some fixed T timesteps. The time horizon shifts after processing jobs during that timestep, with the job metadata vectors updated and resource image advancing by one row. As the time horizon shifts, the energy available from renewables (and battery) dictates the availability of resources for placing new jobs. The scheduler agent continuously observes the state - consisting of jobs, resources, and resource/power availability - to make scheduling decisions.

QoS Value: Users may have different utility functions, i.e., users are willing to pay different amounts for different jobs based on their importance. The user picks the required QoS for that job based on the user's willingness to pay for the job (e.g., spot instances [3–5]). The QoS value is specified as a percentage of the time the user wants his job to run. The qos_violation_time, ($expected\_finish\_time \div Qos\ Value$), specifies the upper bound by which the job must finish executing. If a job remains in the system past qos_violation_time, it incurs negative rewards every time step after that. The higher the QoS value, the closer the job's completion time to the expected_finish_time. If a user wants 0.95 (95%) QoS value and specifies expected_finish_time $= 10\ hours$, then the job must be completed within 10.5 $hours$. Expressing QoS value in percentages gives an upper bound of when a user can expect his job to finish. The idea is similar to Least Attained Service (LAS) [25] in that if preempted, a job that has received more service is suspended and later restarted.

3.1.3 Actions

The action space for a datacenter with ready_pool size n is a set of $n+2$ discrete options $\mathcal{A} = \{j_0, j_1, \ldots, j_n, suspend, no\_op\}$. The actions $\{a = j_i, \forall i \leq n\}$ schedule the ith ready_pool job j_i on available resources. The job's colored rectangle is added to the first available slot in the resource image with enough free space to schedule it. The action $a = suspend$ is used to suspend an incomplete job and replace it with one of higher value. The suspend action is work preserving, in that a suspended job resumes from the point it was stopped at and not from the beginning. The suspended jobs are re-queued after updating the remaining run time, along with the other ready jobs. Although our scheduler framework supports checkpoint and restart capability [18], the feature was turned off for the experiments discussed in this paper. Finally, the action $a = no\_op$ means that the scheduler agent does not want to schedule (e.g., resources requirements cannot be satisfied) or suspend any jobs in that timestep. In Fig. 2, $action = 1$ (at ready_pool[1]) schedules the yellow job to run on the available resources.

3.1.4 Rewards

The DRL scheduler's objective is realized with rewards that the agent receives. Rewards, which are scalars given by the reward function $\mathbf{R}(s_t, a_t, s_{t+1})$, are a combination of the positive reward or associated cost for the action in a given state. Some actions collect positive rewards, while other actions accrue negative costs. For instance, if a job, j, is running on a resource, it collects a positive reward proportional to the job's value. A job's value, $j._{value}$, is calculated based on the type of resources requested, duration, and QoS value. If a job is delayed and QoS violated, it collects a negative reward. Negative reward indirectly encourages fairness, ensuring low QoS value jobs are not delayed or starved. Other costs and rewards can be incorporated into the reward function. Our DRL scheduler's objective is to maximize the total job value from finished jobs, $|J_{finished}|$ expressed as,

$$Total\ Job\ Value = \sum_{i=1}^{|J_{finished}|} j_i.value \tag{1}$$

A direct calculation of value is the price the user is willing to pay to run a job. Total Job Value is both an application-centric and resource-centric metric; the emphasis is on processing as many user jobs as possible, which may increase resource utilization. By processing as many jobs as possible, we essentially maximize the total value we gain from running those jobs. Even a small improvement in total job value can generate millions of dollars in savings for the service providers. Other common objective functions (utilization, makespan, and system throughput) are driven by system-centric parameters that enhance throughput and utilization rather than improving the utility of application processing. These systems treat resources as if they cost the same price and the results of all applications have the same value, even though this may not be the case..

3.2 Renewable Energy Forecasting

Forecasting is crucial for integrating variable renewable energy (VRE) resources such as wind and solar into datacenters. The difference between forecasted output and actual generation is forecast error. Factors that affect forecast performance include forecast time-horizon, local weather conditions, and weather data availability. By integrating VRE forecasts into the scheduling system, datacenter operators can anticipate up- and down-ramps in VRE generation to balance load and generation in intra-day and day-ahead scheduling.

With shorter timescales, accurate VRE generation forecasting can help reduce the risk of incurring penalties. Over longer timescales, improved VRE generation forecasting based on accurate weather forecasting can help better plan long-running jobs (suspending and resuming the jobs appropriately). The forecasting accuracy decreases with the increase in the forecast time horizon. Thus, selecting a proper time horizon before designing a forecasting model is key to maintaining the accuracy of forecasting at an acceptable level [24].

Additionally, Fig. 1 shows that brown energy can contribute to the electric grid connected to the datacenter. It may not be acceptable to reject or delay some jobs (e.g., jobs with high QoS requirements) if it is possible to execute them with a small additional amount of brown energy. In this case, the datacenter faces a multi-criteria optimization problem comprising the selection of power sources and the scheduling of jobs. Similarly, the use of batteries also results in a multi-criteria optimization problem since the datacenter administrator can decide when to use the additional power from the battery. Multi-criteria optimization is ongoing, and we will cover this topic in our future work.

3.3 Energy Storage Devices (ESDs)

ESDs act as a buffer to smooth out intermittent power from renewables, shifting energy from peak generation time-of-day (charging) to low generation periods (discharging). Batteries store the excess energy from wind and solar, increasing the contribution from renewable resources and reducing the electric grid's need. This translates to reduced electricity costs, lower carbon emissions, and highly reliable services.

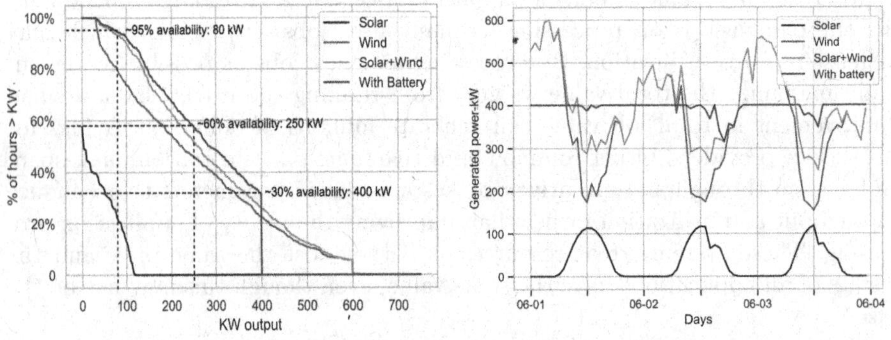

(a) % of time available power exceeds a given value from renewables and battery.

(b) Power generation: solar (peak 120 kW), wind (peak 600 kW), June, 2019.

Fig. 3. Power generation and power availability from wind and solar

Figure 3a shows the probability that total expected power will exceed a given value for each of renewable sources and combinations from data calculated hourly across the 2019 calendar year at the GLEAMM [1] site. For example, a datacenter of 240 kW total electrical draw can expect to have its energy needs met at least 60% of the time entirely by the solar array and wind farm. Approximately 80 kW or more will be available at least 95% of the time for critical infrastructures - such as storage, networking, and control functions of the computational cluster - entirely from the renewables. Under ideal conditions, Fig. 3b (red line) shows the power (over 3-days in June 2019) from renewables and power available with battery on site. Under normal conditions, the power generation from solar and wind is much more volatile.

4 DRL Scheduling Agent

We train our scheduling agent with a custom variant of the Deep Actor-Critic RL framework (Sect. 2.1). The datacenter simulator (Sect. 3) with ready_pool size n is converted to a RL environment that takes an action index $< n + 2$ and returns a new state and reward. States are tuples containing both the resource image and array of job metadata (Sect. 3.1), while the reward function can be adjusted to reflect the goals of our scheduling system. This paper focuses on optimizing the total (monetary) value of completed jobs; the reward at timestep t is the total value of all completed jobs at that timestep. Our agent learns to select jobs from the ready_pool that maximize total job value with the help of three DNNs.

The *encoder* combines the state information in the resource allocation image and job metadata array and produces a compact vector representation. The resource allocation image is processed by convolutional layers common in computer vision applications, while the job array is passed through standard feed-forward layers.

The two representations are then normalized for stability and concatenated together before a final sequence of layers condenses them to a vector $\tilde{s} \in \mathbb{R}^{128}$ that summarizes the current state of the scheduling environment. The *actor* network takes $\tilde{s}$ as input and outputs probabilities for selecting all $n + 2$ scheduling actions. The *critic* also takes $\tilde{s}$ as input and outputs $q \in \mathbb{R}^{n+2}$, where $q[i]$ is an estimate of the total monetary value that we expect to achieve in the future when beginning in the current state and taking the ith action.

In an actor-critic method, the actor is trained to assign higher probabilities to actions that the critic determines will lead to higher monetary value. The critic then uses the improved actor to better estimate the expected return of selecting each action. Both networks rely on the state representation $\tilde{s}$ learned by the encoder network. Separating the encoder in this way lets us share parameters across the actor and critic training processes and reduces overall network size. However, the encoder parameters are updated alongside the critic but not the actor for stability reasons.

Additionally, we are interested in learning to mimic or improve upon the decisions of heuristic schedulers. Learning from fixed datasets of prior experience is the topic of Offline RL [22], and applying standard ("online") actor-critics without the ability to test the policy in the environment and confirm the outcome can lead to value overestimation [21]. Therefore, we adjust the training process when using offline data so that the actor network learns to mimic the scheduling decisions in the dataset, as long as the critic network suggests those actions are an improvement over what the actor would have done otherwise.

The training process is outlined in Algorithm 1. Our specific implementation includes several additional details that have been shown to improve stability and performance; the online version of `RARE` is closest to discrete SAC [8,15] while the offline variant is implemented similarly to CRR [32].

Algorithm 1: RARE Training Process

Input: Batch Size B, Learning Rate α, Online $True/False$, Discount γ
Initialize: Encoder Net g_ψ, Actor Net π_θ, Critic Net Q_ϕ

if *Online* **then**
  Input: Datacenter Simulator Env with Dynamics $\mathbf{T} : \mathcal{S} \times \mathcal{A} \rightarrow \mathcal{S}$ and Reward Function $\mathbf{R} : \mathcal{S} \times \mathcal{A} \times \mathcal{S} \rightarrow \mathbb{R}$
  Initialize: Replay Buffer $\mathcal{D} \leftarrow \{\}$
else
  Input: Advantage Samples k, Replay Buffer with pre-provided transitions $\mathcal{D} \leftarrow \{(s_i, a_i, r_i, s'_i), \dots\}$
end
for *training step* $t \in \{0, \dots, T\}$ **do**
  if *Online* **then**
    // sample an action from the policy
    $a_t \sim \pi_\theta(g_\psi(s_t))$
    // advance datacenter sim and receive next state and reward
    $s'_t \leftarrow \mathbf{T}(s_t, a_t)$, $r_t \leftarrow \mathbf{R}(s_t, a_t, s'_t)$
    // add transition to the replay buffer
    $\mathcal{D} \leftarrow \mathcal{D} \cup \{(s_t, a_t, r_t, s'_t)\}$
  end
  Randomly Sample Batch of B transitions $\{(s_i, a_i, r_i, s'_i)\}_{i=0}^{i=B} \sim \mathcal{D}$
  // the encoder embeds the resource image and job metadata into a single array
  Let $\tilde{s}_j := g_\psi(s_j)$
  // critic loss (where $\not\nabla$ cancels gradient contributions)

$$\mathcal{L}_{critic} \leftarrow \frac{1}{B} \sum_{i=0}^{i=B} \left(\left(Q_\phi(\tilde{s}_i, a_i) - \mathop{\mathbb{E}}_{a' \sim \pi_\theta(\tilde{s}'_i)} \left[(r_i + \not\nabla \gamma (Q_\phi(\tilde{s}'_i, a') \right] \right)^2 \right)$$

  if *Online* **then**
    // online actor loss (see [15]). train the actor to maximize the Q-function.

$$\mathcal{L}_{actor} \leftarrow \frac{1}{B} \sum_{i=0}^{i=B} \left(\mathop{\mathbb{E}}_{a' \sim \pi_\theta(\tilde{s}_i)} \left[-Q_\phi(\tilde{s}_i, a') \right] \right)$$

  else
    // estimate the advantage function, $A(s, a)$, by comparing the value of a to the average value of actions sampled from the policy in a given state.
    Let $\hat{A}(\tilde{s}_i, a_i) := Q_\phi(\tilde{s}_i, a_i) - \frac{1}{k} \Sigma_0^k Q_\phi(\tilde{s}_i, a' \sim \pi_\theta(\tilde{s}_i))$
    // offline actor loss (see [32]). supervised regression to copy actions with positive advantage (where $\mathbb{1}_{\{x\}}$ is 1 if x is *True* else 0)

$$\mathcal{L}_{actor} \leftarrow \frac{1}{B} \sum_{i=0}^{i=B} \left(-\mathbb{1}_{\{\hat{A}(\tilde{s}_i, a_i) > 0\}} \log \pi_\theta(a_i | \tilde{s}_i) \right)$$

  end
  // update neural nets by gradient descent
  $\psi \leftarrow \psi - \alpha \nabla_\psi \mathcal{L}_{critic}$, $\phi \leftarrow \phi - \alpha \nabla \phi \mathcal{L}_{critic}$, $\theta \leftarrow \theta - \alpha \nabla_\theta \mathcal{L}_{actor}$,
end
Output: Trained Scheduling Policy $\pi_\theta(g_\psi(s))$

5 Evaluation

This section evaluates the DRL scheduler's performance with different workloads, power availability at the green datacenter and explores the effects of design choices on the performance. Before presenting the results, we briefly discuss the workload and experimental setup.

5.1 Experimentation Conditions

Our green datacenter simulator compares different resource allocation and scheduling policies using various workloads and power availability settings. Our datacenter simulator (Sect. 3) integrates resources, jobs, power supply from renewables (Sect. 3.2) and ESDs (Sect. 3.3). We have not explicitly modelled networking, storage and I/O overhead. These overheads can be incorporated into the model by adding start/end delay to each job's start and end times. The flexible design of our datacenter simulator allows exploring various design options that can potentially improve the DRL scheduler's performance. For the following experiments, we modeled a small-scale (10 to 50 resources) and a medium-scale datacenter (100 to 300 resources).

5.2 Evaluation Metrics

The metric used for evaluating the DRL scheduler's performance is the *Total Job Value* (Sect. 3.1.4) from running the jobs. The *Total Job Value*, accumulated during evaluation, includes a total value for all the jobs that complete on time. The higher the *Total Job Value*, the better. We repeated each experiment 10 times, with new seed, and found the error margin between runs was insignificant.

We also evaluate traditional heuristic scheduling policies, including: Shortest Job First (SJF), Quality of Service (QoS), Highest Value First (HVF), and First Come First Serve (FCFS) for comparison. With the SJF heuristic policy, the job with the shortest runtime is picked first. The job with the highest QoS value (refer Sect. 3.1.2) is scheduled first with the QoS scheduling policy. The highest value job is scheduled first with the HVF policy, and the job with the earliest enter_time is scheduled using FCFS. Our framework does not support backfilling during scheduling; we will incorporate this feature in our future work.

5.3 Workload

The datacenter simulator consists of a cluster with different resource types. Jobs arrive at the cluster in an online manner in discrete timesteps. We assume that the resource demand of each job is known upon arrival; i.e., the resource requirements of each job j is given by the vector $r_j = (r_{j,1}, r_{j,2})$, and T_j is the duration of the job. We assume each job has a fixed allocation (no malleability), such that r_j must be allocated continuously from when the job starts execution until completion. If a job gets suspended, then the job's remaining run time is updated when the job resumes.

5.3.1 Synthetic Workload

We used a synthetic workload where each job consists of meta-data, including job-id, resource requirement (#cpus, #gpus), and job duration. Jobs arrive online according to a *Poisson process.* The average job arrival rate, λ, determines the average load on the cluster. We chose the job duration and resource requests such that 70% of the jobs are short jobs with a duration between $1t$ and $10t$ chosen uniformly. The remaining are long duration jobs chosen uniformly from $10t$ to $30t$ for a time horizon of 48. Each job can request a maximum of 50% of the total resources, picked randomly. Synthetic workload provides more nuanced control over simulation parameters (e.g., job arrival rate, job distribution) while allowing us to study the scheduler's behavior under a wide range of conditions [10,11].

5.3.2 HPC Workload

We trained and evaluated the RARE scheduler using Argonne National Laboratory (ANL) Intrepid HPC workload [6]. The logs contain several months' accounting records (from 2009) from the Blue Gene/P system called Intrepid. The ANL HPC workload is an old data set, but it has similar characteristics to modern workloads in terms of job arrival rates, resource requirements, and job duration. We made additional changes to the job logs to compensate for missing information. For example, we added GPU requirements to the job requests because Intrepid job logs did not have GPU jobs. Similarly, ANL logs do not have a QoS parameter. We added QoS value (ranging between 0.1 to 0.9, refer §3.1.2) for each job during training and evaluation.

5.3.3 Power Availability

We use synthetic power and real power prediction data traces in our experiments. When using synthetic power traces, the power availability level, e.g., 90%, means that 90% of the resources are turned on (10% resources turned off) for that time step (refer Fig. 2). The real power prediction data (solar and wind) is from GLEAMM [1] datacenter. The GLEAMM center is a microgrid equipped with 150 kW solar power and three wind turbines connected to the facility, each with 300 kVA of expected power generation.

5.4 Results

First, we evaluate our DRL scheduler with synthetic and HPC workloads. Second, we demonstrate the DRL scheduler's adaptability to the intermittent power supply. Third, we evaluate design choices, namely extended planning horizon and increasing ready_pool size, that significantly increase the performance of the DRL scheduler compared to heuristics. Finally, we show that the DRL scheduler can learn to imitate the existing heuristic policies and improve performance over those heuristic policies.

5.4.1 Performance with Synthetic and HPC Workloads

Performance with Synthetic Workload and Power Data: This section demonstrates the DRL scheduler's performance with the increasing number of resources. We modeled a small and medium scale datacenter and maintained the workload and power availability at 100%. The *Total Job Value* obtained compared to heuristic scheduling policies is plotted in Fig. 4.

Analysis: From Fig. 4, the DRL scheduler performs 18% to 25% better for small scale datacenter and 2% to 20% better for medium scale datacenters compared to heuristic policies. As the number of resources increases (≥50), the DRL scheduler's performance closely matches (2% to 6% better) the performance of QoS and SJF policies. The DRL scheduler's state space increases as the problem size increases (100 to 300 resources). As the state space increases, the DRL scheduler must explore more states to decide on the best action in any given step. Given the vast state space (for resources ≥50), the agent cannot explore all possible state-action pairs within the fixed episodic limits. Therefore, the performance difference between DRL scheduler and heuristic policies narrows with a larger state space. This huge state-space problem can be alleviated by splitting the state space into smaller sizes. We will investigate this approach in the future.

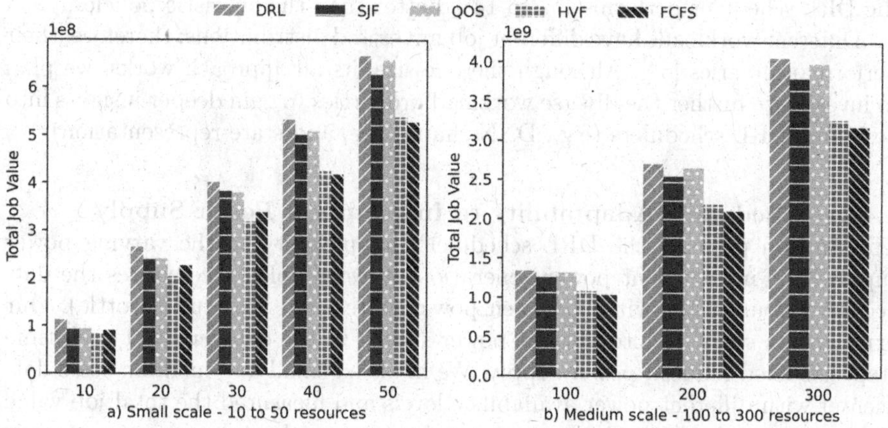

Fig. 4. DRL scheduler's performance vs. heuristic scheduling policies with varying resource pool size (small to medium scale datacenter)

Performance with ANL Workload and Real Power Prediction Data: We modeled a small scale datacenter (10 to 30 resources) with ANL HPC job workload and maintained the job arrival rate at 100%. Additionally, we used the actual power prediction data from the GLEAMM datacenter to simulate a real-world green datacenter powered by renewables and battery (no brown energy).

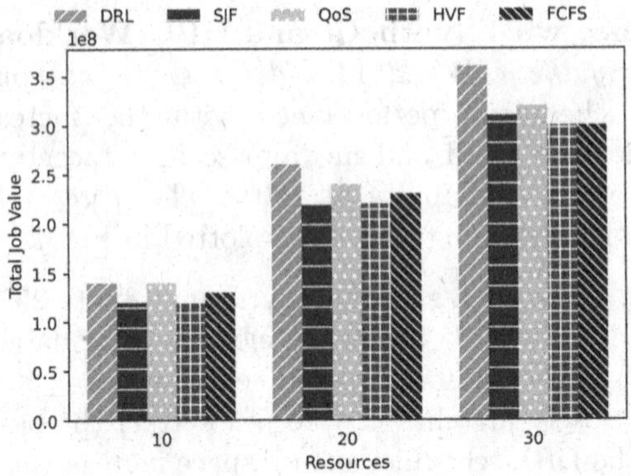

Fig. 5. DRL scheduler's performance vs. heuristic scheduling policies with ANL workload and GLEAMM power data

Analysis: Figure 5 shows the performance of the DRL scheduler compared to heuristic policies on the ANL workloads and real power prediction data from GLEAMM. For 10 resources, the DRL scheduler's performance matches the QoS and is 5% to 10% better than other scheduling policies. For 20 and 30 resources, the DRL scheduler performs 7% to 14% better than the heuristic policies.

Different workloads have different job mixes and distributions; therefore, their performance varies [34]. Although the one-size-fits-all approach works, we plan to investigate further the diverse workload properties to gain deeper insights into designing DRL schedulers (e.g., DNN shape, size, and state representation).

5.4.2 Scheduler's Adaptability to Intermittent Power Supply

This section presents the DRL scheduler's adaptability to the varying power supply. The intermittent power generation by renewables necessitates the datacenter resources to switch between power states (off, idle, full throttle). Our experiments simulate intermittent power supply to the datacenter at each time step, not fixed reduced power supply. We modeled small and medium-scale datacenter with different power availability levels and measured the total job value obtained at each level. The resource pool size expands and contracts at every timestep (Fig. 2), based on power availability. The job arrival rate is kept constant at 100% for all the power availability levels. We did not simulate adaptive throttling to dynamically manage the datacenter load since it is out of the scope of this paper.

Analysis: In Fig. 6, we plotted the total job value with varying power supply (100%, 90% and 80%) for small and medium size cluster. For small-scale cluster (Fig. 6a, b and c), the DRL scheduler performs 9% to 13% better (10 and 20 resources) and 8% to 12% better (50 resources) than heuristic policies. For medium-scale cluster (Fig. 6d), the DRL scheduler performs 1% better than QoS policy and 5% to 20% better than other heuristic policies. The greedy heuristic policies, like SJF, do not plan for the future by design. On the contrary, the DRL scheduler observes the resource availability changes in the future and intelligently schedules suitable jobs maximizing total job value. As observed in the previous section, the performance difference between DRL scheduler and heuristic policies narrows (300 resources) with a larger state space.

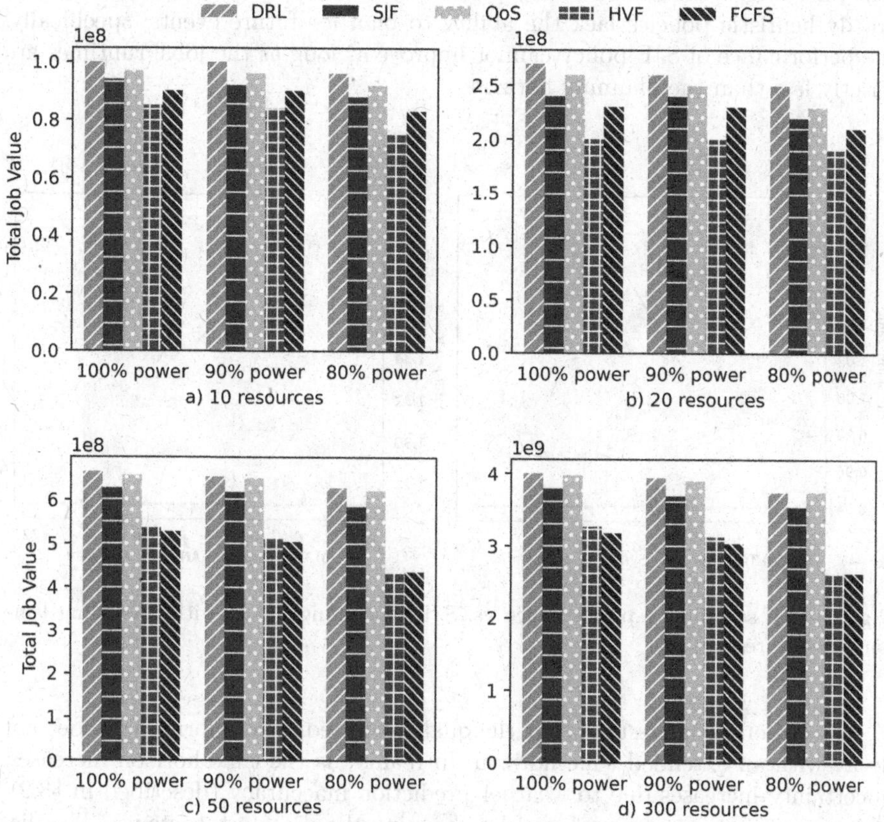

Fig. 6. DRL Scheduler's performance with varying power supply - small and medium scale datacenter

5.4.3 Extended Planning Horizon

Typically, the renewable energy predictions are generated for a 24−*hour* (day ahead) window. More recently, researchers have developed better prediction models that can predict (with relative accuracy) power generation for extended time windows (2–3 d) [19]. This subsection investigates the DRL scheduler's performance with various planning horizons, namely 36, 48, 60, and 72 time units. For this experiment, we used synthetic workload and 100% power to isolate the performance implications of the extended planning horizon.

Analysis: From Fig. 7, as the planning horizon increases from 36 to 72, the DRL scheduler performs 4% to 14% and 6% to 10% better than SJF heuristic policy for synthetic and ANL HPC workloads, respectively. The DRL scheduler seeks to maximize the future cumulative rewards over some predefined planning horizon (a.k.a, time horizon). With a shorter planning horizon, TH=36, the DRL scheduler might be limited to *myopic* decisions yielding immediate gains. The greedy heuristic policies lack the ability to plan for future events; specifically, the performance of SJF policy cannot improve as long as the jobs' runtimes are strictly less than the planning horizon.

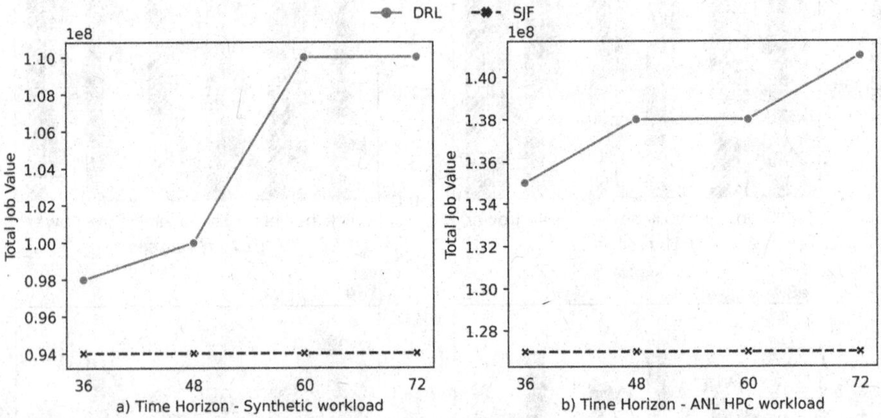

Fig. 7. DRL scheduler's performance vs. SJF scheduling policy with increasing time horizon - 10 resources

Our experiments assume that the quality of predictive information does not decay with an extended time horizon. In reality, as the time horizon increases, uncertainty increases due to weather prediction inaccuracy (described in §3.2). This uncertainty can be captured by changing the $discount\ factor, \gamma$. The discount factor determines how much the DRL agent cares about rewards in the distant future relative to those in the immediate future. If $\gamma = 0$, the agent will be completely myopic and only learn about actions that produce an immediate reward. For our experiments above, we set $\gamma = 0.99$. We note that optimization problems become computationally-intensive (due to state-space explosion) with longer time horizons. In the future, we will identify the limits beyond which extending the time horizon will yield ineffective results for the DRL scheduler.

5.4.4 Varying Readypool Size

This section evaluates the performance of different scheduling policies as the ready_pool size varies. The size of the ready_pool (described in Sect. 2) is fixed for any given problem size because the DNN's shape cannot change dynamically during training or evaluation. The DRL scheduler can only select one or more jobs in the ready_pool at each step. On the other hand, typical heuristic schedulers can select one or more jobs from all of the waiting jobs in the system. This experiment demonstrates that limiting the list of jobs (ready_pool size) does not affect the performance of the DRL scheduler. For this experiment, we used 10 resources, synthetic and ANL workloads with 100% power supply to study the effect of ready_pool size on the quality of the results produced by the DRL scheduler.

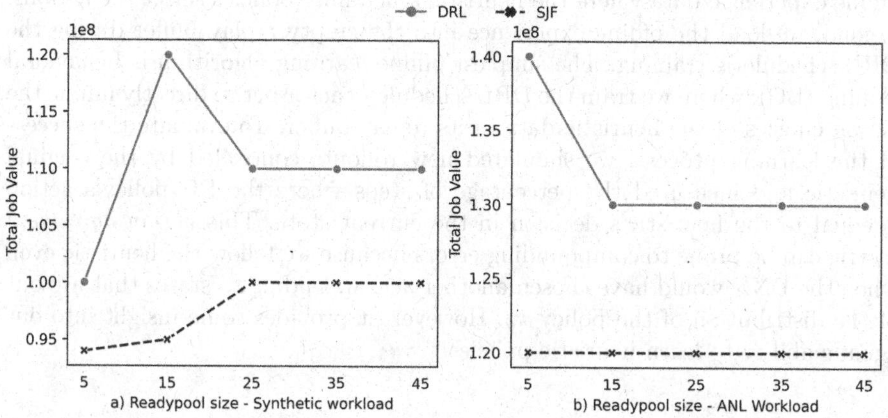

Fig. 8. DRL scheduler's performance vs. SJF scheduling policy with varying *ready_pool* sizes - 10 resources

Analysis: Figure 8a shows the DRL scheduler's performance (synthetic workload) compared to SJF scheduling policy with varying ready_pool sizes. The DRL scheduler performs best with a ready_pool size of 15, an 18% improvement over SJF. The DRL scheduler's performance decreases for ready_pool sizes of 25 and higher but still performs 4% to 7% better than SJF. On the other hand, the SJF policy always picks the smallest job, and the performance stays constant even when we increase the ready_pool size because the jobs' lengths are within a certain distribution (described in Sect. 5.3.1). Even if more jobs are visible (in the ready_pool) to the SJF scheduler, the job lengths are likely to be similar.

Figure 8b shows the DRL scheduler's performance with ANL HPC workload. The DRL scheduler performs 10% better than SJF when the ready_pool size is 5 and 7% better for ready_pool size 15 and above. Whereas, with the synthetic workload, the DRL scheduler's performance increases, with ANL HPC workload, the performance decreases as ready_pool size increases. We showed that having a smaller set of ready_pool jobs does not affect the DRL scheduler's overall performance. Further, we believe that the graph trends for the two workloads are different due to the differences in the job distributions. We plan to investigate further with other workloads.

5.4.5 Behavioural Cloning and Offline RL

While DRL can learn efficient scheduling strategies, it often takes hundreds of thousands of timesteps to explore the datacenter environment and adapt from a randomly initialized DNN policy. Following the recent success of Offline RL [22], we can try to learn a scheduling policy from a fixed dataset of prior experience collected from existing heuristic schedulers.

We used a synthetic workload with 100% power supply on a small cluster (20 resources). First, we collected 20 rollouts (sequences of 100–200k samples) of offline experience data where the heuristic scheduling policies select the actions. Second, we load the offline experience into the empty replay buffer during the DRL scheduler's training. The simplest offline learning algorithm is behavioral cloning (BC), where we train the DRL scheduler's actor net to directly mimic the action choices of the heuristic data in its replay buffer. To evaluate the success of the learning process, we simulated new rollouts controlled by the original heuristic and measured the percentage of steps where the BC policy's action is equal to the heuristic's decision in the current state. This *action agreement* metric can be prone to compounding errors because we follow the heuristic even when the DNN would have chosen another action, leading to states that are out of the distribution of the policy π_θ. However, it provides some insight into our agent's ability to learn heuristic policies.

Table 1. DRL scheduler's action agreement of BC and performance improvement over BC with Offline learning

20 Resources	SJF	QoS	HVF	FCFS
Action Agreement (BC)	98%	71%	75%	80%
Offline Improvement	2%	5%	19%	7%

Analysis: The results for 20 resource environment are shown in Table 1. We also experiment with fully offline RL (Algorithm 1 with `Online` = False), where we use reward information to mimic heuristic actions only when our trained critic network interprets those actions to be an improvement over what the current policy π_θ would have done otherwise. This approach improves upon BC in terms of percentage increase in Total Job Value shown in the second row of Table 1.

Another interesting direction is whether our offline agent can learn from multiple heuristic policies. We collected rollouts from SJF, QoS, HVF, and FCFS on a 50 resource environment and trained the offline version of RARE on a replay buffer filled evenly with actions from each heuristic. We then measured the action agreement of the DRL policy with each of the original heuristics, and found: SJF (64%), QoS (7%), HVF (31%), and FCFS (16%). This suggests that the offline algorithm learns to favor the SJF heuristic, which performs well in the 50 resource datacenter (Fig. 6), and easier to mimic SJF than QoS.

6 Related Work

6.1 Heuristics Schedulers

Resource allocation or scheduling has been extensively studied in the literature. Tetrisched [30] is a scheduling system implemented for repetitive analytics jobs in datacenters. Tetrisched plans ahead in time using a Mixed Integer Linear Programming (MILP) constraint solver to optimize job placement. Gandiva [33] scheduler, implemented on top of Kubernetes, exploits intra-job predictability (time taken for each mini-batch iteration) to time-slice GPUs efficiently across multiple jobs leading to low job latency. These schedulers do not demonstrate their suitability in green datacenter environments. To address the intermittent power supply from renewables, the existing heuristics schedulers [13,20,28] delay the deferrable jobs until the renewable power is adequate or the electricity price is low before the soft deadline of the jobs expires. Deferring the jobs may lead to poor QoS for the users. Additionally, these implementations use hand-crafted heuristics-based scheduling techniques, and reasoning about these heuristics' interactions is complicated and becomes intractable as the number of variables and heuristics increases.

6.2 RL Schedulers

The Spotlight [12] partitions the agent's neural network training operations onto different devices (CPUs and GPUs) for fast model execution. The RL scheduler in [17] is designed to minimize the makespan of DAG jobs considering both task dependencies and heterogeneous resource demands. DeepEE [26] proposes improving datacenters' energy efficiency by considering the jobs scheduling and cooling systems concurrently. The goal, in [26], is to reduce cooling costs in a datacenter rather than optimize job scheduling. The scheduler in [27] implements a co-scheduling algorithm based on an adaptive RL by combining application profiling and cluster monitoring. Smoother [23] is renewable power-aware middleware. This work's primary focus is to provide sustained power to the datacenter with stored energy rather than learning to adapt job scheduling given intermittent power supply.

The RL schedulers discussed above do not have power variability as part of the system's internal state. When we consider power intermittency as part of the system state, it changes the problem setting completely. Additionally, the works discussed above treat the RL schedulers as black boxes without exploring crucial system design parameters that significantly improve overall performance. Further, each of these works is designed for specific environments and workloads and therefore cannot be directly compared with one another or used in other settings. Our implementation is a dynamic system with power variability encoded in the system's internal state. Our DRL scheduler's primary focus is to schedule jobs in green datacenters effectively, not predicting renewable energy production, reducing electricity consumption or carbon emissions.

7 Conclusion

Datacenters operate 24X7, guzzling megawatts of electricity, relying heavily on brown energy. Brown energy is expensive and harmful to the environment as brown energy generation releases gigatons of greenhouse gases. Concerns regarding carbon emissions have led organizations to raise the bar by adopting a goal of matching their power consumption with renewable energy.

The difficulty with using renewables to power datacenters is intermittent energy generation, accompanied by inaccuracies in power predictions. The degree of inaccuracy varies from one renewable energy source to another, requiring smart systems and system software to carefully balance and intelligently adapt computing to energy generation. The existing heuristic and RL schedulers are not designed for complex dynamic green datacenters. Additionally, the existing RL schedulers do not explain or explore the system design configurations that lead to better performance with proper tuning.

To address these shortcomings, we propose a unified green datacenter scheduler, RARE, that allows experimenting with synthetic and real workloads and integrates various renewable energy sources along with Energy Storage Devices (batteries). We showed that our DRL scheduler performs better than heuristics-based algorithms in the dynamic green datacenter environment for synthetic and real HPC workloads for a cluster of up to 300 resources. The DRL scheduler adapts exceptionally well to the intermittent power supply (synthetic and actual power prediction data). We demonstrated that accurately tuning the system parameters like planning horizon and ready_pool size leads to increased performance. Finally, we show that the DRL scheduler can effectively learn from and improve the existing systems using Offline Learning techniques.

References

1. GLEAMM Facility at TTU. https://www.depts.ttu.edu/gleamm/
2. Lancium Inc. https://lancium.com
3. Amazon ec2 spot instances. Accessed May 2022. https://aws.amazon.com/ec2/spot/
4. Azure spot virtual machines. Accessed May 2022. https://azure.microsoft.com/en-us/pricing/spot/
5. Ambati, P., Bashir, N., Irwin, D., Shenoy, P.: Waiting game: optimally provisioning fixed resources for cloud-enabled schedulers. In: Proceedings of the International Conference for High Performance Computing, Networking, Storage and Analysis. SC 2020, p. 14. IEEE Press, Atlanta (2020). articleno 67
6. ANL: The argonne national laboratory intrepid log (2009). https://www.cs.huji.ac.il/labs/parallel/workload/l_anl_int/
7. Bashroush, R.: Data center and ICT energy consumption: a fact-check on "factchecking" (2020). https://www.linkedin.com/pulse/data-center-ict-energy-consumption-fact-check-rabih-bashroush
8. Christodoulou, P.: Soft actor-critic for discrete action settings. arXiv preprint arXiv:1910.07207 (2019)
9. Facebook: Facebook sustainability. https://sustainability.fb.com

10. Feitelson, D.: Workload modeling for performance evaluation, pp. 114–141, January 2002
11. Feitelson, D.: Resampling with feedback – a new paradigm of using workload data for performance evaluation (2021). https://youtu.be/JAvha-eM3G4
12. Gao, Y., Chen, L., Li, B.: Spotlight: optimizing device placement for training deep neural networks. In: Proceedings of the 35th International Conference on Machine Learning. In: Proceedings of Machine Learning Research (2018)
13. Goiri, I.N., Le, K., Nguyen, T.D., Guitart, J., Torres, J., Bianchini, R.: Greenhadoop: leveraging green energy in data-processing frameworks. In: Proceedings of the 7th ACM European Conference on Computer Systems, EuroSys 2012 (2012)
14. Google: We're sourcing clean energy for a better future. https://www.google.com/about/datacenters/renewable/
15. Haarnoja, T., Zhou, A., Abbeel, P., Levine, S.: Soft actor-critic: Off-policy maximum entropy deep reinforcement learning with a stochastic actor (2018)
16. Hindman, B., et al.: Mesos: a platform for fine-grained resource sharing in the data center. In: Proceedings of the 8th USENIX Conference on Networked Systems Design and Implementation, NSDI 2011 (2011)
17. Hu, Z., Tu, J., Li, B.: Spear: optimized dependency-aware task scheduling with deep reinforcement learning. In: 2019 IEEE 39th International Conference on Distributed Computing Systems (ICDCS) (2019)
18. Jain, T., Cooperman, G.: CRAC:: Checkpoint-restart architecture for CUDA with streams and UVM. In: Proceedings of the International Conference for High Performance Computing, Networking, Storage and Analysis, SC 2020, IEEE Press (2020)
19. Jee, C.: Deepmind's AI is predicting how much energy Google's wind turbines will produce (2019). https://www.technologyreview.com/2019/02/27/239459/deepmind-creates-algorithm-to-squeeze-more-out-of-wind-power/
20. Krioukov, A., et al.: Design and evaluation of an energy agile computing cluster. Technical Report, EECS Department, University of California, Berkeley (2012). http://www2.eecs.berkeley.edu/Pubs/TechRpts/2012/EECS-2012-13.html
21. Kumar, A., Fu, J., Soh, M., Tucker, G., Levine, S.: Stabilizing off-policy q-learning via bootstrapping error reduction. In: Advances in Neural Information Processing Systems, vol. 32 (2019)
22. Levine, S., Kumar, A., Tucker, G., Fu, J.: Offline reinforcement learning: tutorial, review, and perspectives on open problems. arXiv preprint arXiv:2005.01643 (2020)
23. Liu, X., Hua, Y., Liu, X., Yang, L., Sun, Y.: Smoother: a smooth renewable power-aware middleware. In: 2019 IEEE 39th International Conference on Distributed Computing Systems (ICDCS) (2019)
24. Muhammad Naveed Akhter, Saad Mekhilef, H.M.N.M.S.: Review on forecasting of photovoltaic power generation based on machine learning and meta heuristic techniques (2018). https://doi.org/10.1049/iet-rpg.2018.5649
25. Narayanan, D., Santhanam, K., Kazhamiaka, F., Phanishayee, A., Zaharia, M.: Heterogeneity-aware cluster scheduling policies for deep learning workloads. In: 14th USENIX Symposium on Operating Systems Design and Implementation (OSDI 20), pp. 481–498. USENIX Association, November 2020. https://www.usenix.org/conference/osdi20/presentation/narayanan-deepak
26. Ran, Y., Hu, H., Zhou, X., Wen, Y.: Deepee: joint optimization of job scheduling and cooling control for data center energy efficiency using deep reinforcement learning. In: 2019 IEEE 39th International Conference on Distributed Computing Systems (ICDCS) (2019)

27. Souza, A., Pelckmans, K., Tordsson, J.: A hpc co-scheduler with reinforcement learning. In: Klusáček, D., Cirne, W., Rodrigo, G.P. (eds.) Job Scheduling Strategies for Parallel Processing (2021)
28. Sun, Q., Ren, S., Wu, C., Li, Z.: An online incentive mechanism for emergency demand response in geo-distributed colocation data centers. In: Proceedings of the Seventh International Conference on Future Energy Systems. e-Energy 2016 (2016)
29. Terascale: https://terrascale.org
30. Tumanov, A., Zhu, T., Park, J.W., Kozuch, M.A., Harchol-Balter, M., Ganger, G.R.: Tetrisched: global rescheduling with adaptive plan-ahead in dynamic heterogeneous clusters. In: Proceedings of the Eleventh European Conference on Computer Systems (2016)
31. Venkataswamy, V., Grimshaw, A.: Scheduling in data centers running on renewable energy with deep reinforcement learning. In: 2nd workshop on Machine Learning for Computing Systems, hosted at SC 2020 (2020)
32. Wang, Z., et al.: Critic regularized regression. Adv. Neural Inf. Process. Syst. **33**, 7768–7778 (2020)
33. Xiao, W., et al.: Gandiva: introspective cluster scheduling for deep learning. In: 13th USENIX Symposium on Operating Systems Design and Implementation (OSDI 18) (2018)
34. Zhang, D., Dai, D., He, Y., Bao, F.S., Xie, B.: Rlscheduler: an automated HPC batch job scheduler using reinforcement learning. In: Proceedings of the International Conference for High Performance Computing, Networking, Storage and Analysis, SC 2020 (2020)

Dynamic Management of CPU Resources Towards Energy Efficient and Profitable Datacentre Operation

Christos Kalogirou(✉), Christos D. Antonopoulos, Spyros Lalis, and Nikolaos Bellas

University of Thessaly, Volos, Greece
{hrkalogi,cda,lalis,nbellas}@uth.gr

Abstract. Energy reduction has become a necessity for modern datacentres, with CPU being a key contributor to the energy consumption of nodes. Increasing the utilization of CPU resources on active nodes is a key step towards energy efficiency. However, this is a challenging undertaking, as the workload can vary significantly among the nodes and over time, exposing operators to the risk of overcommitting the CPU. In this paper, we explore the trade-off between energy efficiency and node overloads, to drive virtual machine (VM) consolidation in a cost-aware manner. We introduce a model that uses runtime information to estimate the target utilization of the nodes to control their load, identifying and considering correlated behavior among collocated workloads. Moreover, we introduce a VM allocation and node management policy that exploits the model to increase the profit of datacentre operators considering the trade-off between energy reduction and potential SLA violation costs. We evaluate our work through simulations using node profiles derived from real machines and workloads from real datacentre traces. The results show that our policy adapts the nodes' target utilization in a highly effective way, converging to a target utilization that is statically optimal for the workload at hand. Moreover, we show that our policy closely matches, or even outperforms two state-of-the-art policies that combine VM consolidation with VFS – the second one, also operating the CPU at reduced voltage margins – even when these are configured to use a static, workload- and architecture-specific target utilization derived through offline characterization of the workload.

Keywords: Energy efficiency · Dynamic CPU management · Dynamic VM consolidation · Cost-effective datacentre operation

1 Introduction

Modern datacentres have a significant energy footprint, which accounts for approximately 2%–3% of the worldwide energy consumption [9]. In fact, CPUs are responsible for up to 60% of the total energy consumption of compute

D. Klusáček et al. (Eds.): JSSPP 2022, LNCS 13592, pp. 131–151, 2023.
https://doi.org/10.1007/978-3-031-22698-4_7

nodes [8]. Therefore, optimizing the energy efficiency of these nodes is a first-class concern for both designers and operators of large-scale datacentres.

Techniques such as virtual machine (VM) consolidation [5,7] promote energy efficiency at the datacentre-level by creating opportunities to switch off nodes. The challenge is to balance between packing VMs to the nodes as densely as possible, and avoiding node overloads that will trigger Service Level Agreement (SLA) violation penalties. At the node-level, dynamic voltage and frequency scaling (VFS) [13], available on most modern processors, enables the dynamic, joint manipulation of CPU voltage (V) and frequency (f) to support potentially more power- and energy-efficient operating points, according to the characteristics of the workload. Our recent work in [15] goes a step further, exploiting CPU voltage guardbands to enable even more energy-efficient operation by configuring CPUs outside their normal (V, f) envelope, with only slightly increased crash probability (if managed carefully).

Dealing with this multi-parametric configuration and optimization space is far from trivial. Scheduling, configuration and resource management policies for the cloud often use static thresholds to drive their decisions [4,15] with node target utilization thresholds being a typical example. This popular approach has low design complexity, however (a) selection of the optimal static threshold requires *a priori* knowledge of the workload, which may not always be realistic, (b) it fails to capture inter-node variations of workload characteristics at any given time, (c) it fails to capture system-wide workload variations in time, and (d) the value of the optimal threshold is also sensitive to hardware characteristics and configuration.

In this paper, we tackle the aforementioned weaknesses with a policy which dynamically adapts target node utilization thresholds. This is achieved by analyzing the workload characteristics observed in the past and predicting short-term future behavior. Moreover, we quantify the correlation among collocated workloads on each node in order to identify a sweet-spot between high node utilization and risk of SLA violation penalties due to unexpected load increases, which may lead to node overloads. More specifically:

- We introduce a scalable, analytic and architecture-agnostic model to estimate target CPU utilization for individual nodes in a datacentre, exploiting knowledge on the past behaviour of the VMs scheduled on these nodes. These adaptive utilization targets favor high VM consolidation, while controlling the risk of node overloads.
- We find that, in order to achieve this dual goal, the policy needs to identify correlations between the CPU capacity requests of co-scheduled VMs and consider them when deciding on node utilization targets.
- The proposed method works fully online, without a priori knowledge regarding the workload of the datacentre, nor requiring any pre-training.
- We introduce an adaptive VM management and node configuration policy that exploits the aforementioned adaptive thresholds for VM consolidation, together with VFS and with CPU configuration at reduced voltage margins,

considering the cost of SLA violation penalties due to both node overloads and crashes (due to operation with reduced margins).
- We perform simulations to evaluate our approach using real datacentre workload traces and realistic node parameters ((V, f) steps, voltage margins, power consumption to the plug, failure probability) derived from real systems with two different processor architectures, an Intel Xeon E3-1120 v5, and an ARM-based Ampere Computing X-Gene 3.

To the best of our knowledge, this is the first work that combines per node target CPU utilization adaptivity with VFS and relaxed CPU voltage guardbands in a cost-centric approach, to increase the profit of cloud infrastructure providers exploring the trade-off between energy cost and potential SLA violation penalties. Our results show that our adaptive policy manages to always outperform two state-of-the-art policies using statically optimal target CPU utilization values derived via pre-characterization of the workload at hand on the respective architecture: (a) a policy that combines VM consolidation with VFS [3], and (b) a policy which also exploits reduced CPU voltage guardbands on top of VM consolidation and VFS [15].

2 Background

In this section, we briefly outline the notation and some basic assumptions used in our adaptive model introduced in Sect. 3. We use a notation and assumptions compatible to those in [15].

2.1 System Model

We assume a datacentre with nodes $n_i, 1 \leq i \leq N$. Each node has limited memory MEM_i. All nodes have the same CPU, which can operate at different nominal voltage-frequency points (V, f), where (V_{max}, f_{max}) offers maximum performance. For each nominal point, there is a reduced voltage configuration (V^r, f) with $V^r < V$, offering the same performance at lower power consumption. However, in this case the node may fail with probability $Pfail > 0$, whereas $Pfail = 0$ for nominal configurations. We assume crash failures, where the node stops working and all hosted VMs stop running. Modeling and tolerating silent data corruptions that might occur due to CPU undervolting is beyond the scope of this work.

Different jobs are submitted for execution, packaged as virtual machines $VM_m, 1 \leq m \leq M$ with formally declared resource requirements in respective SLAs. Let MEM_m^{SLA} be the required memory and $C_{m,f_{max}}^{SLA}$ be the CPU capacity at f_{max} for VM_m as per its SLA. Notably, when the CPU operates at $f < f_{max}$, the effective CPU capacity as per the SLA becomes $C_{m,f}^{SLA} \geq C_{m,f_{max}}^{SLA}$ (the increase depends on the sensitivity of the VM to frequency scaling).

We partition time into periods and assume that VMs arrive and terminate at their boundaries. Further, we divide each period in K timeslots of duration

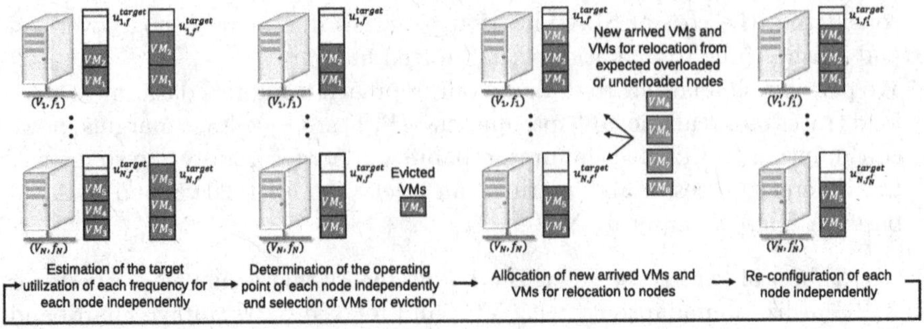

Fig. 1. Overview of the proposed approach.

$slotT$ (the total duration of a period is $prdT = K \times slotT$). Let $C^{req}_{m,f,p}$ be the actual CPU capacity requirements of VM_m for frequency f throughout period p. Note that $C^{req}_{m,f,p} \leq C^{SLA}_{m,f}$, i.e., in some periods the VM may not need the full CPU capacity as per its SLA.

Let $C^{alloc}_{m,f,p,k}$ be the CPU capacity at frequency f that is allocated to VM_m in the kth timeslot of p. If the host node is overloaded, the VM may get less capacity than needed, $C^{alloc}_{m,f,p,k} < C^{req}_{m,f,p}$. Furthermore, the restart of VM_m on a node in period p (due to an eviction from its old host) takes R_m time slots (linearly dependent contractually agreed memory footprint of VM_m) thus $C^{alloc}_{m,f,p,k} = 0, 1 \leq k \leq R_m$. We assume VMs to be stateless, therefore they can be restarted without needing elaborate migration. Also, if the host of VM_m crashes (due to operation with reduced voltage), $C^{alloc}_{m,f,p,k} = 0, 1 \leq k \leq K$ for all slots of the period.

2.2 VM Allocation Approach

When a period ends, the target utilization, VM allocation and operating point is decided for each node, so as to minimize the expected cost for the datacentre due to the node's energy consumption and SLA violation penalties – the latter apply in case of node overload as well as in case the VM remains unavailable because it is being restarted on another node or the host node crashes.

Our approach is divided in the following main steps, illustrated in Fig. 1. (1) We estimate the target node utilization for each CPU frequency based on the current VM allocation and load, in order to identify expected node overloads for each operating point and pick the VMs that need to be evicted from the node to avoid overload. (2) We select the best nominal operating point of each node considering the trade-off between the node's energy cost and SLA violation penalties due to restart of the evicted VMs on other nodes. (3) We allocate evicted VMs and newly arrived VMs to nodes, respecting the selected operating point and target utilization of each node. At this point, we consider activating additional nodes or deactivating underutilized nodes. (4) We re-configure each node considering the updated VM allocation, exploiting operation at reduced voltage margins for additional cost gains selecting the operating point in a cost-driven manner. Note that steps (1), (2) and (4) are performed using only local data of the node. Thus, the approach is scalable even for large datacentres.

3 Node-Level Estimations

We introduce a model that considers the trade-off between the energy cost and potential SLA violation penalties. In contrast with previous work [15], this model does not require in advance knowledge and characterization of the workload, but instead quantifies and adapts to workload characteristics at execution time. Moreover, it estimates the cost at the level of the entire system, even though scheduling decisions are taken at the node level. Hence, our approach is: (a) easily applicable in realistic settings, (b) scalable, and (c) cost-effective even for large datacentres. In this section we discuss in detail the estimation of the different costs involved, while in Sect. 4 we focus on the adaptation to workload characteristics.

3.1 Target CPU Utilization and VM Evictions

Each node n_i has a target CPU utilization $u_{i,f,p}^{target}$ for n_i in period p for CPU frequency f. This serves as a conservative upper bound for the CPU load to be assigned to the node, so as to avoid node overload in case some of the hosted VMs request more CPU capacity than expected. When the period ends, the target utilization is adjusted for the next period $p+1$ based on the current VM allocation and a tentative frequency f_i, possibly selecting some VMs for eviction to avoid overloads.

The tentative VM evictions are captured via matrix $Evct$, where $Evct[i, f_i, m, p+1] = 1$ if VM_m is to be evicted from n_i assuming operation at f_i in $p+1$, else 0. Similarly, we use $Rem[i, f_i, m, p+1]$ to encode whether VM_m will remain on n_i in $p+1$. This exploration is done for each of the supported CPU frequencies, in order to find the best option for n_i. Note that any VM allocation must respect the full memory requirements of each hosted VM, i.e., $\sum_{m=1}^{M} Rem[i, *, m, p+1] \times MEM_m^{SLA} \leq MEM_i$.

3.2 Load Estimation

We estimate the CPU requirements of each VM_m for frequency f in the next period $p+1$ as $\hat{C}_{m,f,p+1}^{req} = \overline{C}_{m,f,p}^{req}$, where $\overline{C}_{m,f,p}^{req}$ are the VM's mean CPU requirements over the past periods up to p adjusted to f.

Then, the estimated load for n_i assuming operation at f_i, based on the VMs that will remain on the node in the next period, is calculated as

$$\hat{load}_{i,f_i,p+1}^{rem} = \sum_{m=1}^{M} Rem[i, f_i, m, p+1] \times \hat{C}_{m,f_i,p+1}^{req} \quad (1)$$

We also estimate the load of each VM to be evicted from n_i and restarted on another node. However, we do not know the hosts of these VMs nor the respective CPU frequencies in the next period. As an approximation, we estimate the load of the evicted VMs for each supported frequency f as

$$\hat{load}^{vms}_{i,f_i,p+1,f} = \sum_{m=1}^{M} Evct[i, f_i, m, p+1] \times \hat{C}^{req}_{m,f,p+1} \tag{2}$$

And then we estimate the total load of the VMs to be evicted from n_i for the entire system, by weighing the above load for each frequency according to the nodes' operating frequencies during the previous period p

$$\hat{load}^{evct}_{i,f_i,p+1} = \sum_{f \in F} \frac{nodes_{f,p}}{nodes_p} \times \hat{load}^{vms}_{i,f_i,p+1,f} \tag{3}$$

where $nodes_{f,p}$ is the number of nodes that operated at f in p, and $nodes_p$ is the number of nodes that were active in p.

Thus, the total estimated VM load related to n_i (for the node and the system as a whole) assuming it will operate at f_i in the next period $p+1$, is

$$\hat{load}_{i,f_i,p+1} = \hat{load}^{rem}_{i,f_i,p+1} + \hat{load}^{evct}_{i,f_i,p+1} \tag{4}$$

3.3 Energy Cost Estimation

The estimated energy cost of each active node n_i that will host one or more VMs in the next period, assuming it will be configured to operate at (V_i,f_i), is calculated as

$$\hat{costE}^{rem}_{i,V_i,f_i,p+1} = P_{node}(V_i, f_i, \hat{u}_{i,f_i,p+1}) \times prdT \times price_{en} \tag{5}$$

$$P_{node}(V, f, u) = A + B \times f \times V^2 \times u \tag{6}$$

$$\hat{u}_{i,f_i,p+1} = min(\hat{load}^{rem}_{i,f_i,p+1}, 1) \tag{7}$$

where $price_{en}$ is the energy price and $\hat{u}_{i,f_i,p+1}$ is the estimated node utilization for the next period based on the estimated load as discussed in Sect. 3.2. Function $P_{node}(V, f, u)$ returns the node's power consumption when the CPU operates at (V,f) with utilization u, based on a linear power estimation model [15] where A and B are platform-specific constants for the node's static and dynamic power consumption, respectively.

The energy cost due to the load of the VMs that will be evicted from n_i is approximated as follows. First, the individual cost of each evicted VM_m if hosted on a node configured to operate at (V,f) is

$$\hat{costE}^{vm}_{i,m,f_i,V,f,p+1} = P_{vm}(V, f, \hat{C}^{req}_{m,f,p+1}) \times prdT \times price_{en} \tag{8}$$

$$P_{vm}(V, f, u) = \frac{u}{\overline{u}^{target}_{f_i,p}} \times A + B \times f \times V^2 \times u \tag{9}$$

In this case, the CPU utilization factor for the dynamic component of the power estimation function is set to the expected CPU load of VM_m in the next period $\hat{C}^{req}_{m,f,p+1}$. We also factor the static power consumption component with the ratio of that load to the mean target CPU utilization of all nodes configured to operate at f_i in the previous period p, let $\overline{u}^{target}_{f_i,p}$, as a proxy for the likelihood of that particular VM eviction leading to the activation of a new node in $p+1$.

Then, we estimate the total energy cost for the entire system of all VMs that will be evicted from n_i, as

$$\hat{costE}^{evct}_{i,V_i,f_i,p+1} = \sum_{(V,f)\in VF} \Big(\frac{nodes_{V,f,p}}{nodes_p} \times \sum_{m=1}^{M} Evct[i,f_i,m,p+1] \times \hat{costE}^{vm}_{i,m,f_i,V,f,p+1}\Big) \tag{10}$$

weighing the contribution of each operating point in the same spirit this done for the load estimation in Eq. 3.

Thus, the total estimated energy cost related to n_i (for the node and the system as a whole) assuming it will operate at (V_i,f_i) in the next period $p+1$ is

$$\hat{costE}_{i,V_i,f_i,p+1} = \hat{costE}^{rem}_{i,V_i,f_i,p+1} + \hat{costE}^{evct}_{i,V_i,f_i,p+1} \tag{11}$$

3.4 SLA Violation Cost Estimation

We estimate the CPU capacity $\hat{C}^{alloc}_{i,m,f_i,p+1,k}$ allocated to VM_m hosted on n_i in the kth timeslot of period $p+1$ as follows. If n_i $\hat{load}^{rem}_{i,f_i,p+1} \leq 1$ then $\hat{C}^{alloc}_{i,m,f_i,p+1,k} = \hat{C}^{req}_{i,m,f_i,p+1}$, else (if the node is overloaded) $\hat{C}^{alloc}_{i,m,f_i,p+1,k} < \hat{C}^{req}_{i,m,f_i,p+1}$ since the node's CPU capacity is divided among the VMs proportionally to their requirements (all VMs have the same priority). Also, $\hat{C}^{alloc}_{i,m,f_i,p+1,k} = 0$ in timeslots where VM_m is restarting as well as in all timeslots of the period if n_i crashes.

Whenever VM_m does not get the requested CPU capacity, the datacentre provider has to pay a penalty to the customer. We consider the *Percentage Price Refund* (*PPR*) model [11] where the penalty is a percentage of the VM price for the duration of the violation, depending on the percentage of the CPU capacity that was not allocated w.r.t. to the SLA requirements. More specifically, the expected violation cost for VM_m for the kth timeslot of period $p+1$ is

$$\hat{costV}^{vm}_{m,f_i,p+1,k} = \begin{cases} q_m \times \frac{C^{SLA}_{m,f_i} - \hat{C}^{alloc}_{m,f_i,p+1,k}}{C^{SLA}_{m,f_i}} \times price_m, \\ \text{if } \hat{C}^{alloc}_{m,f_i,p+1,k} < \hat{C}^{req}_{m,f_i,p+1} \\ 0, \text{if } \hat{C}^{alloc}_{m,f_i,p+1,k} = \hat{C}^{req}_{m,f_i,p+1} \end{cases} \tag{12}$$

where q_m reflects the severity of the violation and $price_m$ is the price charged for executing VM_m per timeslot.

We then calculate the total estimated SLA violation cost for n_i for the entire period $p+1$, as follows

$$\hat{costV}_{i,f_i,p+1} = \sum_{m=1}^{M}\sum_{k=1}^{K} Rem[i, f_i, m, p+1] \times \hat{costV}^{vm}_{m,f_i,p+1,k} \tag{13}$$

This equation captures node overloads and VM restarts during normal operation, let $\hat{costV}^{nofail}_{i,f_i,p+1}$, as well as the case where n_i crashes and does not run any VM, let $\hat{costV}^{fail}_{i,f_i,p+1}$.

3.5 Total Estimated Node Cost

Based on the above, the total estimated operational cost related to n_i (for the node and the system as a whole) assuming it will operate at (V_i,f_i) in the next period $p+1$ is

$$\begin{aligned} \hat{cost}_{i,V_i,f_i,p+1} = Pfail \times \hat{costV}^{fail}_{i,f_i,p+1} + \\ (1 - Pfail) \times (\hat{costE}_{i,V_i,f_i,p+1} + \hat{costV}^{nofail}_{i,f_i,p+1}) \end{aligned} \tag{14}$$

calculated by weighing the cost of normal node operation vs a node crash with the corresponding probabilities.

We assume that if a node fails it does so for an entire period during which it does not run any VMs and does not consume any energy.

4 Adaptive Target CPU Utilization

The target node utilization for the next period $u^{target}_{i,f,p+1}$ is set with some slack, so that the node can handle load beyond the estimated $\hat{C}^{req}_{i,f_i,p+1}$ without being overloaded. This is subject to an interesting trade-off: High utilization targets result in more energy-efficient hence also greener and lower cost operation. However, if future CPU requests of the VMs are underestimated and overshoot the CPU capacity of the node, SLA violations will occur, incurring penalties for the operator.

In addition, potential correlation between different collocated VMs further perplexes the estimation of a good CPU utilization target. Let $C^{ratio}_{m,p} = \frac{C^{req}_{m,f_{max},p}}{C^{SLA}_{m,f_{max}}}$ be the percentage of the CPU requirements of VM_m in period p with respect to the contractually promised CPU capacity, both at frequency f_{max}. Figure 2 illustrates the C^{ratio} of eight VMs from Google traces [19] over 10 periods. Each line corresponds to a different VM. One can identify clusters of VMs with similar, positively correlated $C^{ratio}_{m,p}$ variations (lines of the same color). Moreover, VMs in the blue and green cluster are characterized by a rapid increase of their requested CPU capacity at period 10, while the red cluster has the opposite trend to the blue one.

If decisions on target CPU utilization do not consider such phenomena, they are highly likely to lead to node overloads. On the one hand, the identification of positively correlated VMs should encourage more conservative values of target CPU utilization. On the other hand, the co-execution of anti-correlated VM clusters on the same node can protect against overloads due to dynamic workload changes: when one cluster increases its requests, its counterpart tends to decrease them, thus balancing the total load on the host node. This allows for more aggressive (higher) CPU utilization targets, and a more energy-efficient usage of the available resources.

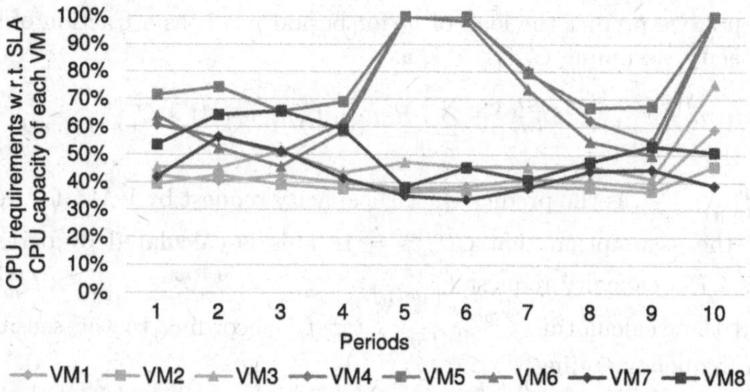

Fig. 2. CPU pressure of different VMs w.r.t their contractual (SLA) maximum CPU requirements, over consecutive periods.

To address the aforementioned challenges, at period boundaries we evaluate, separately for each node n_i, the past behavior of its assigned VMs and decide a new value for $u_{i,f,p+1}^{target}$ for the following period. The estimation process involves the following steps: (1) For every pair (VM_l, VM_m) of VMs on the node we quantify the Pearson correlation $corr_{(l,m),p}$ between the C^{ratio} of VM_l and VM_m during periods up to p. (2) We use linear regression to estimate the CPU capacity requests of every VM_m on the node, given the capacity requests of a different VM_l for the next period, according to $corr_{(l,m),p}$. (3) We pessimistically assume that on the next period a specific VM_l will request its maximum contractually agreed CPU capacity, i.e., $\hat{C}_{l,p+1}^{ratio} = 1$. Given this assumption and the correlations determined in step (2), we reach a conservative estimation of the respective total node load. (4) We repeat steps (2)–(3) using each VM on the node as the baseline for the estimation, and then use the highest (most pessimistic) load estimation for period $p+1$ to set the new target CPU utilization for the node. Below we provide more details about these steps.

In step (2) we first apply linear regression, as modelled by Eq. 15, to predict the C^{ratio} of VM_m in period $p+1$ assuming we know the C^{ratio} of VM_l on the same period:

$$\hat{C}_{(m|l),p+1}^{ratio} = \alpha_{(m|l),p} \times \hat{C}_{l,p+1}^{ratio} + \beta_{(m|l),p} + \epsilon_{(m|l),p} \quad (15)$$

where $\alpha_{(m|l),p}$ is the slope of the regression line, $\beta_{(m|l),p}$ is the intercept, and $\epsilon_{(m|l),p}$ is the error of the prediction. We calculate $\alpha_{(m|l),p} = corr_{(m,l),p} \times \frac{std_{m,p}}{std_{l,p}}$, where $std_{l,p}$ and $std_{m,p}$ are the standard deviations of the C^{ratio} of VM_l and VM_m respectively, over past periods up to p. To derive $\beta_{(m|l),p}$, we first calculate the mean C^{ratio} of VM_m and VM_l up to period p, let $\overline{C}^{ratio}_{m,p}$ and $\overline{C}^{ratio}_{l,p}$, respectively. Then, we set $\epsilon_{(m|l),p} = 0$ and solve Eq. 15 for $\beta_{(m|l),p}$, using $\overline{C}^{ratio}_{m,p}$ and $\overline{C}^{ratio}_{l,p}$ in place of $\hat{C}^{ratio}_{(m|l),p+1}$ and $\hat{C}^{ratio}_{l,p+1}$. Finally, since our goal is to avoid node overloads, we conservatively set $\epsilon_{(m|l),p}$ to the maximum absolute error between the predicted values of our model and the observed real values over past periods.

In step 3, we predict the load of n_i for period $p+1$, as a fraction of its total CPU capacity, assuming $\hat{C}^{ratio}_{l,p+1} = 1$, as

$$\hat{load}^{pre}_{i,l,f_i,p+1} = C^{SLA}_{l,f_i} + \sum_{m \neq l} Rem[i, f_i, m, p+1] \times \hat{C}^{pre}_{(m|l),f_i,p+1} \tag{16}$$

where $\hat{C}^{pre}_{(m|l),f_i,p+1}$ is the predicted CPU capacity request by VM_m for frequency f_i under the assumption that $\hat{C}^{ratio}_{l,p+1} = 1$. This is calculated by deriving the predicted CPU capacity request $\hat{C}^{pre}_{(m|l),f_{max},p+1} = \hat{C}^{ratio}_{(m|l),f_{max},p+1} \times C^{SLA}_{m,f_{max}}$ at f_{max} and then calculating $\hat{C}^{pre}_{(m|l),f_i,p+1}$ for f_i (according to the sensitivity of VM_m to frequency scaling).

Finally, in step 4, after performing the above for each VM hosted on n_i, we determine the highest (most pessimistic) load across all scenarios, let $\hat{load}^{max}_{i,f_i,p+1}$. We then use this value to set the new target CPU utilization for n_i at f_i in $p+1$:

$$u^{target}_{i,f_i,p+1} = u^{target}_{i,f_i,p} \times \left(1 + \frac{1 - \hat{load}^{max}_{i,f_i,p+1}}{\hat{load}^{max}_{i,f_i,p+1}}\right) = \frac{u^{target}_{i,f_i,p}}{\hat{load}^{max}_{i,f_i,p+1}} \tag{17}$$

where we adjust the previous target based on the relative slack $\frac{1-\hat{load}^{max}_{i,f_i,p+1}}{\hat{load}^{max}_{i,f_i,p+1}}$ between the most pessimistic load and full node utilization, asymptotically pushing the maximum expected CPU requests on the node close to (yet lower than) full utilization. A negative slack indicates that the node is at risk for an overload, thus the target utilization is lowered. If, on the other hand, the slack is positive, there is CPU capacity available for hosting more VMs, and the target utilization is increased. As an exception, if $u^{target}_{i,f_i,p+1} > \hat{load}^{max}_{i,f_i,p+1}$, we set $u^{target}_{i,f_i,p+1} = u^{target}_{i,f_i,p}$. This guards against the corner-case of having enough spare CPU capacity on n_i just because it did not host "enough" VMs in p, as in this case a further increase of the target utilization would introduce the risk of excessive arrival of additional VMs on n_i, leading to an overload.

5 VM Allocation and Node Configuration Policy

In this section, we introduce Adaptive Target Utilization and Configuration (*ATUC*), a VM allocation policy which dynamically adjusts the target utilization and configuration of each node to increase the profit of datacentre providers.

The optimization target is to minimize the predicted cost-to-load ratio of each node for the next period

$$\hat{CL}^{ratio}_{i,V_i,f_i,p+1} = \frac{\hat{cost}_{i,V_i,f_i,p+1}}{\hat{load}_{i,f_i,p+1}} \tag{18}$$

where the nominator and denominator of the fraction comes from Eq. 14 and Eq. 4, respectively. Note that this involves only local information, as discussed in Sect. 3.2, Sect. 3.3 and Sect. 3.4.

Algorithm 1. Selection of nominal operating point (V_i',f_i') and evicted VMs for n_i in the next period $p+1$.

Input: $vmsHost_{i,p}$, $u^{target}_{i,*,p+1}$
Output: (V_i', f_i'), $vmsEvct_{i,p+1}$

$minCLRatio \leftarrow \infty$
for each nominal (V_i, f_i) and $u^{target}_{i,f_i,p+1}$ **do**
  $Rem[i, f_i, m, p+1] \leftarrow 1, \forall m \in vmsHost_{i,p}$
  $Evct[i, f_i, m, p+1] \leftarrow 0, \forall m \in vmsHost_{i,p}$
  $\hat{load}^{rem}_{i,f_i,p+1} \leftarrow$ calculate based on Equation 1
  while $\hat{load}^{rem}_{i,f_i,p+1} > u^{target}_{i,f_i,p+1}$ **do**
    $minRestartCost \leftarrow \infty$
    for each $m : Rem[i, f_i, m, p+1] = 1$ **do**
      $vmRestartCost \leftarrow \sum_{k=1}^{R_m} \hat{costV}^{vm}_{m,f_i,p+1,k}$
      if $vmRestarCost < minRestartCost$ **then**
        $minRestartCost \leftarrow vmRestartCost$
        $vmEvct \leftarrow m$
      end if
    end for
    $Rem[i, f_i, vmEvct, p+1] \leftarrow 0$
    $Evct[i, f_i, vmEvct, p+1] \leftarrow 1$
    $\hat{load}^{rem}_{i,f_i,p+1} \leftarrow$ calculate based on Equation 1
  end while
  $\hat{CL}^{ratio}_{i,V_i,f_i,p+1} \leftarrow$ calculate based on Equation 18
  if $\hat{CL}^{ratio}_{i,V_i,f_i,p+1} < minCLRatio$ **then**
    $minCLRatio \leftarrow \hat{CL}^{ratio}_{i,V_i,f_i,p+1}$
    $(V_i', f_i') \leftarrow (V_i, f_i)$
  end if
end for
$vmsEvct_{i,p+1} \leftarrow \{m : Evct[i, f_i', m, p+1] = 1\}$

The *ATUC* policy consists of the following main steps:

1) Estimation of target CPU utilization for each frequency: We use the methodology discussed in Sect. 4 to estimate the new target utilization for each node independently. More specifically, we estimate $u_{i,f_i,p+1}^{target}$ for the next period $p+1$, for each node n_i and for each supported CPU frequency step f_i.

2) Cost-driven node configuration and VM eviction: Given $u_{i,f_i,p+1}^{target}$ for each f_i, we select the best operating point for each node n_i independently in $p+1$ and the VMs to be evicted in this case. At this point, we focus on VM (re)assignment and only consider nominal operating points ($Pfail = 0$). The decision whether to configure the node to operate at reduced voltage margins (where $Pfail > 0$) is taken in the last step of the policy.

The high-level logic of this step is given in Algorithm 1 (while some values can be calculated incrementally, we refer to the previously introduced equations for more clarity). The algorithm takes as input the VMs hosted on n_i in the previous period p, and the node utilization targets for each CPU frequency in the next period $p+1$, and produces as output the nominal operating point and the VMs to be evicted from n_i for that period. The logic is briefly as follows. For each nominal CPU operating point, starting from the previous VM allocation (lines 3–4) and the corresponding estimated load (line 5), the VMs with the smallest SLA violation cost due to restart on another node (lines 7–14) are tentatively selected for eviction (lines 15–16) and the expected node load is recalculated (line 17), until the load does not exceed the target utilization. Note that the evicted VMs are assumed to be hosted on a non-overloaded node (the cost only comes from the time slots needed to restart the VM). Then, the operating point in question is preferred if the respective cost-to-load ratio is better than the one of the current selection (19–22). The final (best) selection results after performing this check for all nominal operating points.

3) Assignment of unallocated VMs to nodes and switch-off of underutilized nodes: At this point there are two types of unallocated VMs that need to be assigned to nodes: the VMs selected for eviction in the previous step and newly arrived VMs (if any). In a first step, we use the approach in [15] (best fit decreasing allocation) to assign unallocated VMs to nodes. In a second step, we adopt the technique in [5] to identify severely underutilized nodes and switch them off, by relocating the VMs accommodated on them (as above).

4) Cost-driven re-configuration of nodes at a nominal or reduced voltage margins operating points: Finally, based on the new VM allocation, the CPU of each node is configured to the most cost-effective operating point. This is done by examining all (V, f) configurations that do not violate the target utilization, and selecting the one that minimizes the respective cost-to-load ratio for each node independently according to Eq. 18. In this step, reduced voltage configurations are considered as well, taking into account the probability of node crash and the respective SLA violation costs as per Eq. 14.

6 Experimental Evaluation

In this section, we evaluate the *ATUC* policy via simulations. For these experiments, we use real-world traces and hardware parameters derived from real

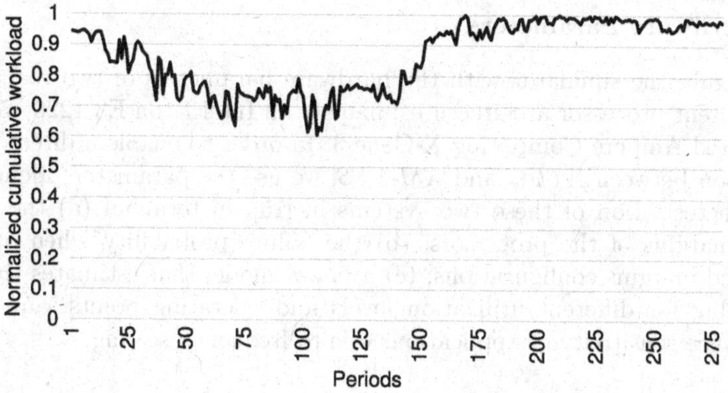

Fig. 3. Cumulative CPU load (normalized w.r.t the maximum cumulative CPU load) variation in time (across different periods).

platforms. We also compare *ATUC* against *LrMmt* [3], which combines VM consolidation with VFS, and *XM-VFS* [15], which exploits configuration of reduced CPU voltage margins on top of these two techniques. Both these policies use a static target CPU utilization value, which is derived by offline characterization of the workload and the platform architecture at hand.

6.1 Experimental Setup

For our simulations, we use the CloudSim toolkit [6], a popular framework for evaluating cloud policies, which already supports mechanisms such as VM consolidation and configurable node hardware parameters. We extend CloudSim to implement our system model (Sect. 3) and the *ATUC* policy (Sect. 5), including target utilization adaptivity at the node granularity (Sect. 4).

We use real values for the energy price [2] (\$0.14 per KWh) and the range price of the VMs [1] (\$0.0062 – \$0.896 per hour). Our simulated workload consists of 10,000 VMs from Google traces [19], for a period of one day. Figure 3 illustrates the cumulative CPU load for this workload for each period (the values are normalized to the maximum cumulative CPU load during the simulated period). This dataset combines different interesting characteristics. During the first half of the day, it is characterized by a low frequency CPU load variation, combined with significant high frequency fluctuations. On the second half, the cumulative load does not vary (however the CPU requests of individual jobs still follow different, varying patterns — not visible in the figure). The mean cumulative normalized CPU load is 0.86, with a standard deviation of 0.12.

We assume the policy is invoked every 300 s (we select the same scheduling period as in [3], which is also the default for CloudSim). The execution time of the policy is negligible, particularly considering that job scheduling in large scale cloud systems is performed at orders of magnitude lower frequency compared with the OS scheduling frequency on individual nodes.

6.2 Hardware Parameters

We configure the simulator with the hardware parameters of two real systems with different processor architectures, namely an Intel Xeon E3-1220 v5 and an ARM-based Ampere Computing X-Gene 3. In order to enable a direct and fair comparison between *ATUC* and *XM-VFS*, we use the parameters identified by the characterization of these two systems in [15], in terms of (a) the reduced voltage margins of the processors, (b) the failure probability when operating at reduced margins configurations, (c) a power model that estimates the power at the plug for different utilization levels and operating points, and (d) the performance sensitivity of applications due to frequency scaling.

Table 1. Intel Xeon E3-1220 v5 and ARM-based ampere computing X-Gene 3 operating points.

Intel platform			ARM platform		
Frequency (GHz)	Nominal Voltage (mV)	Reduced Voltage (mV)	Frequency (GHz) (mV)	Nominal Voltage (mV)	Reduced Voltage (mV)
2.0	850	666	0.4	880	790
2.5	922	741	1.3	880	790
3.0	1075	865	2.2	880	830
3.3	1147	929	3.0	880	840

More specifically, Table 1 gives the parameters of the (V, f) pairs (nominal and reduced margins) used for the Intel and the ARM platforms. The failure probability for a scheduling period of 300 seconds, when the processors operate at reduced voltage margins configurations, is $Pfail = 0.000579$. As in [15], we assume crash failures (no silent data corruptions). Also, when the CPU is at nominal conditions, it operates with a negligible failure probability. Power at the plug, is calculated using linear model $A + B * V^2 * f * u$, where A and B are platform-specific constants of the model, V is the voltage, f is the frequency and u is the utilization of the processor. For the Intel platform $A = 34.01$ and $B = 18.98$, whereas for the ARM platform $A = 52.48$ and $B = 34.38$ [15].

6.3 Threshold and Cost Convergence

ATUC adjusts the target utilization of each node independently, adapts VM allocation to nodes, and hardware configuration according to the dynamic workload requirements, in order to minimize the cost for the operator. It is important for *ATUC* to be resilient to sub-optimal initial values of the target utilization (u^{target}), as historical data of VM behavior are not available during the first periods of the simulations.

Figure 4 presents $\overline{u^{target}}$ (the mean target utilization of the nodes) for each period for different initial u^{target} values (different solid lines). The dashed lines

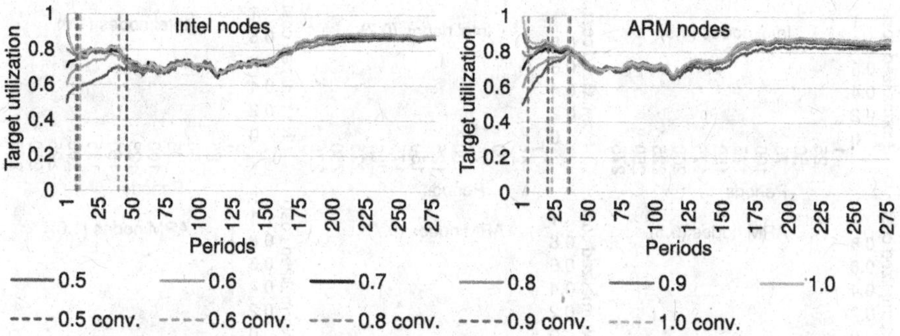

Fig. 4. $\overline{u^{target}}$ per period for different initial values of u^{target} $(0.5 - 1.0)$.

mark (for the initial u^{target} with the same color) the time of convergence with the $\overline{u^{target}}$ timeseries for an initial target utilization of 0.7. We select 0.7 as the baseline for the convergence study as it is roughly in the middle of the range of evaluated initial target utilization values.

We observe that *ATUC* is resilient to the "sub-optimal" choice of the initial value of u^{target}, as it eventually converges to similar $\overline{u^{target}}$ values in all cases. However, the convergence time depends on that initial value. Lower initial values (0.5 and 0.6) converge later, as *ATUC* is conservative when increasing the target utilization, in order to avoid node overloads. For example, recovering from a low initial u^{target} of 0.5 requires 46 and 36 periods for the Intel and ARM platform, respectively. On the other hand, the convergence from higher initial values of u^{target} (0.8, 0.9 and 1.0) is quick, as *ATUC* decreases the target utilization rapidly when at risk for node overloads. As an example, $\overline{u^{target}}$ estimations reached with initial $u^{target} = 1.0$ and 0.7 (baseline) converge within just 11 and 23 periods for the Intel and ARM nodes, respectively. Overall, *ATUC* adjusts the target utilization within the ranges of 0.64 - 0.89 and 0.64 - 0.88 for the Intel and the ARM, respectively.

Apart from the resilience of $\overline{u^{target}}$ estimates to the initial value, we also study the cost breakdown per period for different initial u^{target} values to evaluate the cost of convergence. We perform experiments for low (0.5), high (1.0) and the baseline (0.7) initial values for u^{target}. Figure 5 illustrates the results, where the green, yellow, blue and red areas represent the cost of energy, and the cost of SLA violations due to VM relocation, node overloads and node crashes, respectively. All costs have been normalized, for each of the two architectures (Intel and ARM), w.r.t. the total cost during the first period of execution with an initial $u^{target} = 0.5$. Similarly to the previous figure, for the experiments with initial $u^{target} = 0.5$ and 1.0 we use vertical dashed lines to illustrate the convergence time of the target utilization timeseries w.r.t to that for 0.7.

As expected, the case of an initial u^{target} of 0.5 introduces a higher cost (dominated by the energy cost) for both platforms, compared with the other two cases (0.7 and 1.0) for the periods before convergence of the target utilization, as the

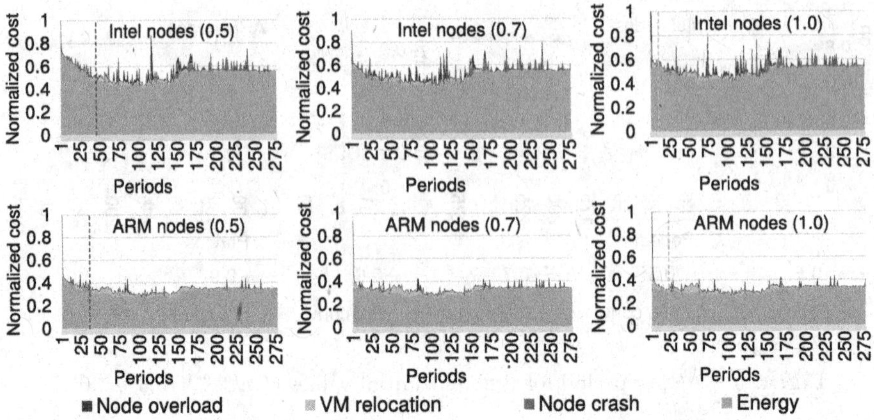

Fig. 5. Normalized cost per period for initial values of target utilization of 0.5, 0.7 and 1.0.

resulting low adaptive target utilization leads to the activation of more nodes. On the other hand, although a high u^{target} (1.0) achieves the lowest energy cost at the first periods, the total cost is higher due to node overloading. However, once convergence is reached, we observe that the energy cost pattern is similar, irrespective of the initial u^{target} selection. More specifically, after convergence, the relative energy cost difference between algorithm invocations with initial estimates 0.5 and 1.0, and the invocation with 0.7 is in the order of 1.76% and 1.55% respectively for the Intel platform. The respective relative energy cost differences for the ARM platform are 2.3% and 1.65%. In conclusion, *ATUC* manages to recover from sub-optimal initial values of the target utilization, asymptotically introducing similar energy cost per period, irrespective of the value of target utilization used for the initialization of the adaptive estimation algorithm. In the next section, we focus on the total cost, also including SLA violation penalties.

6.4 *ATUC* Total Cost of Operation

As we discussed in Sect. 6.3, *ATUC* manages to recover from sub-optimal initial values of u^{target} achieving, after convergence, a low relative energy cost difference w.r.t. the baseline initial u^{target} case. In this section, we evaluate the effectiveness of *ATUC* regarding the total cost, also including the periods of sub-optimal operation until convergence. Figure 6 illustrates the results. Similarly to Sect. 6.3, we itemize the cost as energy cost and SLA violation penalty cost (node crash, VM relocation, node overload). For each architecture, cost is normalized w.r.t. the cost achieved by setting the initial value of $u^{target} = 0.7$.

We observe that a low initial value (0.5) results in the highest cost, for both platforms. This is expected, as in this case *ATUC* (i) requires the longest time to recover from this sub-optimal initial target utilization value, and (ii) during this time the estimated target CPU utilization of nodes remains lower than needed to

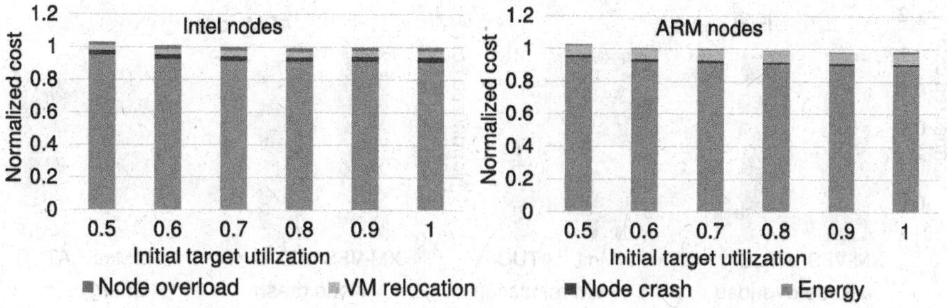

Fig. 6. Normalized (total) cost for different initial values of u^{target}.

achieve overload-safe operation for the architecture and workload at hand, hence the policy activates a higher number of nodes, which consume more energy. However, even in this case the total cost is only 2.98% and 2.46% higher compared with the baseline initial value for the Intel and ARM nodes, respectively. For all other initial values, we observe that the cost is similar, for both platforms. These results confirm that *ATUC* manages to recover not only quickly but also cost-effectively from adverse values for the initial setting of u^{target}.

6.5 Comparison of *ATUC* with State-of-the-Art Policies

In this section, we compare *ATUC* with *XM-VFS* and *LrMmt* in terms of energy and cost efficiency. The statically optimal target CPU utilization threshold is a function of the workload and the performance elasticity of the architecture along different (V, f) operating points. Work in [15] has experimentally confirmed this; after brute-force evaluation of different target utilization thresholds, it was determined that both *XM-VFS* and *LrMmt* introduce the minimum cost at the essentially the same target CPU utilization threshold, which is equal to 0.8 on Intel nodes and 0.7 on ARM nodes. In this work, we focus on evaluating whether *ATUC* can match the efficiency of these policies, which need in advance characterization of the workload to derive the optimal static target utilization (which is quite unrealistic for several real-world settings). The performance of these policies is highly dependent on the quantification of an appropriate static target utilization for the specific workload at hand. If the workload is not characterized in advance, or if it is characterized on a non-representative sample, performance is significantly penalized, even for small deviations of the target node utilization from the statically optimal value. For example for the workload in our evaluation, *XM-VFS* may introduce 14.65% higher cost on Intel nodes for a static target utilization of 0.65 (instead of the optimal 0.8).

Thanks to the effective adaptation employed by *ATUC*, the initial u^{target} value does not significantly affect cost (Sect. 6.4), therefore we set it at 0.7 for all these experiments. Figure 7 presents the results of the comparison between *ATUC* and the two state-of-the-art policies for the Intel and ARM platforms. Once again, we itemize the cost incurred due to energy consumption and the

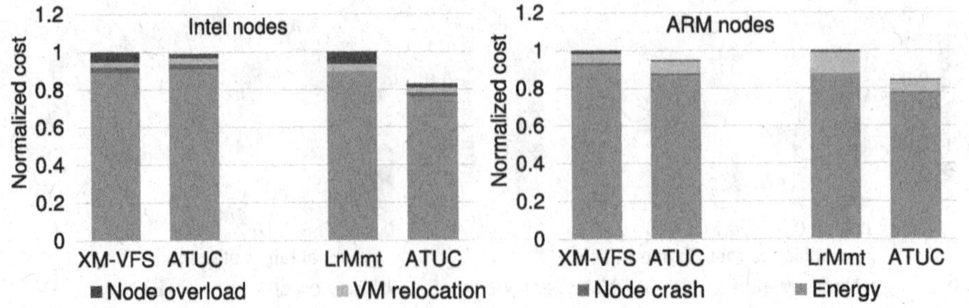

Fig. 7. Cost comparison of *ATUC* with *LrMmt* and *XM-VFS*.

different sources of SLA violation penalties. All costs are normalized w.r.t. the total cost of the policy we compare against on the corresponding platform.

We observe that *ATUC* is not inferior to policies requiring in advance knowledge of workload characteristics. Instead, it manages to outperform them in all cases, even compared with *XM-VFS* which also exploits reduced CPU voltage margins.

Specifically, with *ATUC* the percentage of penalty cost due to node overloads over the total cost is 2.27% for Intel and 0.51% for ARM nodes on average. The respective contribution of overload penalty to the total cost is higher for both the other policies: with *XM-VFS* it accounts for 5.41% (Intel) and 1.67% (ARM) of the total cost, whereas with *LrMmt* for 6.39% (Intel) and 0.85% (ARM).

ATUC reduces the SLA violation penalties due to overloads at the expense of a slightly higher energy cost compared against *XM-VFS* for the Intel platform, however, still achieving 0.85% cost gains against a policy that uses an optimal static target utilization for the current workload. In the case of the ARM platform, beyond reducing SLA penalties due to overloads, *ATUC* also achieves energy gains over *XM-VFS*, resulting in 5.1% net cost gains. Moreover, *ATUC* manages to reduce the cost of crashes (red area) by 19.65% and 29.52% compared with *XM-VFS* for the Intel and ARM platform, respectively.

Comparing *ATUC* with *LrMmt*, we observe that *ATUC*, beyond reducing SLA violation costs due to node overloading, it also reduces the penalties due to VM relocations managing to adapt to the dynamic workload requirements. There are also energy gains against *LrMmt*, however, given that — unlike *ATUC* and *XM-VFS* — *LrMmt* does not exploit configuration at reduced margins, these energy gains come mainly from operation at reduced margins. The cost gains of *ATUC* against *LrMmt* are 17.06% for the Intel and 15.61% for the ARM nodes.

In summary *ATUC*, with zero-knowledge of the workload, manages to dynamically identify favorable points in the energy reduction vs. SLA penalties tradeoff, thus outperforming *XM-VFS* and *LrMmt*, which use a statistically optimal target utilization, obtained via offline pre-characterization of the workload. The effective, adaptive estimation of the target CPU utilization is a key contributor towards the gains achieved by *ATUC*. In turn, a key feature of the estimation process is quantifying and considering the correlation between collocated workloads. If this correlation is overlooked, the operating cost achieved by *ATUC* is 24.52% higher due to the larger number of node overloads.

7 Related Work

Making educated decisions on the trade-off between energy cost and potential SLA violation penalties is a challenging, yet necessary undertaking towards cost reduction for cloud infrastructure providers. VM consolidation is a commonly used technique that tries to consolidate VMs to fewer nodes (without triggering SLA violations) to create opportunities to switch nodes off. The authors in [12,17] propose heuristics to increase the energy gains when applying VM consolidation.

Handling the aforementioned trade-off is further complicated by the dynamic variations of typical cloud workloads, which – if not guarded-against through overallocation of resources – may affect the quality of service (QoS) received by the end-users, increasing the SLA violation cost. The work in [10] uses Reinforcement Learning (RL) to adapt to a dynamic environment, while reducing the energy consumption and preserving the performance of the system. Work in [22] introduces an adaptive, multi-threshold framework to categorize the nodes according to their load to drive VM management considering both energy consumption and SLA violations. Authors in [14] discuss an approach to satisfy the maximum response time requirements in multi-tier applications for Cloud, detecting and resolving bottlenecks and predicting the optimal configuration. The study in [20] uses fuzzy logic to estimate a lower and upper utilization threshold of the nodes, which is used to characterize nodes as underloaded or overloaded, and to optimize the VM placement in order to reduce energy consumption and SLA violation penalties. The authors in [5] deal with the dynamic resource requirements of VMs, proposing heuristics for VM allocation and methods for estimating a target utilization threshold for the nodes. Authors in [21] deal with the dynamic workload problem, proposing two regression-based algorithms to estimate the upper utilization threshold of the nodes and detect overloads, combined with an algorithm that selects VMs from overloaded nodes, minimizing the VM migration time. In contrast with [5] and [21], our policy – apart from detecting node overloads – considers the target utilization of the nodes for the mapping of VMs to nodes, both for new VMs and for relocated ones. Moreover, unlike policies in [5] and [21], *ATUC* does not employ arbitrary safety parameters, which directly affect the energy vs. SLA penalty costs trade-off.

Apart from VM consolidation, works that combine VM management with DVFS can exploit opportunities for additional energy gains, as DVFS allows processors to operate at more power-efficient states. The work in [16] discusses the importance of combining VM consolidation with DVFS in datacentres. The study in [18] introduces an algorithm that employs an adaptive threshold estimation to improve the performance through task replication, while saving energy through DVS. Authors in [3] extend the policies in [5]. They combine VM consolidation with DVFS, and achieve significant energy gains compared with [5]. Our previous work in [15] combines VM consolidation and DVFS with CPU configuration at reduced voltage margins, aggressively reducing energy at the expense of an increased probability of crashes. However, similarly to *LrMmt*, the best performing policy in [3], they exploit a static CPU utilization target estimated through offline workload characterization. Our work combines adaptivity, VM consolidation, DVFS and CPU operation at reduced margins in a cost-driven profit maximization approach. It also exploits online analysis of past VM behavior, rather than offline pre-characterization, to reduce the risk of costly, hard to predict and mitigate node overloads.

8 Conclusions

In this paper, we introduced an adaptive VM scheduling and node configuration policy (*ATUC*). Our policy identifies profitable points in the multiparametric space of VM-node mappings and node CPU configurations, using exclusively information collected at execution time. We combine a scalable, architecture-agnostic, statistical model that estimates a target CPU utilization for each node independently, considering VM allocations to the node and runtime information on past CPU usage of the VMs, with VM consolidation, VFS and CPU operation at reduced voltage margins. We evaluated our approach through simulations, using real datacentre workload traces and hardware parameters derived from real Intel- and ARM-based systems. We found that *ATUC* outperforms, in all cases, two state-of-the-art policies (*XM-VFS* and *LrMmt*) that assume *a priori* workload knowledge and use offline characterization to derive an optimal static target utilization for the workload at hand.

References

1. Amazon EC2 pricing. https://aws.amazon.com/ec2/pricing/
2. Eletric Power Monthly. https://www.eia.gov/electricity/monthly/
3. Arroba, P., Moya, J.M., Ayala, J.L., Buyya, R.: Dynamic Voltage and Frequency Scaling-aware dynamic consolidation of virtual machines for energy efficient cloud data centers. Concurrency Comput. Pract. Experience **29**(10), e4067 (2017)
4. Beloglazov, A., Abawajy, J., Buyya, R.: Energy-aware resource allocation heuristics for efficient management of data centers for cloud computing. Future Gener. Comput. Syst. **28**(5), 755–768 (2012)
5. Beloglazov, A., Buyya, R.: Optimal online deterministic algorithms and adaptive heuristics for energy and performance efficient dynamic consolidation of virtual machines in cloud data centers. Concurrency Comput. Pract. Experience **24**(13), 1397–1420 (2012)
6. Calheiros, R.N., Ranjan, R., Beloglazov, A., De Rose, C.A., Buyya, R.: CloudSim: a toolkit for modeling and simulation of cloud computing environments and evaluation of resource provisioning algorithms. Softw. Pract. Exp. **41**(1), 23–50 (2011)
7. Cao, Z., Dong, S.: An energy-aware heuristic framework for virtual machine consolidation in cloud computing. J. Supercomput. **69**(1), 429–451 (2014)
8. Dayarathna, M., Wen, Y., Fan, R.: Data center energy consumption modeling: a survey. IEEE Commun. Surv. Tutorials **18**(1), 732–794 (2016)

9. Engbers, N., Taen, E.: Green Data Net. Report to IT Room INFRA. European Commission. FP7 ICT 2013.6.2;2014 (2016)
10. Farahnakian, F., Liljeberg, P., Plosila, J.: Energy-efficient virtual machines consolidation in cloud data centers using reinforcement learning. In: 2014 22nd Euromicro International Conference on Parallel, Distributed, and Network-Based Processing, pp. 500–507, February 2014. https://doi.org/10.1109/PDP.2014.109
11. Garg, S.K., Gopalaiyengar, S.K., Buyya, R.: SLA-based resource provisioning for heterogeneous workloads in a virtualized cloud datacenter. In: Xiang, Y., Cuzzocrea, A., Hobbs, M., Zhou, W. (eds.) ICA3PP 2011. LNCS, vol. 7016, pp. 371–384. Springer, Heidelberg (2011). https://doi.org/10.1007/978-3-642-24650-0_32
12. Ghribi, C., Hadji, M., Zeghlache, D.: Energy efficient VM scheduling for cloud data centers: exact allocation and migration algorithms. In: 2013 13th IEEE/ACM International Symposium on Cluster, Cloud, and Grid Computing, pp. 671–678, May 2013. https://doi.org/10.1109/CCGrid.2013.89
13. Herbert, S., Marculescu, D.: Analysis of dynamic voltage/frequency scaling in chip-multiprocessors. In: 2007 ACM/IEEE International Symposium on Low Power Electronics and Design (ISLPED), pp. 38–43, August 2007. https://doi.org/10.1145/1283780.1283790
14. Iqbal, W., Dailey, M.N., Carrera, D., Janecek, P.: Adaptive resource provisioning for read intensive multi-tier applications in the cloud. Future Gener. Comput. Syst. **27**(6), 871–879 (2011)
15. Kalogirou, C., et al.: Exploiting CPU voltage margins to increase the profit of cloud infrastructure providers. In: 2019 19th IEEE/ACM International Symposium on Cluster, Cloud and Grid Computing (CCGRID), pp. 302–311. IEEE (2019)
16. von Laszewski, G., Wang, L., Younge, A.J., He, X.: Power-aware scheduling of virtual machines in DVFS-enabled clusters. In: 2009 IEEE International Conference on Cluster Computing and Workshops, pp. 1–10, August 2009. https://doi.org/10.1109/CLUSTR.2009.5289182
17. Lee, Y.C., Zomaya, A.Y.: Energy efficient utilization of resources in cloud computing systems. J. Supercomput. **60**(2), 268–280 (2012)
18. Liu, W., Du, W., Chen, J., Wang, W., Zeng, G.: Adaptive energy-efficient scheduling algorithm for parallel tasks on homogeneous clusters. J. Netw. Comput. Appl. **41**, 101–113 (2014)
19. Reiss, C., Wilkes, J., Hellerstein, J.L.: Google cluster-usage traces: format + schema. Technical report, Google Inc., Mountain View, CA, USA, November 2011. revised 2014-11-17 for version 2.1. Posted at https://github.com/google/cluster-data
20. Salimian, L., Esfahani, F.S., Nadimi-Shahraki, M.H.: An adaptive fuzzy threshold-based approach for energy and performance efficient consolidation of virtual machines. Computing **98**(6), 641–660 (2016)
21. Yadav, R., Zhang, W., Kaiwartya, O., Singh, P.R., Elgendy, I.A., Tian, Y.C.: Adaptive energy-aware algorithms for minimizing energy consumption and SLA violation in cloud computing. IEEE Access **6**, 55923–55936 (2018)
22. Zhou, Z., et al.: Minimizing SLA violation and power consumption in Cloud data centers using adaptive energy-aware algorithms. Future Gener. Comput. Syst. **86**, 836–850 (2018)

Optimization of Execution Parameters of Moldable Ultrasound Workflows Under Incomplete Performance Data

Marta Jaros(✉) and Jiri Jaros

Faculty of Information Technology, Centre of Excellence IT4Innovations, Brno University of Technology, Brno, Czech Republic
{martajaros,jarosjir}@fit.vutbr.cz

Abstract. Complex ultrasound workflows calculating the outcome of ultrasound procedures such as neurostimulation, tumour ablation or photoacoustic imaging are composed of many computational tasks requiring high performance computing or cloud facilities to be computed in a sensible time. Most of these tasks are written as moldable parallel programs being able to run across various numbers of compute nodes. The number of compute nodes assigned to particular tasks strongly affects the overall execution and queuing times of the whole workflow (makespan) as well as the total computational cost.

This paper employs a genetic algorithm searching for a good resource distribution over the particular tasks, and a cluster simulator evaluating the makespan and cost of the candidate execution schedules. Since the exact execution time cannot be measured for every possible combination of the task, input data size, and assigned resources, several interpolation techniques are used to predict the task duration for a given amount of compute resources. The best execution schedules are eventually submitted to a real cluster with a PBS scheduler to validate the whole technique.

The experimental results confirm the proposed cluster simulator corresponds to a real PBS job scheduler with a sufficient fidelity. The investigation of the interpolation techniques showed that incomplete performance data can successfully be completed by linear and quadratic interpolations keeping the maximum mean error below 10%. Finally, the paper introduces a user defined parameter instructing the genetic algorithm to prefer either the makespan or cost, or find a suitable trade-off.

Keywords: Task graph scheduling · Workflow · Genetic algorithm · Moldable tasks · Makespan estimation · Performance scaling interpolation

1 Introduction

All fields of science and engineering use computers to reach new findings, while the most compute power demanding problems require High Performance Computing (HPC) or Cloud systems to give answers to their questions. The problems

D. Klusáček et al. (Eds.): JSSPP 2022, LNCS 13592, pp. 152–171, 2023.
https://doi.org/10.1007/978-3-031-22698-4_8

being solved nowadays are often very complex and comprise a lot of various tasks with mutual dependencies describing different aspects of the investigated problem. Their computation can be formally described using scientific workflows [2], also referred to as task graphs [22].

Ultrasound computing workflows aim at various applications of the ultrasound such as neurostimation, tumour ablation, targeted drug delivery, or photoacoustic imaging [23]. The goal of ultrasound treatment workflows is to asses the outcome the treatment and adjust the parameters of the ultrasound traducers to deliver the acoustic energy into desired area while preventing any damage to heathy tissue. The goal of photoacoustic imaging is to reconstruct the tissue structure by running an iterative inverse ultrasound models on signals recorded at the body surface [20]. Since the wavelength of the ultrasound signals are very small compared to the investigated area, e.g. human head or chest, and there are tight deadlines by when the simulation outcome has to be delivered, it is necessary to optimize the workflow execution to reduce both the execution time as well as the cost.

The execution of scientific workflows on HPC systems is performed via communication with the HPC front-end, also referred to as the job scheduler [11]. After the workflow data has been uploaded to the cluster, the workflow tasks are submitted to the computational queues where waiting until the system has enough free resources, and all task dependencies have been resolved (predecessor tasks have been finished).

Modern HPC schedulers implement advanced techniques for efficient task and resource management [12]. However, the queuing time, computation time and related cost depend on the task execution parameters provided at submission. These parameters include the required execution time accompanied by the number of compute nodes, cores and accelerators, the amount of main memory and storage space, and more and more frequently, the frequency and power cap of various hardware components. In most cases, only experienced users are endowed by sufficient knowledge to estimate these parameters appropriately knowing the size of the input data for particular tasks. In other cases, default parameters may be chosen leading to inefficient workflow processing.

Complex compute tasks are usually written as moldable distributed programs being able to exploit various amounts and types of computing resources, i.e., they can run on different numbers of compute nodes. However, the moldability is often limited by many factors, the most important of which being the domain decomposition [4] and parallel efficiency (strong scaling) [1]. The goal of the workflow execution optimization is posed as the assignment of suitable amount of compute resources to individual tasks in order to minimize the overall computation time and cost.

While the field of rigid workflow optimization, where the amount of resources per task is fixed or specified by the user in advance, has been thoroughly studied, and is part of common job schedulers such as PBSPro [11] or Slurm [28], the autonomous optimization and scheduling of moldable workflows has still been an outstanding problem, although firstly opened two decades ago in [8].

During the last decade, many papers have focused on the prediction of rigid workflow execution time and enhancing the HPC resource management. For example, Chirkin et al. [5] introduces a makespan estimation algorithm that may be integrated into job schedulers. Robert et al. [22] gives an overview of task graph scheduling algorithms. The usage of genetic algorithms addressing the task scheduling problems has also been introduced, e.g., a task graph scheduling on homogeneous processors using genetic algorithm and local search strategies [13], and performance improvement of the used genetic algorithm [19]. However, a handful works have taken into the consideration the moldability and strong scaling behavior of particular tasks, their dependencies and the current cluster utilization [3,7,27].

In all cases, the estimation of the makespan and optimization of the tasks execution parameters rely on the performance database storing strong and weak scaling. However, it is often not possible to benchmark the execution time for all possible combinations of the task type, task inputs and execution parameters. If a task has already been executed with given inputs and execution parameters, the execution time can be retrieved from the performance database. However, for unseen combinations, some kind of interpolation or machine learning techniques have to be used.

In our previous work [16], Genetic Algorithms (GA) [10] and a simple cluster simulator were used to find optimal execution parameters for various workflows on systems with on-demand and static allocations. This paper follows up with our previous work and its main goals are to (1) prove that GA is able to find execution plans for different workflows when using incomplete performance datasets, (2) prove a trade-off parameter to find different solutions meeting contradictory optimization criteria can be introduced, and finally (3) extend the cluster simulator by adding support for backfilling and considering the initial cluster workload. The resilience of the optimization techniques will be investigated on several scenarios and validated against the real workflow makespan measured on the Barbora supercomputer[1].

2 Automatic Optimization of Workflow Execution Parameters

Selection of suitable execution parameters for workflow tasks plays a crucial role in scheduling process and the maskespan/cost optimization. A naive selection of the execution parameters often leads to various unpleasant situations such as unnecessarily long waiting times and idling nodes if high amounts of compute resources were chosen, or on the other hand, premature task termination and crashes if the amount of compute resources was not sufficient.

Even having enough experience with applications used within the workflow, setting the execution parameters properly to get good performance is a difficult and tedious task. The key to get short makespan is to look at the workflow as a

[1] IT4Innovations, Czech republic, https://docs.it4i.cz/barbora/introduction/.

whole. There are many dependencies among tasks and selection of best execution parameters for each task independently may lead to a suboptimal solution since there is a limited total amount of resources offered by the HPC facilities.

Although batch schedulers implement several optimization methods and heuristics to maintain high cluster utilization and low queueing times, bad execution parameters spoil their submission schedules, e.g., when tens of tasks enter the queue asking for 24 h allocations but actually finishing after an hour.

2.1 k-Dispatch Workflow Management System

Molding scientific workflows during the scheduling process goes beyond the capabilities of common batch job schedulers which schedules tasks independently only paying attention to their dependencies and requires the resource requirements to be specified in advance. For the modlable workflow scheduling, a workflow management system sitting in between the end user and the batch job scheduler is required [18,24]. k-Dispatch [18] is a Workflow Management System (WMS) [6,26] allowing the end users to submit complex workflows with associated data via a simple web interface and have them automatically executed on remote HPC facilities. Although oriented on the ultrasound community and the popular k-Wave acoustic toolbox [24], its general design allows simple adaptation to other workflows and toolboxes by integrating new task graphs, registering new binaries and adding performance tables.

k-Dispatch consists of three main modules depicted in Fig. 1: Web server, Dispatch database and Dispatch core. The user applications, e.g., a standalone medical GUI, Web application, or Matlab interface, communicate with the Web server using the secured HTTPS protocol and REST API. The Dispatch database holds all necessary information about the users, submitted workflows, jobs, computational resources, available binaries and the performance data collected over all executed tasks suitable for the execution time estimation. The Dispatch core is responsible for planning, executing and monitoring submitted workflows. The communication with HPC and cloud facilities is done via SSH and RSYNC protocols. For more information, please refer to [18].

2.2 Workflow Optimization Within k-Dispatch

The optimization algorithm providing suitable parameters for particular tasks of the workflow is integrated inside the Dispatch core. It is composed of four modules: Optimizer, Estimator, Evaluator and Collector [16].

The Optimizer is based on a Genetic Algorithm implemented in the PyGAD library [9] and its parameter settings have been thoroughly investigated in [16]. The goal of the Optimizer is to generate high quality candidate solutions, each of which holding a list of execution parameters for all tasks in the workflow. In the simplest case, a candidate solution is a vector where the position of the task is given by a breath first traversal through the workflow task graph and the value determines the number of compute nodes to be used. Although several heuristics has been proposed to optimize the execution parameters [7,14,27], they have

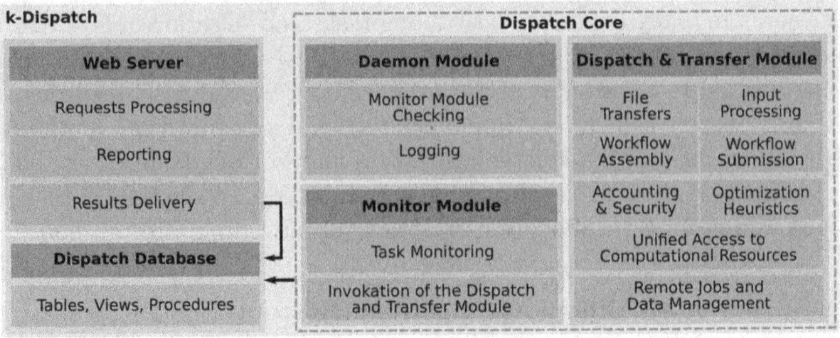

Fig. 1. k-Dispatch's modules and a brief description of the actions each module is responsible for. Arrows show the communication between Dispatch Core, Web Server and Dispatch Database.

strong limitations such as no dependencies among tasks or monotonic strong scaling. The genetic algorithm allows to solve any instance of the optimization problem.

The Estimator is responsible for estimating the execution time for particular tasks based on their input data and the amount of required resources. The Estimator incorporates various interpolation heuristics to reckon up missing values in strong and weak scaling.

The Evaluator uses a simplified simulator of job scheduler called Tetrisator [16], which takes a candidate schedule, simulates its execution on a given cluster and calculates the workflow makespan and cost. Tetrisator is a one-pass simulator of an HPC system with a predefined number of uniform computing nodes. It is inspired by the default strategy of the PBS job scheduler. In this paper, its functionality was extended by the backfilling technique allowing smaller jobs to overtake larger ones if no delays is introduced. The tasks are submitted to the simulator in the order defined in the candidate solution. Workflows may contains multiple dependencies among inner tasks, and the initial cluster workload may be defined, i.e., the cluster is not empty at the workflow submission time.

As soon as a satisfactory solution is found, the workflow is submitted to the real cluster and executed. Upon finishing the execution, the execution times for all tasks are collected by the Collector and stored in the performance database. This data is used to gradually improve the accuracy of the Estimator.

2.3 Estimator Module and Interpolation Techniques

There are many factors that may affect the execution time of a given task. Obviously, the most important ones are the size of the problem stored in the input file and the amount of resources assigned to the task. However, there might be many additional aspects significantly impacting the execution time such as data distribution and load balance, varying time complexity of the algorithms

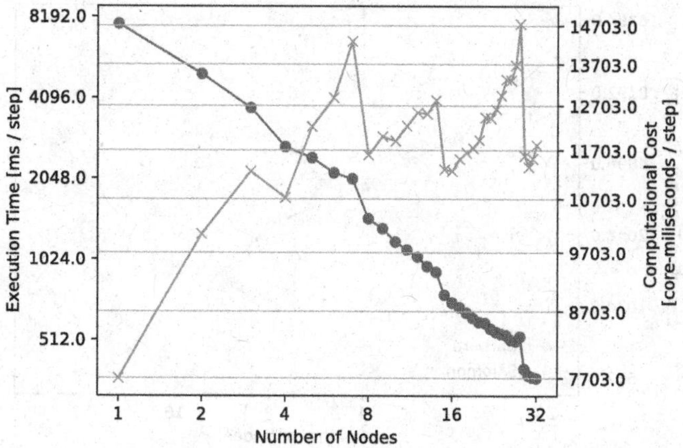

Fig. 2. Red line shows the strong scaling of the k-Wave code measured for a domain size of 1024^3 grid points on the Barbora cluster. Blue line shows the evolution of the computational cost when more nodes are added. (Color figure online)

used, additional task parameters and the amount of data being stored during the task execution.

As a practical example, let us talk about the MPI implementation of the k-Wave toolbox [15] simulating (non)-linear propagation of ultrasound wave through a heterogeneous absorbing medium. The scaling of the execution time and cost for one specific problem instance on the Barbora cluster with 36 processor cores per node can be seen in Fig. 2. Here, a domain of 1024^3 grid points is partitioned into 2D slabs and distributed over various numbers of compute nodes (1 to 32). The red curve shows the execution time per one simulation time step (the whole simulation usually executes tens of thousands of time steps).

Although this strong scaling curve looks almost ideal, several sudden drops in the execution time can be observed. These drops are the consequences of well balanced workload distribution. For example, if we cut the domain into 512 slices, we can distribute the work over 512 ranks mapped onto 512 cores. Since k-Wave is a memory and network bound application, it is often advantageous to undersubscribe the computing nodes and use higher aggregated memory and network bandwidth. On the Barbora cluster, we can spread 512 ranks over 15 to 28 nodes in a round robin fashion. Since the efficiency of such distribution is decreasing, the scaling curve is flattening toward 28 nodes. However, when 29 nodes are allocated to the task, the domain can be cut into 1024 slices leading to a much better workload distribution and significantly lower execution time. This imperfect workload distribution also renders into the simulation cost since there is a direct proportion between the parallel efficiency and the related cost. The blue curve shows several local minima and maxima in the execution cost which provide very suitable execution parameters or should be avoided, respectively.

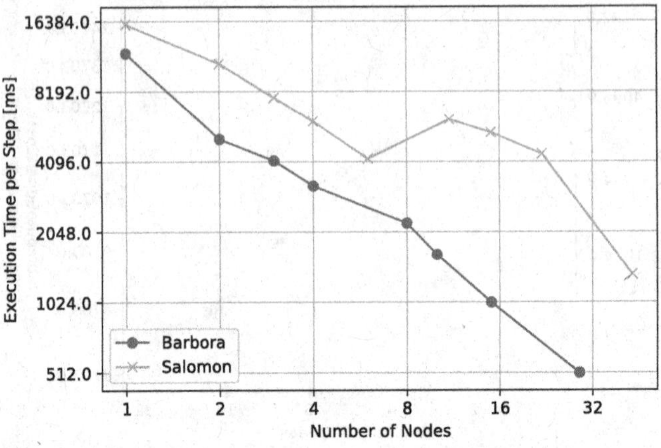

Fig. 3. Strong scaling of the k-Wave code execution time measured for 1024^3 domain size on the Barbora (36 cores/node) and Salomon (24 cores/node) cluster.

Let us note that having a complete performance dataset with all possible input sizes, numbers of nodes, and other tens of simulation parameters is computationally intractable. When having incomplete performance datasets where some points on the scaling curve are missing, the interpolation should rather overestimate the execution time to prevent premature task termination. Even more important question is how the scaling curve changes when a previously unseen domain size is used. In this situation, it is necessary to estimate both the shape and the position of the scaling curve from measured strong and weak scaling. As interpolation functions, linear and quadratic interpolation were used.

Finally, the scaling curves may change significantly among different machines. One such an example can be seen in Fig. 3 where the same problem is solved on Barbora (36 Cascade Lake cores per node) and Salomon (24 Haswell cores per node). Not only is the curve shifted due to a lower node performance, but it has a very different shape in the second half. This may be the effect of a different interconnection network topology, but also current cluster utilization. In this case, it may be very hard to use any interpolation. Thus when a new cluster is connected to k-Dispatch, a few benchmark runs for the most typical simulation settings are performed to get a minimum amount of performance data.

2.4 Evaluator Module Improvement

Since our previous work [16], Tetrisator has been extended by implementing the backfilling technique [21] to simulate the real batch scheduler more accurately.

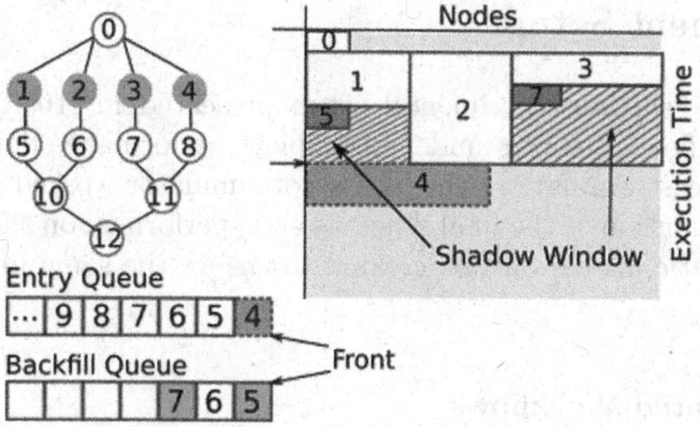

Fig. 4. The state of the entry and backfill queues when the task no 4 is about to be executed. Workflow tasks came to the entry queue in the execution order. Tasks 0–3 have already been executed. When task 4 is to be executed, the scheduler (depicted as schedule on the right) gets short of free nodes, and allows task 5 and 7 to overtake task 4 and fill the *shadow window.*

Tetrisator schedules tasks in the same order as they come to the HPC system (breadth first traversal of the workflow) [16]. The tasks are waiting in an entry queue until executed. A task at the front of the entry queue is ready for execution when all the task dependencies have been fulfilled and there are enough free resources. If this condition is not met, backfilling may find its place. Provided that the execution time of the waiting task will not be postponed and any task dependencies will not be offended, tasks requiring smaller amount of resources may overtake the waiting task. The task to be backfilled is calculated in a so called *shadow window.* The implemented algorithm is depicted in Fig. 4.

Real batch schedulers[2] may implement more sophisticated criteria for backfilling. For example, user and task priorities may be taken into account when deciding which tasks may overtake the waiting ones (fair-share policy). Since we mainly aim at static allocations where users do not compete, this calculation is omitted, i.e., all tasks and users have the same priority and only task dependencies are considered.

The implemented backfilling algorithm considers a queue of jobs that could be possibly backfilled, i.e., the *backfill queue* of length n and width of 1. n stands for a positive number of tasks that have the capability to be backfilled. Width of 1 means that the dependent tasks on the direct candidates to backfill are not considered. In other words, let us have task A actually being calculated, task B waiting for task A and other two tasks C and D. Task D depends on task C. Task C is not dependant on any other task and since not offending the execution time of task B, it can be directly added to the backfill queue. Task D could be also executed and finished within the *shadow window* as task C as well as still not running out of available resources, however, since dependent on task C it is not added to the *backfill queue* (attacking width of 2).

2 https://docs.it4i.cz/general/job-priority/.

3 Experiment Setup

This paper follows the experimental setup presented in [16] to evaluate the developed workflow schedules under incomplete performance database. For the makespan and cost evaluation, the Tetrisator simulator worked with a 54 node cluster. The validation of the final schedules was performed on the Barbora cluster, where a static allocation was created to ensure the same initial conditions for all tests.

3.1 Investigated Workflows

This paper uses two typical biomedical ultrasound workflows applied in the ultrasound neurostimulation and photoacoustic imaging, see Fig. 5. Both workflows consist of two types of tasks. The simulation tasks (ST) executing the k-Wave MPI solver represent heavy parallel jobs running for a few hours. The ST tasks were limited to use between 1 and 32 nodes (36 - 1152 cores). The data processing tasks (PT) perform data pre-processing, post-processing, aggregation, etc. The PT tasks have a linear time complexity and almost perfect scaling. Since their runtime is on the order of minutes, only one or two nodes depending on the amount of memory requested are used.

The first workflow starts with a single PT task generating input files for the ST tasks. Consequently, a few independent trains of ST-PT-ST tasks are executed. Finally, the results from all trains are aggregated using a parallel reduction tree composed of PT tasks. The second workflow starts by running a few ST tasks operating on the same input file, but with different parameters. The results are aggregated into a single output file using a parallel tree reduction. But this time, the result is used by the following wave of ST tasks. In practise, this workflow is repeated in a loop until some error metric calculated by the last PT task is satisfied.

3.2 Used Datasets

Let us here define the datasets used in our experiments along with their short description:

- **Dataset A**. Reference strong scaling of the k-Wave code measured on a domain size of $1024 \times 1024 \times 1024$ grid points using 1–32 nodes.
- **Dataset 1A**. Based on *Dataset A* but having only 16 values including peaks and values in between them.
- **Dataset 2A**. Based on *Dataset A* but having only 8 values excluding peaks.
- **Dataset B**. Reference strong scaling of the k-Wave code measured on a domain size of $810 \times 810 \times 810$ grid points using 1–32 nodes.
- **Dataset 1B**. $810 \times 810 \times 810$ domain interpolated for 1–32 nodes using the quadratic interpolation from the known domain sizes: $512 \times 512 \times 512$, $648 \times 648 \times 648$, $1024 \times 1024 \times 1024$.

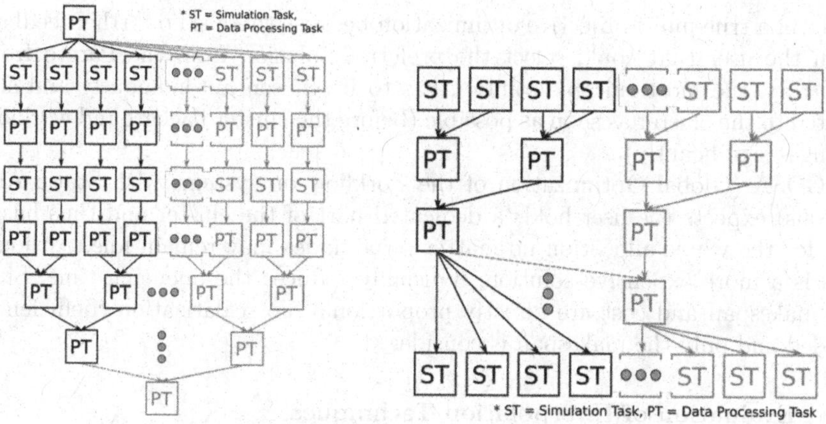

Fig. 5. The structure of investigated workflows. The heavy simulation tasks are interleaved with light data processing tasks. The parts highlighted in black show the minimal workflow structure consisting of 20 and 11 tasks, respectively. The parts displayed in grey show how the workflow structure can grow. (Color figure online)

3.3 Tetrisator Validation Against Real Cluster

To compare the simulator output with the real execution carried out in a dedicated queue comprising 54 nodes of the Barbora cluster, an artificial schedule based on the first workflow type was created. This workflow contained 20 tasks, (8 heavy STs alternated with 12 light PTs). The execution times of particular tasks were taken from the *Dataset A*. The number of simulation time steps inside the ST tasks were reduced to make the workflow finish in less that 1 h. To prevent premature termination, a safety cap of 10% calculated from the estimated execution time was added to each task. The real execution time actually covers net computing time as well as overheads such as the computing node initialization. Performed experimental scenario expects no initial workload, i.e., the cluster was empty when the workflow was submitted and executed. The obtained experimental results are then compared against two evolved execution plans employing Tetrisator with backfilling switched on and off.

3.4 Workflow Schedule Quality Measures

The quality of the developed workflow schedules is evaluated by a fitness function the Optimizer calls after the execution trace has been created by Tetrisator. This work investigates two different fitness functions: GODA and GOSA.

GODA (Global Optimization of the workflow on systems with on-Demand Allocations) calculates the makespan over the longest critical path including queueing times. However, the execution cost considers only truly consumed resources. This is a typical cluster operation with users competing for resources. Since having two contradictory criteria, a user-defined scalarization parameter α is used to balance between the execution time and cost. The algorithm cannot perform a true multi-objective optimization because there is no further feedback from the user that could select the preferred solution from the Pareto front. Contrary, the most suitable solution has to be chosen autonomously and submitted to the cluster as soon as possible (before the cluster background workload changes significantly).

GOSA (Global Optimization of the workflow on systems with Static Allocations) expects the user holds a dedicated part of the cluster and thus has to pay for the whole allocation no matter some nodes may remain idle. Although this is a more expensive solution, it usually reduces the queueing time. Since the makespan and cost are directly proportional, no scalarization coefficient is needed and only the makespan is considered.

3.5 Evaluation of Interpolation Techniques

To estimate missing execution time for a particular task, domain size, and number of nodes, two different interpolation techniques from the Python's *scipy* package [25] were used. After a thorough investigation in [17] and new experiments performed in the paper, a linear and quadratic `interp1d` interpolations were chosen. Very similar results to the quadratic interpolation were also obtained by cubic spline `CubicSpline` with the `bc_type` parameter set to `natural`. Unfortunately, the use of the default value of `bc_type` caused high oscillations and strong underestimations of the execution time. Therefore, we decided to use a quadratic interpolation instead.

Three different experiments with the interpolation functions were conducted. The goals of particular experiments were

- to estimate missing points on the strong scaling curve for a domain size of 1024^3 grid points defined by the points with ideal scaling ($N\%(P*36) \approx 0$), where N is the domain size and P is the number of nodes, see Fig. 8.
- to estimate missing points on the strong scaling curve for a domain size of 1024^3 grid points when having also points in the middle of the intervals between two points with ideal scaling, see Fig. 8.
- to reconstruct a completely unknown scaling curve for an unseen domain size from the data stored in the performance database. In this example, scaling curves for 512^3, 648^3 and 1024^3 were used to estimate the one for 810^3 grid points, see Fig. 9. The domain sizes chosen progressively double the total number of grid points.

As the measure of the interpolation quality, a mean relative error was used, see Eq. (1).

$$meanError = \frac{1}{N}\sum_{i=0}^{N}(\frac{|a_i - b_i|}{a_i}) \tag{1}$$

where a denotes the measured execution time, b the interpolated execution time, and N is the total number of the compute nodes (32).

In all cases, we can tolerate a small overestimation but shall avoid underestimation which leads to premature job termination and necessary resubmission with prolonged execution time.

4 Experimental Results

This section presents and discusses (1) the similarity of the workflow execution schedule to the one executed on a real HPC cluster, and (2) the error reached by the interpolation techniques.

4.1 Simulated Execution Plans Reliability

The following figures point out the differences between simulated execution plans created by Tetrisator and the real executions performed in the dedicated queue on Barbora. Figure 6 shows the scenario where no initial workload is expected and all 54 nodes are fully available at submission time. As expected, the simulated makespan by Tetrisator with backfilling switched off is a bit pessimistic causing the overestimation by 15%. On the contrary, it can be seen that the simulated makespan by Tetrisator using backfilling is underestimated by 3%. This underestimation is, however, caused by cumulative error produced by slight delays of individual task execution times on the cluster.

Our observations suggest that the real PBS cluster scheduler works in the same manner as Tetrisator. This means the tasks within the workflow are submitted to the real cluster in the same order as they are processed by the Tetrisator, and their submission time is more or less the same. Thus, the tasks are also executed one by one in the same manner as arriving to the cluster. The changes in the order happen when a task has to wait for free resources (Fig. 7).

4.2 Interpolation Functions Accuracy

Figure 8 shows the measured and interpolated strong scaling curves on a domain composed of 1024^3 grid points. Inspecting the scaling curve created by a linear interpolation, a very close match can be seen. When interpolating using values where the scaling is close to the optimal, the mean interpolation error reaches 4%. After adding the values from the middle of particular intervals, the error drops below 0.8%. Unfortunately, the interpolated values for sparser training data are mostly underestimated, which can be corrected by a small bias or picking the points with the worst instead of best workload distribution.

When repeating the same experiment with a cubic spline and a quadratic interpolation, the mean error gets higher up to the level of 12% and 7%, respectively, depending on the number of known values. The high error is caused by several oscillations, and more specifically, by the extrapolation error where the execution time is extremely underestimated.

The 4% error of the linear interpolation reaches the level of uncertainty of real execution time measurement on clusters due to unstable node, network and I/O performance. The suitability of the linear interpolation can be also attributed to a very good scaling of the ST tasks without any significant anomalies. Since parallel codes have to show good scaling to be deployed in production runs, linear interpolation is expected to work well for most such codes.

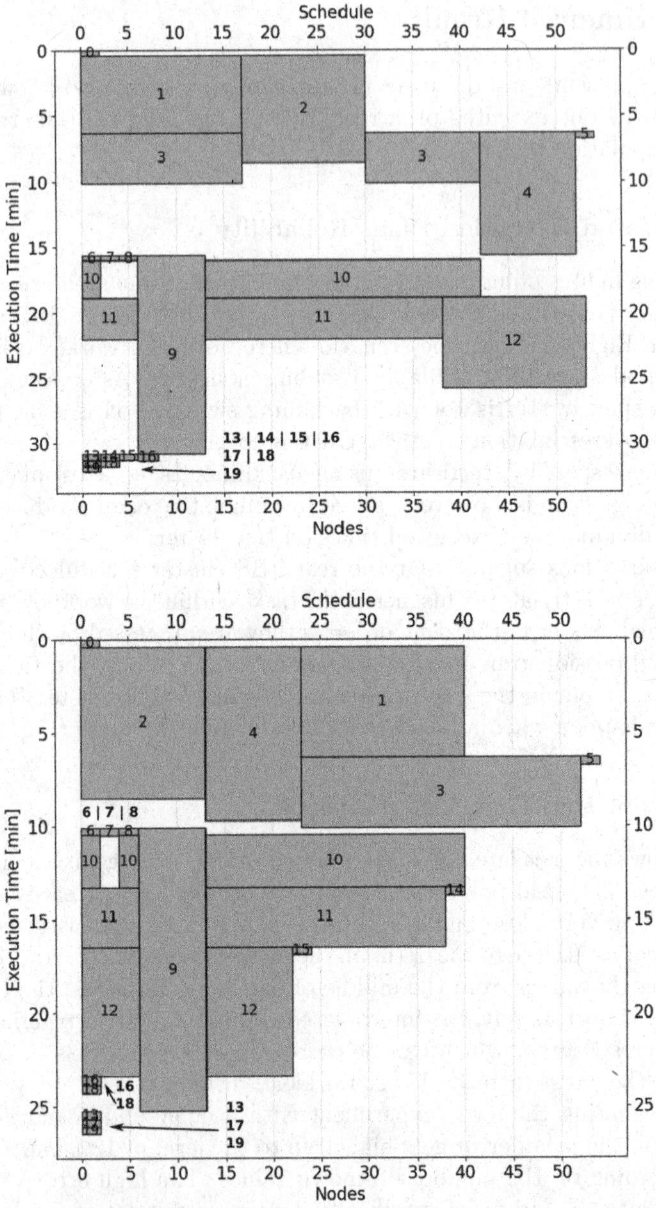

Fig. 6. Two simulated execution schedules. The top one with backfilling switched-off and the makespan reaches 32.1 min, and the bottom one implementing backfilling and finishing earlier in 26.4 min.

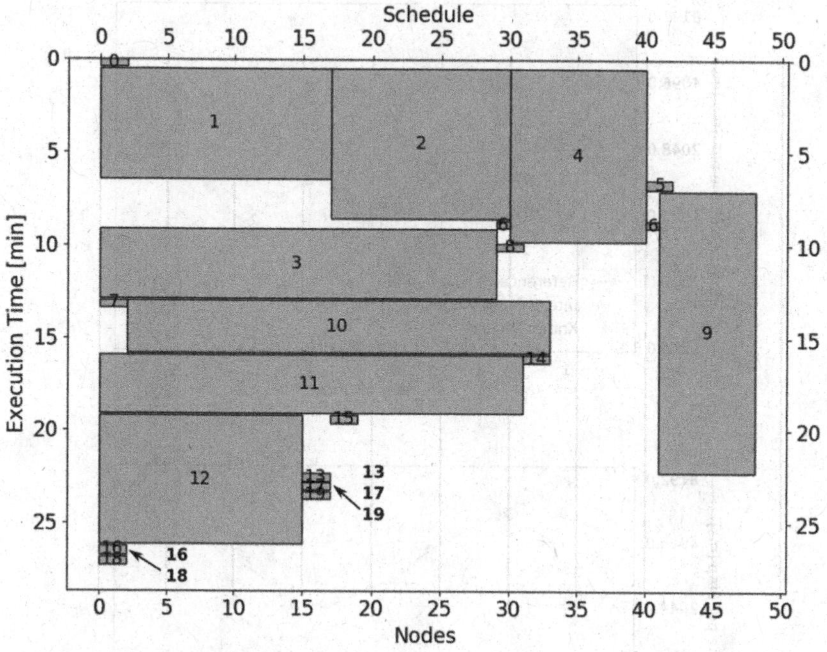

Fig. 7. Real execution of the workflow on Barbora finishing in 27.3 min.

The second experiment attempts to estimate the strong scaling for an unknown domain size, see Fig. 9. The figure reveals that the interpolation method rather overestimate the scaling curve. When repeating this experiment with a linear and a natural cubic spline interpolations, we got the mean error of 25.4% and 13.5%, respectively, while the quadratic interpolation and the cubic spline with `bc_type` parameter set to default produced better estimates reaching the mean error at a level of 10.5%. The explanation is quite simple. While the strong scaling of the ST tasks on a given domain size is almost linear, the algorithm has an asymptotic time complexity of $O(n \log n)$. Moreover, the ST tasks heavily employ fast Fourier transform which is very sensitive to the domain size and its prime factors. The quadratic interpolation thus better capture the nature of ST tasks.

The conclusion is to use a linear interpolation to estimate values on known scaling curves while using a quadratic interpolation when the domain size has not been seen before. It is important to say that the k-Wave code is highly tuned and scales very well. Employing a code the scaling of which is more "wild" with many peaks or a dramatic slowdowns may become a challenge. When using different

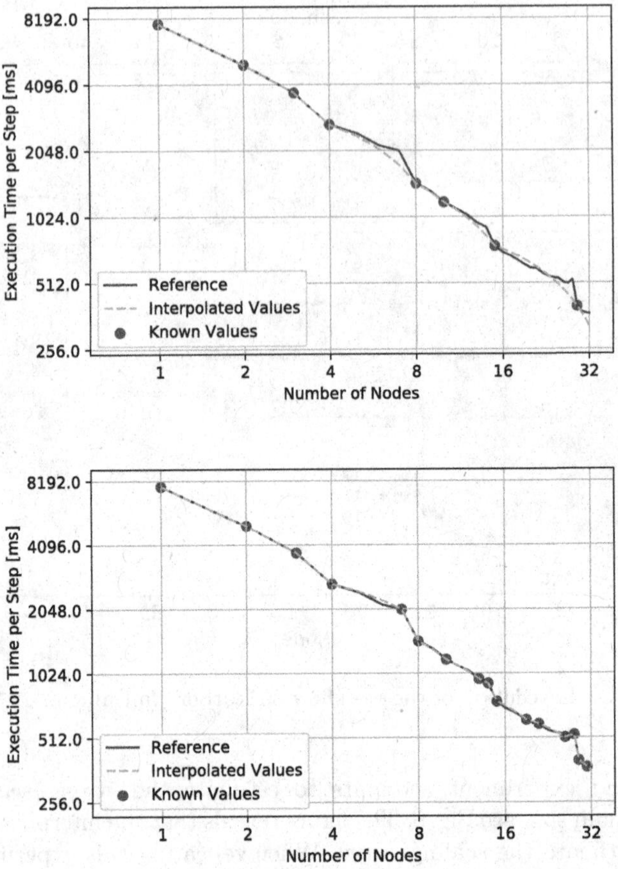

Fig. 8. Reference and interpolated strong scaling of ST tasks for a domain size of 1024^3 grid points with a linear interpolation calculated from 8 and 16 known values, respectively. In the top figure, values in unexpected peaks were selected intentionally to see how much the value would be underestimated.

parallel codes, it may be beneficial to use a different interpolation for unknown domain sizes corresponding to the asymptotic time complexity. Moreover, if the scaling is relatively stable, it may be possible to construct a scaling equation and use a fitting methods to set its coefficients using known performance data. Alternatively, we may try to interpolate the known points using a various polynomial interpolations and based on the error make a decision about a selection of the interpolation method.

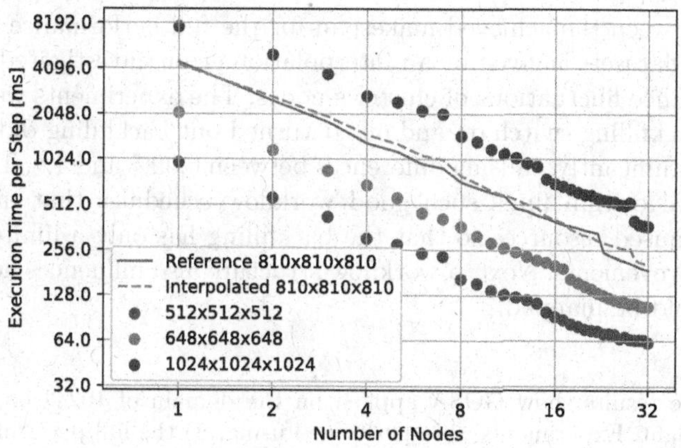

Fig. 9. Reference and interpolated strong scaling of ST tasks for an unknown domain size of 810^3 grid points with a quadratic interpolation.

4.3 Impact of Interpolation on Schedule Makespan and Cost

This section investigates the quality and accuracy of the developed schedules when using the performance database containing all data, only a subset, or no data for particular domain size.

Figure 10 shows the makespan and cost of the best workflow schedules developed for the GODA situation on a known domain size of 1024^3 grid points, with all, 8 and 16 performance values. These experiments also use different values of the α scalarization coefficient (only three values of α are used in figure for better visibility). The schedules were collected over twenty independent runs of the genetic algorithm. The Pareto fronts (lines in the plot) for the same values of α are close to each other confirming that by employing interpolation methods on incomplete datasets we are able to achieve very similar results. When using *Dataset 2A* containing only 8 performance values, the solutions found may be deflected from that ones evolved using dense dataset. This actually does not mean that found solutions are bad, they just overlap the area where solutions for different value of α would be expected. Next, it can be seen that solutions for different α form isolated clusters. This implies we can affect the execution plan to prioritize different criteria. At this point, it is important to note that the execution plan may be adjusted in makespan by a factor of 10.0 while in computational cost by a factor of 1.7. The factors vary and the cost factor is such small due to the highly optimised code used. This is a very promising result showing that when the interpolation is reasonably accurate, the impact on the best solution developed by the Optimizer is rather small.

Table 1 summarizes conducted experiments of GOSA expressing the quality of the execution schedules as makespan. The table may be divided into two parts. The left one is for the domain size of 1024^3 where missing strong scaling values were completed by a linear interpolation. The right one is for the domain size of 810^3 which was fully interpolated using a quadratic interpolation. The difference between the achieved makespan for the full performance dataset and interpolated datasets is given by an interpolation error (investigated in Sec. 4.2) and performance fluctuations of cluster's nodes. The experiments were provided with both backfilling switch on and off. It turned out backfilling did not impact the results significantly, causing differences between 0.09% and 4%. This suggests the genetic algorithm finds such good workflow schedules that minimize the amount of unused resources so that the backfilling has only a limited space for schedule improvements. Next, a workflow structure also influences how good the workflow could be mapped.

Table 1. The results show GOSA applied on the domain of 1024^3 on the left and 810^3 on the right. Experiments were performed using (1) the full performance dataset without interpolation, (2) the partial performance dataset of 8 and 16 known values, respectively, and completed using linear interpolation, and (3) the full performance dataset created using quadratic interpolation. The table depicts average (Avg), minimum (Min) and maximum (Max) obtained values of makespan in minutes. The percentage difference between experiments with partial and full performance datasets is also depicted.

1024 x 1024 x 1024		**40 Tasks**		**80 Tasks**		**810 x 810 x 810**		**40 Tasks**		**80 Tasks**	
		Makespan [min]	**Diff. [%]**	**Makespan [min]**	**Diff. [%]**			**Makespan [min]**	**Diff. [%]**	**Makespan [min]**	**Diff. [%]**
GOSA	**Avg**	**29.70**	-	**58.31**	-	**GOSA**	**Avg**	**14.82**	-	**30.05**	-
with no	**Min**	27.75	-	55.74	-	**with no**	**Min**	14.07	-	28.32	-
interp.	**Max**	35.10	-	61.07	-	**interp.**	**Max**	16.88	-	31.76	-
GOSA with	**Avg**	**29.19**	**1.72**	**59.23**	**1.57**	**GOSA**	**Avg**	**17.08**	**15.25**	**33.11**	**10.18**
linear interp.	**Min**	27.29	1.65	55.27	0.84	**with quadratic**	**Min**	15.44	9.70	31.27	10.41
(Dataset A1)	**Max**	33.25	5.27	65.47	7.21	**interpolation**	**Max**	18.85	11.64	36.67	15.44
GOSA with	**Avg**	**26.74**	**9.98**	**51.06**	**12.44**						
linear interp.	**Min**	24.87	10.36	49.05	12.00						
(Dataset A2)	**Max**	30.33	13.58	56.46	7.55						

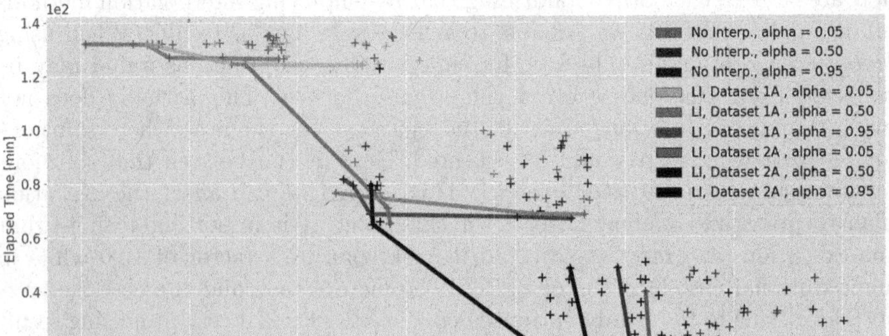

Fig. 10. Pareto front together with dominated solutions showing the evolved schedules for workflows of 11 tasks not requiring interpolation, and two experiments both using linear interpolation (LI) but differing in the content of the performance dataset.

5 Conclusions

The paper has investigated the optimization of moldable ultrasound workflow executions under incomplete performance database where the execution times for some combination of tasks, input data and amount of resources are not known and have to be estimated. Consequently, the paper has proven the workflow execution on a cluster can be simulated and this simulator can be integrated in the k-Dispatch's optimization module. Although being a one-pass PBS-based simulator, the estimations provided are sensible. The simulator gives accurate estimations especially for workflows executed on dedicated resources where other workload is known. The cross validation of an artificial and the real schedules created by the PBS job scheduler on Barbora show a good general match.

The experimental results indicate that linear interpolation works well in situations the input data has been seen before and the task has already been executed using a few execution parameters configurations. In such cases, the missing performance data can be calculated with a very small error below 4%. From our experience, linear interpolations appear to be generally applicable on parallel codes with good strong scaling. On the other hand, if the input data has not been seen before, the execution time has to be estimated from similar inputs by interpolating between known strong/weak scaling curves. In this case, a quadratic interpolation worked sufficiently well for our codes, however, the error may reach 10%. This can be attributed to used codes having $O(N \log N)$ time complexity. For codes with different time complexity, higher polynomial interpolations may produce better results.

The paper also confirms that it is possible to find different schedules that prioritize various criteria using the trade-off parameter α. The proposed optimization algorithm constructs the Pareto front offering different suitable schedules. Users, however, (1) are not aware of what tasks are executed within the workflow, (2) may not know what solution to choose, and finally (3) the Pareto fronts are calculated just before the workflow execution and this information is not available at submission time to k-Dispatch. This is the reason why a multi-criteria optimization is transformed to an easier form where users can express their preferences between two criteria (makespan vs. computational cost) using, e.g., a slider bar just before workflow submission to k-Dispatch.

The developed schedules tend to overestimate the execution time, which is partially caused by imperfect interpolation, and a reserve of 10% added to the workflow to avoid premature termination. Nevertheless, the error between developed and real schedules fits within a 15% margin, which is considered to be acceptable for most users.

5.1 Future Work

There are two directions we would like to follow in our future work. First, we would like to include the information about the actual cluster utilization into the cluster simulator. This will allow us to better simulate workflow execution in on-demand allocations where the user competes with others. It may have an impact on the shape of the developed schedules because tasks asking for more resources sit longer in the queue. Using smaller amounts of resources thus may improve the workflow makespan. Second, we would like to examine more advanced machine learning techniques to improve the interpolation accuracy once the performance database includes tens of thousands of records.

Acknowledgments. This work was supported by the Ministry of Education, Youth and Sports of the Czech Republic through the e-INFRA CZ (ID:90140). This work was supported by Brno University of Technology under project numbers IGA FIT/FSI-J-22-7980 Acceleration of Selected Evolutionary Communication Techniques for Solving Combinatoric Tasks and FIT-S-20-6309 Design, Optimization and Evaluation of Application Specific Computer Systems.

References

1. Amdahl, G.M.: Validity of the single processor approach to achieving large scale computing capabilities. In: Proceedings of the April 1820 1967 Spring Joint Computer Conference, vol. 23(4), pp. 483–485 (1967)
2. Bharathi, S., Chervenak, A., Deelman, E., Mehta, G., Su, M.-H., Vahi, K.: Characterization of scientific workflows. In: Third Workshop on Workflows in Support of Large-Scale Science, pp. 1–10. IEEE (2008)
3. Bleuse, R., Hunold, S., Kedad-Sidhoum, S., Monna, F., Mounie, G., Trystram, D.: Scheduling independent moldable tasks on multi-cores with GPUs. IEEE Trans. Parallel Distrib. Syst. **28**(9), 2689–2702 (2017)
4. Chan, T.F., Mathew, T.P.: Domain decomposition algorithms. Acta Numer **3**, 61–143 (1994)
5. Chirkin, A.M., et al.: Execution time estimation for workflow scheduling. Future Generat. Comput. Syst. **75** (2017)
6. Deelman, E., Vahi, K., Juve, G., et al.: Pegasus: a workflow management system for science automation. Future Generat. Comput. Syst. (2014)
7. Dutot, P.-F., Netto, M.A.S., Goldman, A., Kon, F.: Scheduling moldable BSP tasks. In: Feitelson, D., Frachtenberg, E., Rudolph, L., Schwiegelshohn, U. (eds.) JSSPP 2005. LNCS, vol. 3834, pp. 157–172. Springer, Heidelberg (2005). https://doi.org/10.1007/11605300_8
8. Feitelson, D.G., Rudolph, L.: Toward convergence in job schedulers for parallel supercomputers. In: Feitelson, D.G., Rudolph, L. (eds.) JSSPP 1996. LNCS, vol. 1162, pp. 1–26. Springer, Heidelberg (1996). https://doi.org/10.1007/BFb0022284
9. Gad, A.F.: Geneticalgorithmpython: Building genetic algorithm in python (2021)
10. Goldberg, D.E.: Genetic algorithms in search, optimization, and machine learning. Addison-Wesley Longman, Boston (1989)
11. Henderson, R.L.: Job scheduling under the portable batch system. In: Feitelson, D.G., Rudolph, L. (eds.) JSSPP 1995. LNCS, vol. 949, pp. 279–294. Springer, Heidelberg (1995). https://doi.org/10.1007/3-540-60153-8_34
12. Hovestadt, M., Kao, O., Keller, A., Streit, A.: Scheduling in HPC resource management systems: queuing vs. planning. In: Feitelson, D., Rudolph, L., Schwiegelshohn, U. (eds.) JSSPP 2003. LNCS, vol. 2862, pp. 1–20. Springer, Heidelberg (2003). https://doi.org/10.1007/10968987_1
13. Izadkhah, H.: Learning based genetic algorithm for task graph scheduling. Applied Computational Intelligence and Soft Computing (2019)

14. Jansen, K., Land, F.: Scheduling Monotone Moldable Jobs in Linear Time. In: 2018 IEEE International Parallel and Distributed Processing Symposium (IPDPS), pp. 172–181. IEEE, May 2018
15. Jaros, J., Rendell, A.P., Treeby, B.E.: Full-wave nonlinear ultrasound simulation on distributed clusters with applications in high-intensity focused ultrasound. Int. J. High Perfor. Comput. Appli. **30**(2), 137–155 (2016)
16. Jaros, M., Jaros, J.: Performance-cost optimization of moldable scientific workflows. In: Klusáček, D., Cirne, W., Rodrigo, G.P. (eds.) JSSPP 2021. LNCS, vol. 12985, pp. 149–167. Springer, Cham (2021). https://doi.org/10.1007/978-3-030-88224-2_8
17. Jaros, M., Sasak, T., Treeby, B.E., Jaros, J.: Estimation of execution parameters for k-Wave simulations. In: Kozubek, T., Arbenz, P., Jaroš, J., Říha, L., Šístek, J., Tichý, P. (eds.) HPCSE 2019. LNCS, vol. 12456, pp. 116–134. Springer, Cham (2021). https://doi.org/10.1007/978-3-030-67077-1_7
18. Jaros, M., Treeby, E.B., Jaros, J., Georgiou, P.: k-dispatch: A workflow management system for the automated execution of biomedical ultrasound simulations on remote computing resources. In: Platform for Advanced Scientific Computing Conference, pp. 1–10. ACM (2020)
19. Omara, F.A., Arafa, M.M.: Genetic algorithms for task scheduling problem. J. Paral. Distrib. Comput. **70**(1), 13–22 (2010)
20. Poudel, J., Lou, Y., Anastasio, M.A.: A survey of computational frameworks for solving the acoustic inverse problem in three-dimensional photoacoustic computed tomography. Phys. Med. Biol. (2019)
21. Rajaei, H., Dadfar, M.: Comparison Of backfilling algorithms for job scheduling in distributed memory parallel system. In: 2006 Annual Conference and Exposition Proceedings, ASEE Conferences, pp. 11.339.1-11.339.12 (2007)
22. Robert, Y.: Task Graph Scheduling. In: Encyclopedia of Parallel Computing, pp. 2013–2025 (2011)
23. Szabo, T.L.: Diagnostic Ultrasound Imaging: Inside Out (2014)
24. Treeby, B., Cox, B.: k-wave: Matlab toolbox for the simulation and reconstruction of photoacoustic wave fields. J. Biomed. Opt. **15**, 021314 (2010)
25. Virtanen, P., Gommers, R., Oliphant, T. E. A. O.: Fundamental algorithms for scientific computing in python. SciPy 1.0. Nat. Methods **17**, 261–272 (2020)
26. Wolstencroft, K., Haines, R., Fellows, D., et al.: The taverna workflow suite: designing and executing workflows of web services on the desktop, web or in the cloud. Nucleic Acids Res. **41**(W1), W557–W561 (2013)
27. Ye, D., Chen, D.Z., Zhang, G.: Online scheduling of moldable parallel tasks. J. Sched. **21**(6), 647–654 (2018). https://doi.org/10.1007/s10951-018-0556-2
28. Yoo, A.B., Jette, M.A., Grondona, M.: SLURM: simple linux utility for resource management. In: Feitelson, D., Rudolph, L., Schwiegelshohn, U. (eds.) JSSPP 2003. LNCS, vol. 2862, pp. 44–60. Springer, Heidelberg (2003). https://doi.org/10.1007/10968987_3

Scheduling of Elastic Message Passing Applications on HPC Systems

Debolina Halder Lina(✉), Sheikh Ghafoor, and Thomas Hines

Tennessee Tech. University, Cookeville, TN, USA
dlina@tntech.edu

Abstract. Elastic parallel applications that can change the number of processors while being executed promise improved application and system performance, allow new classes of data and event-driven highly dynamic parallel applications, as well as provide the possibility of predictive proactive fault tolerance via shrinkage in increasingly larger and more complex HPC systems, where the mean time between component failures is decreasing. There are several challenges for elastic application to become mainstream: 1) a clear understanding of programming models for elastic applications, 2) adequate support from message passing libraries, middleware, and resource management systems (RMS), and 3) thorough investigation of scheduling algorithms. Scheduling elastic jobs requires communication between running jobs and the RMS, keeping track of pending jobs, and prioritizing jobs to expand or shrink at a certain point in time. These challenges make the task of finding an optimal schedule challenging. We have proposed three different scheduling algorithms to schedule elastic applications along with six different candidate selection policies to prioritize the shrinkable applications and investigated their impact on system and application performance. We have studied the impact of workload characteristics and algorithms on performance. Our simulations results indicate that workload characteristics as well as the range of elasticity (flexibility) of the elastics applications impact the system and application performance.

Keywords: Elastic applications · Malleable · Evolving · Scheduling

1 Introduction

High Performance Computing (HPC) systems are growing in capacity, complexity, and heterogeneity [5,23]. The upcoming and current large HPC systems have hundreds of thousands of computing cores in addition to networking and other components. On the other hand, parallel applications that generally run on such systems are also growing increasingly complex. They are increasingly data and event-driven and dynamic in nature. The current generation of message passing parallel applications can not change resources (grow or shrink in terms of resource usage) once they start executing. According to Feitelson [8], a malleable application can grow or shrink in response to commands by the resource management system and an evolving application can also grow or shrink, but the

D. Klusáček et al. (Eds.): JSSPP 2022, LNCS 13592, pp. 172–191, 2023.
https://doi.org/10.1007/978-3-031-22698-4_9

application itself decides when it needs to change size. We will refer to malleable and evolving applications as elastic applications. Currently, there is no or limited support from runtime libraries and/or resource management systems (RMS) for such applications.

One use case for elastic applications is for dynamic applications whose computational needs are not known when the application is launched. Consider an application that simulates both airflows around an airplane and the stresses on the frame from the airflow. If the stress simulation determines that a crack appears then the computational needs to simulate the airflow may increase by an order of magnitude. Using current inelastic (rigid) applications, the way to deal with this would be to give the application the worst-case number of nodes (which may be difficult to compute), wasting resources. An elastic application could automatically request more nodes from the system at the time they are needed. If no crack appears then there would be no need to waste resources for that potentiality. Another potential benefit of elastic applications is that it gives a way for applications to proactively respond to failures. If a node is giving signs of impending failures, such as temperatures running too hot, then the system could instruct the application to shrink down, off the failing node. Elastic applications provide a path to maximum possible utilization by expanding or shrinking applications. Elastic applications would open up the potential for new highly dynamic applications that are not developed as there is no support for running them. There is no support because there are no applications that need it. Breaking this cycle would allow opportunities for a new generation of applications.

There are many challenges to realizing elastic applications. Current applications use a distributed memory model. Data is transferred by message passing. The number of shared memory nodes remains fixed for the lifetime of the application. Elastic applications will need to reorganize their data as they shrink or grow. The nature of the reorganization would depend on the application. A parameter sweep application might simply need to migrate some runs to a new node. An iterative grid-based application might need to completely redistribute the data to a new rectangular layout. The resource manager will need to communicate with running and the elastic applications in order to allocate more or preempt (shrink) resources. Likewise, the application will need to be able to give up or acquire more resources. Evolving applications will need to request more resources. This may potentially involve multiple phases as the resource manager offers resources and the application counteroffers. Current resource managers only need to consider pending applications in the queue and keep track of used and free nodes. An elastic job scheduler will need to make decisions about when to grow or shrink malleable applications, as well as respond to evolving applications' requests to grow or shrink. This will need to be done in a way that is fair to inelastic and elastic applications.

We have proposed three algorithms to schedule workloads containing elastic as well as non-elastic (traditional rigid) jobs. Each algorithm has been evaluated with a different policy to select a running malleable job to preempt resources.

We have run a number of simulations to observe the impact of these different policies on different types of workloads. We have used modified workload traces from real systems [17,24] as well as synthetic workloads. Our simulation results indicate that as the workload increases the impact of candidate selection policy gradually becomes insignificant. We also found that the distribution of elastic jobs in the workload impacts the performance gain. Our simulation results are consistent with several previous works that the presence of elastic application in the workload improves both system and application performance compared to the same workload with rigid applications only.

The rest of the paper is organized as follows. Section 2 provides a brief discussion of related works found in the literature. Our elastic application model is presented in Sect. 3, followed by a description of scheduling algorithms and candidate selection policies in Sect. 4. The experimental results are presented in Sect. 5. Finally, Sect. 6 presents our conclusion and planned future works.

2 Related Works

Research in the field of elastic parallel systems is not as extensive compared in other HPC areas. The simplest way of expanding and shrinking is to checkpoint the application state at some point in time and then again start the application from that point with a different number of processors. This approach has been implemented by Vadhiyar and Dongarra [27] as the Stop Restart Services (SRS) framework. ReSHAPE, developed by Sudarsan et al. [25] combines a scheduler with a reconfiguration library for iterative MPI applications. The Parallel programming framework, AMPI [15], is built on top of Charm++ [13]. AMPI implements MPI as user level threads. Recently, Iserte et al. [11] have designed a library DMRlib which provides a series of predefined communication patterns for data-redistribution and communication with the RMS. They have designed a communication API using which Nanos++ OmpSs [1] can communicate with the Slurm resource manager [28]. CooRMv2 is an RMS to ensure efficient scheduling of non-predictable evolving applications developed by Klein et al. [16]. Process Management Interface-exascale (PMIx) is an abstract set of interfaces using which applications and tools can interact with the different components of the System Management Stack (SMS) as well as different SMS components can also interact with each other [3,19]. The PMIx standard provides APIs for applications to request allocation of additional resources, extend the reservation on currently allocated resources, and release currently allocated resources. These APIs are still being developed, yet to provide support for full flexibility, and have not been adopted by production RMSs.

Kale et al. [14] have designed a simple scheduling algorithm for elastic job schedulers where all jobs are initially allocated with their minimum number of processors and the rest of the processes are shared equally among the jobs considering the maximum allowable resources of a particular job. Utrera et al. [26] have proposed an algorithm that mainly focuses on reducing the average waiting time. Gupta et al. [10] have proposed a split-phase scheduling algorithm where shrinkage requests are performed asynchronously. D'Amico et al. [4] have proposed a dynamic slowdown-driven (SD) policy to schedule rigid and malleable jobs to reduce average response time. Iserte et al. [12] have modified Slurm and implemented a reconfiguration policy using the moldable submission mechanism of Slurm. Prabhakaran et al. [20] have proposed a scheduling algorithm to run evolving jobs with rigid jobs but they have only considered expansion. They have extended the algorithm to schedule rigid, malleable, and evolving jobs together [21].

Research on scheduling elastic applications is at an early stage. Recent research mainly focuses on the impact of different scheduling parameters on performance, but how workload characteristics impact performance along with scheduling algorithms has not been investigated adequately. Similarly, the communication and negotiation aspect between RMS and elastic applications has been under investigation.

3 Application Model

Before developing the scheduling algorithms, we developed a model for elastic application and their interaction with the RMS. We made the following assumptions for our proposed model and algorithms:

- All applications in the workload are parallel applications.
- Only processors are considered as resources.
- The HPC system is homogeneous and communication time between any pair of processors are identical.
- An elastic application can run on any number of processors between a predefined minimum and maximum allowable processors (this may not hold true for some applications).
- The overhead of interaction between a running application and the RMS is negligible.

An elastic message-passing application consists of *ph* phases and the number of resources allocated to the application does not change during a phase. Changing a phase involved a change in the number of resources either in response to the application request or the RMS request.

A phase ph_i can be defined by three tuples-

$$< R_i, W_i, T_i >$$

where R_i is the allocation of phase i, W_i is the amount of computation done at that phase and T_i is the execution time of the phase. The total runtime of the application T is a summation of all T_i.

A phase change may involve data re-distribution as the number of processors changes. So, the total time of a phase consists of five components: computation time tw, parallel overhead to, data reorganization cost td, synchronization cost ts, and other overhead such as process creation or terminations tp. So,

$T_i = tw_i + to_i + td_i + ts_i + tp_i$. The parallel overhead of an application in general increases and computation time decreases as the number of processors increases and vice versa when the workload remains constant. We have modeled the parallel overhead as a certain percentage ($x\%$) of total execution time before any phase change. The remaining$(1 - x\%)$ time is required for computation. x varies from application to application. Let us assume that, the application has p_i and p_{i+1} processors at phase i and phase $i+1$. So,

$$to_{i+1} = to_i/p_i * p_{i+1}$$

$$tw_{i+1} = tw_i * p_i/p_{i+1}$$

Data-redistribution cost depends on two variables- the total number of processors involved in change and change in the number of processors. The data distribution cost decreases if the total number of processors involved is increased. Again, data redistribution cost increases with the increase in the difference in the number of processors. For example, the data distribution cost of 8 to 16 processors is lower than the data distribution cost of 4 to 16 processors. The total number of processors involved is 24 and 20, and the difference in processors is 8 and 12, respectively. Synchronization cost varies from application to application state and does not depend on the change in resources. Though synchronization cost depends on the current resources of the application, we are ignoring that for simplification.

$ts_{i+1} = \sigma$, where σ varies from application state to application state. Total processor involved in phase change $p_{total} = p_i + p_{i+1}$. Change in processor $p_{difference} = |p_i - p_{i+1}|$. Then, data redistribution cost-

$$td_{i+1} = \alpha * p_{difference} + \beta/p_{total}.$$

Here, α and β are constants. Other overhead like processor creation or deletion cost is directly proportional to the number of new processors. So,

$$tp_{i+1} = b * p_{difference}$$

where b is the cost of one processor. We have used [9] as the execution model of the elastic parallel application in this study.

4 Scheduling Algorithms

To simulate different scheduling algorithms and visualize their impact on different performance metrics, we have used a discrete event simulator. We have followed the pattern from [9]. The following data structure is used in the algorithms described in this section:

- system state:
  - Idle processors (p_c): Number of idle processors

    - total processors (p_t): Number of total processors
    - Running job list (J_r): List of all currently running jobs
    - Running malleable job list (J_rm): List of all currently running malleable jobs
    - Pending job list (J_p): List of all pending jobs yet to be scheduled
- Candidate schedule:
    - List of job to start list (J_s): Jobs that are scheduled to be started at this time
    - Agreement List (A): List of expansion and shrinkage that needs to be done at this time
- Shrinkable malleable job list (J_sm): List of malleable jobs that need to be shrunk
- Required number of processors p_r: Number of processors that are required by a job for execution

The main scheduling algorithm is described in Algorithm 1.

Algorithm 1. Main Scheduling Algorithm (FCFS & easy backfilling with evolving request priority over pending job with maximizing throughput)

input: The current system state
output: A candidate schedule & system state

(schedule evolving request)#SatisfyEvolvingRequest()
(schedule initial allocation)#InitialAllocation()
if $length(J\_p) > 0$ and $length(J\_rm) > 0$ **then**
    (schedule pending jobs by shrinking malleable jobs)#SchedulePendingJob()
end if
if $p\_c > 0$ and $length(J\_rm) > 0$ **then**
    (expand running malleable jobs if possible)#ExpandRunningMalleableJobs()
end if
while $length(A)$ **do**
    Take the first agreement
    Calculate negotiation cost (Similar to [9])
    execute agreement
    return J_s and A
end while

Main Scheduling Algorithm

The algorithm SatisfyEvolvingRequest() is described in Algorithm 2. As evolving requests are given the highest priority, first the algorithm tries to schedule the evolving request with idle resources. If enough idle resources are not found, the algorithm tries to allocate necessary resources by shrinking malleable jobs. The candidate for shrinkage is chosen by select_shrinkable_job() algorithm. The select_shrinkable_job() algorithm is described later in this section.

The initial allocation is based on FCFS with an easy backfilling scheduling policy [18]. The algorithm is described in Algorithm 3. If there are jobs in

Algorithm 2. SatisfyEvolvingRequest(system state)

```
input: system state
output: A & system state
if Shrinkage Request then
    Add shrink to A
    Update system state
else
    Allocate idle resources
    if Enough idle resources not found then
        J_sm = select_shrinkable_job()
        if length(J_sm) not zero then
            Add the shrinkages to A
            Add the expansion to A
            Update system state
        end if
    end if
end if
return A and system state
```

the pending job list and running malleable job list, the algorithm then tries to schedule pending jobs by shrinking running malleable jobs using the SchedulePendingJob() algorithm. The algorithm is detailed in Algorithm 4.

Algorithm 3. InitialAllocation(J_p, system state)

```
input: J_p, system state
output: J_s, J_p, system state
for each job in J_p do
    if p_c == 0 then
        return J_s, J_p, system state
    end if
    if job.p_r ¡= p_c then
        add the job to J_s
        update system state
    end if
end for
return J_s, J_p, system state
```

The ExpandRunningMalleableJob() algorithm expands running malleable jobs if idle resources are available after scheduling pending jobs. As expanding any job will result in higher system utilization, jobs with the highest runtime are chosen for expansion with the motivation to reduce average turnaround time.

We have proposed three different algorithms to select the shrinkable malleable jobs. Algorithm 5 does not look at any system or application state. It tries to shrink jobs if enough resources are not found. For the rest of the paper, we

Algorithm 4. SchedulePendingJob(J_p)

Input: J_p
Output: A, J_s

```
for each job in J_p do
    if Job is malleable then
        p_r = minimum processor that is required to run the job
    end if
    (J_sm), J_s, system state = select_shrinkable_job()
    if length(J_sm)! = 0 then
        Add shrinkages to agreement list
        Add the job to job_to_start_list and remove from pending queue
        Update system state
    end if
end for
```

will refer to it as "Default". Algorithm 6 looks at the running applications first and sees if any application ends in the next t seconds. If it is the case, then the application waits for that application to finish before it shrinks any new application. We will refer to this algorithm as "Application" for the rest of the paper. Algorithm 7 looks at the system utilization before shrinking any job. If the utilization is greater than $u\%$, it does not shrink any job. For the rest of the paper, we will refer to this algorithm as "System". In each algorithm, malleable jobs are sorted according to a certain priority. These techniques are described later in this section. Algorithm 8 tries to shrink running malleable jobs and allocate necessary resources. The technique to set these priorities is called the candidate/ victim selection technique.

Algorithm 5. Algorithm 01 for selecting shrinkable jobs (SelectShrinkableJob (J_rm, p_r))

input: J_rm and p_r
output: (J_sm) , J_s & system state

```
Sort the running malleable jobs according to priority
for each job in the sorted list do
    J_sm, J_s, system state = AllocateResource(job, p_r, system state)
end for
return empty list, J_s, system state
```

Setting Priority of Malleable Jobs (Candidate/Victim Selection Techniques)

We have used multiple policies to define the priority of malleable applications. These are called candidates of victim selection techniques. The priorities are described below:

- Random, r: Jobs are randomly selected without considering any parameter. Jobs selected first have the highest priority.

Algorithm 6. Algorithm 02 for selecting shrinkable jobs (SelectShrinkableJob (J_rm, p_r))

input: J_rm and p_r
output: (J_sm), J_s & system state

```
if there is a job which is about to end in next t sec then
    return empty list, J_s, system state
end if
Sort the running malleable jobs according to priority
for each job in the sorted list do
    if the job is not x% done then
        J_sm, J_s, system state = AllocateResource(job,p_r, system state)
    end if
end for
return empty list, J_s, system state
```

Algorithm 7. Algorithm 03 for selecting shrinkable jobs (SelectShrinkableJob (J_rm, p_r))

input: J_rm and p_r
output: (J_sm), J_s & system state

```
if utilization is greater than u% then
    if there is a job which is about to end in next t second then
        return empty list, J_s, system state
    end if
end if
Sort the running malleable jobs according to priority
for each job in the sorted list do
    J_sm, J_s, system state = AllocateResource(job, p_r, system state)
end for
return empty list, J_s, system state
```

Algorithm 8. AllocateResource(job, p_r, system state)

input: job, p_r, system state
output: (J_sm), J_s & system state

```
needed resource allocation = p_r
if available_shrinkable_resources of job ≥ p_r then
    shrinkable resources = needed resource allocation
    needed resource allocation = 0
    add pending job to J_s
else
    needed resource allocation -= available shrinkable resources
    shrinkable resources = available resource allocation
end if
Add the malleable job to J_sm
if needed resource allocation = 0 then
    Return J_sm, J_s, system state
end if
Return J_sm, J_s, system state
```

- Gain, g: Initially, every job has a gain (g) value set to 0. Every time a job expands or shrinks, the gain changes. For expansion, the number of expanded cores is added to the gain. For shrinkage, the number of shrunk cores is subtracted from gain. The job with the highest gain has the highest priority.
- Shrinkable Resources, sr: If the application is running on $P_{current}$ processors and the minimum processor for the application is P_{min}, then the application has $P_{current} - P_{min}$ shrinkable resources (sr). The application with the highest sr has the highest priority. If two applications have the same shrinkable resources, the application with the highest current resources has the highest priority.
- No. of expansion, e: The job with the highest number of expansions (e) has the highest priority.
- Adaptation Cost, a: The job with the lowest adaptation cost has the highest priority.
- Time, t: The job with the lowest remaining runtime (t) has the highest priority.

4.1 Evaluation Metrics

We choose average turnaround time to measure application performance and utilization to indicate system performance.

If the arrival time of a job i is Ta_i and completion time is Tc_i, and the workload has total n jobs then average turn around time (TAT) is -

$$average\ TAT \sum_{i=1}^{n} \frac{Tc_i - Ta_i}{n}$$

System utilization indicates the fraction of CPU cycles that has been used during the execution of the workload. If the scheduled span of a workload is SS and total processors is p, then total cpu cycle, $C_{total} = SS * p$. Let us assume that the CPU cycle used by an application i is C_i. If the application has total ph phases and the execution time and processor of phase p is T_p and P_p respectively then,

$$C_i = \sum_{p=1}^{ph} T_p * P_p$$

If the workload has total n jobs then,

$$utilization = \sum_{i=1}^{n} \frac{C_i}{C_{total}}$$

5 Experiment and Results

5.1 Workload

Selecting a workload to simulate a scheduling algorithm needs special attention. The workload should emulate the workload running on a cluster. Input data for simulating scheduling algorithms can be obtained in two ways. One is to derive it from workload traces of the existing HPC system and the other is to generate them using different workload models. For our study, we have used two real workloads and one synthetic workload. We have chosen the LLNL Atlas [17] and the KIT for HLR II [24] logs from the parallel workload archive [7]. We will refer to these two workloads as LLNL and KIT, respectively. For both workloads, we have considered the first 10,000 jobs for simulation. In order to increase the load and see the impact of that, we have further modified these two workloads. We have created two shrunk versions of LLNL and KIT by shrinking the inter-arrival time by 5% and 35% respectively. The modified workloads are referred to as LLNL-shrunk and KIT-shrunk respectively. In addition to the real workloads, one synthetic workload has been generated using Downey's model [6]. A workload containing 10,000 jobs was created with a cluster size of 10,000 processors. The model parameters to generate the workload are listed in Table 1.

Table 1. Parameters of Downey's model to generate synthetic

#Jobs	rho	seed	Job width ($ln(T_r)$)		Job size ($ln(P)$)	
10,000	0.75	17	Min	Max	Min	Max
			5.69	9.91	0.69	8.51

Table 2 summarizes the workloads. The max processor and min processors are the maximum and the minimum number of processors a job has in the workload, respectively. The relevant parameters of the workloads are:

Table 2. Workloads for simulation

Workload	# of jobs	Max processor	Min processor	Total processors	% of shrinkage in interarrival time
LLNL	10,000	9160	1	9,216	–
LLNL_shrunk	10,000	9160	1	9,216	5%
KIT	10,000	10,240	1	24,048	–
KIT_shrunk	10,000	10,240	1	24,048	35%
Synthetic	10,000	4994	2	10,000	–

- Id: A unique identifier for the jobs in the workload
- Type: A job can be of three types- rigid, malleable and evolving

- Arrival, T_a: Job arrival time
- Runtime, T_r: Execution time of a job
- Processors, P: Number of desirable processor allocation
- Minimum Allowable processor, p_{min}: Minimum required resource allocation for a job. p_{min} is equal to P for rigid jobs.
- Maximum Allowable Processor, p_{max}: Maximum allowable processor allocation of a job. p_{max} is equal to P for rigid jobs.

Creating Elastic Workload. All the workloads mentioned in Sect. 5.1 are rigid. We have generated an elastic workload by randomly selecting jobs to be elastic. If in a certain workload $x\%$ of jobs are elastic, then $x/2\%$ of them are malleable, and $x/2\%$ of jobs are evolving. For every workload, we have made in total 10 elastic versions with $10, 20, 30, 40, 50, 60, 70, 80, 90$, and 100% elastic jobs. Every elastic job has maximum and minimum processor requirements. We have selected 800% of P to be the maximum (p_{max}) and 50% of P to be the minimum (p_{min}) allowable resources.

Evolving jobs make expansion and shrinkage requests to the simulator. We refer to these requests as evolving requests. We choose the total number of evolving requests submitted by an evolving job chosen randomly from a predefined maximum and minimum. We have selected the event type (expansion or shrinkage) from a Bernoulli Distribution with a higher probability to be expansion. Then, we have chosen the number of processors involved in the evolving event from a predefined maximum and minimum. The time of occurrence of each evolving event is selected at a percentage of the remaining computation. The percentage is also chosen from a predefined minimum and maximum.

5.2 Experimental Setup

The discrete event simulator has been implemented using Python 3.4.1. Results shown in this section reflect the average of 10 runs. We have chosen the predefined parameters used in this simulation from an educated guess. Parameters were chosen to be the following:

- t in Algorithm 6 and 5 is set to be 5 s.
- u in Algorithm 5 is set to be 80.
- Maximum negotiation cost is set to be 0.05 s and minimum negotiation cost is set to be 0.005 s.
- Parallel overhead defined in the mathematical model (Sect. 3) is set to be between 0.5% to 1%.
- α and β defined in the mathematical model of Sect. 3 are randomly chosen from a uniform random distribution of 0.005 to 0.05.
- Synchronization cost defined in the mathematical model of Sect. 3 is randomly chosen from a uniform random distribution of 0.015 s to 0.1 s.
- Maximum and minimum evolving events requested by an evolving application are set to be 4 and 1 respectively.
- Probability of an evolving event to be an expansion event is set to be 0.8
- Expansion event can occur anytime when 30% to 60% of work is left.

5.3 Results

In all cases, including elastic application into the workload improves performance over only rigid workload. The performance of the only rigid workload is shown in the dotted line in all the plots of this section. Figures 1, and 2 show the comparison of algorithm System, Application, and Default in terms of average turnaround time, and system utilization of KIT workload, respectively. The algorithm System attains the best system utilization for all candidate selection techniques but performs worst in terms of average turnaround time. Algorithms Application and Default perform in a similar manner.

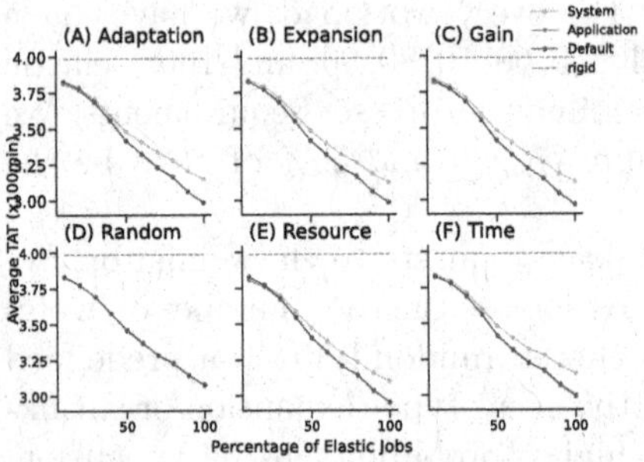

Fig. 1. Average turnaround time of KIT workload with different algorithms

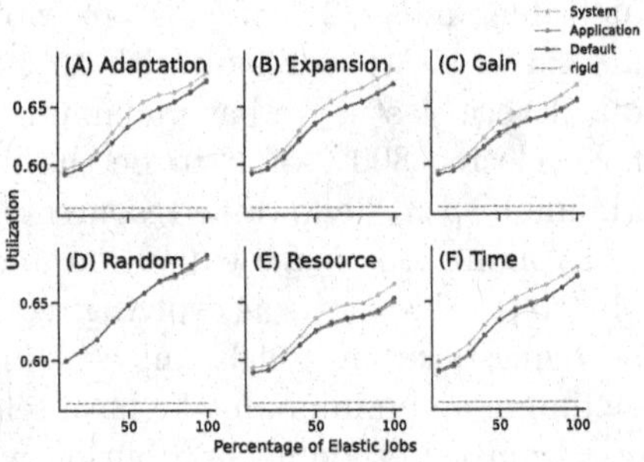

Fig. 2. System utilization with KIT workload and different algorithms

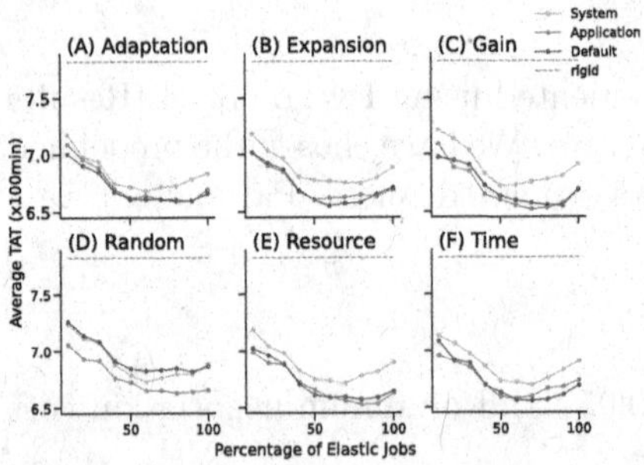

Fig. 3. Average turnaround time of KIT_shrunk workload with different algorithms

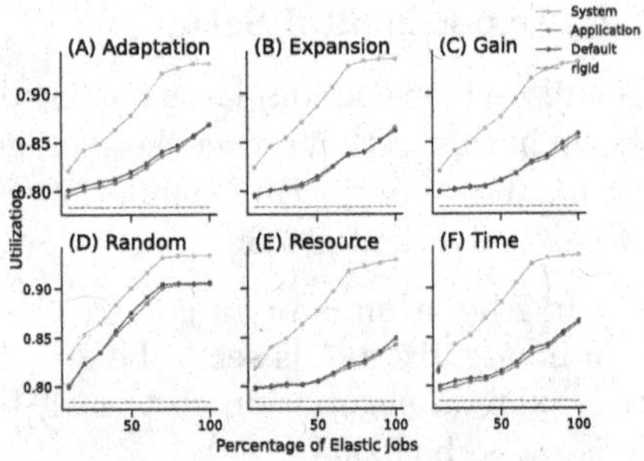

Fig. 4. System utilization with KIT_shrunk workload and different algorithms

Figures 3, and 4 show the comparison of Algorithm System, Application, and Default in terms of average TAT, and system utilization of KIT_shrunk workload, respectively. Random performs the best in terms of utilization for all three algorithms. The algorithm System attains the best system utilization

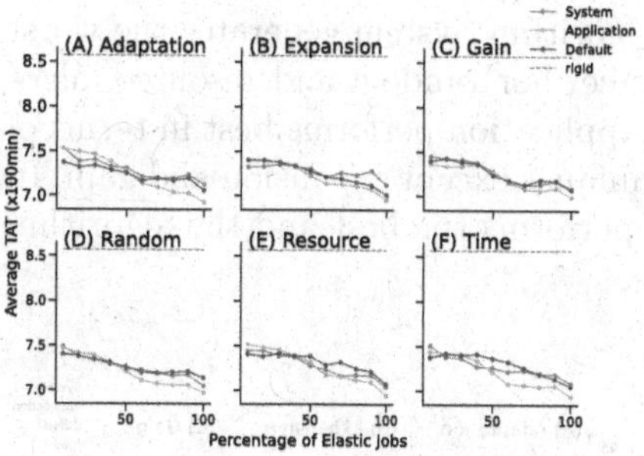

Fig. 5. Average turnaround time of LLNL workload with different algorithms

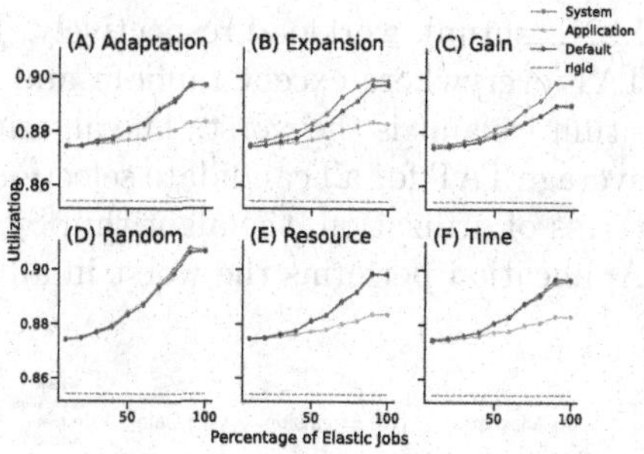

Fig. 6. System utilization with LLNL workload and different algorithms

for all candidate selection Algorithms but performs the worst in terms of average turnaround time. The algorithm Application performs the best in terms of average turnaround time (see Fig. 3).

Figures 5 and 6 show the comparison of algorithm System, Application, and Default in terms of average turnaround time, and system utilization of LLNL workload respectively. The algorithm System has the worst average TAT in the case of adaptation, expansion, and gain. The algorithm Default has the worst average TAT in the case of random, resource, and time. The algorithm Application provides the best TAT in all cases. In terms of utilization, the algorithm System gets the best turnaround time for adaptation, expansion, gain, and random. Algorithm Default generates the best utilization for resources and time. The worst TAT comes from the algorithm Application in case of adaptation, expansion, resource, and time, and from the algorithm Default in case of gain and random.

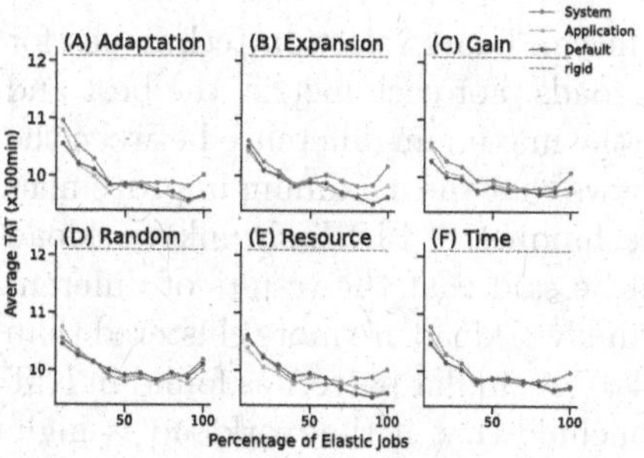

Fig. 7. Average turnaround time of LLNL_shrunk workload with different algorithms

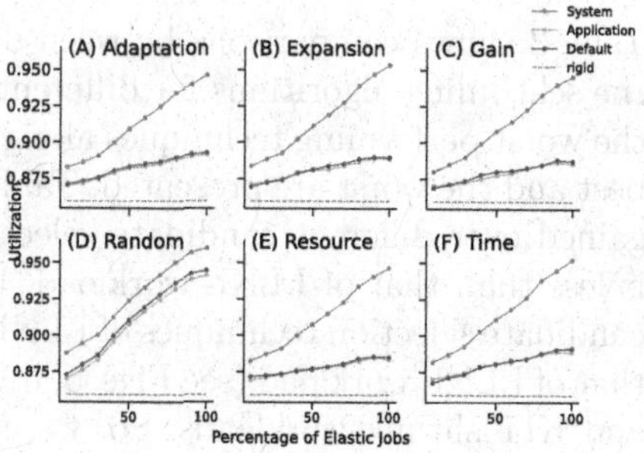

Fig. 8. System utilization with LLNL_shrunk workload and different algorithms

Figures 7 and 8 show the comparison of Algorithm System, Application, and Default in terms of average turnaround time, and system utilization of

LLNL_shrunk workload respectively. The algorithm System generates the worst TAT everywhere except random and resource. For random and resource, algorithm Default is the worst. The algorithm Application performs best in terms of average TAT for all candidate selection techniques except expansion and gain. In terms of utilization, the algorithm System performs the best and the algorithm Application performs the worst in all cases.

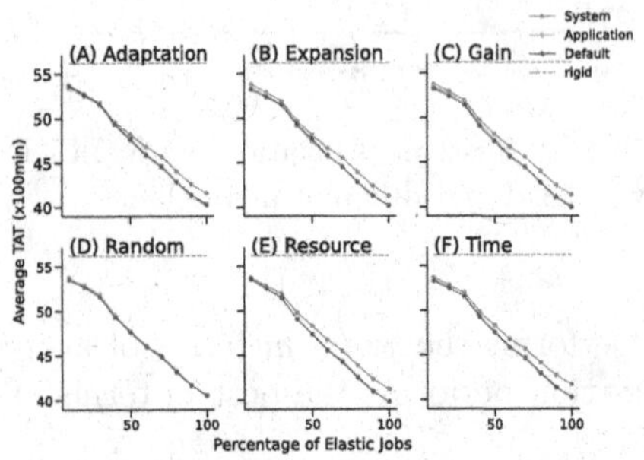

Fig. 9. Average turnaround time of synthetic workload with different algorithms

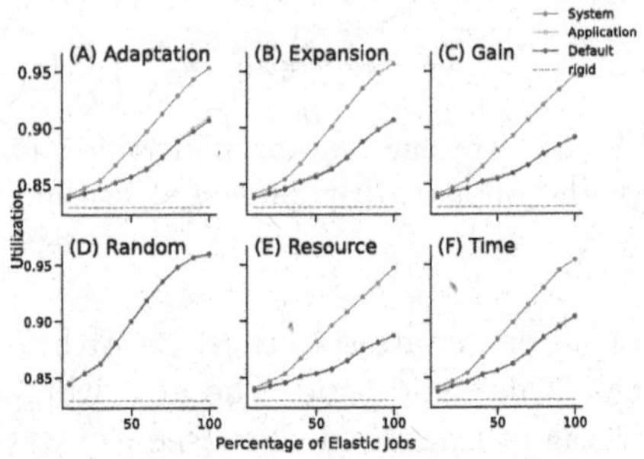

Fig. 10. System utilization with synthetic workload and different algorithms

Figures 9 and 10 show the comparison of algorithm System, Application, and Default respectively in terms of average TAT, and system utilization of Synthetic workload, respectively. In terms of average TAT and utilization, the results of the algorithm Application and Default are clustered together. The algorithm System is the best in terms of utilization and the worst in terms of average TAT.

5.4 Analysis

Table 3 shows comparisons between different candidate selection techniques for the scheduling algorithms for different workloads. For each metric, the best and the worst performing techniques along with the maximum difference between the best and the worst are presented. Table 3 shows that the maximum improvement gained over different candidate selection techniques of LLNL_shrunk workload is less than that of LLNL workload. It can be said that the results of different candidate selection techniques of LLNL_shrunk workload are more clustered than that of LLNL workload (see Figs. 5, 6, 7 and 8). A similar pattern is found in KIT and KIT_shrunk workloads. So, we can conclude that if the workload is high, the difference in performance between different candidate selection techniques becomes insignificant. Table 3 also shows that in terms of average TAT gain performs the best and random performs the worst in most of the cases. In terms of utilization, random performs the best, and resource performs the worst in most cases.

The performance of Synthetic workload increases as the percentage of elastic jobs increases. For other workloads, the increase saturates and stops at some

Table 3. Maximum improvement achieved by using different candidate selection techniques at any percentage of elastic jobs

Workload	Algorithm	Average TAT			Utilization		
		Best	Worst	Max difference	Best	Worst	Max difference
LLNL	Application	Gain	Random	2.62% at 40% elastic jobs	Random	Resource	8.075% at 70% elastic jobs
	System	Gain	Resource	2.09% at 100% elastic jobs	Random	Resource	3.65% at 70% elastic jobs
	Default	Random	Resource	3.08% at 30% elastic jobs	Random	Resource	9.0% at 90% elastic jobs
LLNL_shrunk	Application	Adaptation	Random	1.45% at 70% elastic jobs	Random	Time	3.23% at 90% elastic jobs
	System	Gain	Random	2.19% at 60% elastic jobs	Random	Time	1.65% at 90% elastic jobs
	Default	Resource	Random	2.36% at 100% elastic jobs	Random	Gain	2.49% at 90% elastic jobs
KIT	Application	Gain	Random	3.21% at 70% elastic jobs	Random	Resource	10.25% at 50% elastic jobs
	System	Adaptation	Random	3.04% at 20% elastic jobs	Random	Resource	3.11% at 40% elastic jobs
	Default	Gain	Random	5.7% at 70% elastic jobs	Random	Resource	10.9% at 50% elastic jobs
KIT_shrunk	Application	Gain	Random	1.23% at 80% elastic jobs	Random	Resource	0.85% at 90% elastic jobs
	System	Gain	Time	1.66% at 100% elastic jobs	Random	Resource	1.33% at 60% elastic jobs
	Default	Gain	Random	2.84% at 100% elastic jobs	Random	Resource	1.31% at 90% elastic jobs
Synthetic	Application	Gain	Random	1.51% at 60% elastic jobs	Random	Resource	8.58% at 80% elastic jobs
	System	Gain	Time	1.09% at 90% elastic jobs	Random	Resource	3.6% at 70% elastic jobs
	Default	Gain	Random	1.79% at 90% elastic jobs	Random	Resource	3.47% at 70% elastic jobs

point. Figures 11 and 12 shows the distribution of total jobs and the elastic jobs of KIT_shrunk workload and Synthetic workload when 30% and 60% of the workload are elastic respectively. The distribution for KIT, LLNL, and LLNL_shrunk workloads is similar to KIT_shrunk workloads. From these figures, we can see that in the case of Synthetic workload there are always elastic jobs present in the workload which is not the case for other workloads. For this reason, the Synthetic workload shows constant improvement with the increase in the percentage of elastic jobs.

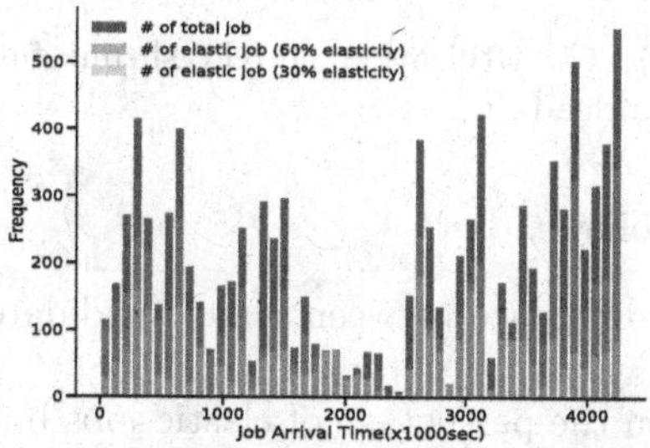

Fig. 11. Distribution of elastic job in KIT_shrunk workload

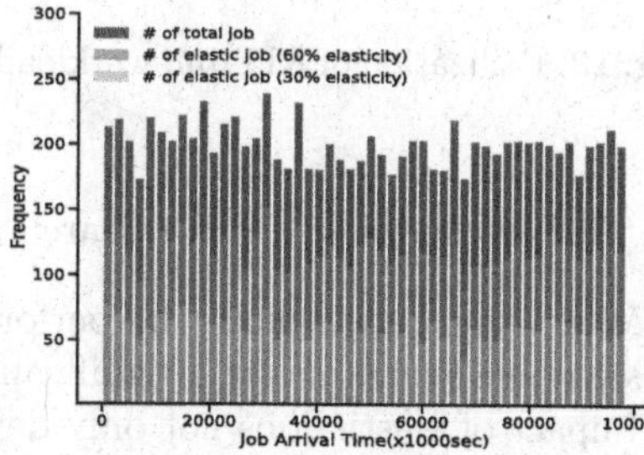

Fig. 12. Distribution of elastic job in synthetic workload

For KIT workload and KIT_shrunk workload, no algorithm can achieve utilization above 91% (see Figs. 2 and 4). The possible reason for this can be fragmentation and/or adaptation and negotiation overhead. Elastic jobs have a limit on how much they can expand. As a result, fragmentation can still exist even after the full expansion of all running elastic jobs. Again, the job distribution over time may be in such a way that at any point in time, there may not be any elastic job running at the cluster, and the cluster may remain underutilized. Also, adaptation cost and negotiation cost cause some utilization loss. To investigate this further, we have created another version of KIT and KIT_shrunk workload where every elastic job has a maximum resource of 24048 (equal to cluster size) and a minimum resource of 1. We refer to this phenomenon as 100% flexibility. We call these versions KIT_full workload and KIT_shrunk_full workload, respectively. Figures 13 and 14 show the utilization of KIT_full and KIT_shrunk_full workloads, respectively. Utilization of KIT_full workload saturates at 90%, but utilization of KIT_shrunk_full workload saturates at 98.5%. This proves that the KIT_full workload still has fragmentation as the inter-arrival time is high as well as adaptation and negotiation overhead. On the other hand, KIT_shrunk_full workload losses 1.5% utilization due to adaptation cost and negotiation cost. Also, from the figures, a knee is visible in the utilization curve. After a certain point, utilization saturates and does not improve with the increase in percentage elastic jobs. At 100% flexibility, improvement in utilization saturates at a certain percentage of elastic jobs.

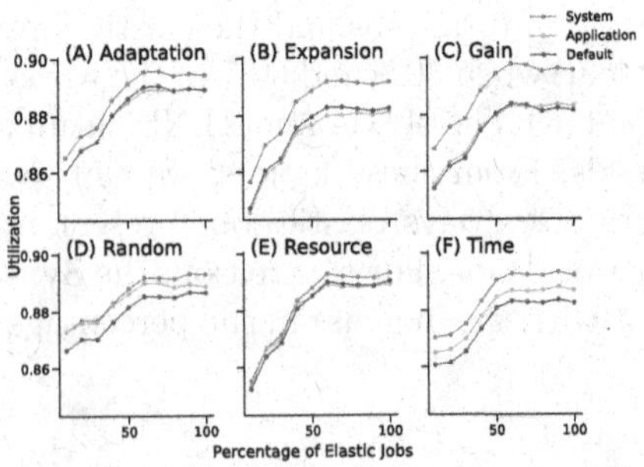

Fig. 13. Utilization of KIT_full workload

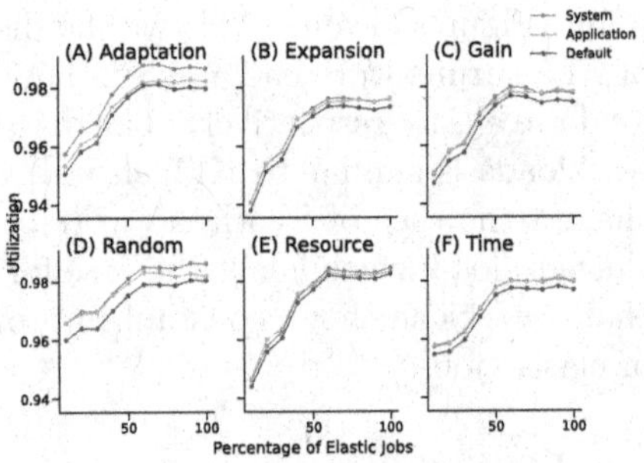

Fig. 14. Utilization of KIT_shrunk_full workload

The key findings of this research are as follows:

- When the load is high, the performance difference between many candidate selection techniques is insignificant.
- Impact of elastic jobs not only depends on the percentage of elastic jobs but also depends on the distribution of elastic jobs over time. The more uniform the distribution of elastic jobs over time is, the more evident the impact is.
- Even introducing 100% flexibility, utilization may not be 100% due to adaptation cost, negotiation cost, and fragmentation. Fragmentation may still remain due to the limit on the expansion capability of running elastic jobs.
- Algorithm System (Algorithm 7) always gets the highest system utilization. In most of the cases, the Algorithm Application (Algorithm 6) gets the lowest average TAT.

- In terms of average TAT, the case study shows that gain performs the best and random performs the worst in most cases. In terms of utilization, random performs the best and resource performs the worst in most cases.
- In all cases even a low percentage of elastic jobs (as low as 10% of the total job) improves the performance.

6 Conclusion and Future Works

The main objective of our research is to propose and evaluate different scheduling strategies for elastic applications under different workloads. We have proposed three different scheduling algorithms, and for every algorithm, we have proposed six candidate selection techniques to prioritize shrinkable jobs. We have evaluated the proposed algorithms using modified workload traces from real systems as well as synthetic workloads. The following are the main observations from our study: 1) With the increased workload, the difference in performance improvement between the proposed candidate selection techniques becomes insignificant. 2) The impact of elasticity not only depends on the number of elastic jobs but also depends on their distribution over time in the workload. The more uniform the distribution of elastic jobs over time is, the more constant the improvement will be with the increase in elasticity. 3) We have observed that even with 100% flexibility, 100% utilization can not be achieved. Adaptation and negotiation overhead limits the maximum achievable utilization. 4) In all cases, workload with elastic applications improves both system and application performance compared to the same workload with rigid workload only. 5) Even with a very small percentage of elasticity (as low as 10%), both system and application performance improved.

One of the limitations of the study is that the HPC systems we derived the workload traces for our simulation no longer represent current large HPC systems such ORNL Summit, Fugaku, etc., or upcoming systems like ORNL Frontier. In addition, simulation parameters such as adaptation cost used for simulation were derived from educated estimates based on sample runs of an iterative structured grid application running on a medium-size cluster. Experiments with the real application at scale should be used to estimate the value of such parameters. These limitations are mostly due to time, effort, allocation and access to large HPC systems, and availability of real workload traces from systems like Summit. Our planned future work includes: 1) investigating candidate selection policies for job expansion, 2) the impact of the ratio of malleable and evolving jobs in the workload on performance (all our workload has 50% malleable 50% evolving). It is difficult to estimate the execution time of an application if the number of processors is changed in the middle of execution. There exists some model to estimate the total execution time of an application on different sets of processors [2,22]. Further exploration/extension of such models for estimation of execution time on a different number of processors can be investigated.

References

1. Ayguade, E., Badía, R., Labarta, J.: OmpSs and the Nanos++ runtime
2. Bhimani, J., Mi, N., Leeser, M., Yang, Z.: New performance modeling methods for parallel data processing applications. ACM Trans. Model. Comput. Simul. (TOMACS) **29**(3), 1–24 (2019)
3. Castain, R.H., Hursey, J., Bouteiller, A., Solt, D.: PMIx: process management for exascale environments. Parallel Comput. **79**, 9–29 (2018)
4. D'Amico, M., Jokanovic, A., Corbalan, J.: Holistic slowdown driven scheduling and resource management for malleable jobs. In: Proceedings of the 48th International Conference on Parallel Processing, pp. 1–10 (2019)
5. Dongarra, J.: Report on the Fujitsu Fugaku system. University of Tennessee-Knoxville Innovative Computing Laboratory, Technical report ICLUT-20-06 (2020)
6. Downey, A.B.: A parallel workload model and its implications for processor allocation. Clust. Comput. **1**(1), 133–145 (1998)
7. Feitelson, D.G.: Parallel workload archive (2007). http://www.cs.huji.ac.il/labs/parallel/workload
8. Feitelson, D.G., Rudolph, L.: Toward convergence in job scheduling for parallel supercomputers (1996)
9. Ghafoor, S.K.: Modeling of an adaptive parallel system with malleable applications in a distributed computing environment. Mississippi State University (2007)
10. Gupta, A., Acun, B., Sarood, O., Kalé, L.V.: Towards realizing the potential of malleable jobs. In: 2014 21st International Conference on High Performance Computing (HiPC), pp. 1–10. IEEE (2014)
11. Iserte, S., Mayo, R., Quintana-Ortí, E.S., Beltran, V., Peña, A.J.: DMR API: improving cluster productivity by turning applications into malleable. Parallel Comput. **78**, 54–66 (2018)
12. Iserte, S., Mayo, R., Quintana-Orti, E.S., Pena, A.J.: DMRlib: easy-coding and efficient resource management for job malleability. IEEE Trans. Comput. **70**(9), 1443–1457 (2020)
13. Kale, L.V., Krishnan, S.: Charm++ a portable concurrent object oriented system based on C++. In: Proceedings of the Eighth Annual Conference on Object-Oriented Programming Systems, Languages, and Applications, pp. 91–108 (1993)
14. Kalé, L.V., Kumar, S., DeSouza, J.: A malleable-job system for timeshared parallel machines. In: 2nd IEEE/ACM International Symposium on Cluster Computing and the Grid (CCGRID 2002), pp. 230–230. IEEE (2002)
15. Kale, L.V., Zheng, G.: Charm++ and AMPI: adaptive runtime strategies via migratable objects. In: Advanced Computational Infrastructures for Parallel and Distributed Applications, pp. 265–282 (2009)
16. Klein, C., Pérez, C.: An RMS for non-predictably evolving applications. In: 2011 IEEE International Conference on Cluster Computing, pp. 326–334. IEEE (2011)
17. Minh, T.N., Wolters, L.: Modeling parallel system workloads with temporal locality. In: Frachtenberg, E., Schwiegelshohn, U. (eds.) JSSPP 2009. LNCS, vol. 5798, pp. 101–115. Springer, Heidelberg (2009). https://doi.org/10.1007/978-3-642-04633-9_6
18. Mu'alem, A.W., Feitelson, D.G.: Utilization, predictability, workloads, and user runtime estimates in scheduling the IBM SP2 with backfilling. IEEE Trans. Parallel Distrib. Syst. **12**(6), 529–543 (2001)
19. Polyakov, A.Y., Karasev, B.I., Hursey, J., Ladd, J., Brinskii, M., Shipunova, E.: A performance analysis and optimization of PMIx-based HPC software stacks. In: Proceedings of the 26th European MPI Users' Group Meeting, pp. 1–10 (2019)

20. Prabhakaran, S., Iqbal, M., Rinke, S., Windisch, C., Wolf, F.: A batch system with fair scheduling for evolving applications. In: 2014 43rd International Conference on Parallel Processing, pp. 351–360. IEEE (2014)
21. Prabhakaran, S., Neumann, M., Rinke, S., Wolf, F., Gupta, A., Kale, L.V.: A batch system with efficient adaptive scheduling for malleable and evolving applications. In: 2015 IEEE International Parallel and Distributed Processing Symposium, pp. 429–438. IEEE (2015)
22. Raeder, M., Griebler, D., Baldo, L., Fernandes, L.G.: Performance prediction of parallel applications with parallel patterns using stochastic methods. In: Sistemas Computacionais (WSCAD-SSC), XII Simpósio em Sistemas Computacionais de Alto Desempenho, pp. 1–13 (2011)
23. Schneider, D.: The exascale era is upon us: the frontier supercomputer may be the first to reach 1,000,000,000,000,000,000 operations per second. IEEE Spectr. **59**(1), 34–35 (2022)
24. Soysal, M., Berghoff, M., Klusáček, D., Streit, A.: On the quality of wall time estimates for resource allocation prediction. In: Proceedings of the 48th International Conference on Parallel Processing: Workshops, pp. 1–8 (2019)
25. Sudarsan, R., Ribbens, C.J.: ReSHAPE: a framework for dynamic resizing and scheduling of homogeneous applications in a parallel environment. In: 2007 International Conference on Parallel Processing (ICPP 2007), p. 44. IEEE (2007)
26. Utrera, G., Tabik, S., Corbalán, J., Labarta, J.: A job scheduling approach to reduce waiting times. Technical report, Technical University of Catalonia, UPCDAC-RR-2012-1 (2011)
27. Vadhiyar, S.S., Dongarra, J.J.: SRS: a framework for developing malleable and migratable parallel applications for distributed systems. Parallel Process. Lett. **13**(02), 291–312 (2003)
28. Yoo, A.B., Jette, M.A., Grondona, M.: SLURM: simple Linux utility for resource management. In: Feitelson, D., Rudolph, L., Schwiegelshohn, U. (eds.) JSSPP 2003. LNCS, vol. 2862, pp. 44–60. Springer, Heidelberg (2003). https://doi.org/10.1007/10968987_3

Improving Accuracy of Walltime Estimates in PBS Professional Using Soft Walltimes

Václav Chlumský and Dalibor Klusáček(✉)

CESNET a.l.e., Brno, Czech Republic
{vchlumsky,klusacek}@cesnet.cz

Abstract. Job walltime estimates are used by current batch schedulers to optimize the performance and predictability when scheduling parallel jobs on the computing resources. Since the user-provided estimates are inaccurate and often overestimated, system administrators often seek ways to improve them artificially using some form of walltime predictor. In this work, we present our real-life experience with deploying such a predictor using the *soft walltime* feature available in PBS Professional resource manager. Our results indicate that the applied solution is working properly, significantly increasing the accuracy of user-provided estimates. We share our experience when tuning the scheduler, discussing several problems that occurred along the way. Also, we provide a comparison of how the system behavior evolved once soft walltimes were deployed in production. Last but not least, we publish collected workload traces along with this paper to allow other researchers to further study and extend our work.

Keywords: Job · Scheduling · Soft walltime · Estimate · Prediction · PBS

1 Introduction

This paper is addressing the problem of inaccurate user-provided job walltime estimates [7,8,12]. Inaccurate estimates cause holes to be left in the schedule during backfilling [10] as jobs appear to be too long for them to fit in. This may lead to a well known scenario, where only very short jobs can use the holes in the schedule, resulting in an SJF-like behavior (Shortest Job First) that can compromise other system's goals such as fair job ordering [16].

This paper is motivated by our real-life experience when maintaining the PBS Professional resource manager in the Czech national distributed computing infrastructure *MetaCentrum* [9]. As we have already discussed in our previous work [7], our users are no exception to the widely documented behavior of common HPC system users. They tend to use rather overestimated job walltime estimates in order to decrease the chance that their job will be prematurely killed due to running out of time. So the most common scenario is that users

D. Klusáček et al. (Eds.): JSSPP 2022, LNCS 13592, pp. 192–210, 2023.
https://doi.org/10.1007/978-3-031-22698-4_10

choose the maximum allowed runtime of a queue and then use it as the walltime estimate.

This well-known fact [15,16] motivated several researchers to either develop some form of runtime prediction technique or find a significant incentive for individual users to improve the accuracy of their runtime requests [2,8]. While the problem itself and various walltime prediction techniques have been studied extensively, we saw very little practical deployment of these techniques in practice. One of the reason was that mainstream resource managers did not provide tools to easily implement walltime predictors. This has changed in 2017 when PBS Professional introduced the so called *"soft walltime"* feature—a tool designed to simplify walltime predictor deployment [14].

In our earlier work [7], we used historical workload traces and a simulator to evaluate the impact of various walltime predictors in simulated HPC system. Those simulations were designed in order to give us a hint whether it is worth the effort to use the soft walltime in practice. Since the results were promising, we have decided to use soft walltimes generated by walltime predictor in our HPC system. This paper summarizes our current experience and lessons learned along the way.

The main contributions of this paper are following. In Sect. 2, we provide detailed description of our predictor and its integration in the HPC system. We discuss the evolution of the walltime predicting algorithm and—using real-life data—we illustrate problems that were observed and required our attention during the development. Section 3 analyzes the accuracy of the predictor in great detail, showing how even relatively simple predictor can improve the accuracy of job walltime estimates. Next, we analyze how the system performance has changed since the soft walltime has been deployed and used (Sect. 4). We believe that this paper is one of the first reports that documents the impact of soft walltimes in real environment. We conclude the paper in Sect. 5 and provide the developed predictor and all workload traces used in this study to the scheduling community.

2 Soft Walltime Adoption in CERIT-SC

In this paper we are using real data from the *CERIT-SC* partition of *MetaCentrum* infrastructure. CERIT-SC manages the second largest partition in our infrastructure [1]. It consists of 6,656 CPUs and it has its own instance of PBS server. This allowed us to use it as a "guinea-pig" in our efforts to introduce soft walltimes in MetaCentrum.

2.1 Inaccurate Estimates

To demonstrate the level of inaccuracy of user-provided estimates we present Fig. 1 that shows how jobs are distributed according to their user-provided walltime and their actual runtime. Clearly, the curves are very different and do not match at all as users provide rather overestimated walltimes. This means that the scheduler is using very inaccurate data when constructing reservations for

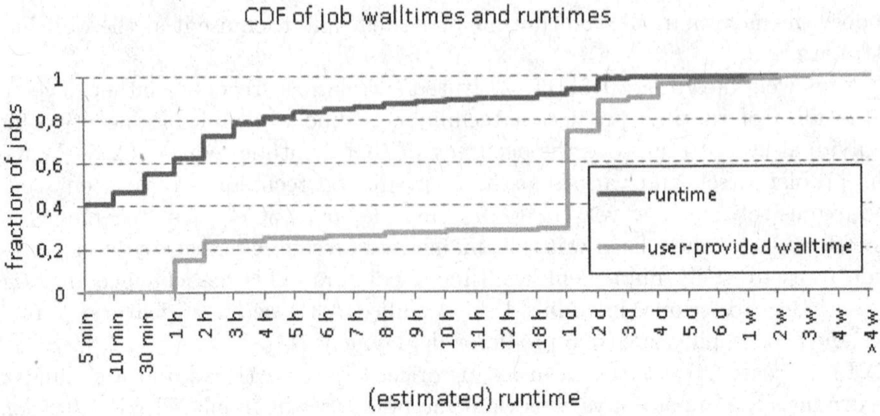

Fig. 1. Cumulative distribution functions of user-provided walltimes and actual job runtimes. User-provided estimates are significantly overestimated.

top jobs[1], predicting job start times, or trying to find small-enough jobs to be backfilled.

2.2 Soft Walltime Functionality

Soft walltimes in PBS are designed to safely *refine* user-provided job walltime (runtime) estimates. When enabled, the scheduler does not use user-provided estimates but instead uses so-called soft walltimes for all scheduling operations. Most importantly, it uses them to create job reservation(s) and perform backfilling. Soft walltimes are safe from the point of view of the user, because jobs are not killed when their soft walltimes are exceeded. As usual, a job is only killed when it exceeds its original, user-provided estimate. Unlike the walltimes which represent hard limit on job runtime, soft walltimes can be underestimated. In such situation the soft walltime is increased by a factor of two. This process can be repeated until either the job completes or the original walltime limit is reached. Underestimated soft walltimes should be avoided (if possible) because they can invalidate guaranteed start times for top jobs [13]. An important security feature is that soft walltimes cannot be (by default) specified or modified by users. Only the manager (system administrator) is allowed to set them up, typically using the so-called *job hook* script. This guarantees that users cannot obtain unfair priority in backfilling by providing very low (unrealistic) soft walltimes. More details on soft walltimes can be found in the PBS documentation [13,14].

This paper is not focusing on discussing various runtime prediction techniques. Instead, we will proceed with the details of our solution and we kindly

[1] In PBS Professional, not every waiting job gets a reservation. Only a predefined number of high priority jobs (per queue) has guaranteed (latest) start times and these are called top jobs. Remaining jobs can be backfilled around top jobs provided they will not interfere with their reservations.

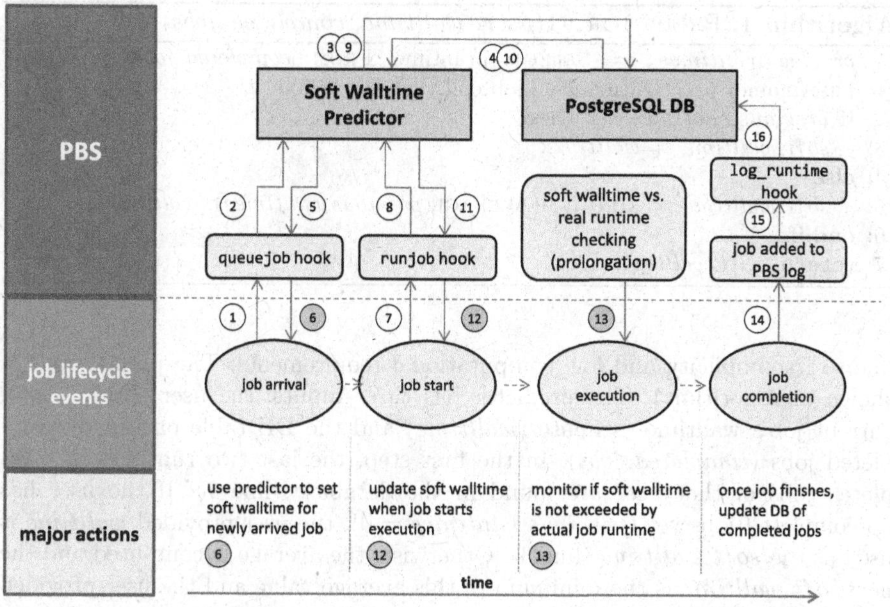

Fig. 2. The scheme of soft walltime generation used in CERIT-SC system.

refer to existing works that discuss various techniques for walltime refinement, e.g., the survey from Seneviratne and Witharana [11] or Soysal et al. [15].

2.3 Soft Walltime Predictor Implementation

The soft walltime feature was enabled by implementing a very simple predictor. The predictor uses a small PostgreSQL database that collect statistics about previously completed jobs of each user. The SQL database is hosted on the main server and all SQL-related operations are performed using PBS hooks. No operations are needed on the MoMs (execution nodes) due to security reasons (no SQL connections to the server-side database). As designed in PBS, soft walltime can be set either upon job arrival, job modification or when a job starts (using hook events: `queuejob`, `modifyjob` and `runjob`).

In our implementation, soft walltime is first generated upon each job arrival and is later updated when the job starts its execution. Once the job completes and is recorded in the PBS accounting log, we add its parameters into the PostgreSQL database to keep it up-to-date. Figure 2 depicts the current implementation and the main events + communication used to generate and maintain soft walltimes.

The predictor used for soft walltime generation is very simple and underwent two major upgrades since its first deployment in October 2021. The first version (v1) used simple arithmetic average of the last two previous runtimes of completed jobs of a given user [17]. This solution was used as a baseline

Algorithm 1. PREDICTOR_V1(*user*, *walltime*, *completed_jobs*)

```
1: previous_runtimes := SELECT j.runtime FROM completed_jobs j WHERE
   j.user_name=user ORDER BY j.job_end_time DESC limit 2;
2: if previous_runtimes = ∅ then
3:    soft_walltime := walltime;
4: else
5:    soft_walltime := MINIMUM(AVERAGE(previous_runtimes), walltime);
6: end if
7: return soft_walltime;
```

due to its simplicity and low computational requirements. The pseudo-code is shown in Algorithm 1. The predictor has three inputs: the user name (*user*), current job's walltime estimate (*walltime*) and the DB table of already completed jobs (*completed_jobs*). In the first step, the last two runtimes of completed jobs of that user are found in the database (line 1). If the user has no completed jobs yet (*previous_runtimes* $= \emptyset$), the user-provided *walltime* is used as the *soft_walltime* (line 3). Otherwise, the average is computed and the new *soft_walltime* is the minimum of this average value and the user-provided *walltime* (line 5).

This predictor was used for roughly three weeks and its performance was then analyzed. Although it reduced absolute estimate errors significantly, it had one major flaw which was obvious and critical—it generated too many predictions that were underestimated. This was a big problem because it meant that the scheduler had to perform many soft walltime prolongations (see Sect. 2.2) which implied that existing reservations previously computed by the scheduler (using overly optimistic soft walltimes) were not valid and top jobs were delayed. We performed detailed analysis and realized that *by adding a fixed reserve* to every generated soft walltime (+15 min) we should be able solve this problem in most cases. This simple modification was added to the predictor at the beginning of November 2021.

Although this modification reduced the number of underestimated soft walltimes, it only worked for users with fairly stable job runtimes. Sadly, there are users in our system with highly spread job runtimes. Notably, we are dealing with users that have highly varying runtimes within a single batch of jobs[2]. To demonstrate this problem we provide Fig. 3 that shows every job submission of a given user within the first week of November 2021. Vertical axis represents job runtime while the horizontal axis is the job submission time.

It is clear, that with such highly spread runtime distribution it makes no sense to use simple arithmetic mean to "guess" next job's runtime. This finding motivated us to develop a more robust predictor. For this purpose, we have developed a simple event-driven simulator which emulated job submissions and completions in the system and allowed us to test the accuracy of various

[2] In this context, job batch is the set of jobs submitted into the system by a given user in a short time frame, e.g., during few minutes.

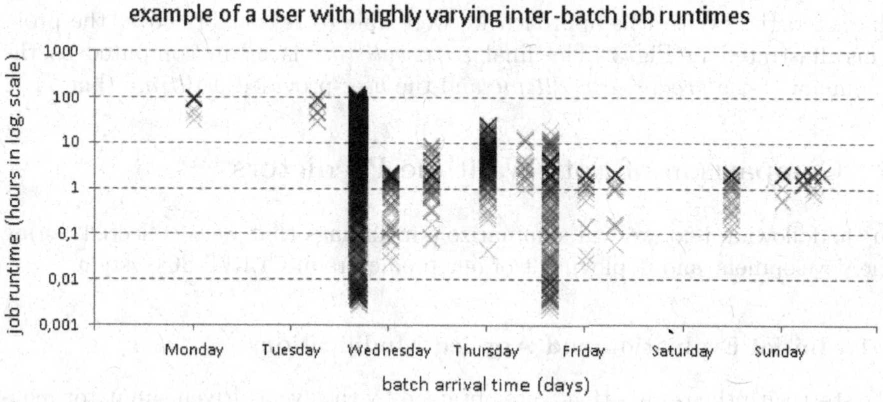

Fig. 3. Varying job runtimes (hours in log. scale) of several job batches submitted during one week by a given user.

Algorithm 2. PREDICTOR_V3(*user*, *walltime*, *completed_jobs*)

1: *walltime_usages* := SELECT (j.runtime/j.job_walltime) as walltime_usage FROM *completed_jobs j* WHERE j.user_name=*user* ORDER BY j.job_end_time DESC limit 15;
2: **if** *walltime_usages* = ∅ **then**
3: *soft_walltime* := *walltime*;
4: **else**
5: *max_walltime_usage* := MAXIMUM(*walltime_usages*);
6: *predicted_walltime* := (*max_walltime_usage* · *walltime*) + 900;
7: *soft_walltime* := MINIMUM(*predicted_walltime*, *walltime*);
8: **end if**
9: **return** *soft_walltime*;

---

predictors. The final solution abandoned the original average runtime and instead focuses on the recent relative walltime usage. It is represented by Algorithm 2 and works as follows.

First, we compute so called *walltime_usage* ratio for the 15 most recently completed jobs. The *walltime_usage* is computed as the ratio of job runtime to its walltime (*j.runtime/j.job_walltime*). The *walltime_usages* list is used to collect these ratios (line 1). Next, we choose the maximum of these values. The maximum relative walltime usage is then used to multiply the user-provided job walltime (line 6) producing the *predicted_walltime* (which includes 900 s corresponding to the 15 min-long reserve). It represents a conservative strategy, where the prediction is calculated using the known relative accuracy of user's recent estimates. By choosing the *max_walltime_usage* (i.e., by choosing a job where the difference between actual and estimated runtime was minimal), this technique aims to minimize the number of cases where the new soft walltime will be underestimated. At the same time, since the predictor only uses 15 recent jobs it reflect aging and orients itself more on the recent user's workload characteristics. With this approach we were able to reasonably cover the problems illustrated in Fig. 3. The final *soft_walltime* is again computed as the minimum of the *predicted_walltime* and the user-provided *walltime* (line 7).

3 Comparison of Soft Walltime Predictors

In the following text we will summarize our findings that were collected during the development and deployment of our predictors in CERIT-SC system.

3.1 Initial Evaluation and Applied Modifications

We start with the results that were obtained by the event-driven simulator mentioned in the previous section. This simulator used real workload and realistically emulated job submissions and completions. Therefore, we were able to replay job arrivals and test all three variants of our predictor and compare their accuracy. Figure 4 illustrates the development of our predictor (v1, v2 and v3 variants). In this figure, we show absolute estimate errors (hours in log. scale) with respect to the used predictor. As a reference we also include errors of the original user-provided estimates (walltime). In order to distinguish between under- and overestimation, we first order errors in the increasing order for each used predictor. Next, we compute absolute values of these (ordered) errors and plot them using the log. scale. The resulting curves thus have a typical "V"-shape where the left part (decreasing) represents absolute values of negative errors (i.e., underestimated predictions) and the right part (increasing) corresponds to the overestimations (positive errors).

Clearly, original walltimes are never underestimated since they represent the upper bound of allowed runtime. From this experiment, which covers 67K jobs, we can see that the initial average-based predictor (predictor_v1) generated a lot of underestimated soft walltimes (over 40% of jobs were underestimated). The addition of 15 min reserve (predictor_v2) reduces this unwanted situation, yet still nearly 31% of all jobs are underestimated. The predictor based on relative walltime usage (predictor_v3) produced the best results (less than 12% jobs is underestimated). While not so critical, the negative yet natural effect of predictor_v3 is the fact that jobs are typically quite overestimated with respect to predictor_v2 and v1.

3.2 Analysis of Soft Walltime Accuracy

Unlike the previous experiment which used identical workload and performed predictions using a simulator the following analysis is solely based on *results collected from the real system.* In the first part, we compare our three predictors as they were deployed during the time. While the underlying workload is not identical we can still observe how the different predictor variants (v1, v2 and v3) performed with respect to the original user-provided estimates.

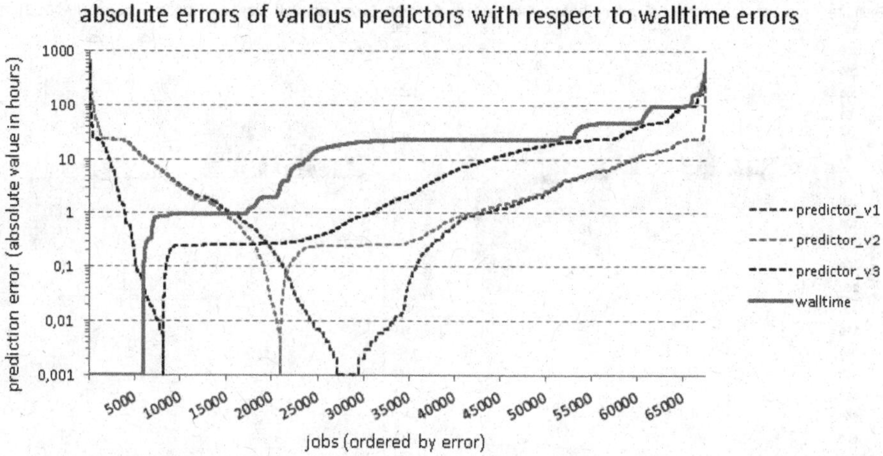

Fig. 4. The ratio and level of under- and overestimation with respect to different soft walltime predictors.

Figure 5 uses the actual data from the system to show the distribution of runtime estimate errors. It consists of 3 boxplots, each covering one time period—October 2021, November 2021 and December 2021–January 2022, respectively. In the first period (October 2021) predictor_v1 was used. It was replaced in November 2021 with the predictor_v2 which was replaced with predictor_v3 that has been used since December 2021. Each boxplot shows the distribution of errors both for the given predictor (v1, v2 or v3) and the original user-provided estimates. Moreover, the errors are divided into three groups according to the actual runtime of the job. The first group represents short jobs (runtime [0, 2] hours), the second group contains all medium jobs (runtime (2, 24] hours) while the third group consists of long-running jobs (runtime $\geq$ 24 h).

Figure 5 shows how the aforementioned predictors improved the quality of walltime estimates with respect to those provided by users. Also, it shows how the quality of predictions was further improved with those two major modifications that were performed in November (Fig. 5 top right) and December (Fig. 5 bottom left). As we can see, predictor_v1 used in October 2021 produced a lot of underestimated soft walltimes (Fig. 5 top left) and its performance was thus not acceptable. Clearly, the added 15 min reserve applied in predictor_v2 significantly decreased the underestimation of soft walltimes as can be seen, e.g., from the reduced spread and better lower quartile value (long jobs). The second modification deployed in December 2021 (predictor_v3) further reduced the errors of generated soft walltimes. Version v3 clearly generates soft walltimes that are much more accurate than user-provided estimates (Fig. 5 bottom left).

We have also analyzed the accuracy of soft walltimes on a per-user basis. These results are shown in Fig. 6. This figure compares the average absolute errors of user-based walltimes and generated soft walltimes. Also, for each user we show the number of jobs they have submitted into the system. In general, soft

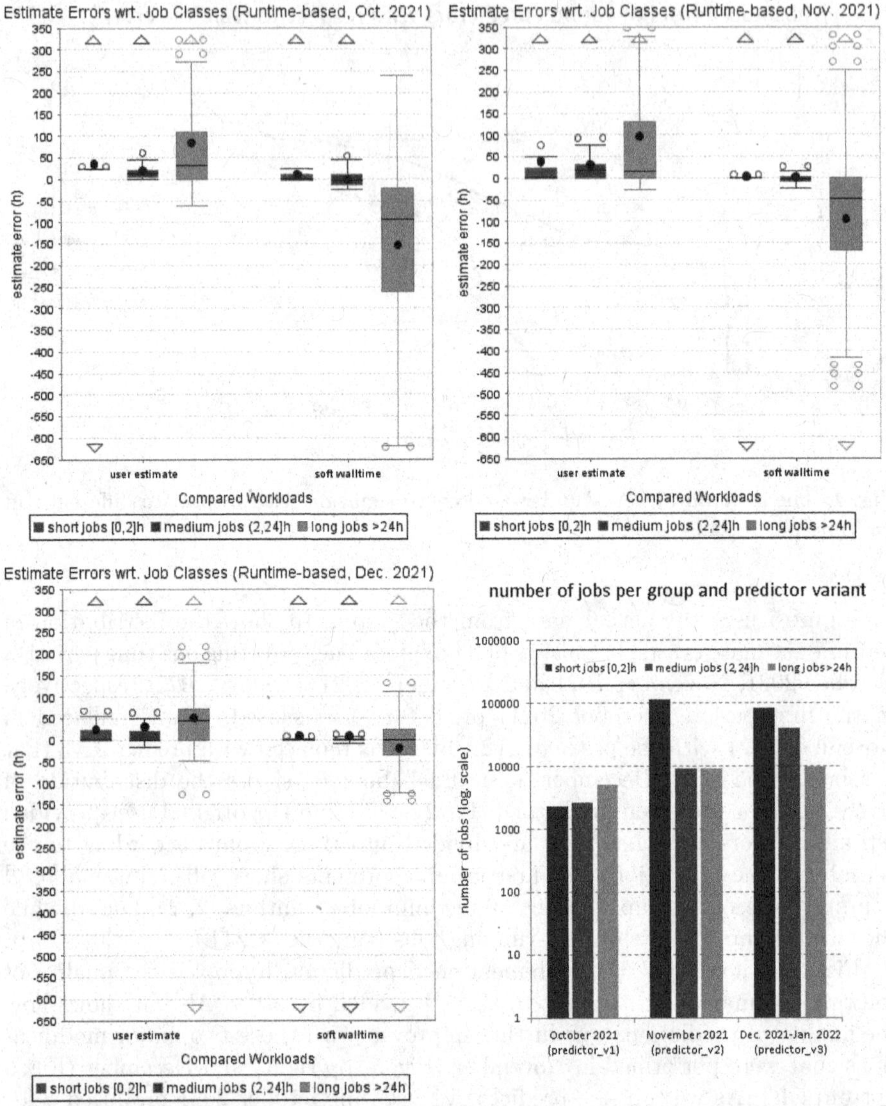

Fig. 5. The impact of two major upgrades of the soft walltime predictor with respect to the initial October version (top left). Both the November and the December upgrades (top right and bottom left) decreased errors significantly. All boxplots have the same scale of y-axis. Bottom right chart shows the number of jobs per job group and epoch.

walltime-based estimates were more accurate for 91% of users (on average). For the remaining 9% users, the average deterioration was rather small. The biggest and smallest deteriorations we have observed were 26 min and 36 s, respectively. While the drawbacks of soft walltimes were minor, the improvements were very

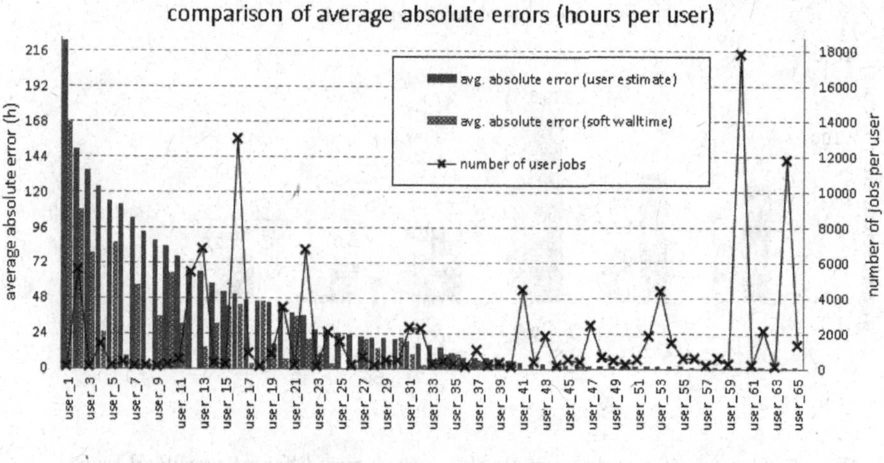

Fig. 6. Comparison of average absolute errors per user.

clear. For example, for 77% of users the average improvement in the accuracy was greater than 24 h, i.e., the average error of user-based estimates was reduced by more than 24 h thanks to the application of soft walltime predictor.

Last but not least, we have used other existing historical workload traces to test if our predictor_v3 would work in other systems too. Beside our workload from CERIT system (2022), we have chosen several older workloads from the Parallel Workloads Archive: KIT FH1 (2020), MetaCentrum (2013), HPCN (2006), SDSC SP2 (2000), and CTC SP2 (1997). As can be seen, these workloads cover both recent and decades old systems, thus representing a very variable mixture of input data. The results of this comparison are presented in Fig. 7 using the average absolute error metric (hours in log. scale). We can see that even simple technique like predictor_v3 decreases significantly the average error that is embedded in user-provided runtime estimates.

3.3 Soft Walltime Caveats

During the deployment of soft walltimes in the CERIT-SC system we have also analyzed the *impact of using soft walltimes*. During this process we have come up with a set of "caveats" that one should keep in mind when using soft walltimes. The first one is the danger that originates from underestimated soft walltimes and we have already discussed this caveat in Sects. 2.2 and 3.1. The second caveat relates to the way jobs are routed into queues. In our system, user-provided walltime limit is one of the major factor that influences to which queue his or her job will be routed to. Simply put, the system has several queues with different maximum allowed walltime limits. "Short" queues can access larger

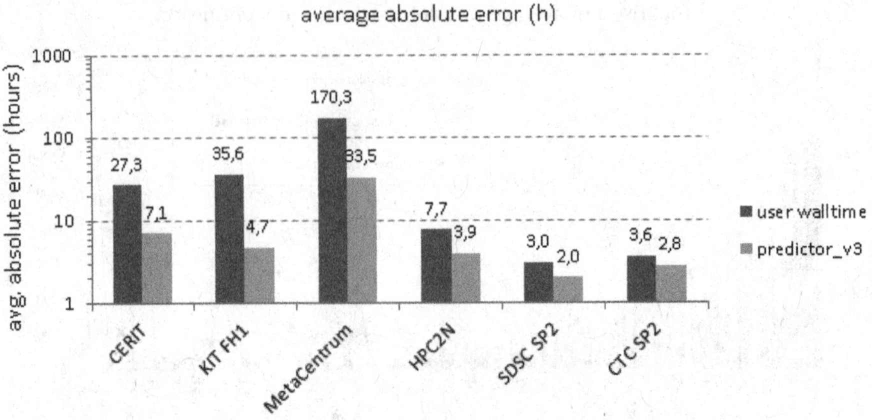

Fig. 7. Comparison of average absolute errors per different workload traces.

pools of nodes while "long" have smaller pools of available nodes. These node pools are overlapping and the limits are used to increase the chance that short jobs will not be hugely delayed by long running jobs from long queues. However, jobs are always routed by user-provided walltimes and soft walltimes do not change this at all, unless the system is reconfigured to allow such soft walltime-based routing. It means that although the job may be considered as "short" by the scheduler it cannot be moved into a proper "short" queue and will remain in the "long" queue (in default settings). Therefore, jobs having long walltimes and small soft walltimes cannot use those larger pools of nodes that are available to "short" queues. As a result, these jobs thus may experience larger wait times compared to jobs from "short" queues.

Figure 8 shows this caveat in practice. On the left side, we present job (top) and error (bottom) distribution when jobs are grouped according to their real runtime. We can see that short and medium jobs are the most common (63% and 30%) while long jobs are scarce (7%). On the other hand, when jobs are grouped according to their queue (right) the job-to-group distribution is much different (33%, 42% and 25%) since many jobs are overestimated by users, thus ending up in "wrong" queues.

This difference then also changes completely the distribution of estimate errors. In the former case (runtime-based grouping) soft walltimes are underestimated for 50% of long jobs while in the latter case (queue-based job grouping) soft walltimes are underestimated for only 25% of jobs from long queues. Similarly, user-provided estimates are much worse when considering long queues (right) instead of long jobs (left). The output from this caveat is that the system administrator must closely monitor system performance on the per-queue basis as the introduction of soft walltimes will likely cause that resource-restricted queues (e.g., "long" queues in our case) will contain lots of jobs that may be more suitable for other system partitions (e.g., those used by "short" queues).

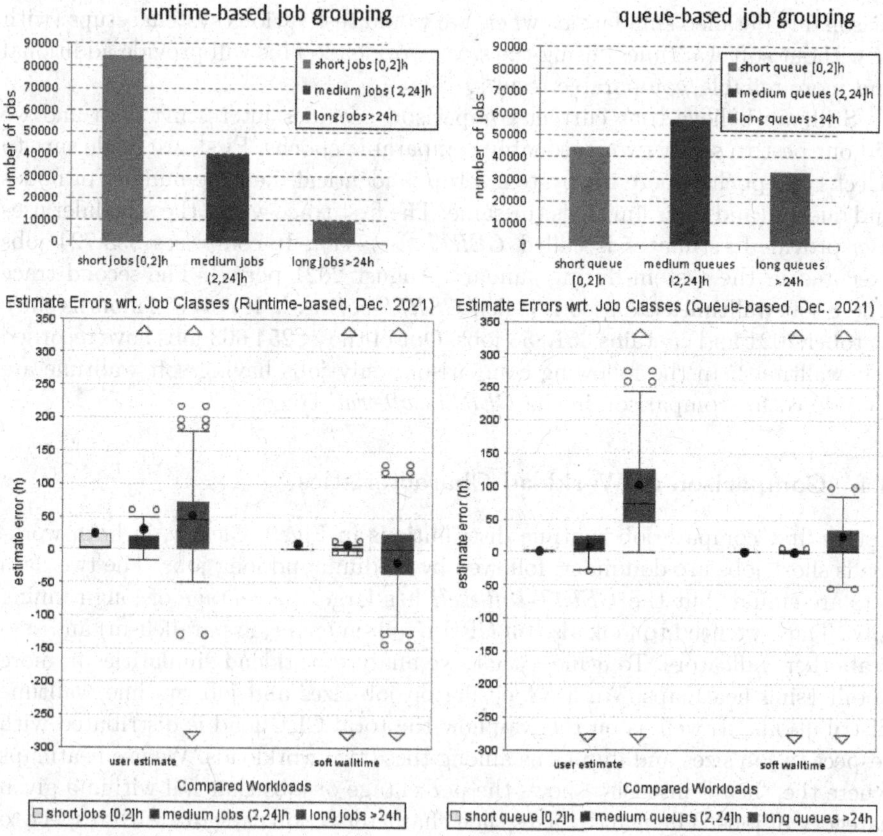

Fig. 8. Job (top) and error (bottom) distribution according to the runtime-based (left) and queue-based (right) job grouping. 3.4× more jobs fall into the "long" category when grouped according to their system queues (right). Both boxplots have the same scale of y-axis.

Not only this may limit the system performance but it can also degrade the impact of using soft walltimes.

4 Comparison of System Performance

In the final part of our evaluation we compare how the system performed *prior* and *after* soft walltimes were introduced. We will compare two data sets from CERIT-SC system and analyze their differences. Since we are using real data from the system, this comparison has some inevitable shortcomings. Clearly, we are comparing two different workloads thus we cannot directly compare selected metrics and draw immediate conclusions from such comparison. Instead, we will provide side by side workload comparison and discuss observed trends in the processed workloads. In the future, we plan to extend this work by performing reasonably detailed simulations where we would test various system setups (with or without soft walltimes) using the same workload. This will provide additional and more reliable/comparable results.

Still, we believe that current comparison provides interesting data and we did our best to select two reasonably comparable epochs. First, we made sure to select two epochs where the system setup is identical, i.e., the number of nodes and queues (and their limits) is the same. The first trace where the scheduler uses user-provided estimates is called *CERIT-user-wall.* It comprises 935,724 jobs executed in the system during January–August 2021 period. The second trace where soft walltimes are used is called *CERIT-soft-wall.* It covers 4 months since October 2021 and contains 351,853 jobs. Out of these, 254,663 jobs have recorded soft walltime[3]. In the following comparison, only jobs having soft walltime are considered for comparison in the *CERIT-soft-wall* trace.

4.1 Comparison of Workload Characteristics

Let us first compare job runtime distributions in Fig. 9. Clearly, in both workloads short jobs are dominant, followed by medium and long jobs. The two data sets are similar but the *CERIT-soft-wall* has larger percentage of long-running jobs. Thus, we need to look also on CPU requirements (job parallelism) and several other indicators. To achieve that, we analyze workload similarities in more detail using heatmaps. We are focusing on job sizes and job runtime/walltime distributions, as well as on the way how the total CPU load is distributed with respect to job sizes and durations among these two workloads. We use heatmaps where the "heat" intensity shows the percentage of jobs that fall within a given category of jobs. The y and x axes then characterize job category with respect to their CPU demands and runtime/walltime, i.e., y-axis denotes the required number of CPUs while x-axis divides jobs into categories according to their runtime or walltime, respectively.

Figure 10 (top) shows that both workloads are quite similar with respect to their CPU requirements and actual job runtime. In both cases, the majority of jobs requires at most 32 CPUs (99.7% and 99.8% of jobs, respectively). Also, the majority of jobs requires at most 1 day to execute (93.9% and 86.7% of jobs, respectively).

The middle row in Fig. 10 shows, that both workloads have very coarse grained user-provided estimates. Many jobs simply use the maximum allowed queue runtime limit as their walltime[4]. When compared to the real runtimes (see top row in Fig. 10), this heatmap clearly shows how the user-provided estimates are overestimated in both workloads. For example, according to user provided estimates in CERIT-soft-wall workload only 38.6% of jobs is expected to execute within 2 h, while in reality 68.1% of all jobs run for less than 2 h.

[3] The difference is caused by the fact that it takes some time before we collect enough data for each user to produce soft walltimes.

[4] In our case, those are 2, 4 and 24 h, 2, 4 and 7 days and 2, 4 or >4 weeks.

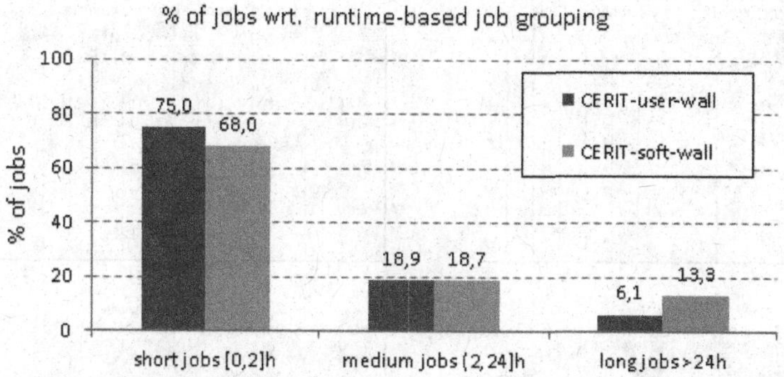

Fig. 9. Job distribution (%) into the three common job runtime categories for CERIT-user-wall and CERIT-soft-wall workload traces.

The last row in Fig. 10 compares the use of CPU hours with respect to job classes. Here, the "heat" intensity shows the percentage of total used CPU hours that are consumed by a given category of jobs. It shows that also the overall CPU utilization is quite similar for *CERIT-user-wall* and *CERIT-soft-wall* workloads, i.e., the majority of CPU time is consumed by long-running jobs (>1 day) in both workloads (71.0% and 81.1% of CPU time, respectively). CERIT-soft-wall's higher use of CPU hours (in long jobs category) is related to the higher number of long-running jobs (see Fig. 9).

Clearly, although the two workloads are not identical, they both have similar patterns, i.e., utilized CPU hours are mostly consumed by long-running jobs while at the same time, most jobs are rather short, requesting less than 40 CPUs. Based on these similarities, we now compare those two workloads by means of job wait time and bounded slowdown.

4.2 Comparison of Wait Time and Bounded Slowdown

In this section, we use two optimization criteria to compare CERIT-user-wall and CERIT-soft-wall traces—job wait time and bounded slowdown [4]. Job slowdown is the ratio of the actual response time of the job to the response time if executed without any waiting. By definition, job slowdown is always ≥1. As pointed out by Feitelson et al. [4], slowdown reflects users' notion of system responsiveness through measuring if jobs are completed within the time proportional to the job length. In another words, it prefers completion of shorter jobs in a shorter time horizon in comparison with time consuming jobs where a longer waiting is acceptable. Since the whole idea behind soft walltime is to allow the scheduler to "find shorter jobs" and backfill them efficiently we have used these two metrics in our comparison.

In nearly all existing traces (ours included), many jobs have very short runtime. This often represents jobs that ended prematurely right after their start due to some error. These short jobs then skew slowdown distribution (their slowdowns are huge). Therefore, we use so called *bounded slowdown* [3,4], where

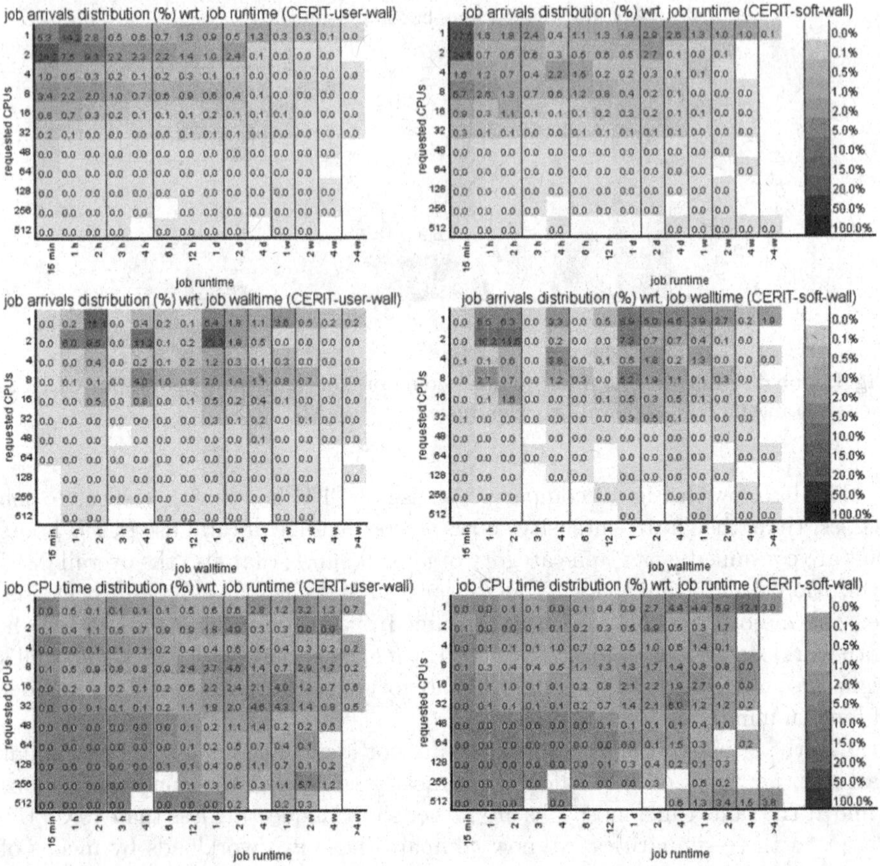

Fig. 10. Comparison of CERIT-user-wall (left) and CERIT-soft-wall (right) workload traces according to their job runtime distribution (top), job walltime distribution (middle) and utilized CPU hours (bottom).

the minimal job runtime is guaranteed to be greater than some predefined time constant, in our case 10 min[5].

Figure 11 shows the distribution of job wait times (left) and bounded slowdowns (right) for the CERIT-user-wall and CERIT-soft-wall traces. Let us start with the wait time comparison. We can see, that there is a significant difference in the shape of wait time distributions. Soft walltime-driven scheduler (CERIT-soft-wall) seems to distribute high wait times to the long-running jobs, which is natural for backfill-like scheduler. In the original walltime-driven workload (CERIT-user-wall), both short and medium jobs have significantly different wait

[5] Other values such as 10 s [3,4] or 1 min [18] are used as well in the literature. In CERIT-SC, 10 min is the recommended minimal runtime of regular job. Shorter jobs are not recommended due to excessive overhead related to their (frequent) processing.

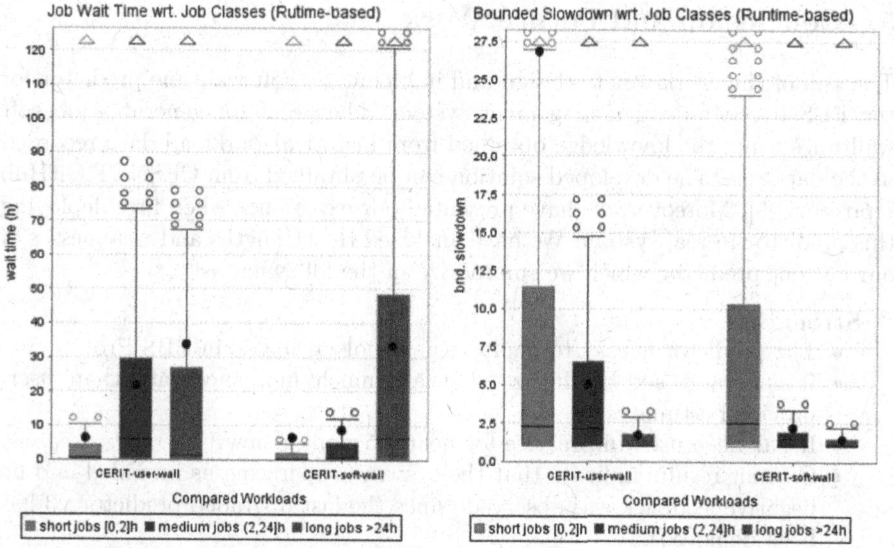

Fig. 11. Wait time (left) and slowdown (right) distributions for CERIT-user-wall and CERIT-soft-wall traces.

time distribution, with medium jobs waiting the most. This is an indication that more diverse soft walltimes enable the scheduler to pick shorter jobs more easily and schedule them first. In other words, the wait time distribution in CERIT-soft-wall trace is satisfactory for us, as we expect the system to follow the trend of prioritizing shorter jobs[6]. Again, we must highlight the limitation of this comparison, i.e., we are comparing different workloads. As was already discussed in Sect. 4, instead of directly comparing the observed *values* we are only discussing "shapes" and "trends" here. Direct comparison of wait time values would be quite misleading as the underlying workloads are different.

The distribution of job slowdowns is shown in Fig. 11 (right). Here, we see that the long wait times of medium jobs in CERIT-user-wall trace result in rather significant slowdowns as well. For example, the slowdown median for short and medium jobs is very close in CERIT-user-wall trace. On the other hand, CERIT-soft-wall trace has more "natural" slowdown distribution, where largest slowdowns are related to short jobs and decrease as job runtime increases (see the distribution of medium jobs and long jobs). Again, this indicates that the application of soft walltimes helps the scheduler to find suitable jobs for backfilling, which leads to lower wait times and thus reduces their slowdown.

[6] This is also coupled with fair-share based job ordering which we use to prioritize less active users over those who utilize the system heavily.

5 Conclusion and Future Work

The aim of this work was to design and implement a soft walltime predictor for the PBS Pro workload management system. The predictor generates job soft walltimes using the knowledge obtained from historical workload data recorded in the database. The developed solution can be obtained from CESNET GitHub repository [5]. Moreover, we have presented our experience when first deploying this predictor in real system. We have analyzed the strengths and weaknesses of our current predictor which we summarize in the following list:

- **Strengths**
  - The predictor is easy to deploy using tools available in PBS Pro.
  - It generates soft walltimes that are much more accurate than user-provided estimates.
  - It has been used in practice for nearly 5 months now.
  - Current results indicate that the system is operating as intended and no negative feedback was observed (since the last upgraded predictor_v3 has been deployed).
- **Weaknesses**
  - Current predictor does not enable to generate different soft walltimes for different job classes of a single user (even if we know that the user has different job classes).
  - As a result, all jobs of a given user are treated as "identical" and their soft walltime is generated using the same scaling factor at the given moment (see *max_walltime_usage* in Algorithm 2).
  - Due to the current limitations in PBS Pro, there is limited possibility to update job soft walltime before job start (soft walltime can be modified only upon job arrival or when it starts but not while it is waiting in a queue). This means that the scheduler may work with rather "old" soft walltimes that are only updated when the job finally starts.

Also, we provide real workload trace that contains generated job soft walltimes. This trace has been published in the JSSPP workloads archive [6], hosted at the JSSPP workshop page: https://jsspp.org/workload/. Using this real-life data we have analyzed the accuracy and impact of our approach. We believe this is one of the first publicly available reports on practical application of soft walltimes.

In the future, we want to extend our existing work by detailed simulations that would increase our understanding of how the refined estimates influence the performance of the scheduler. Also, we would like to use such simulations to test new variants of soft walltime predictor that would focus on the current weaknesses (see above).

Acknowledgments. We kindly acknowledge the support and computational resources supplied by the project "e-Infrastruktura CZ" (e-INFRA LM2018140) provided within the program Projects of Large Research, Development and Innovations Infrastructures.

References

1. CERIT Scientific Cloud, August 2022. http://www.cerit-sc.cz
2. Chiang, S.-H., Arpaci-Dusseau, A., Vernon, M.K.: The impact of more accurate requested runtimes on production job scheduling performance. In: Feitelson, D.G., Rudolph, L., Schwiegelshohn, U. (eds.) JSSPP 2002. LNCS, vol. 2537, pp. 103–127. Springer, Heidelberg (2002). https://doi.org/10.1007/3-540-36180-4_7
3. Feitelson, D.G.: Experimental analysis of the root causes of performance evaluation results: a backfilling case study. IEEE Trans. Parallel Distrib. Syst. **16**(2), 175–182 (2005)
4. Feitelson, D.G., Rudolph, L., Schwiegelshohn, U., Sevcik, K.C., Wong, P.: Theory and practice in parallel job scheduling. In: Feitelson, D.G., Rudolph, L. (eds.) JSSPP 1997. LNCS, vol. 1291, pp. 1–34. Springer, Heidelberg (1997). https://doi.org/10.1007/3-540-63574-2_14
5. Soft walltime predictor implementation, August 2022. https://github.com/CESNET/softwalltime-predictor/
6. JSSPP workloads archive, August 2022. https://jsspp.org/workload/
7. Klusáček, D., Chlumský, V.: Evaluating the impact of soft walltimes on job scheduling performance. In: Desai, N., Klusáček, D., Cirne, W. (eds.) JSSPP 2018. LNCS, vol. 11332, pp. 15–38. Springer, Cham (2018). https://doi.org/10.1007/978-3-030-10632-4_2
8. Lee, C.B., Schwartzman, Y., Hardy, J., Snavely, A.: Are user runtime estimates inherently inaccurate? In: Feitelson, D.G., Rudolph, L., Schwiegelshohn, U. (eds.) JSSPP 2004. LNCS, vol. 3277, pp. 253–263. Springer, Heidelberg (2004). https://doi.org/10.1007/11407522_14
9. MetaCentrum, February 2022. http://www.metacentrum.cz/
10. Mu'alem, A.W., Feitelson, D.G.: Utilization, predictability, workloads, and user runtime estimates in scheduling the IBM SP2 with backfilling. IEEE Trans. Parallel Distrib. Syst. **12**(6), 529–543 (2001)
11. Seneviratne, S., Witharana, S.: A survey on methodologies for runtime prediction on grid environments. In: 7th International Conference on Information and Automation for Sustainability, pp. 1–6. IEEE (2014)
12. Smith, W., Taylor, V., Foster, I.: Using run-time predictions to estimate queue wait times and improve scheduler performance. In: Feitelson, D.G., Rudolph, L. (eds.) JSSPP 1999. LNCS, vol. 1659, pp. 202–219. Springer, Heidelberg (1999). https://doi.org/10.1007/3-540-47954-6_11
13. Non-destructive walltime, February 2022. https://community.openpbs.org/t/pp-482-non-destructive-walltime/587/4
14. Soft walltime documentation, February 2022. https://pbspro.atlassian.net/wiki/spaces/PD/pages/42532871/PP-482+Soft+Walltime
15. Soysal, M., Bergho, M., Streit, A.: Analysis of job metadata for enhanced wall time prediction. In: Desai, N., Klusáček, D., Cirne, W. (eds.) JSSPP 2018. LNCS, vol. 11332, pp. 1–14. Springer, Cham (2018). https://doi.org/10.1007/978-3-030-10632-4_1
16. Tsafrir, D.: Using inaccurate estimates accurately. In: Frachtenberg, E., Schwiegelshohn, U. (eds.) JSSPP 2010. LNCS, vol. 6253, pp. 208–221. Springer, Heidelberg (2010). https://doi.org/10.1007/978-3-642-16505-4_12

17. Tsafrir, D., Etsion, Y., Feitelson, D.G.: Backfilling using system-generated predictions rather than user runtime estimates. IEEE Trans. Parallel Distrib. Syst. **18**(6), 789–803 (2007)
18. Vasupongayya, S., Chiang, S.-H.: On job fairness in non-preemptive parallel job scheduling. In: Zheng, S.Q. (ed.) International Conference on Parallel and Distributed Computing Systems (PDCS 2005), pp. 100–105. IASTED/ACTA Press (2005)

Re-making the Movie-Making Machine

James Vanns(✉) and David Galeano

Industrial Light & Magic, a Lucasfilm Ltd., Company, San Francisco, USA
jvanns@ilm.com
https://www.ilm.com

Abstract. The visual effects (VFX) industry has for decades been actively developing and running job and resource management systems (JARMS) under the guise of "render farms". Rarely have we sought to share our work, stories, and problems beyond our niche bubble with the wider HPC community. With this paper we hope to break that cycle and introduce you to how we at Industrial Light & Magic (ILM) support our ever-changing diverse workloads at scale to produce high quality imagery for major motion pictures and television such as *Jurassic World* and *The Mandalorian.* We then share recent development efforts to prepare us for our biggest challenge yet: *ABBA Voyage.* These developments are the result of practical improvements to a production scheduler yielding higher throughput, reduced waste and makespan, and increased insight into internal metrics. We also briefly discuss how we developed tooling to aid in trace-based simulations to gain confidence in production upgrades.

This is the printed edition featuring greyscale images and dashed line types in line graphs. The original digital edition retains the coloured images and lines, which some readers may find offer a greater definition and distinction between data points, for example.

Keywords: Scheduling · Render farm · Batch schedulers · High performance computing · Cluster management

1 Introduction

The VFX industry has relied upon compute farms to parallelise the tasks required to render frames for film since the mid-to-late 1990 s. For ILM this has scaled from a few dozen MIPS cores at a single location to nearer 100k x86 cores per location, now numbering 5 across the globe.

A VFX shot (generally a run of frames uninterrupted by a cut or edit) may comprise of, but is not limited to, camera tracking, environment or set extension, 3D modelling, animation, texture painting, FX & Simulations, lighting & shading, and 2D compositing. These disciplines work on a single shot as it moves towards completion, and the process is colloquially referred to as "the pipeline" (although this is a simplification). Many of these stages submit work as jobs to the farm and range in complexity depending on the shot.

Supported by Industrial Light & Magic.

D. Klusáček et al. (Eds.): JSSPP 2022, LNCS 13592, pp. 211–232, 2023.
https://doi.org/10.1007/978-3-031-22698-4_11

As an artist (our end user - not a scientist) iterates over refinements to their work, many versions are "rendered" on the farm. For each re-render, adjustments to the resource requirements plus parameters specific to the DCC (digital content creation) tool are made, though they are opaque to the scheduler.

With such a heterogeneous workload running on the farm, where task types are diverse, the corresponding resource requirements are also varied. The precedent constraints between tasks that model the job structure also change with this diversity, contributing to the overall system complexity.

1.1 Basic Concepts

For ILM, concurrency comes in many forms; we work on multiple shows at a time (e.g. *The Book of Boba Fett*, *Eternals*, *Red Notice* etc.) and these are often at different stages of development and vary in complexity. A single shot can be developed by different departments at the same time (e.g. modelling, animation) especially when these iterations are versioned. Finally, we achieve task concurrency on the farm by executing many tasks simultaneously through parallel directed acyclic graphs (DAGs).

Shows generally work to different deadlines (internal, director approval, trailers etc.) and many shots are prioritised over others according to these deadlines (due dates). Individual users themselves may also wish to rank their own submissions to the farm. However, the farm is a company resource and digital resource managers (DRMs) have the tricky job of juggling conflicting objectives such as farm throughput/high utilisation vs. competing show priorities & resource contention.

Finally, each discipline or stage in this VFX pipeline demands diverse resources of varying quantities to accomplish their task. Consumable resources available on a host include CPU, GPU, RAM and local disk space (we don't factor in network bandwidth). Static resources include things such as OS release, GPU chipset, SIMD instruction set etc.

From a global pool, consumable tokens include software licences, often expensive resources hotly contended between shows. Each vendor licence may come with a different sharing scheme - an opportunity to pack and cut costs.

All these packing dimensions lead to task shapes and corresponding holes on compute nodes ranging from 1 CPU and 512MB RAM to 96 CPUs and 128GB RAM, and every combination & permutation in between. These shapes can of course influence the runtime of the task, assuming the task can parallelise well (many renderers do) on a multi-core host. Task types are so diverse that normalised runtimes range from 30 s (e.g. data moves) to several days (e.g. machine learning) and are bounded by different resources (e.g. I/O or GPU). Despite this, most tasks are compute-heavy requiring high core counts, fast clock speeds and SIMD instructions.

It's worth noting that across VFX, rarely is a runtime or duration estimate (from the user) assigned to a task and doesn't contribute to scheduling decisions made by the system. Historically, it's been widely accepted that workloads are simply too unpredictable since many commands, once they execute, are black boxes to the scheduler; scene parameters in the input file(s) significantly affect the render times and resources consumed.

2 Background

Star Wars Episode I: The Phantom Menace began production in 1997 and since then ILM adopted use of its proprietary ObaQ/DOALL [6] distributed scheduling system. This system delivered hundreds of feature films and millions of frames until it was eventually superseded 2 decades later in 2020 by a centralised dispatch system, Coda [11], developed at a sibling company, Walt Disney Animation Studios (WDAS).

2.1 Coda

In 2017 work began to adapt the WDAS system for the ILM pipeline. During this period we developed additional Coda tooling, maintained & supported the existing ObaQ system, integrated Coda into our software stack all the while still delivering films. By 2019 we were coordinating the production of rendered frames through Coda and had scheduled ObaQ for decommission. As ILM began adopting version 5.1 of Coda, WDAS continued to develop version 6. We were unable to interupt our own integration and migration plans to accommodate this additional change. Therefore, ILM remained on the 5.1 release, which is the codebase we forked and maintained internally.

2.2 Production Proven

Coda 5.1 had already proven itself in production both at WDAS and ILM. At Disney, Coda had delivered animation features such as *Frozen* and *Moana* and at ILM, before the advances in this paper were required, we delivered, among others, *Star Wars: The Rise of Skywalker*. The success of Coda at both studios, despite their workflows being different, gave us confidence enough to develop it further to meet the demands of more challenging shows.

2.3 Architecture

The Coda architecture is designed such that system responsibilities reflect components often shared by similar systems (see Fig. 1). The reflector is a central communications broker where every message flows through it via topical channels - every other Coda component communicates through it; there is no other direct peer transport. The *rgoferd* daemon receives submissions and control actions, the *rqinfod* daemon caches data to answer queries and the *rdispatcher*, the primary focus of this paper, is the decision engine behind core allocation, task-to-node mapping, prioritisation and dispatch.

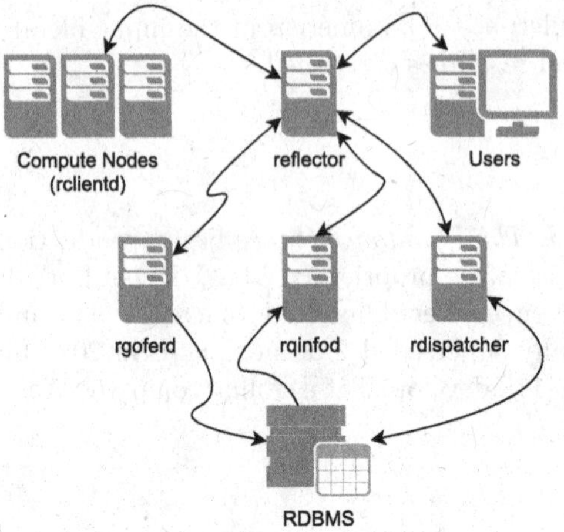

Fig. 1. The coda architecture

2.4 Concepts and Configuration

Coda assigns CPUs or cores to so-called pools. Typically each show would have a set of pools assembled in a hierarchical structure (to reflect work type, discipline or priority as they see fit), and a DRM would discuss with the show their requirements and set a core entitlement for these pools accordingly. Any show under-utilising their entitlement of any given pool implicitly permits other pools to borrow from them, leading to speculative execution with a preemption penalty. In other words, tasks are killed and requeued if running speculatively and an entitled pool now requires its cores back to fulfil a demand. Each pool effectively models a priority queue implemented as a heap and tasks are placed according to an ordinal priority. A synthetic structure illustrating a pool configuration is given below in Fig. 2.

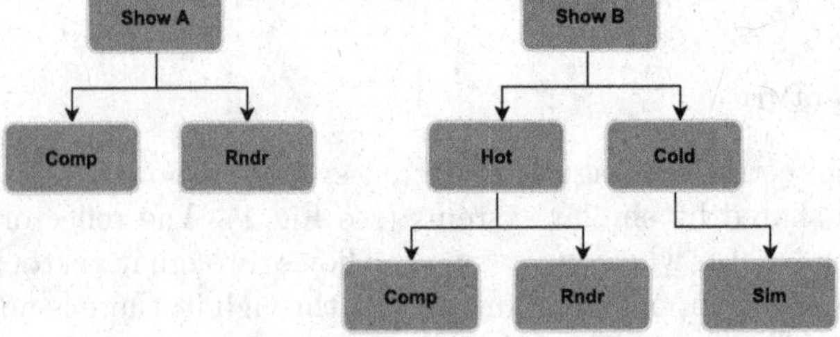

Fig. 2. An example of how CPU Pools can be arranged according to requirement

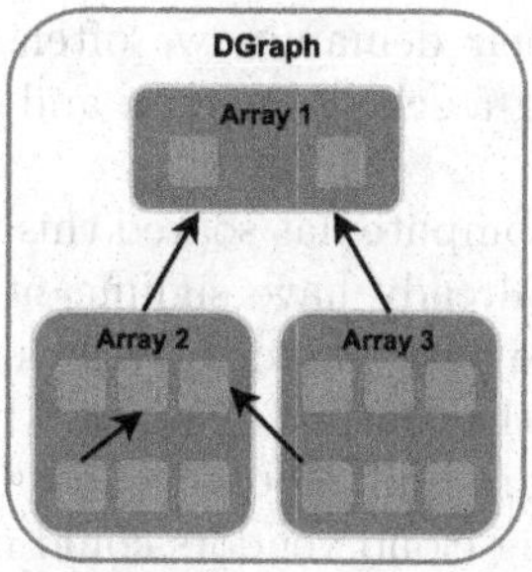

Fig. 3. Illustrating the nested encapsulation of a dgraph (innermost squares represent tasks, arrows represent dependencies)

Coda models jobs as "dgraphs" (dependency graph) and these contain *arrays*, which in turn are comprised of *tasks*. An array is often used to represent a frame range, each task thus rendering a frame of the film. Precedent constraints are defined as dependency expressions in *JavaScript* (rather than a DAG directly) between any of these 3 layers. Each instance of an object in a dgraph had a unique identifier, a fully qualified ID being `9876.1.1000`, for example. Metadata attributes, expressed as `key=value` pairs, can also be set at any level, as there exists a hierarchy between them. Thus the lowest level (a task) can inherit values through its ancestry. Reserved metadata keys describe common attributes such as required resources, user, command, dependencies, priority etc. whereas others such as title, shot name or task type are informational only and used in reporting or display data for UIs. Figure 3 demonstrates the job composition. Although a job or dgraph is a container of arrays and an array is a container of tasks, the rdispatcher component is concerned only with eligible tasks (those with no pending predecessor tasks).

2.5 Scale and Complexity

The growth of a render farm at ILM is steady and expands to accommodate increased workload. More shows concurrently, greater complexity (e.g. resolution, number of characters in frame), new CG technologies (virtual production, machine learning etc.) all make demands of the farm in ways we've not experienced before. At its peak, the on-premises render farm in London is now 40% larger than 4 years ago when we delivered *Ready Player One*. Cloud bursting has also allowed us to expand capacity flexibly when required - our Singapore studio recently ran at 3x its normal 30k core capacity for a week to meet a deadline. Since introducing Coda across the globe, we even launched an entirely new studio in Sydney which now runs at 50k cores. The sum of ILMs regular on-premise core count now exceeds a quarter of a million and we regularly peak at 40x that for our task-queued cores, which is a lot of work to chew through!

With these sizes, the dimensionality of resources, diversity of workload and pressure of deadlines, we began to experience regular problems in production.

As the larger sites scaled their demands, we often found Coda was unable to examine enough tasks during a scheduling run and overall farm utilisation was low.

The popularity of cloud compute has soared this past decade, but VFX facilities such as ILM not only already have significant investment in existing on-premises renderfarms but are also bounded by jobs often requiring low-latency, high-frequency IOPS during the runtime of a task. Much of the pipeline that supports tasks as they execute are built upon decades of assumed high-performing NFS filers, which is something cloud vendors could not guarantee. It is also cost prohibitive and time consuming to synchronise the data between them. However, renderfarms are often extended by cloud-compute VMs during peak periods and thus we 'burst' into the cloud when required. Suitable tasks (those with a known high-compute to low-IO ratio) are guided via a series of labels or tags to cloud VMs, otherwise they remain on-premise only.

In an attempt to provide some idea on film complexity and growth, these metrics may be of some use. However, note that they are simplified a great deal in an attempt to make them more discernible. Table 1 shows that *Star Wars: The Rise of Skywalker* was rendered at a greater resolution than the previous two films of the Skywalker saga, which contributes to its near 2x increase in average core hours per frame. In addition to this, we can state that Episode 9 took in excess of 367,000,000 core hours to render!

Table 1. Final render report statistics for star wars

Film	Year	Shot count	Resolution	Aspect ratio	Core hours/Frame
Episode VII	2015	1696	2k	1.77	650
Episode VIII	2017	1840	2k	1.77	1511
Episode IX	2019	1719	4k	2.37	2720

2.6 Problem Statement

With each facility handling a share of the *ABBA* workload plus their own additional film & TV projects, we'd reached a point where the main scheduling component, rdispatcher, struggled to handle the increased load. This was causing disruption to the service since queue wait times for our users became unsatisfactory even though we'd not yet reached the forecasted peak demand. A project was proposed to deal with the fundamental issues we faced, and planned phases to tackle each of them.

Our first challenge was improving our ability to correlate events on a timeline - reports from users or production and the performance of system components, modules etc. We lacked this visibility, and without it, would be unable to easily identify root-causes of performance degradation. This work is covered in Sect. 3. Section 4 then details the cycles[1] we spent identifying the specific bottlenecks

[1] An agile development process. See [10].

and eradicating them. Section 5 presents the necessity of improved tests and how we tackled them, since before now, testing representative production workloads simply didn't exist.

It's worth emphasising here that a keen reader will come to realise that our paper surveys the merit of a series of pratical code and architectural changes introduced over time to a production dispatcher. A dispatcher that is not only an integral part of an intricate software pipeline used by thousands but also that it must continue to service users and deliver films, remaining available at all times to receive jobs and dispatch matched tasks to compute nodes. The paper doesn't discuss any switch of job shop scheduling dispatch rules, for example, since the majority of scheduling systems in VFX are often solutions in queueing theory and packing due to the lack of a temporal dimension in the decision criteria. We hope that the successes of this project will grant us the freedom and, crucially, the time to evaluate alternative job scheduling strategies in the future. Where relevant, each of the following sub-sections may refer to particular scheduling or dispatch algorithms implemented in code.

3 Observability

One of our initial challenges was understanding the system performance; where it struggled and why. The very motivation behind this project was to handle increased load (more tasks, more nodes) and we already had at hand, reports of dispatch problems at each site and a modicum of metrics to refer to. However, nothing rich enough to provide greater insight - no key performance indicators (KPI) or engineers' view of the farm and its operational state.

3.1 Logging

To ease the selection of useful log entries that could drive data on a dashboard, we concentrated on rewriting each log line according to a semi-structured format that made extraction and understanding easier. Choosing concise, descriptive text removed previous ambiguity and improved readability and parsing. New messages were also added to expose previously unavailable data. Log lines were extracted and sent, via a handler, in real-time to fluentd [2] for processing before storing in Elasticsearch [1] (ES). The fluentd processing engine was able to generate ES document mappings automatically via the `key=value` pairs present in some of the logs.

3.2 Dashboard

With ES as a data source we now had enough information to build a Grafana [5] dashboard. The aim with this dashboard was to give us, as maintainers of the software and system, useful diagnostic information to quickly narrow down dispatch problems in production. We were able to derive KPIs and, among others, produce resource distributions via binning and a task distribution by priority band for each pool. This latter metric was useful, since one of the primary problems we faced was identifying the flood of tasks to a pool and where in the corresponding heap they were located (guided by their priority). Coda was originally designed to honour absolute (task) order by priority with respect to its pool. A pool's priority queue could effectively be blocked by 100s of 1000s of "undispatchable"[2] tasks, thus starving 1000s of others at a lower priority (Figs. 5 and 6). This, we found, contributed to the overall low utilisation of the render farm. Figures 4 through 7 provide some small insight into the panels on our dashboard.

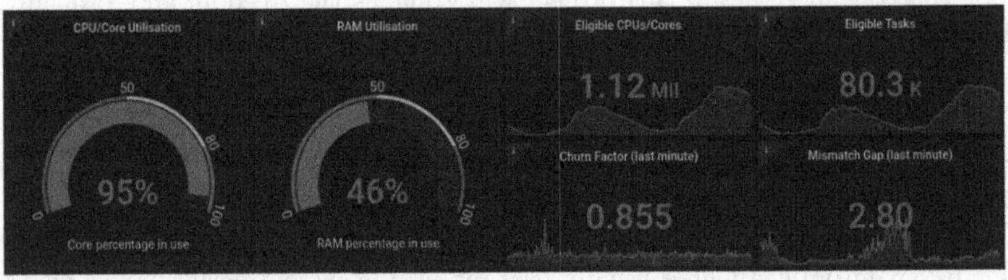

Fig. 4. The high-level overview of an render farm (24h period)

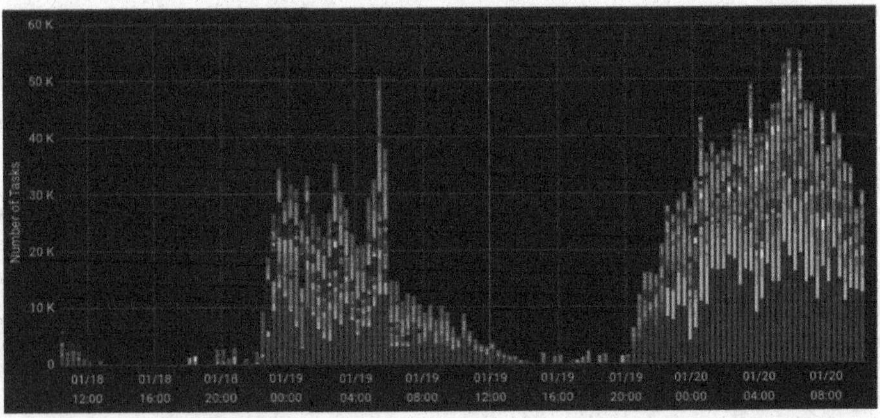

Fig. 5. Distribution of tasks by priority band per pool (pool names omitted)

[2] Tasks unable to be dispatched due to scarce resources, exceeded limitations etc.

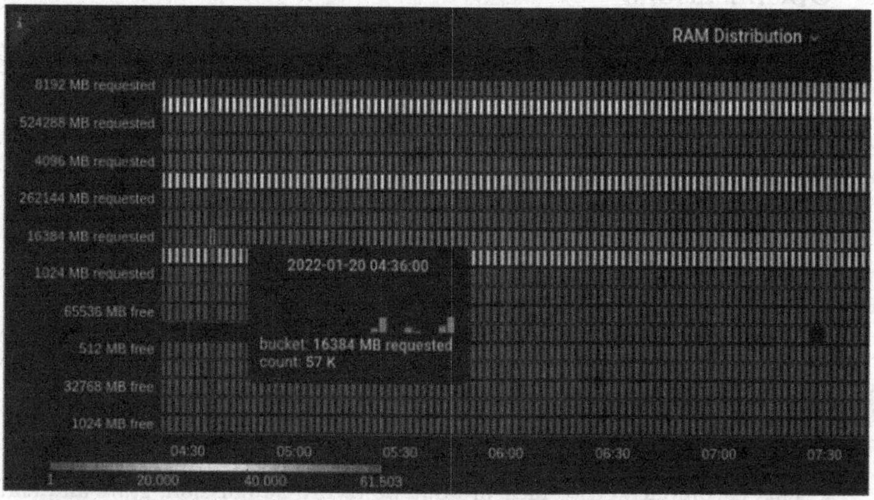

Fig. 6. Requested & Free RAM binned in powers of 2 shown as a Heatmap

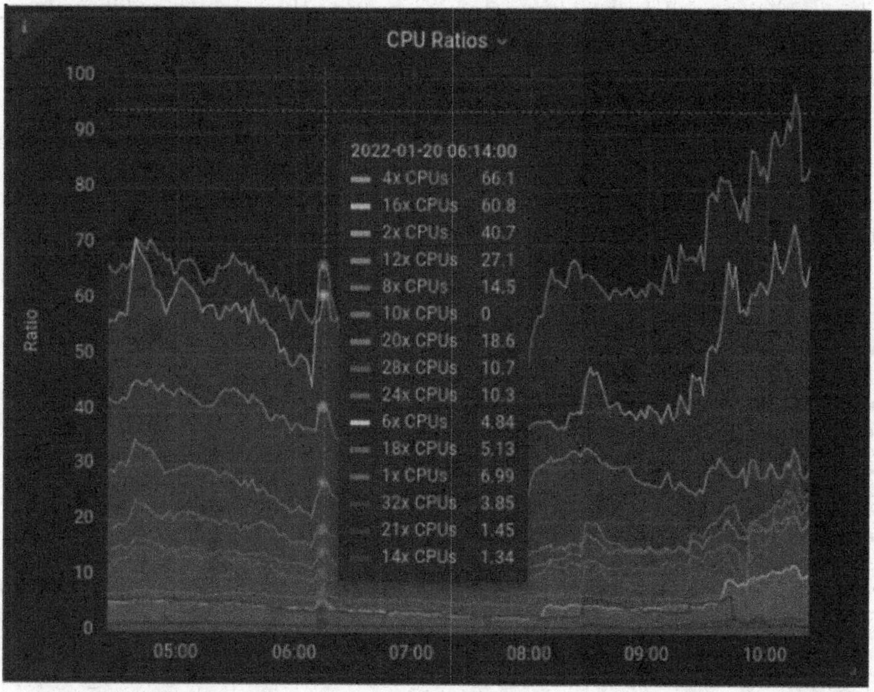

Fig. 7. Distribution of CPUs as a ratio of requested to available. I.e 66x more 4-core slots are required than available to fulfil the queued amount.

4 Optimisations

In order to measure the effectiveness of Coda we employ the following metrics:

- Is the farm busy? Idle machines are a waste of money.
  - This can be measured in real-time.
- Is the farm busy with effective work? Discarding work is a waste of money.
  - This can only be measured accurately in retrospect, tasks may take many hours to complete and they could be killed at any time for different reasons.
- Are pools filling their assigned quotas?
  - This can be measured in real-time.
- Are the hardware resources available on the machine hosting the dispatcher service used effectively? An idle machine is a waste of money.
  - This can be measured in real-time.
- Are high priority tasks completed before lower priority ones?
  - This is complicated to measure but we record submission, start and end times, the number of times the task was examined, the reasons why it was not dispatched, all the status changes, etc. All this information could be used in retrospect to compare dispatch times versus other tasks.

These metrics need to be interpreted in context, there is a big difference in monitored values when there are only one hundred eligible tasks versus when there are hundreds of thousands of them.

We take into account all the metrics when we check the status of the farm and the effect our changes have on its performance. Each of the following subsections report on the major developments required to improve all of these metrics, effectively producing a survey on our recent work. The process as a whole was iterative and relied upon repeated profiling & testing both in production and through simulations (see Sect. 5.4).

4.1 Thread Model

The original implementation had a fixed number of worker or dispatch threads servicing all pools, the main loop being similar to;

```
CPUPool *pool = nullptr;
const bool use_round_robin = true;
while ((pool = select_next_pool(use_round_robin))) {
   Task *task = pool->get_highest_ranking_task();
   if (task != nullptr && examine(task)) {
      Host *host = match_host(task);
      if (host != nullptr) {
         host->manage(task);
         dispatch(task, host);
      }
   }
}
```

This was not optimal for these primary reasons:

1. The process of selecting a pool required access to shared global data that had to be protected by a mutex, which effectively serialised the threads and avoided potential parallelism.
2. Selecting a pool was not free, sometimes it was more expensive to select a pool than to actually examine a task for dispatch, which acted as an unwanted dispatch-rate throttle.

Simply increasing the number of dispatch threads in this model was not providing a noticeable improvement in dispatch rates. We also observed the CPU utilisation of the machine hosting the service was almost never above 40%. These machines had 88 logical cores and they were underutilised. Our hottest metric here was the considerable voluntary context switching performed.

Our primary objective throughout the project was in effect, to increase farm throughput. At the root of this problem was the way in which tasks in a pool formed a priority queue, relying on the mechanics of a heap data structure. The highest priority task was given 1st shot at dispatch. If, due to constraints or limits, this task was unable to be dispatched the next in line was given the same chance. This iterative process drove the core of the dispatcher and thus a low priority task was given a chance to execute if a higher priority task could not be dispatched. However, the queue(s) had begun to grow so large and resources for high priority items become so constrained, that lower priority tasks were denied this opportunity since the dispatcher was not fast enough to reach the bottom of the heap. This was our optimisation goal!

Replace Static Pool. Changing the model to have a separate thread per pool rather than a shared pool of worker threads, improved examination and dispatch rates. The few stages of the new thread loop was now:

1. Select the highest priority task from the pool.
2. Examine, match, and dispatch the selected task, if possible.
3. Back to 1

With this model the main serialisation point and the repeated work of selecting a pool were avoided. This feature was introduced in the milestone release 0.19.12, and is included in the results produced for Figs. 9 and 10.

Work Stealing. The previous change improved our examination and dispatch rates but it did not take advantage of all the CPU cores available on the dispatcher machine when the number of active pools was small. To compensate for this, we implemented a work stealing system for idle pools which worked in the same way the previous thread model worked, by first selecting an active pool to dispatch a task from. With this change we had the best of both threading models, automatically changing from one system to another depending on the number of active pools and some thread-to-pool affinity where possible. This feature was introduced in the milestone release 0.19.16, and is included in the results produced for Figs. 9 and 10. A later release, which included a throttle to prevent the work-stealing mode being too aggresive (denying other threads access to shared data) is also included and labelled as 0.20.4.

4.2 Parallelisation

Reduce Serialisation Points. Despite the thread model improvements, rdispatcher was still unable to take full advantage of all the CPU cores available on the host. Careful analysis and profiling highlighted several global mutexes that were serialising many operations. We removed or avoided several of those global locks and managed to improve our overall parallelism.

Reduce Cost of Critical Sections. Several global locks still remained that were required for the effective and safe work of the dispatcher service. In order to reduce the impact of those locks we reduced the amount of work done in critical sections in order to reduce the amount of time threads were waiting on locks. Some improvements were, for example, to move safe calculations outside of critical sections. We also identified computation that could be carried out in parallel since it did not require access to shared data, or only required read-only access to shared data.

4.3 Redundant Calculations

Reuse *JavaScript* Engines In Sect. 2.4 we highlighted that precedent constraints were implemented as JavaScript (JS) expressions between the graph vertices. We discovered that each JS engine used to evaluate task dependencies were recreated every time those dependencies were checked (which happened frequently). We changed the code to create and reuse one single JavaScript engine per thread, effectively removing the heavy cost of recreating them. This feature was introduced in the milestone release 0.19.13, and is included in the results produced for Figs. 9 and 10.

Cache Regular Objects. We identified several strings that were reconstructed regularly. By caching these strings we traded off a small increase in memory usage by a massive reduction in string operations, further reducing the load on the memory allocator and avoiding the work required to recalculate those strings.

Introduce 128-Bit Integers. Tasks are sorted by priority, and the one with the highest value is examined and dispatched first. This ordinal priority was a composite of many individual priorities and the final value computed for comparison was the 40-character string (stored internally as UTF-16) representation of these concatenated priorities. The string operations required to generate and to compare that value appeared high on profiling sessions. Careful examination of the values used to generate that string showed that we could encode the same amount of information as a 128-bit integer, converting only to strings when we had to present that value for debugging purposes. This change allowed the compiler to generate far fewer yet more efficient instructions provided by a big reduction in string operations that otherwise ranked highly during profiling sessions. The results produced for Figs. 9 and 10 feature this improvement and is present in release 0.20.13.

Replace Strings with Integers. The task state and event system used strings as identifiers which required many string comparisons by the state machine and the event system. The number of different values was fixed and small, which meant that it was relatively easy to convert into integer values. This change again removed a large amount of string comparisons from the profiler sessions.

4.4 Memory Footprint

Many routine bug fixes contributed to an overall reduction in memory footprint and the associated cost or overhead introduced by an allocator continuously trying to manage memory. There were two modifications we made however, where the significance is worth highlighting. Eventually, we reduced the mean memory consumption by 50%.

Share a Fixed State Hierarchy. A finite state machine was created for each task, and with hundreds of thousands of tasks active at each single run, and millions more inactive but in cache, meant a significant amount of memory allocations were duplicated for this graph. Upon investigation we concluded that the state graph was fixed and constant during the runtime of the service and that we could generate the graph at startup time and to share it with all the tasks. The original implementation of the state machine was very generic, allowing for dynamic and variable state graphs, but the actual usage of the state machine was actually static once the service had started. This change saved millions of memory allocations, significantly helping to reduce the load on the memory allocator. This feature was introduced in the milestone release 0.19.14, and is included in the results produced for Figs. 9 and 10.

Reduced Temporary Objects. Several components of the dispatcher service were creating too many temporary objects, often unnecessarily. Carefully rewriting the code to reuse or reduce the number of temporary objects improved the load on the allocator.

4.5 Memory Allocator

Our profiling sessions often showed the memory allocator (tcmalloc [4]) as responsible for up to 30% of the CPU usage. After some investigation and testing we identified a more suitable allocator (mimalloc [7]) which now rarely exceeds 1% of the CPU usage according to the profiler. The previous allocator was not suitable for the amount of CPU cores and threads and the memory allocation patterns our service required.

4.6 Stability

Serialise State Changes. The original implementation allowed task state modifications from multiple threads at the same time. There were mutexes attempting safe operations but there were several race conditions that contributed to abnormal operations. For example, dispatching the same task twice to two different clients at the same time or task metrics being accounted for on the wrong pool. By serialising task state modifications we removed the race conditions and improved the behaviour of the system.

Generic Bug Fixes. There were logical bugs that affected the correct behaviour of the service. For example the recalculation of available CPU cores was returning negative values for overallocated clients, and those negative values were wrongly affecting the cache structures used to identify clients that provided the required amount of resources for a task.

4.7 Asynchronous Events

Simplified and Streamlined Event System. The Qt [9] event system was used heavily in the original implementation but it's generic applicability was not performant enough for our needs. We recorded latencies in excess of 1 min between when an event was emitted until it was processed, due to the sheer amount of events we were generating (sustaining peaks of 400,000 events per minute), and due to the cost of processing each individual event. By implementing a much simpler and specific event system we reduced both CPU and memory usage and greatly reduced event processing latency. This feature was introduced in the milestone release 0.20.0, and is included in the results produced for Figs. 9 and 10.

Simplified and Streamlined Timer System. As part of the implementation of the new event system we also implemented our own timer system highly integrated with the event system and tailored to our simple and specific requirements, further reducing memory and CPU overhead.

4.8 Networking

Reduced Data Copies. We identified a redundant data copy every time we received a message from the network. We receive hundreds of thousands of JSON-encoded messages per minute, each averaging 2.3KB. Removing this redundant buffer, among a few other trivial optimisations, increased our throughput by up to 50% at times.

Remove Shared Sockets. We were using a single socket for all the messages sent and received, and because of the way messages were encoded we needed to serialise access to that socket, otherwise headers and bodies of different messages could interleave and corrupt the communication between the endpoints. Because the number of threads using the socket was small it was feasible to create a separate socket for each thread which allowed us to parallelise network operations more efficiently.

4.9 Work Distribution

Spread Dependency Checking Evenly. The system often has hundreds of thousands of tasks waiting on others to complete. Depending on the job type, these dependency checks can be quite complex (E.g. FX simulations). The dispatcher service employs several worker threads constantly running those dependency checks and originally it was observed that some threads had 10 times the work than others, which resulted in some dependencies taking a lot longer to be satisfied than others just because the thread handling the checks was extremely busy. We identified that the key used to distribute the work among the worker threads was not evenly distributed because it only depended on the ID of the dgraph owning the task (again, see Fig. 3). After comparing several alternative hash algorithms, we settled on choosing the popular FNV-1a [3] and switched to combining the fully qualified ID. This resulted in a near perfect balance of work across available threads. This feature was introduced in the milestone release 0.20.1, and is included in the results produced for Figs. 9 and 10.

Revised Thread Count. Each subsystem of the dispatcher service has its own number of dedicated threads, and in some cases the number of worker threads too small, this was identified by the latency of processing work items. Simply increasing the number of worker threads on those subsystems improved the responsiveness of the whole system. We now routinely examine the CPU usage of each worker thread in order to identify subsystems that may require additional resources.

4.10 Waste Reduction

Ordered Preemptive Task Selection. When a pool has reached its allocated farm quota it is still allowed to dispatch work to clients but that work is deemed speculative, and hence can be preempted at any point by a regular task entitled to run. By ordering speculative tasks according to their running time and by selecting the one(s) with the least amount of work done, we reduced the amount of wasted core-hours on the farm.

Ordered In-place Promotion (IPP). When the dispatcher has the option to promote a speculatively running task over dispatching a new task of the same shape and belonging to the same pool, it does so to reduce "lost" core hours (a form of waste). To further improve the selection of these otherwise preemptable tasks, we now order by runtime in decreasing order ensuring to promote the longest-running task first.

Recovery of "ghost" Tasks. Sometimes clients become unresponsive and after a specific amount of time. Without hearing any status updates from these hosts, we consider the tasks running on them as "dead", and we proceed to dispatch the task to another client. But in many cases the lack of updates was due to some temporary reason such as network congestion, machine overload etc. and the client is still functioning correctly and the tasks are still running. We are now able to identify these situations and to recover those dead tasks that are still running, hence avoiding the wasted effort of dispatching that task to another machine and starting over.

5 Simulations and Testing

An obstacle often inhibiting the adoption of new or upgraded critical software in production is sufficient and relevant testing. Can we with good confidence guarantee that *a)* we won't degrade the service and *b)* achieve our objective(s) such as handle increased load?

5.1 Coda in a Box (CIAB)

The system components listed in Fig. 1 run across a variety of powerful host systems in production. Developers don't have this luxury and bringing up a system and all its components including several compute clients was cumbersome. To simplify this step we adopted a container approach early on, running all components sandboxed and managed via utility scripts. This container could then also be run on a single powerful machine sufficient to handle greater loads, although running 1000 s of rclientd processes remained impractical.

5.2 Integration Tests

To identify regressions we wrote short integration tests that create tasks using the public API and verify that they run successfully within a time limit. We test a fair amount of the internal functionality through these tests (though not everything) - enough to detect obviously broken builds. We run the integration tests in a CI/CD fashion, as a vanguard before any other test.

5.3 Saturation Tests

For more comprehensive testing we created saturation tests. We create 280k tasks with dependencies between them and distributed among 50 different pools. Every minute we issue thousands of random changes to those tasks, such as priority increments or pool migrations. These task modifications helped us to identify and subsequently fix many race conditions. The tests may take up to one hour to run and require a machine with dozens of cores in order to run properly. We run these tests extensively during development when profiling and are good indicators of improved or degraded performance. The results illustrated through Figs. 9–10 are produced from this script.

5.4 Simulation

At the heart of the Coda system is the reflector (see Fig. 1) and a rich set of messages pass through it - every message necessary, in fact, to replicate a production workload targeted at a separate test system. We developed "refractor", a tool that simulates a render farm given the recorded input stream of another.

In capture mode it simply listens, as a read-only client, to a source reflector (from a production system) for all the messages necessary to rebuild jobs, mimic compute nodes and gather configuration data. This data, once processed, is then serialised to disk ready to replay on a separate test system at will (though there is also a real-time mode).

Refractor can replay recorded input streams, on a test system. It submits the jobs exactly as a user would retaining structure, resource requirements, priority etc. It also creates and configures as many compute nodes as recorded ready to accept the tasks scheduled by the test dispatcher. However, each node is an object in code rather than a real machine. Tasks don't execute the command a user intended but rather sleeps for the known duration, which was encoded into the stream as completed tasks were observed.

This new tool gave us the ability to simulate a render farm at the scale we expect in production. Moreover, it also gave us representative jobs and compute node configurations such that we were able to better simulate the behaviour of a production system under the same conditions (e.g. artificial user limits, resource sharing & scarcity, error rates etc.).

We found that the refractor tool is also limited by the number of "in-flight" ascynchronous events *Python 3* can handle. Some of our larger simulations are constrained by this and as such, may reconsider its implementation in the future.

6 Results

We provide results measured from simulations through refractor and our saturation script, plus metrics recorded in production. We also demonstrate the improved resource utilisation of the host machine the dispatcher runs on.

6.1 Simulation & Saturation

Our trace data replayed through versions old and new (denoted via their semantic versioning) consistently demonstrate improved performance when compared. Figure 8 shows an overall better farm utilisation for two runs of the same trace data. Note that version 0.20.11 was allowed to complete whereas 0.18.3 was terminated prematurely due to time pressure. Since the saturation tests take less time to complete we've been able to run each milestone release through our simplified sampling pipeline to produce graphs that clearly demonstrate the incremental improvements each version introduces. The oldest release, 0.18.2, featured only the additions we made to increase insight and observability (see Sect. 3) before tackling the required performance improvements covered in later sections. This same release, 0.18.2, also featured a curious inaccuracy in reporting throughput; the counters were actually sampled periodically and then extrapolated to produce an imprecise value rather than its true rate. Thus the dispatch rate present in Fig. 10 is actually likely to closely follow 0.18.3, which introduced a fix for this bug. CPU utilisation however, was unaffected by this and remains true in Fig. 9. Figure 10 shows improved task handling by the dispatcher resulting in a makespan reduction of 75% between 0.18.3 and the latest release, 0.20.13. It clearly illustrates the efficiency gains of the newer system, and these results remain consistent even under increased load (i.e. greater rclientd counts).

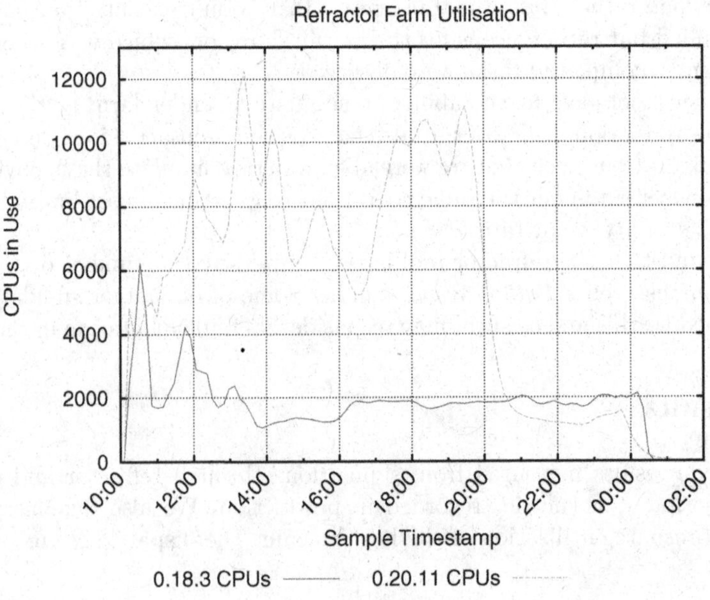

Fig. 8. CPU Utilisation of the refractor render farm using a 15h trace from our San Francisco studio

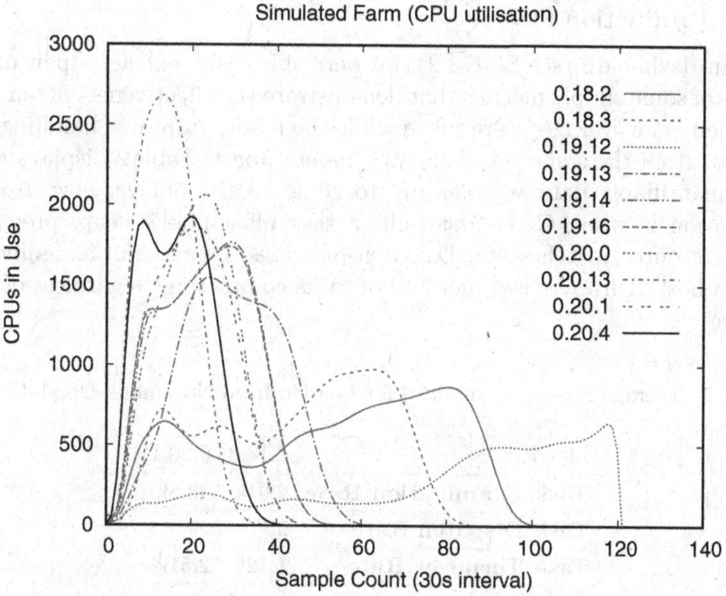

Fig. 9. CPU Utilisation during saturation tests of all major milestone releases

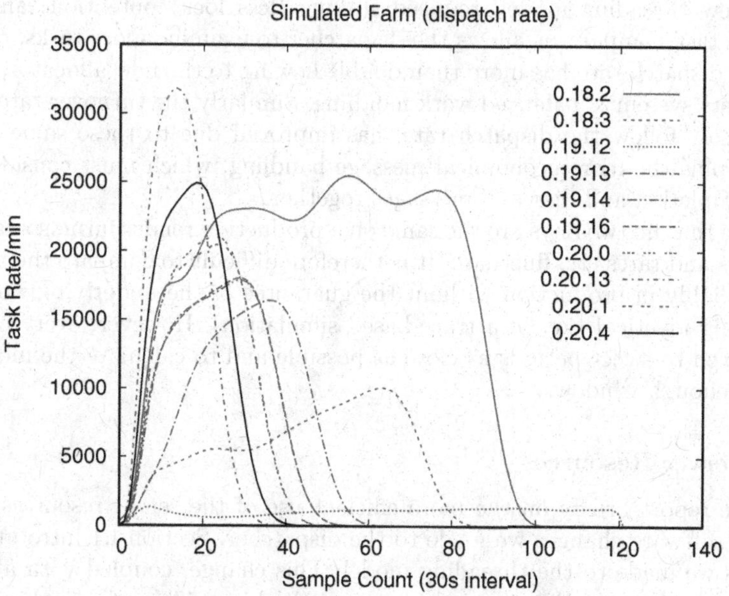

Fig. 10. Task dispatch rates during saturation tests of all major milestone releases (higher and shorter is better)

6.2 In Production

Using our dashboard (see Sect. 3.2), we were able easily extract a pair of 3 week averages of some simple metrics that demonstrate the effectiveness of our work in production. The averages were taken while the render farm was handling similar workloads from the same set of shows a month apart. Table 2 displays a subset of the quantifiable data we measure to compare the old vs. new dispatcher. Examination is when Coda first pulls a task off a pool's heap, preparing to attempt resource matches etc. Dispatch indicates a successful assignment of a task to a host. Turnover is a measure of tasks completing (regardless of success or failure).

Table 2. Average rates (per minute) for London from November–December 2021

Metric	0.18.3	0.20.11
Task Examination Rate	2.01k	43.8k
Task Dispatch Rate	953	2k
Task Turnover Rate	1.12k	2.51k

The examination rate illustrates a typical 20x improvement in throughput - the new threading model, reduced stalling (less lock contention) and more efficient task comparator allows the dispatcher to examine more tasks, quicker.

The dispatch rate has more than doubled owing to the new allocator, rewritten events system & balanced work handling. Similarly the turnover rate, which will closely follow the dispatch rate, has improved due to these same optimisations plus the more economical message handling, which must consider both task completion and dispatch messages together.

Note that no two days are the same on a production render farm, so naturally numbers and rates etc. fluctuate. It is therefore difficult to compare the two versions reliably in production without the guarantee of the underlying workloads remaining identical (i.e. in a trace-based simulation). However, every care has been given to select periods as close as possible and to calculate the mean over a large enough window.

6.3 Server Resources

Here we report briefly on the more efficient use of the server resources following the software changes we made to the dispatcher. Section 4.1 introduced the changes we made to the threading model. This change, coupled with attempts to reduce lock contention to a minimum, resulted in a 50% reduction in context switching and a corresponding boost in on-CPU time. We're finally exceeding the 40% CPU utilisation threshold mentioned in Sect. 4.1. This efficiency gain is reflected in the examination rate given above in Sect. 6.2. Figures 11 & 12 respectively, illustrate clearly the improved CPU utilisation for two separate 7 day periods for a similarly loaded system.

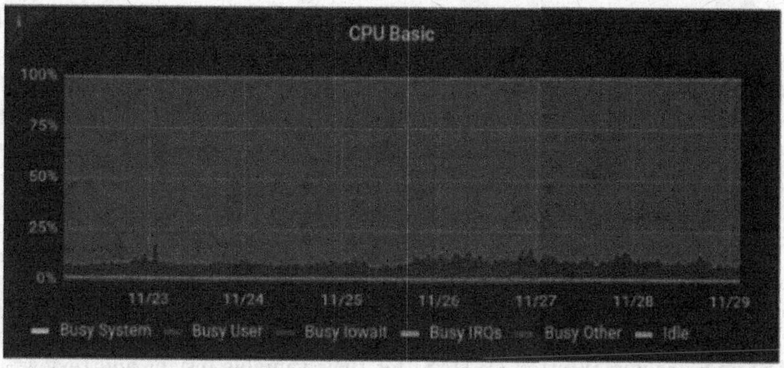

Fig. 11. CPU Utilisation of the server under rdispatcher 0.18.3

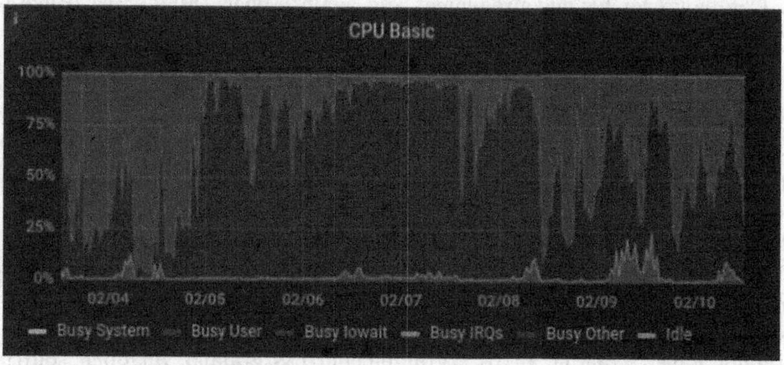

Fig. 12. CPU Utilisation of the server under rdispatcher 0.20.11

7 Future Work

This paper has concentrated only on the changes necessary to improve our current production scheduler and makes no mention of any research into alternatives. However, we have experimented with several ideas we wish to revive, to further maximise our general render farm utilisation.

We're keen to quickly compare common benchmarks such as the minimisation of makespan, mean user wait-time, resource fragmentation etc., when trace data is run through different scheduling policies or established dispatching rules from [8] (e.g. FCFS/ERD, SJF, LRPT, WSPT etc.). Similarly, we wish to evaluate the different packing strategies available to us such as NF, BF, FFD etc. as well as our own proprietary algorithms. To this end we'd begun work on a pluggable/modular framework where combinations of these can be composed quickly and tested offline without the need of production systems.

Many scheduling policies require some knowledge of expected task runtimes and we've already disclosed that rarely do we have this information available as decision criteria. However, in order to evaluate the suitability of deadline scheduling with preemptive backfill through the aforementioned framework, we must first tackle this problem. To this end, we had some success experimenting with simple attribute-based grouping and unsupervised clustering of tasks and, through ARIMA and EWMA, forecasting runtimes for the tasks categorised by these clusters. The framework again supports pre-processing refinement stages such as this prior to the main scheduling run.

We hope to resurrect these efforts in R&D in the near future and bring them closer to conclusion and, ideally, production.

Acknowledgements. The authors would like to thank Andre Prado (ILM) and Tommy Burnette (ILM) for their support and feedback, and Kevin Constantine (WDAS) and Graham Whitted (WDAS) for their valuable insight and reviews of the paper, not to mention their considerable contributions to Coda over the years at WDAS - we are grateful for your collaboration! We'd like to also thank Jason Cox (The Walt Disney Company) for his encouragement and again, review. Finally, we'd like to also thank Christian Dahlberg (ILM) for his contributions to the larger project.

References

1. Elastic: Elasticsearch. https://www.elastic.co/elasticsearch, an index+search analytics engine
2. Fluentd: Fluentd. https://www.fluentd.org, an open source data collector
3. Fowler, G., Noll, L.C., Vo, K.P.: Fnv-1a. https://www.ietf.org/archive/id/draft-eastlake-fnv-17.txt, a non-cryptographic hash function
4. Google: Tcmalloc. https://github.com/google/tcmalloc, a memory allocator
5. Grafana Labs: Grafana. https://grafana.com/oss/grafana, an open source web-based visualisation platform
6. Industrial Light & Magic: ObaQ. https://www.linuxjournal.com/article/6783, a public disclosure of the ObaQ/DOALL Render Farm Queuing System
7. Microsoft: mimalloc. https://github.com/microsoft/mimalloc, a memory allocator
8. Pinedo, M.: Scheduling Theory, Algorithms and Systems, chap. 7. 1 edn., Prentice Hall, Hoboken (1995)
9. Qt Group: Qt. https://www.qt.io, a cross-platform application development framework
10. Singer, R.: Shape Up - Stop Running in Circles and Ship Work that Matters. Basecamp (2019). https://basecamp.com/shapeup/webbook
11. Walt Disney Animation Studios: Coda. https://www.disneyanimation.com/technology/coda, a public disclosure of the Coda Render Farm Queuing System

Open Scheduling Problems

Using Kubernetes in Academic Environment: Problems and Approaches

Viktória Spišaková[1(✉)], Dalibor Klusáček[2], and Lukáš Hejtmánek[1]

[1] Institute of Computer Science, Masaryk University, Brno, Czech Republic
{spisakova,xhejtman}@ics.muni.cz
[2] CESNET, a.l.e., Prague, Czech Republic
klusacek@cesnet.cz

Abstract. In this work, we discuss our experience when utilizing the Kubernetes orchestrator (K8s) to efficiently allocate resources in a heterogeneous and dynamic academic environment. In the commercial world, the "pay per use" model is a strong regulating factor for efficient resource usage. In the academic environment, resources are usually provided "for free" to the end-users, thus they often lack a clear motivation to plan their use efficiently. In this paper, we show three major sources of inefficiencies. One is the users' requirement to have interactive computing environments, where the users need resources for their application as soon as possible. Users do not appreciate waiting for interactive environments, but constantly keeping some resources available for interactive tasks is inefficient. The second phenomenon is observable in both interactive and batch workloads; users tend to overestimate necessary limits for their computations, thus wasting resources. Finally, Kubernetes does not support fair-sharing functionality (dynamic user priorities) which hampers the efforts when developing a fair scheme for Pod/job scheduling and/or eviction. We discuss various approaches to deal with these problems such as scavenger jobs, placeholder jobs, Kubernetes-specific resource allocation policies, separate clusters, priority classes, and novel hybrid cloud approach. We also show that all these proposals open interesting scheduling-related questions that are hard to answer with existing Kubernetes tools and policies. Last but not least, we provide a real workload trace from our installation to the scheduling community which captures these phenomena.

Keywords: Cloud · HPC · Scheduling · Kubernetes · Resource management

1 Introduction

In today's world, the usefulness of container-oriented computing is widely recognized. Businesses adopted containers several years ago for their digital services. However, academia started to notice containers as a viable way of supporting research not so long ago.

D. Klusáček et al. (Eds.): JSSPP 2022, LNCS 13592, pp. 235–253, 2023.
https://doi.org/10.1007/978-3-031-22698-4_12

Historically, demanding computations that process data, produce analyses or deliver results of complex workflows are foundations of research. These actions occur on large high performance computing clusters. Specifically, computations are managed by various scheduling systems because there are more requests on resources than resources themselves. Scheduling methodologies have been in active development for at least 30 years and internal design is finely calibrated to provide a variety of important features such as granular resource selection, placement control or topology and affinity as well as fairness. Scheduling systems can have different optimization goals. Some systems focus on maximizing throughput and resource utilization while users' jobs have to wait in queues. Other systems want to avoid starvation, focusing on low latency, thus running new jobs as quickly as possible which in turn often results in decreased resource utilization. Furthermore, resources are often allocated such that overall fairness among users, groups and/or projects is guaranteed.

Resources for scientific computations in academia are in majority offered for free as a result of financing by national governments that earmark funds for research and education. For this reason, academic resource providers need proper scheduling mechanisms as it is the only way to regulate access to resources. This is in contrast to commercial world where access to resources is paid by users which imposes strong and efficient access regulation. This explains why container orchestrators or cloud-management frameworks do not typically provide truly sophisticated HPC-like schedulers to regulate resource access. Especially, a well-performing scheduler in the commercial world equals high profit and vice versa.

A crucial difference between HPC scheduler logic and container orchestrator is that in the HPC world, submitted jobs typically act as a "finite" computations that start, compute and then finish, whereas container orchestrators (e.g., Kubernetes[1]) were developed to accommodate continuous services and long-running stateless applications [15]. Nevertheless, container orchestrators are actively looking for a way of implementing HPC jobs concept. For example, recent versions of Kubernetes (`v.1.21`) feature `Indexed Jobs`[2] that allow static work partition among the workers of a parallel job. The introduction of such resource marks efforts of Kubernetes developers and community to migrate more of HPC and batch workloads into the platform. None of these "extensions" enforces job runtime limit so as of now, container orchestrators do not forbid endless jobs which makes HPC-like scheduling almost impossible.

Besides potentially endless jobs, there is another category of waiting-sensitive workloads—interactive jobs, i.e., jobs that do not run in batch/background but users interactively work with them. This kind of jobs imposes problems to schedulers even in standard HPC installations used in academia.

Another complication for moving HPC workloads to container platform lies in the modus operandi of this platform. Kubernetes orchestrator (K8s) works with

[1] https://kubernetes.io.

[2] https://kubernetes.io/blog/2021/04/19/introducing-indexed-jobs/.

the assumption that every `Pod`[3] can be terminated and restarted. In contrast, typical HPC workload does not expect any interruptions once it has started and terminates only when it has either finished or has reached its allocated walltime limit.

In this paper, we discuss our experience and problems observed when utilizing the Kubernetes container orchestrator in academia. We aim to provide Kubernetes platform that will be fully competitive with traditional HPC infrastructure as well as other types of workload. We see this as challenging and interesting task. The benefits of containerized computations are obvious and are becoming very popular among scientists. The challenge is to come up with a solution that allows "free of charge" computing while being robust and self-regulating. On the other hand, we do not aim to "mimic" HPC-like system including complex HPC scheduler on top of Kubernetes infrastructure, and vice versa Kubernetes infrastructure on top of HPC infrastructure.

The rest of this paper is organized as follows. First, in Sect. 2 we define major scheduling challenges that arise due to the intended use of Kubernetes infrastructure in academic environment. Next, Sect. 3 presents current scheduling capabilities of Kubernetes. In Sect. 4, we propose several ideas on how to solve our scheduling and resource allocation issues. We also discuss the details of our infrastructure setup and provide basic data about the workload trace from our installation (Sect. 5). Finally, we introduce the related work in Sect. 6 and conclude the paper.

2 Scheduling Challenges

Concept of shared, multi-tenant infrastructure is usually adopted in academic environment. Choosing Kubernetes as workload scheduler might be regarded as illogical step because such infrastructures are usually built with HPC schedulers e.g. `SLURM`[4], `OpenPBS`[5]. Moreover, some workload managers e.g. SLURM supports requesting containers[6]. However, there are numerous reasons why we adopted Kubernetes rather than embracing containers in HPC environment.

First of all, Kubernetes is a system developed specifically for deployment, scaling and management of containerized applications. Its deployment stack is optimized for containers which is reflected on easiness of use, high reliability and much more comfortable environment to work with. Kubernetes manages whole container lifecycle and automatically ensures number of desired replicas exist in the system. When choosing workload manager for containers, we were considering not only specialized HPC containers but all sorts of containers—web services, databases, microservice applications and other workload types regularly deployed. We already maintain a fully functional HPC environment where

3 Pods are the smallest deployable units of computing that you can create and manage in Kubernetes.

4 https://slurm.schedmd.com/documentation.html.

5 https://www.openpbs.org.

6 https://slurm.schedmd.com/containers.html.

we learned running containers in such environment has considerable amount of downsides and missing features. We understood users would benefit from opportunity to run wide variety of containerized workflows conveniently on specialized infrastructure. Interests of users seeking HPC characteristics with container technology were secondary and we started to accommodate them later. However, only then we discovered importance of conducting scheduling related research in Kubernetes environment.

Providing multi-tenant infrastructure (HPC or container) requires proper scheduling. Otherwise, vast inefficiencies can appear and lead to resource (money) wasting while irritating the users. We discuss major obstacles that threaten the success and efficiency of the container infrastructure. From infrastructure administrator point of view, we distinguished three major domains of inefficiencies, all coupled with scheduling.

2.1 Endless Computing with Limited Resources

In a standard HPC batch system, each job has a maximum allowed lifetime—the so called walltime limit [17]. Achieving time limit for a workload is not always simple, e.g., in interactive workloads or other long-running services. Therefore, the runtime of a container/Pod is unbounded and unknown, in general [10]. This means that the system (and its users) do not expect the workload will terminate after predefined time. Since the academia is not using pay-per-use model, we lack a clear motivation for the users to terminate their containers/Pods once they are not needed anymore.

At the same time, academia budget is fixed (as users use it for free), i.e., we cannot simply buy another cluster whenever the demand is approaching the available capacity. The absence of the pay-per-use model together with no clear resource-reclaiming policy will inevitably cause another obvious problem—existing resources will be allocated to the users without considering overall fairness. This is in great contrast with common batch HPC installations, where fairness is one of the major optimization goals and is usually enforced by the well known fair-sharing approach [11].

Job starvation is tightly connected to the absence of walltime limit. Users can submit jobs demanding resources that cannot be satisfied because all nodes are occupied by jobs without finite walltime. The problem is more visible with standard Kubernetes scheduler as it is not able to reserve a node for a large job. Without reservation, large job is endlessly preempted by smaller jobs or it can evict smaller jobs from a node, but this solution is not acceptable for (long-running) HPC jobs.

2.2 Interactive Computing

In HPC environment, batch jobs often do not start immediately but reside in a queue and wait until a cluster has enough free resources to execute the job. However, we are witnessing rising popularity of user interest in working with graphical interfaces rather than command line. In the past, we deployed a web

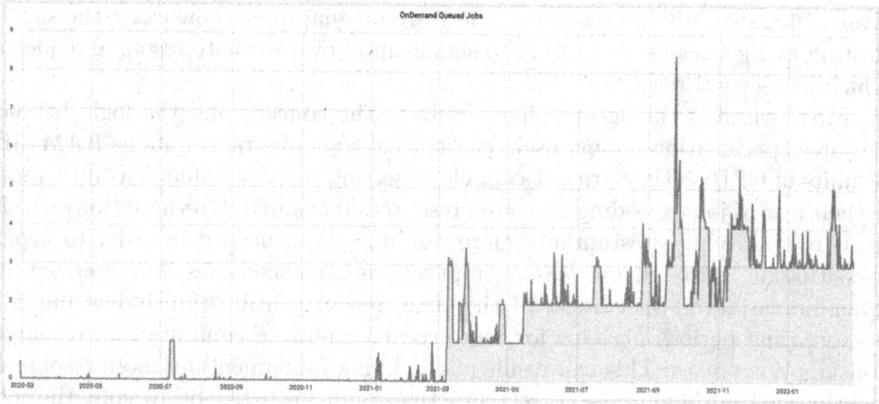

Fig. 1. Time series graph depicting rising popularity of applications spawned from OnDemand portal.

portal *Open OnDemand*[7] as the first step of improving interactive applications' accessibility. Figure 1 shows the growing demand of GUI applications in CERIT-SC, supporting the argument that users seek more comfortable ways of working with graphical interfaces, i.e., interactive use-cases will not likely disappear.

Interactive jobs comprise both interactive CLI jobs, i.e., jobs running purely from command line, and more importantly interactive GUI jobs. The two types should be scheduled and started as soon as possible because they require user interaction to run, e.g., selecting options or filling in password in the GUI. If this is the case, the user has to wait but the job may start after such a long time that the user is not available anymore, thus the job is only blocking resources. A common solution to the *waiting-user* problem is to keep some resources unoccupied so interactive jobs start nearly immediately, thus keeping users active and responsive. On the other hand, resources are likewise blocked needlessly so both situations impose ineffective usage of resources.

One solution suggesting itself is suspending non-interactive jobs in order to accommodate interactive ones. Suspending a job would mean to free its resources and thus letting interactive job run. After interactive job is completed, dormant non-interactive job resumes. Unfortunately, neither HPC nor Kubernetes allow to suspend running jobs which makes interactive computing problematic both in HPC and Kubernetes.

2.3 Overestimation

Specifying precise job resource request is a key precondition for effective job scheduling. This is a well understood requirement in HPC world but container orchestrators are not notably strict about the necessity to specify job resources.

[7] https://openondemand.org.

Even if users specify job resources, there are no guarantees how exact the specification is. As a result, users tend to significantly overestimate resource requests which has several reasons.

First reason is the sheer obliviousness to the concept and the logic behind resource specification—some users can not envision abstract units as RAM GB or units of CPU so they are not capable of setting sensible value. Second reason is their fear of job exceeding allocated resources (causing job termination) which leads to specifying substantially more resources than needed in order to avoid the situation. Last but not least, computations are sometimes characterized by dynamic variation when most of the time, resource utilization is low but for a short time period, perhaps for more complex part of computation, resource consumption spikes. This can result in specifying fundamentally more resources than needed, although the correct practice could probably be to split the job into several units with tailored requirements.

User-induced overestimation causes very low real cluster usage. Here, resource oversubscription (allocating more resources than the physical capacity) is a crucial enhancement to existing systems [2]. According to our experience the *overestimation problem* is more coupled with K8s workloads than HPC where the actual usage-to-request ratio is quite good[8].

As we show in the Fig. 2, users are prone to significantly overestimate Pods' resource requests which in turn leads to inefficient use of those resources. In the upper part of Fig. 2 we show the total used CPU hours and the requested (allocated) CPU hours per K8s namespace. Clearly, there are huge differences both in the amount of used resources as well as in the allocations (Y-axis is in *log* scale). When we normalize these allocations into percents (see Fig. 2 bottom), we can see how poorly those allocated resources are being used. 57.7% of namespaces uses less than 5% of allocated resources. The fact that some namespaces use (way) more than 100% of allocated resources is caused by the Kubernetes allowing Pods to have their CPU limits greater than their guaranteed allocations.

2.4 Problem Summary and Scheduling Objectives

To sum up the challenges that we want to address let us briefly recap the scheduling problem. In ideal scenario, we want to provide a service that will allow immediate start of users' workloads to guarantee interactive-like experience. At the same time, we need to provide this service for free while having a fixed budget (i.e., fixed size of infrastructure). Also, we want to minimize resource wastage. Since these requirements are somehow contradictory, we need to develop a reasonable compromise.

First of all, we need to ensure unused resources will not be wasted but rather used by some suitable (lower priority) workloads. Thankfully, this can be solved quite easily (see Sect. 4.2). The complicated part is how to guarantee quick start for new workloads when, e.g., the infrastructure is full. So far, we foresee several

[8] In our system, HPC workloads typically utilize more than 80% of requested CPU resources.

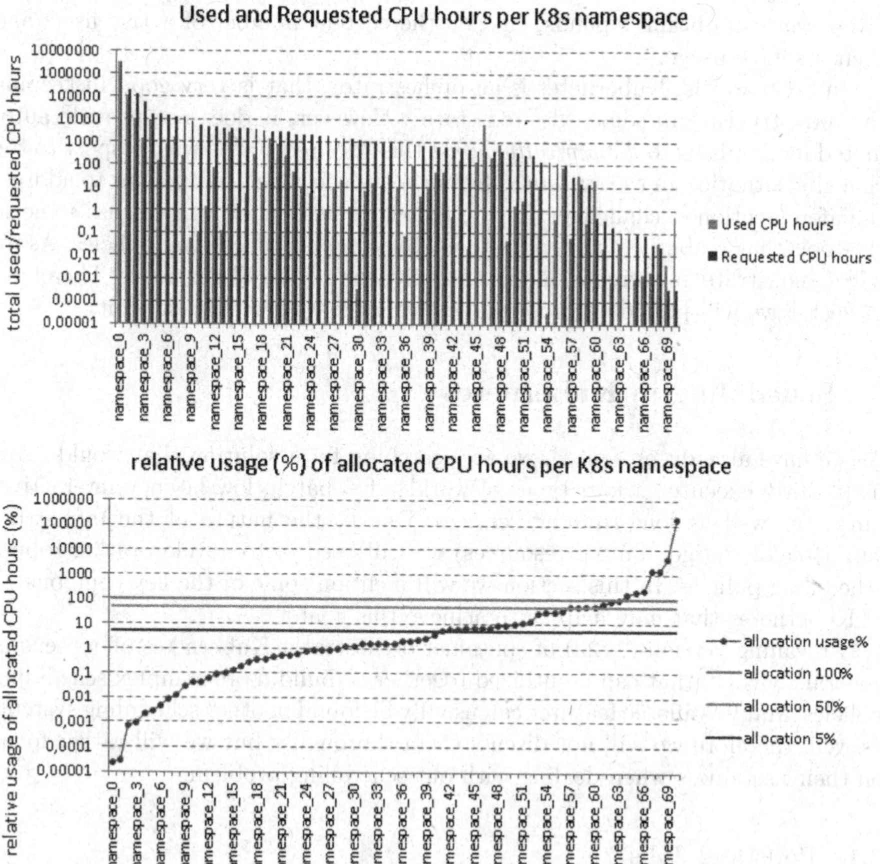

Fig. 2. The comparison of absolute (top) and relative (bottom) usage of requested CPU resources in CERIT-SC Kubernetes (K8s) cluster during the last 90 days. Y-axis in log. scale.

possible directions. The first possibility is to terminate some of those currently executing workloads or guarantee that (at least some) of those executing workload will complete in reasonable time. However, in order to solve this we need to address major problems. Simply put, we need to find a mechanism to select (and assign) priority to users' workloads which in turn will help us to decide which workloads to stop and/or allow to run.

The complication is that this priority mechanism can not be static in general. It is not sufficient to assign each user a fixed priority (or a static share) and keep it intact. This would (in a long run) lead to inefficiencies and/or unfairness. The reasons are obvious—just like in HPC, the "priority" of a given user (tenant) may change in time (for various reasons). Similarly, the size of a "share" that a given user can obtain depends, e.g., on the current number of active users and their resource usage.

In other words, Kubernetes is an orchestrator, that is very good in keeping the infrastructure in some "desired state". However, it does not provide automated mechanisms to *dynamically adjust* this "desired state" with respect to the changing situation in the system. Obviously, we need such component to address the aforementioned challenges. In the following section we will discuss some of the tools that Kubernetes provides to enable complex scheduling policies. As we will demonstrate, it currently lacks the ability to fully fulfill our needs. Therefore, in Sect. 4 we will provide a proposal how to, at least partially, solve it.

3 Scheduling in Kubernetes

As we have already presented, we are searching for a solution that would allow us to fairly execute various types of workloads—batch, low latency interactive, bursty as well as long-running services. Due to the nature of the infrastructure (free of charge, limited resources) we will need to to develop rather robust scheduling policies. In this section we will mention some of the key components of Kubernetes that may help us to achieve this goal.

Prevailing version (`1.22`) of container orchestrator Kubernetes offers several general concepts that can be utilized together to build more complex scheduling policies. Many available features can usually be found in other scheduling systems as well, therefore we will not discuss them thoroughly but we will rather focus on their usefulness when dealing with our scheduling problem.

3.1 Pods and Jobs

In Kubernetes, the basic unit of scheduling is a Pod. It is the smallest deployable unit of computing and contains one or more containers. A Job in Kubernetes is a higher level of abstraction than a Pod. A Job creates one or more Pods and will (try) to execute these Pods until a specified number of them successfully terminate. The important feature of Job is that a *deadline* can be specified and Jobs can be cleaned up by CronJobs, i.e., deleted from the system after their completion. Therefore they can be used for HPC-like jobs with known maximum allowed runtime. Jobs are thus useful building blocks to prevent the "endless computing" scenario mentioned in Sect. 2.1.

3.2 Resource Requests and Limits

Kubernetes uses two types of resource allocation for each container—request and limit—that can be applied to CPU and memory. Request represents guaranteed resources that will be allocated to a container whereas limit is the upper bound of the resources. Standard Kubernetes scheduler makes resource allocation based on requests meaning the scheduler ensures that for both CPU and memory, the sum of their requests (respectively) of all containers scheduled on a node is less than its capacity. CPU limit is a hard upper bound on amount CPU time a container can use. Pod resource request/limit is the sum of the resource requests/limits of that type for each container in the Pod. However, containers share total CPU time and if all containers need more CPU time than their request but less than limit (i.e., several containers use more than they requested), performance degradation can be observed but container runtimes do not terminate jobs or containers for excessive CPU usage.[9]

On the other hand, memory limit imposes strict regime—if container exceeds the limit, the system kernel terminates the process that attempted the allocation and it is likely that the Pod will be evicted if memory shortage appears on the physical node. As scheduler allocates resources solely according to requests, it can happen that a node is short of resources if many containers exceed request resources. In such a case, container eviction starts and some Pods are terminated and moved to another node. However, there are no checkpoints and Pods are basically restarted.

Apparently, requests and limits can be used as a building block to accommodate bursty workloads with generally low momentary CPU utilization (by setting low requests and generous limits). The problem is that requests and limits cannot be modified for running Pods, neither can running Pods be migrated. To change existing limit or move it somewhere else a Pod must be restarted.

It is worth mentioning that no other resources can be strictly limited (or requested) in Kubernetes scheduler, e.g. network bandwidth, GPU or I/O throughput. Technically, *nvidia add-on*[10] enables manipulation with GPU card in Kuberentes in same manner as CPU but eventually, there are multiple ways how GPU can be used in a container without formal request. To conclude, it is important to think about other computational resources and cover them in future discussions because there are many applications that might not be concerned about CPU time but rather about GPU time or I/O time.

3.3 Priority Classes

Priorities are extensively used in HPC world to indicate users' rights to use resources. Kubernetes offers similar concept called Priority Class[11]. Priority Class demonstrates the importance of a Pod among all other Pods in the cluster or in the pending queue. If a Pod cannot be scheduled due to limited capacity of a cluster, the scheduler attempts to preempt one or more Pods with lower priority in favor of scheduling pending Pods with higher priorities.

Priority classes can be configured as preempting and non-preempting. A workload assigned to non-preempting priority class will stay in the scheduling queue until its resource requests are satisfied. This represents a kind of *silent overtake* when prioritized workload claims resource ahead of others but does

[9] https://kubernetes.io/docs/concepts/configuration/manage-resources-containers/.
[10] https://kubernetes.io/docs/tasks/manage-gpus/scheduling-gpus/.
[11] https://kubernetes.io/docs/concepts/scheduling-eviction/pod-priority-preemption/.

not violently terminate other workloads, with the risk of losing their in-progress computation.

Importantly, while a priority class can be changed, added or even removed, this will not impact already running Pods. In other words, the priority of running Pod can not be changed without restarting that Pod.

3.4 Labels, Affinity, Anti-affinity

Kubernetes understands heterogeneous clusters exist and they feature wide variety of node types. This creates many opportunities for fine scheduling when Pods need to run on same node (e.g. due to sharing cache) or oppositely, Pods run on different nodes in order to lower chance of node failure bringing down all workloads.

If there are circumstances when Pods pose their own preferences concerning nodes, Kubernetes has several ways[12] of employing affinity (or anti-affinity) mainly represented by assigning labels and taints to nodes and nodeSelectors to Pods. Importantly, node taints can be used to repel Pods from specific nodes. Moreover, taints can be used to evict Pods and both taints and labels can be changed dynamically. This features can greatly contribute not only to improve Pod's performance but it can be also used to steer the scheduler toward better decisions.

4 Problem Solutions Using Kubernetes Building Blocks

This section discusses several possible approaches how to deal with the outlined problems shown in the previous sections. Not all of them are directly connected to scheduling, but they rather present different approaches to running workloads in the Kubernetes platform. Whenever possible, *we try to use legacy K8s functionality* instead of using either some third party solution or proposing new components.

4.1 Separate Clusters

The first and by far the easiest solution to assigning resources to multiple competing workloads is creating separate clusters for specific computations (e.g. interactive jobs, HPC jobs, web services). Separate clusters bring the possibility of applying distinct schedulers into each cluster where one might be more suitable than the other for a certain workload type.

However, this is merely a naive solution because it brings overhead for users as well as administrators. Users must be familiar with each cluster's structure in order to decide the most appropriate environment for workloads; they have to control progress at multiple places and eventually they spend more time analyzing infrastructure. Furthermore, administrators must handle several clusters,

[12] https://kubernetes.io/docs/concepts/scheduling-eviction/assign-pod-node/.

provide maintenance and continuous development. On the other hand, analyzing the most executed workload types brings the opportunity to tailor scheduler to specific requirements of the specific workload classes. Still, within a cluster diverse workloads may co-exist, thus bringing back most of the problems mentioned earlier.

4.2 Scavanger Jobs

One of the major problems (see Fig. 2) observed in practice is the low CPU utilization of guaranteed allocations. One way how to increase resource utilization without impacting other users is to deploy so called *scavenger jobs*, i.e., jobs that are reasonably short/small and can be easily terminated and later resumed [9]. Scavenger jobs usually run at low priority and if resources are needed, they are terminated. When a resource becomes free again, scavanger jobs are resumed.

In Kubernetes, the administrator can define preemptible classes for Pods. These Pods then act as scavanger jobs; they get started and terminated according to resources' state. As they can be preempted by the scheduler at any time, eligible users will obtain interactive feedback immediately.

We have evaluated this approach using job preemption to deal with inefficiencies of using shared computational infrastructure. It turned out that preemptible scavenger jobs influence Pod allocations that rely on the interplay of requests and limits (see Sect. 3.2). These concepts are basically contradictory. Scavenger jobs, by their nature, do not leave available resources, so users are unable to utilize more resources than they requested, i.e., use the limit property. Therefore, in the following section we propose a solution for this problem in the form of ad-hoc *placeholder jobs* and we discuss their pros and cons.

4.3 Placeholder Jobs

As we stated above, there are no guarantees of free resources in the range between a Pod's request and its limit. As we observed, adopting scavanger jobs makes all resources above Pod's request almost unusable (as they are occupied). Moreover, in the current version of K8s it is not possible to change the amount of requested resources without container restart[13], so the user (or the scheduler) is unable to deal with this problem by temporarily increasing resource requests.

Until in-place vertical scaler is provided in K8s, there is another possibility to mitigate this problem. Instead of specifying resource requests and limits, we can use a little trick to ensure that there are enough free resources that can be used by user's Pod.

The trick how to obtain free resources (used by scavenger jobs) on a particular node is to create so called placeholder job, i.e., a job that *reserves resources but it does not consume them.* Placeholder job terminates existing scavanger job(s), thus freeing resources for the demanding Pod. Using node affinity, we can easily ensure that the placeholder job runs on the same node as the Pod that

[13] https://github.com/kubernetes/kubernetes/pull/102884.

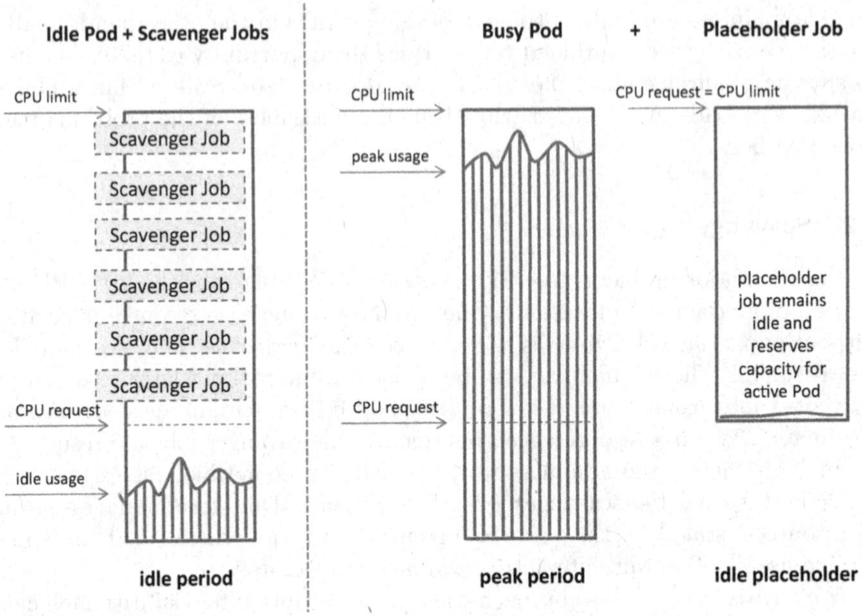

Fig. 3. During idle period scavenger jobs use free resources (left). When Pod's CPU load grows, placeholder job is started thus evicting scavenger jobs and freeing resources for active Pod (right).

needs more resources. This approach works because there is no CPU or memory pinning to particular Pod, so the unused resources (reserved by placeholder) can be consumed by anyone.

Figure 3 illustrates this approach. On the left side we show an idle Pod. Its requested CPUs are low and its (unused) CPU limit is utilized by scavenger jobs. When the load increases (Fig. 3 right), a placeholder job with large CPU request is deployed on that node (evicting low priority scavengers) and the now busy Pod can use its CPUs to the limit.

This solution is not perfect as there are no guarantees that created free resources will be consumed just by the requesting Pod/user. Still, our initial evaluation shows that it is good enough in most situations. We believe that the combination of scavenger and placeholder jobs is currently good solution to keep the utilization high while allowing for quick vertical scaling of selected Pods.

4.4 Unresolved Issues

Native Kubernetes concepts alone are not capable of ensuring fair, efficient, and transparent automated scheduling mechanism. So far, we were able to use some of those building blocks to come up with solutions to several problems. Still, some problems (e.g., fairness) remain unresolved. Let us now discuss some of the directions that can be taken to deal with them.

Hybrid Cloud Approach. The concept of hybrid cloud is now appearing everywhere. Nearly all big cloud providers have already tackled the idea and generally, it is considered as a promising way of computing. The definition of hybrid cloud is not entirely transparent because word "hybrid" itself induces some ambiguity and room for multiple explanations. However, RedHat has come with a list of actions[14] that hybrid cloud should be able to perform and one of them is to *"be able to move workloads between environments"*. We consider this claim as a perfect definition because joining environments—in our context HPC and container-based environments—could represent possibly viable solution to some of the unresolved scheduling problems we discussed. In the first sections of this article, we have introduced complications connected to moving workloads from HPC to container infrastructure, mainly related to resource requests over-estimation and "access control" policies including fairness. We should give it a second thought and admit that for now, some computations perform better in traditional HPC environment, e.g., due to significant resource requests (hundreds of GB of RAM, hundreds of CPUs) or code-optimizations for certain hardware infrastructures. Usually, container-oriented clusters are not composed of large nodes and even if they are, there are limits on the number of containers that can be deployed in a cluster.

Hybrid cloud approach could bring an alternative way of computing where truly HPC workloads would be submitted to HPC environment and other workload types would continue existing as containers. Importantly, HPC schedulers offer better resource division and always allow to fine-tune fairness and job ordering, so offloading large workloads from Kubernetes clusters into HPC cluster would diminish the current need for major changes in K8s's scheduling abilities. Until Kubernetes community creates a way of dealing with HPC-cloud transformation, it would be sufficient to develop a sort of connector for HPC jobs that would connect the two worlds.

While this "outsourcing" may help us to survive for some time, we still need to properly handle truly container-based workloads. Especially, we need to focus on their life cycle which we will discuss next.

Pod Life-Cycle and Resource Draining. Once we have Pods running in our system, we must make sure that only "living" Pods will keep their allocations and all leftover workloads will be evicted and their Pods deleted. Here we propose a naive mechanism which uses priority classes, resource requests and limits. We understand the complexity of scheduling, resource allocation and fairness, and we are aware of the simplicity of the following method.

In the beginning, each workload submitted into the Kubernetes has the same priority and it must provide its specification of resource requirements. Once deployed, the system observes and logs user's utilization of resources for a specified period of time, e.g., three to four days. If the observed resource consumption is close to the requests, no action is needed. If the resource consumption is significantly lower than requested, this workload's priority class is decreased and

[14] https://www.redhat.com/en/topics/cloud-computing/what-is-hybrid-cloud.

the user is informed about this fact together with data and a set of recommendations on how to improve their resource requests. Whatever is the case, the final decision (action Y/N) is stored in a database for further comparisons. After the first *observation time period* the new period begins and same rules apply. Undoubtedly, priority class can not be lowered forever so a proper mechanism handling ignorant users/workloads must be in place. For example, after, e.g., five decreasing periods, the Pod is evicted and deleted. This simple approach guarantees that long-running idle workloads can be preempted or terminated in order to drain resources for new tasks.

Such simple eviction works out of the box only for workloads resembling long stateful services. It is common that cluster hosts burst Pods, on-demand computations or pipelines with fluctuating resource requests. Therefore, during one observation time period, they might present themselves as *resource-intensive* (fully utilizing requested resources) and the next time they can be *resource-dormant* (utilizing near-to-nothing). One solution to that could be enforcing singularity principle, thus letting *one Pod perform only one task* which naturally breaks all pipelines and compound computations into better manageable units. Assigning resource requests to small individual units is more accurate and should contribute to reducing resource wasting.

Accounting, Monitoring, and Control. These approaches will require implementation of a monitoring framework and a "controller" with predefined logic and recent knowledge about the behavior of workloads and/or users in the system. Surely, accounting can be done manually by the administrator, but it does not scale very well. While there exist various accounting and monitoring solutions such as `kubecost`[15], the reactive "controller" is missing and yet needs to be developed. We are convinced that just showing the costs to the user is not enough if the he is not forced to pay the costs. As already mentioned, resources are usually free of charge in academic environments. However, some kind of virtual coins could be adopted as a regulation mechanism. Such approach still requires development, testing, and evaluation to recognize its sufficiency.

5 Real Workload Trace from CERIT-SC Installation

In this section we provide real data from our K8s installation in CERIT-SC system [1]. It is based on Kubernetes cluster version 1.21 consisting of 20 nodes. Each node is equipped with 128 hyperthreaded cores, 512 GB RAM, one NVIDIA GPU card and 7 TB of local SSD storage. In total, the system has 2,560 CPU cores. All of those 20 nodes have worker roles, i.e., they are able to run any Pod. Default limit is 110 Pods per node but it has been increased to 160 Pods per node, so we are able to run up to 3200 Pods on the whole cluster, service jobs are included in this limit.

[15] https://github.com/kubecost/cost-model.

We collected data of all Pods that were executed on the cluster during the July 2021 – May 2022. The workload trace contains information about more than 292,000 Pods. In the workload trace, each Pod occupies one line that contains following (anonymized) data:

- Pod Name
- Pod UUID
- arrival time
- start time
- end time (either completed or killed)
- CPU request
- CPU limit
- RAM request
- RAM limit
- average, minimum and maximum CPU usage
- average, minimum and maximum RAM usage
- requested GPUs
- namespace ID

Since real usage of CPU/Memory resources varies over time and it would not be practical to provide real usage, e.g., for each minute, we (currently) provide data on average, minimum, and maximum real CPU/Memory usage over the runtime of the Pod. Figure 4 shows current distribution of CPU requests and limits (top left) and also illustrates how the values of CPU utilization (avg., min., max.) are spread with respect to Pods' CPU requests. More details can be obtained from the time-series database that records these values periodically. This anonymized workload trace has been published along with this paper in the JSSPP workloads archive [8] which is hosted at the JSSPP workshop page: https://jsspp.org/workload/.

6 Related Work

Aforementioned problems have already been acknowledged by other groups. Even commercial world deals somehow with them as users can opt for enterprise cloud infrastructures which often offer several free deals but in the context of large resource requests, unpaid plans do not provide sensible amount of resources. Enterprise infrastructure can be represented by Amazon AWS[16]. Amazon's paying model is based on per-second billing where user pays only for what he or she uses. Amazon currently offers five plans of reserving computational instances which all introduce various discounts and peculiarities. One of the plans, *Spot Instances*, is based on utilizing unused EC2 capacity in the cloud with significant discount. However, EC2 can reclaim the capacity anytime so when selecting this plan, user sets preferred way of handling evicted workload (hibernate, stop,

[16] https://aws.amazon.com.

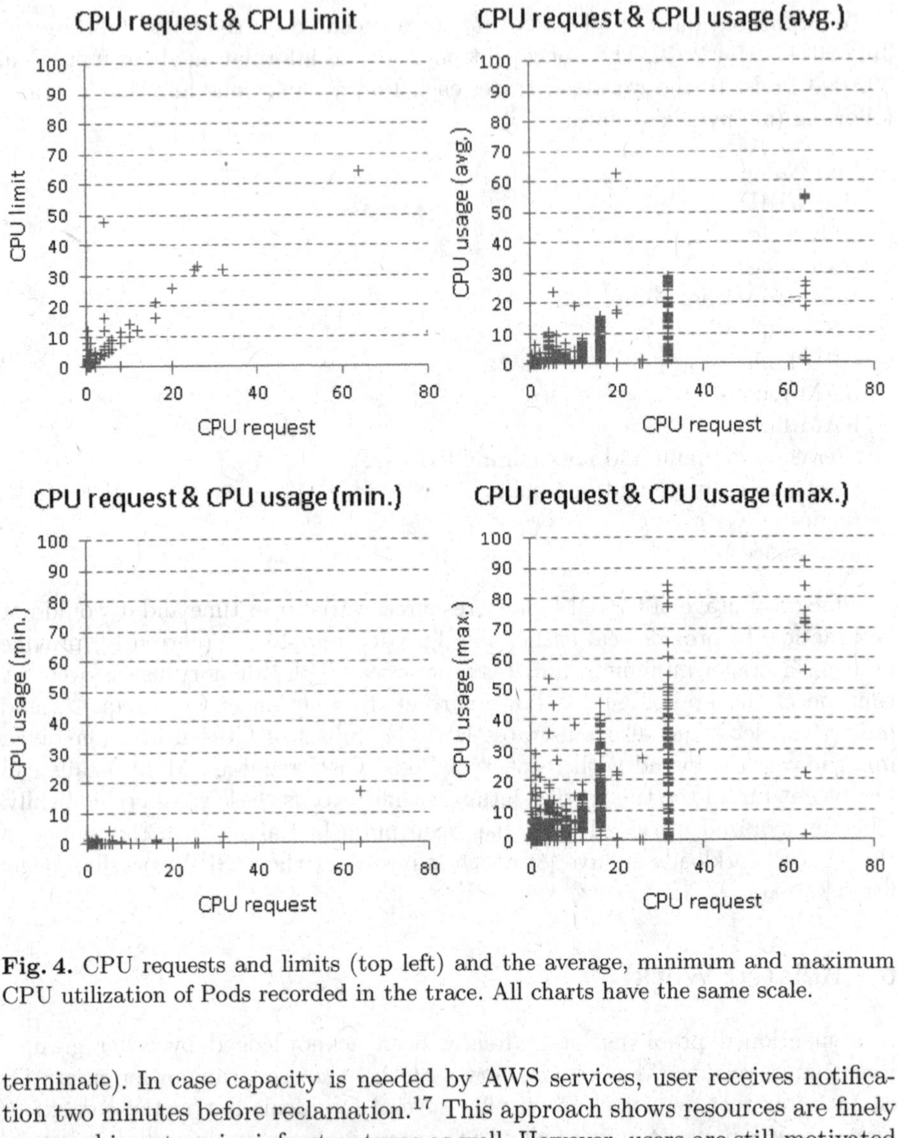

Fig. 4. CPU requests and limits (top left) and the average, minimum and maximum CPU utilization of Pods recorded in the trace. All charts have the same scale.

terminate). In case capacity is needed by AWS services, user receives notification two minutes before reclamation.[17] This approach shows resources are finely managed in enterprise infrastructures as well. However, users are still motivated to think about their requirements because they would have to pay more while infrastructure providers are maximizing earnings.

In the field of container orchestrators, solutions proposed to solve scheduling obstacles are usually crafted only for needs of subjects or as proof of concept without further integration into whole system. The reason is that modern technologies are widely used, open-source hence shaped by outsiders, individuals, enterprises and anyone interested which eliminates the utmost need for academic literature and deep research. Currently, real solutions or novel ideas

[17] https://aws.amazon.com/ec2/spot/.

introductions happen at community discussion forums or at source code management platforms such as *GitHub*[18]. As Randal points out [16]: *"... recent projects such as Docker and Kubernetes are largely written by outsiders providing external commentary rather than by the primary developers of the technologies. As a result, recent academic publications on containers tend to lack the depth of perspective and insight that was common to earlier publications on virtual machines, capabilities, and security in the Linux Kernel. The dialog driving innovation and improvements to the technology has not disappeared, but it has moved away from the academic literature and into other communication channels."*

From published works we choose four that discuss scheduling strategies, fairness resolution and analyze low cluster utilization. We observe that resource allocation issues have become recognized and researchers are trying to invent alternatives to basic Kubernetes scheduler. Still, problems discussed in the works remain unsolved as incorporating any change into the official system is a longer process.

In the work "Availability-driven scheduling in Kubernetes" Farias et al. [3] introduce different Kubernetes scheduling approach based on resource allocation according to promised quality of service (QoS). Their implementation and performed experiments show that QoS-driven scheduling yields better and more reliable service with fairer and more efficient resource division.

Medel et al. propose in their paper "Client-Side Scheduling Based on Application Characterization on Kubernetes" [14] idea that clients should provide a characterization of their applications which would allow scheduler to evaluate the best configuration to deal with the workload at a given moment. The enhanced scheduler design puts emphasis on balancing number of applications in each node and minimizing degradation caused by resource contention. Clients or developers are responsible for providing information about resources used intensively by their applications utilized by scheduler in advance. The solution achieved 20% improvement in a test case compared to basic Kubernetes scheduler but one can argue if user is capable of correctly assessing application's needs, especially in relation to HPC jobs where as mentioned, overestimation is ubiquitous.

Apart from suggesting new scheduling strategies, researchers have noticed non-existence of fairness in Kuberentes [5]. Hamzeh et al. propose a model to calculate and assign resource limits fairly among the Pods in the Kubernetes environment. Authors state that due to early development stage no real case example scenarios could be presented but the work brings interesting view on cloud fair allocation algorithms (DRF [4], MLF-DRS [7] and FFMRA [6]).

Le and Liu in [12] open the work from different perspective where they discuss resource inefficiency of data centers with connection to global emissions and electric energy consumption. Overall, the paper focuses on improving cluster utilization without degrading quality of service. For that purpose, they developed an online resource manager that combines both load balancing and feedback control. Evaluations show that the tool achieved truly higher resource utilization compared to user submitting resource requests.

[18] https://github.com.

Ma and Wang [13] propose a new scheduler on top of standard K8s installation called *Volcano*. It presents some interesting features such as support for efficient batch processing, however it is solely oriented on well-defined set of batch workloads, i.e., it is not a universal solution to our problems.

7 Conclusion

This paper discussed our experience with the Kubernetes container orchestrator and various problems related to the process of scheduling and resource allocation in a containerized environment. Based on existing Kubernetes concepts, we suggest several solutions to existing scheduling challenges such as infinite and interactive computing and/or overestimation of resource requests. Efficient scheduling and resource allocation can not be achieved with current Kubernetes tools easily. While Kubernetes is very good and robust in keeping the infrastructure in some "desired state", it does not provide automated mechanisms to *dynamically adjust* the "desired state" with respect to the changing situation in the system.

The transformation from HPC to containers will not happen in a few months, it is an ongoing, long-lasting process that should be performed by a stable provider to ensure a complete and reliable shift. Since such efforts are not strong enough now, we suggest that a hybrid cloud approach could serve as an interim solution of integrating and merging Kubernetes and HPC environments. Moreover, we offer several resource allocation concepts that might perform well in future versions of Kubernetes. Last but not least, we provide real-life workload trace from our installation to the scientific community.

Acknowledgments. Access to the CERIT-SC computing and storage facilities provided by the CERIT-SC Center, under the program "Projects of Large Research, Development, and Innovations Infrastructures" (CERIT Scientific Cloud LM2015085), is greatly appreciated. We also acknowledge the support supplied by the project "e-Infrastruktura CZ" (e-INFRA LM2018140) provided within the program Projects of Large Research, Development and Innovations Infrastructures.

References

1. CERIT Scientific Cloud, July 2022. http://www.cerit-sc.cz
2. Chen, J., Cao, C., Zhang, Y., Ma, X., Zhou, H., Yang, C.: Improving cluster resource efficiency with oversubscription. In: 2018 IEEE 42nd Annual Computer Software and Applications Conference (COMPSAC), vol. 01, pp. 144–153 (2018). https://doi.org/10.1109/COMPSAC.2018.00027
3. Farias, G., da Silva, V.B., Brasileiro, F., Lopes, R., Turull, D.: Availability-driven scheduling in kubernetes
4. Ghodsi, A., Zaharia, M., Hindman, B., Konwinski, A., Shenker, S., Stoica, I.: Dominant resource fairness: fair allocation of multiple resource types. In: 8th USENIX Symposium on Networked Systems Design and Implementation (NSDI 2011) (2011)

5. Hamzeh, H., Meacham, S., Khan, K.: A new approach to calculate resource limits with fairness in kubernetes. In: 2019 First International Conference on Digital Data Processing (DDP), pp. 51–58 (2019). https://doi.org/10.1109/DDP.2019.00020
6. Hamzeh, H., Meacham, S., Khan, K., Phalp, K., Stefanidis, A.: FFMRA: a fully fair multi-resource allocation algorithm in cloud environments. In: 2019 IEEE SmartWorld, Ubiquitous Intelligence and Computing, Advanced and Trusted Computing, Scalable Computing and Communications, Internet of People and Smart City Innovation, pp. 279–286 (2019). https://doi.org/10.1109/SmartWorld-UIC-ATC-SCALCOM-IOP-SCI.2019.00091
7. Hamzeh, H., Meacham, S., Virginas, B., Khan, K., Phalp, K.: MLF-DRS: a multi-level fair resource allocation algorithm in heterogeneous cloud computing systems. In: 2019 IEEE 4th International Conference on Computer and Communication Systems (ICCCS), pp. 316–321 (2019). https://doi.org/10.1109/CCOMS.2019.8821774
8. JSSPP workloads archive (July 2022). https://jsspp.org/workload/
9. Kane, K., Dillaway, B.: Cyclotron: a secure, isolated, virtual cycle-scavenging grid in the enterprise. In: Proceedings of the 6th International Workshop on Middleware for Grid Computing. Association for Computing Machinery, Inc., December 2008
10. Klusáček, D., Parák, B.: Analysis of mixed workloads from shared cloud infrastructure. In: Klusáček, D., Cirne, W., Desai, N. (eds.) JSSPP 2017. LNCS, vol. 10773, pp. 25–42. Springer, Cham (2018). https://doi.org/10.1007/978-3-319-77398-8_2
11. Klusáček, D., Chlumský, V.: Planning and metaheuristic optimization in production job scheduler. In: Desai, N., Cirne, W. (eds.) JSSPP 2015-2016. LNCS, vol. 10353, pp. 198–216. Springer, Cham (2017). https://doi.org/10.1007/978-3-319-61756-5_11
12. Le, T.N., Liu, Z.: Flex: closing the gaps between usage and allocation. In: Proceedings of the Eleventh ACM International Conference on Future Energy Systems. e-Energy 2020, pp. 404–405. Association for Computing Machinery, New York (2020). https://doi.org/10.1145/3396851.3403514
13. Ma, K., Wang, K.: Introducing Volcano : a Kubernetes native batch system for high performance workload. In: KubeCon Europe. CNCF (2019)
14. Medel, V., Tolón, C., Arronategui, U., Tolosana-Calasanz, R., Bañares, J., Rana, O.: Client-side scheduling based on application characterization on kubernetes, pp. 162–176 (2017). https://doi.org/10.1007/978-3-319-68066-8_13
15. Morris, A.: Choosing the right scheduler for HPC and AI workloads. https://www.hpcwire.com/solution_content/ibm/cross-industry/choosing-the-right-scheduler-for-hpc-and-ai-workloads/
16. Randal, A.: The ideal versus the real: revisiting the history of virtual machines and containers. ACM Comput. Surv. **53**(1) (2020). https://doi.org/10.1145/3365199
17. Tsafrir, D.: Using inaccurate estimates accurately. In: Frachtenberg, E., Schwiegelshohn, U. (eds.) JSSPP 2010. LNCS, vol. 6253, pp. 208–221. Springer, Heidelberg (2010). https://doi.org/10.1007/978-3-642-16505-4_12

Author Index

Printed in the United States
by Baker & Taylor Publisher Services